The Asian American

Series Editor

Roger Daniels, University of Cincinnati

Americanization,
Acculturation,
and Ethnic Identity

Americanization, Acculturation, and Ethnic Identity

The Nisei Generation in Hawaii

Eileen H. Tamura

Foreword by Roger Daniels

University of Illinois Press
Urbana and Chicago

This book is printed on acid-free paper.

Library of Congress Cataloging-in-Publication Data

Tamura, Eileen.
Americanization, acculturation, and ethnic identity : the Nisei
generation in Hawaii / Eileen H. Tamura ; foreword by Roger Daniels.
    p. cm. — (The Asian American experience)
Includes bibliographical references (p.   ) and index.
ISBN 0-252-02031-6 (cl : acid-free paper).
ISBN 0-252-06358-9 (pb : acid-free paper).
    1. Japanese Americans—Hawaii.   2. Hawaii—Race relations.
3. Acculturation—Hawaii.   4. Discrimination—Hawaii.   I. Title.
II. Series.
DU624.7.J3T36 1994
996.9'004956—dc20   93-18118
                                                                          CIP

To my Nisei parents,

Hideo Tamura and Tetsuko Kurisu Tamura

Contents

Illustrations follow page 161

Foreword

Hawaii has long been regarded as a place where the racial tensions that grip the rest of the United States simply do not exist. It is true that since its admission in 1959 our fiftieth state has been the only one with a "non-white" majority and has regularly sent largely Asian American delegations to Congress. But, as Eileen Tamura shows in this insightful analysis, the "color line," what W. E. B. Du Bois called the "problem of the twentieth century," has been very much in evidence since annexation in 1898 and before.

Tamura, a Sansei or third-generation Japanese, writes about the struggles of her parents' Nisei generation to emerge from restricted lives on the sugar plantations and assume its rightful place in Hawaii's society. The major focus of her study is the tensions caused when the second generation of immigrants began to strive toward upward social mobility through the traditional American route of the public educational system, just as most second generation immigrants were doing on the American mainland. And like educational and community leaders on the mainland, the white oligarchs who dominated Hawaii until statehood attempted to use the school system, through its agricultural training programs, to exclude as many of the Nisei aspirants as possible from Hawaii's middle and upper socioeconomic classes.

Tamura's book is significant for at least three reasons. In the first place, it deals with an important part of Hawaii's story and will find a place on the relatively small shelf of books that tell the story of "our Pacific paradise" as it was. In the second place, it provides a useful and unique vantage point from which to reevaluate the American public school system, now under severe bombardment from both revisionist scholars and reactionary politicians. In the third place, this study shows that the struggles of the white leadership to keep the elite segment of Hawaii's system—the English Standard Schools—largely free of "colored" students eerily prefigure some of the less violent devices used by southern school systems in their attempts to resist integration after 1954.

In one respect Hawaii's oligarchs went even further than their south-ern counterparts: they were willing to keep Hawaii a mere territory under federal jurisdiction for decades so that true popular sovereignty, which would come with statehood, could be thwarted. In this they had the overt support of racist mainland politicians. As Mississippi's in-famous John Rankin explained to an Interior Department official at a 1937 hearing, the granting of statehood to Hawaii might result in a "Senator named Moto" (after John P. Marquand's detective). Rankin got the name wrong, but the careers of Daniel Inouye, Spark Matsunaga, and Patsy Takemoto Mink, among others, demonstrate the essential correct-ness of his perception. But before those careers could blossom a long struggle for civil rights in the Islands had to be fought and won.

Eileen Tamura has given us, for the first time, a full account of some of the most important of those strides toward freedom. She has also recounted, with both personal narratives and statistics, the changing generational career lines that are the best evidence of what might be called the coming of age of Hawaii's Nisei.

Roger Daniels

Preface

In the period during and after World War I, the territory of Hawaii became engulfed in an Americanization crusade sweeping the country. On the continental United States the crusade—fueled by wartime hysteria over "foreign" and "un-American" ways—aimed its efforts on the millions of "new" immigrants from southern and eastern Europe. In Hawaii the crusade focused on the Japanese, the largest and most conspicuous immigrant group there. In particular, it focused on the Nisei, the children of Japanese immigrants.

A major theme of this book is the interplay of Americanization and acculturation, two different but related phenomena that sometimes worked in harmony and at other times at cross-purposes. The book develops this theme in successive sections that highlight one or both phenomena: Americanization in part 2, the interplay of Americanization and acculturation in part 3, and acculturation in part 4. Acculturation, which is the larger phenomenon, is what finally occurred.

By acculturation I refer to what the Nisei wanted and actually did achieve—their adaptation to American middle-class life. I distinguish acculturation from Americanization, the organized effort by European Americans and others to force the Nisei to adopt certain so-called American ways and drop Japanese ways.

To understand what happened, it must be kept in mind that not all Caucasians were Americanizers. That is, Caucasians in Hawaii disagreed over what they thought about and hoped for the Japanese. Nor were Japanese homogeneous in thought and deed. Some advocated confrontation, some advised caution, and others kept their distance from the larger community, more concerned with immediate survival than the long-range place of themselves and their descendants in Hawaii and America.

Hawaii's Americanization campaign provides a case study in cultural misunderstanding and miscommunication. The anthropologist Clifford Geertz has pointed to culture as "webs of significance" spun by people, mediating between experience and the perception of that experience. Because of cultural differences, different groups interpret the same events from the perspectives of their own world views.[1]

Both Americanizers and Japanese agreed that the Nisei should adopt American ways, but each group had its own interpretation of what that meant, and as a result, the two groups often talked past each other. Both Americanizers and Japanese agreed that the Nisei should be patriotic American citizens, obey laws, work diligently, and learn to read, write, and speak English. But while Americanizers believed that the Nisei should discard all vestiges of and pride in Japanese culture, become Christians, and stay in their "place" as plantation laborers, Japanese thought the Nisei should fuse the best of Japanese and American cultures and move up the occupational and social ladders. In other words the Japanese believed the Nisei could keep the best of their Japanese cultural heritage while aspiring to American middle-class life. Ironically the Nisei goal of economic advancement was more mainstream American than that of the Americanizers' goal for them, that they be good, docile plantation workers. Issei (Japanese immigrant) leaders gave conflicting advice to the Nisei. On their part the Nisei and their parents were selective in using this advice.

Having come from a status-conscious culture, the Japanese easily adapted to the hierarchical society they encountered in Hawaii, a society dominated by an oligarchy that comprised the social, economic, and political elite in the Islands. But while both Americanizers and Japanese accepted social hierarchy, they drew different conclusions of what that meant for the Japanese in Hawaii. To Americanizers the Nisei children of plantation laborers should remain in their place at the bottom of the social and economic structure. To the Japanese the Nisei's task was to climb up and away from plantation work. Success for the Japanese meant that the Nisei should get an academic, English education, find jobs with good pay and future prospects, and live comfortably as middle-class Americans. Like the Americanizers, the Japanese perceived themselves as belonging at the upper levels of the socioeconomic pyramid.

Rather than seek to change the Anglo-American cultural and economic system, the Nisei sought to fit into it. Those who became successful believed in the American system and gained prominence by playing by its rules, not by challenging them. Yet, while the Nisei sought to acculturate, they were partly inhibited from doing so by white misunderstanding of Japanese culture and by white racism. That is, discrimination encouraged the Japanese to band together and foster pride in the old country, while discouraging close relationships with European Americans.

Nisei as well as Issei participated actively in shaping their own lives in Hawaii. Industrialists, politicians, and school leaders alike found that for all their prestige and power, they had much less control over educational, social, and occupational developments than they would have liked—and less than what some scholars have assumed they had. They failed, for example, to keep Japanese laborers on the plantation, to abolish Japanese language schools, and to keep the children of plantation workers at the bottom of the socioeconomic ladder. While Americanizers controlled public policy, they could not control the actions of workers and their children, who had their own ideas about their futures in Hawaii and America. The Japanese went on strike, moved off the plantation, took the language school issue to court, adapted Buddhism to American society, and used the schools to help rise economically and socially. When school leaders offered the Nisei vocational training in agriculture—an education supposedly appropriate to their station—the Nisei rejected the offer and with it a future as plantation laborers, aspiring instead to the promises of middle-class life.[2]

As the larger community shaped the Nisei, so the Nisei shaped and used the American environment for their own purposes. They sought to conform to American ways on their own terms, adopting some of those ways and rejecting others, and equally important, holding on to what they valued in traditional Japanese culture.

In discussing the experiences of the Nisei and their parents, I refer to other groups in Hawaii and on the continental United States. Rather than attempting an in-depth comparative analysis that would weaken the book's focus, my intent is to provide broad brushstrokes that relate the Japanese experience in Hawaii to the experiences of these other groups.

I should also clarify my use of particular terms. The first of these is *ethnic group.* The anthropologist George DeVos, among others, has pointed out the difficulties of pinning down characteristics common to any group so designated. An ethnic group, he said, is "a self-perceived group of people who hold in common a set of traditions not shared by the others with whom they are in contact." Such traditions often, but not always, include religion, language, history, and geographical origin. Thus Filipinos are an ethnic group, but so also are the Visayan- and Ilocano-speaking subgroups within the Filipino American community. DeVos's definition fits the Territorial Department of Public Instruction (DPI) and census bureau categories used in this book, where ethnic group refers variously to groups with common national origins, such as Japanese and Portuguese, as well as groups with multiple national origins such as Other Caucasians.[3]

Another term, seen frequently in the literature on ethnic groups in the United States, is *racism*. I use the term as defined by Roger Daniels and Harry H. L. Kitano in *American Racism: Exploration of the Nature of Prejudice:* "the belief that one or more races have innate superiority over other races." Daniels and Kitano distinguish racism from ethnocentrism, the latter being "the belief that one's own group is the best or superior to all others." The key difference is the biological basis for racism's assumption of superiority. This definition corresponds with that in *Webster's Third New International Dictionary, Unabridged,* which defines racism as "the assumption that psychocultural traits and capacities are determined by biological race . . . usually coupled with a belief in the inherent superiority of a particular race and its right to domination over others." *Webster's* defines race as "a class or kind of individuals with common characteristics, interests, appearance, or habits as if derived from a common ancestor."[4]

In discussing the different ethnic groups in Hawaii, I use the terms Japanese, Chinese, Korean, and Portuguese to refer to immigrants as well as their children. My reference is to ethnic origins, not national identity, and is in keeping with common usage in Hawaii. To avoid confusion in specific instances, I use the terms Chinese American and Chinese immigrant. In referring collectively to Japanese, Chinese, Korean, and Filipino immigrants and their children, I use the term Asians. During the period under consideration in this study they were referred to as Orientals, a term no longer in general use. Also in keeping with common usage in Hawaii, I reserve the term Hawaiian only in reference to ethnic Hawaiians. Thus a Nisei from Hawaii is a Hawaii Nisei or a Hawaii Japanese; a Hawaiian Japanese is someone who is part-Hawaiian and part-Japanese.

I use interchangeably the terms haole, Caucasian, and European American. I use haole (originally the word in the Hawaiian language for foreigner) as it was used during the period under study, to refer to people of northern and western European ancestry—more specifically, to European Americans other than the Portuguese, Puerto Ricans, or Spaniards. The latter three groups, like the Asians, were brought to Hawaii as plantation workers. Although Territorial DPI and census bureau reports for this period categorized haole as Other Caucasian to distinguish them from the Portuguese, Puerto Ricans, and Spaniards, I use Caucasian rather than Other Caucasian in my narrative, but retain Other Caucasian in the tables and graphs.

In categories of Japanese, Issei refers to immigrants, while Nisei refers to American-born children of Issei. This generational distinction is especially important in this study because Asian immigrants were ineligible for naturalization under American law until 1952, whereas their children born on American soil were citizens under provisions of the

Fourteenth Amendment to the Constitution. Almost all Issei came to the United States between 1885 and 1924, when Japanese immigration abruptly ended, while most Nisei were born between the last decade of the nineteenth century and the third decade of the twentieth century.[5]

During the period of this study Hawaii was a territory of the United States. Hawaii residents referred to the United States as "the mainland" and California, Oregon, and Washington as "the West Coast." I use these terms, since they continue to be used in Hawaii, even after statehood.

Another label popularly used in Hawaii then as well as now is "Pidgin English." It refers to Hawaii Creole English, a language prevalent in the Islands since the 1920s. I use the term Hawaii Creole English, but those I quote call it Pidgin English (see chapters 5 and 9). Hawaii Pidgin English was actually an earlier form of communication that arose when plantation workers who spoke different languages came into contact with each other and minimally with their English-speaking superiors. Plantation children born to Pidgin speaking parents developed a language that linguists call Hawaii Creole English, which has continued to develop and persist to this day.

I have made extensive use of the William Carlson Smith (WCS) collection of student essays housed at the University of Oregon Library and on microfilm at Hamilton Library, University of Hawaii at Manoa. In 1926 and 1927 Smith, a sociologist, visited Hawaii, during which time he asked teachers at ten public and private high schools on most of the islands of Hawaii, at the Territorial Normal and Training School, and at the University of Hawaii to have their students write life history essays based on an extended list of questions Smith provided. The questions focused on early life influences, aspirations, conflicts and accommodations, and relationships with other groups. Smith asked that the questions serve merely as guides, since what he wanted were personal narratives describing experiences, feelings, struggles, disappointments, and hopes. The WCS collection includes about four hundred essays, about half of them written by Japanese Americans. Most of the essays were written anonymously. I identify the writers on the basis of information in their essays, and when possible, I provide dates for the events discussed. In the notes I cite these essays as WCS and provide the reel (R) number, school initials, and student number.[6]

Acknowledgments

In the course of doing the research and writing for this study, I had the good fortune of gaining the assistance of a number of helpful people. I am most deeply indebted to Idus Newby, who was unstintingly generous with his time and scholarly advice, and proved to be an invaluable sounding board and critic. Roger Daniels, the general editor of this series, gave a careful reading of the text and shared his fund of knowledge of Japanese American, Asian American, and American immigration history. His insightful comments, constructive criticisms, and kind encouragement helped make this a satisfying project.

To Edward Beechert, Richard Immerman, and Ann Keppel, who critiqued earlier drafts; Charlene Sato and Kent Sakoda, who helped me improve my discussion of Hawaii Creole English; an anonymous reader who forced me to clarify my thoughts; Morris Lai, who advised me on my statistical data; Kazuyo Sato, who translated materials from the Japanese language newspapers; Judith Hughes, who gave me the idea of exploring the Americanization theme; Ralph Stueber, who pointed me to helpful literature; and Bill Kaneko, who opened doors for me: thank you for your help.

The staff of the Hawaiian Collection at Hamilton Library, University of Hawaii, was most helpful. Special thanks go to Jim Cartwright, Michaelyn Chou, Nancy Morris, and Chieko Tachihata for leading me to invaluable sources. The staff of the Hawaii State Archives was also helpful. Herb Arai in particular found some vital information. The Oral History Project at the University of Hawaii, under the direction of Warren Nishimoto, has produced an outstanding collection of interviews. Michi Kodama-Nishimoto was an especially valuable resource in guiding me to volumes that discussed Issei and Nisei life. Richard Wentworth and his staff at the University of Illinois Press helped me through the publicaton process—Theresa L. Sears, Harriet Stockanes, Lisa Warne-Magro, and Christie Schuetz. Louis Simon, my copy editor, corrected my mistakes and otherwise helped me improve the manuscript.

Because of the assistance and permission of Lynn Ann Davis and Betty

Kam of the Bishop Museum Visual Collection, the staff of the Hawaii State Archives, the Reverend Shugen Komogata, Helen Sato, and Paul Yempuku, I was able to include photographs that enhance the narrative. My appreciation also goes to those who granted me permission to quote from their collections and studies: the Bancroft Library at the University of California, Berkeley, the Watumull Foundation Oral History Project, B. K. Hyams, Mildred D. Kosaki, Jitsuichi Masuoka, and George K. Yamamoto. I am also most grateful to all those who so willingly wrote about their lives and those who consented to be interviewed. Their stories provide a human dimension that enriches the historical record.

Finally, I am indebted to my husband, Dave Raney, who served as an invaluable sounding board for my ideas, provided me with computer expertise, and remained an enthusiastic supporter all the way.

Americanization,
Acculturation,
and Ethnic Identity

Prologue

The Hawaii Setting

About thirteen hundred years before Columbus reached America, the first settlers in Hawaii arrived from the Marquesas, a group of Polynesian islands two thousand miles southeast of Hawaii. They were followed by Tahitians, another group of Polynesians from islands 2,400 miles due south. After a period of repeated long-distance canoe voyaging between Tahiti and Hawaii, contact between the two island groups ended, and for hundreds of years the Hawaiians lived in communal self-sufficiency undisturbed by the rest of the world.[1]

Westerners first came upon Hawaii during the American Revolutionary War. The arrival of English Captain James Cook in 1778, on his third expedition to the Pacific, began a chain of events that radically transformed life in the Islands. News of Hawaii traveled to Europe and America, and before long other Westerners arrived, bringing with them their tools, artifacts, animals, and plants, their ideas and customs, and their diseases.

From 1785 to 1870 Hawaii became a port of call for Westerners engaged in Pacific trade—first furs, then sandalwood, followed by whaling. American traders carried furs from North America to China, and silks, teas, and porcelains from China to Boston, New York, and Philadelphia. Hawaii served as a convenient spot for rest, recreation, and reprovisioning. Soon traders learned that forests in Hawaii were thick with sandalwood, prized by the Chinese for delicately carved boxes and sacred objects, and for incense and oil. To entice the Hawaiian chiefs into commercial activity, traders brought clothes, billiard tables, carriages, and even ships from New England. These the chiefs took in exchange for sandalwood. In 1819, having exhausted the whaling grounds in the South Pacific, whalers moved north to the seas off Japan. Because Japan had closed its ports to foreigners, whaling ships sailed south to Hawaii for reprovisioning and recreation, which meant, all too often, alcohol and prostitution. By 1850, Honolulu and Lahaina had turned from sleepy villages into bustling port towns.[2]

As Hawaiians observed Westerners breaking the *kapu* (taboo) with impunity, the traditional Hawaiian religious system broke down. By the time Protestant missionaries from New England arrived in 1820 to "civilize" and "save" the "natives," the *kapu* system had already been officially abolished, leaving a religious void the missionaries were only too eager to fill.[3]

Governance, too, was affected by Western contact. When Cook arrived in Hawaii, he found the chiefs warring with each other to expand their territory and control. Thirty years later, Kamehameha, more successful than his rivals in using foreign advisors and foreign weapons, emerged victorious. Having brought all of the Islands under his control, Kamehameha took Westerners as advisors and ruled as an absolute monarch. After his death, succeeding monarchs continued to appoint Americans and Britons to government posts as Hawaii developed as a constitutional monarchy.[4]

By 1865, with the depletion of the Pacific whaling grounds, the replacement of whale oil by petroleum, and the demand for sugar in the United States, cultivating sugarcane—grown commercially since 1835—had become Hawaii's dominant industry. The Great *Mahele* (land division) of 1848 had ended the native system of communal land tenure and replaced it with one in which land was private property to be bought and sold. In the aftermath sugar planters were able to buy, lease, or otherwise control vast tracts of land.[5]

The Masters and Servants Act of 1850, which made it legal to import contract laborers (a practice that continued until the United States annexed Hawaii), enabled planters to meet the labor demands of the newly developed plantations. Planters saw foreign indentured workers as the answer to their labor needs. The native Hawaiian population had decreased drastically since the arrival of Westerners, from possibly almost a million to about 82,000 in 1850. Many Hawaiians had signed on as seamen on whalers; others had left for California during the gold rush. Above all, Western diseases such as measles, whooping cough, mumps, influenza, leprosy, and smallpox, to which native Hawaiians lacked immunity, had killed hundreds of thousands. In addition, those who remained were unwilling to perform long hours of backbreaking labor on the plantations. So planters, who wanted cheap, obedient workers for their expanding industry, searched worldwide for them.[6]

The Chinese, the first group of laborers imported for field and mill work, arrived in 1852. Other groups were similarly contracted for by the plantations, including whites from northwestern Europe for skilled or supervisory positions. During the remainder of the nineteenth century and the first half of the twentieth century (only noncontract workers could be recruited after Hawaii became a territory in 1900), other groups followed the Chinese: Portuguese, Norwegians, Germans, Japanese, Puerto Ricans, Koreans, Russians, Spaniards, and Filipinos. The six hundred Norwegians, thirteen hundred Germans, and twenty-four hundred Russians were dwarfed by the multitudes of Asians.[7]

While their land and labor problems were being resolved, sugar planters attacked another obstacle to their prosperity, the high tariff on sugar entering the United States. They sought a reciprocity treaty that would remove the duty on sugar from Hawaii. After several unsuccessful attempts, they succeeded in 1875. Within fifteen years investors and industrialists dramatically increased sugar production, from 25 million pounds in 1875, to more than 250 million pounds in 1890. Hawaii and the United States renewed the treaty in 1887, with the added provision that the United States was to have exclusive use of Pearl Harbor as a naval base.[8]

Then disaster threatened. The McKinley Tariff of 1890 removed the tariff on raw sugar from all foreign countries and gave American sugar producers a bounty payment of two cents a pound. An economic depression in Hawaii followed immediately. To some in the business community, annexation was the only answer to the sugar industry's problem even if it meant an end to the contract labor system. In 1893 the Hawaiian monarchy was overthrown; five years later, the United States annexed the Islands.[9]

A relatively small group of influential haole, many of them decendants of American missionaries, orchestrated the overthrow, set up a provisional government and then a republic, and worked assiduously to have Hawaii annexed by the United States. After annexation in 1898, this elite group ran the government and continued to do so until the 1950s.[10]

The Organic Act creating the territorial government provided for only limited self-government. Except for territorial legislators and a nonvoting delegate to Congress, all other officials were appointed. The U.S. President selected the governor, the secretary (roughly equivalent to lieutenant governor), and all circuit and supreme court judges. Especially before 1930, both Republican and Democratic presidents chose Hawaii's top officials from the haole elite. The governor, in turn, appointed hundreds of local officials. Additionally, he had the power to veto money bills without the threat of legislative override, to decide issues of health, education, welfare, and public works, and to invoke martial law and suspend the right of habeas corpus.[11]

While the territory quickly developed into a vital military center for U.S. Pacific forces, more than half a century passed before Hawaii achieved statehood. Mainlanders objected to Hawaii's predominantly Asian population and distant, insular location, and Hawaii's haole elite gave little more than rhetorical support to the effort. Foremost in their minds was the realization that statehood would end their autocratic control of political and economic life in the Islands.[12]

Thus the Islands remained a territory for six decades. During that time five corporations, popularly known as the Big Five, controlled the sugar industry and the rest of the economy through a system of interlocking directorates. The men who ran the Big Five—Alexander and Baldwin, C. Brewer and Company, Castle and Cooke, Theo. H. Davies and Company, and American Factors—were also active board members of Island banks, utilities, transportation companies, and other large businesses.

These Caucasians also dominated the Republican party, attended Protestant churches, socialized at exclusive clubs, and sent their children to the select, private Punahou School. Hawaii's social structure at the turn of the twentieth century, according to the historian Lawrence Fuchs, "was a curious amalgam of a tropical European colony and a New England settlement."[13]

Below the haole elite was an undersized middle class, also largely Caucasian, especially during the early years of the territory, of craftspersons and small-business people. At the bottom of the socioeconomic scale were the vast majority of Islanders, mostly Asians, who provided the territory with unskilled and semiskilled labor, most of it in arduous plantation fieldwork.[14]

As mentioned earlier, the Chinese constituted the first group of plantation laborers, most of whom arrived before Hawaii was annexed to the United States. Although the Masters and Servants Act had permitted the importation of contract laborers in 1850, it was not until the 1870s that the Chinese began going to Hawaii in large numbers. In all about 46,000 arrived before annexation. Most of them migrated to work on sugar plantations; others, on Chinese-controlled rice plantations. Still others entered the Islands as independent merchants or craftspersons or as workers for Chinese small businesses. Of those who arrived before annexation, 95 percent were males; only after more Chinese women arrived in Hawaii, between 1890 and 1910, did a noticeable population of second generation Chinese emerge.[15]

Portuguese from the Azores and Madeira Islands, arriving between 1878 and 1887 and from 1906 to 1913, constituted the second major ethnic group recruited for sugar plantation work. Because the Portuguese government allowed recruitment only on condition that women and children be included, the more than 17,500 Portuguese came as families. One result was a higher birthrate among the Portuguese compared to the Chinese, so that by 1910 Portuguese outnumbered Chinese in Hawaii, although more than twice as many Chinese had actually been recruited. Because they were imported for plantation work, the Portuguese, although Europeans, were thought of and treated as separate from the haole.[16]

The Japanese followed the Portuguese. Between 1885 and 1924, about 180,000 Japanese arrived in Hawaii, becoming by 1900 the largest ethnic group in the Islands. Partly to offset this dominance, planters recruited other ethnic groups after annexation. Over 5,600 Puerto Ricans, families and single men, arrived in 1901–2 and 1921, as did seven thousand Koreans, mostly men, between 1903 and 1905, and eight thousand Spaniards, families and single men, from 1907 to 1913, though many of the Spaniards quickly left for California.[17]

Filipinos, most of them men, began arriving in 1906. The 1907 to 1908 Gentlemen's Agreement, in which Japan agreed to stop the emigration of laborers to the United States, and a devastating sugar strike by Japanese laborers in 1909, encouraged planters to increase recruitment in the Philippines. By 1932, most of the 126,000 Filipino laborers who migrated to Hawaii during the first half of the twentieth century had arrived. Although a 1924 immigration law excluded Asians from the United States as well as Hawaii, Filipinos could continue to migrate because the Philippines was a U.S. territory and Filipinos were American nationals. The 1935 Tydings-McDuffie Act, granting future independence to the Philippines, closed this loophole for the mainland by imposing a quota of fifty Filipino immigrants a year. But a provision in the act allowed Filipinos to enter Hawaii to meet the territory's sugar needs until the Philippines attained independence in 1946. No attempt was made to invoke this provision until World War II brought about an acute labor shortage. As a result, a group of 6,000 men, 452 women, and 909 children arrived in 1946.[18]

The Japanese were thus only one of many ethnic groups who went to Hawaii to work on sugar plantations. Although all of the groups demonstrated a broadly similar pattern of acculturation, their specific experiences differed. This study focuses on the Japanese experience, particularly among the Nisei.[19]

Part One

❧ ❧ ❧

Background

Chapter 1

Sojourners

Four black ships floated ominously on the placid waters of Tokyo Bay, their cannons pointing menacingly toward shore. It was July 1853, and the American Commodore Matthew Perry had arrived to "open" Japan to the outside world. The commodore's historic visit triggered a chain of events that reverberated throughout feudal Japan. The reverberations eventually touched an archipelago 3,900 miles away in the middle of the Pacific Ocean, the Polynesian kingdom of Hawaii, which had itself been "opened" to the world three quarters of a century earlier.[1]

Perry's visit forced Japan to end the two-centuries-long period of isolation imposed by the Tokugawa shogunate. Once Japan agreed to trade with the United States, other Western powers demanded similar concessions. Japan's weakness in the face of the Westerners' strength touched off a power struggle within Japan. In 1868, fifteen years after Perry's visit, a group of samurai from western Japan succeeded in overthrowing the Tokugawa shogunate and establishing an imperial government in Tokyo. The ensuing period, called the Meiji Restoration, ended the samurai era and Japan's feudal economy.[2]

Well aware of China's failure to control the Western onslaught, Japan's new leaders embarked on a program of reform aimed at transforming the country into an industrial and military power capable of standing up to Western imperialists. They sent students abroad, instituted a nationwide educational system, imported Western technology, and restructured the economy.

In order to industrialize, government officials needed a stable source of revenue. In 1873 they imposed a new tax system that ultimately had a devastating effect on farmers. While taxes on agricultural land had previously been based on the value of the past year's crops, the new system based taxes on the value of the land. Farmers now had to pay fixed taxes regardless of the success of their harvests. If the price of rice was high, their taxes were proportionately small and they prospered. But in 1881 rice prices began to drop, bringing financial ruin to many. From 1883 to 1890 over 367,000 farmers lost their land for failing to pay taxes.[3]

This was the background when, after a series of requests by the Hawaiian government, Japan agreed in 1884 to allow farmers to emigrate to Hawaii to work on sugar plantations beginning the following year. At the suggestion of his Japanese advisors, Robert W. Irwin, agent in Japan for the Hawaiian Board of Immigration, recruited workers in overpopulated and hardpressed rural areas of southwest Japan.[4]

The aftermath was a major population movement. For the first thirteen years, 49,085 immigrants, an average of over 3,700 a year, arrived in Honolulu. The next seven years (1898 to 1904) witnessed an even larger influx of 69,808 Issei, an annual average of over 9,900. Men constituted over 80 percent of these early migrants.[5]

Accompanying the mass of laborers were small numbers of professionals and businessmen: doctors, dentists, bankers, inspectors, and interpreters. These men and their families formed the upper crust of the growing Japanese communities in Hawaii. Japanese physicians, recruited by the Hawaiian government during the first ten years of immigration, provided medical care for laborers. Later, other doctors came on their own to practice in plantation communities or to open offices in Honolulu. Bank officials arrived to run branch offices of the Yokohama Specie Bank and later the Keihin Bank. They handled immigrants' savings. Immigrants also had to deposit 15 percent of their wages to ensure return passage to Japan in case of sickness or death. Unfortunately for the Issei, bank officials sometimes refused to return all the money deposited, and on occasion workers were known to carry a corpse to the bank to force the return of the money due the deceased. Agents of private emigration companies also came to Hawaii, and they too exploited workers. Fees and passage money put immigrants into debt even before they began working, and as a result, many laborers spent up to three years paying off those debts. Inspectors sent by the Japanese government to protect the interests of immigrants proved to be generally unsympathetic to workers facing such problems.[6]

In 1894 the government-sponsored system directed by Irwin ended, and thereafter private Japanese emigration companies contracted to meet the planters' mushrooming demands for laborers. Leaders of the provisional government in Hawaii soon sought to reduce the flow of Japanese immigrants, but pressure from planters blocked effective action.[7]

Most of the Issei came from the southwestern prefectures of Hiroshima, Yamaguchi, Kumamoto, and Fukuoka. Most were sons and daughters of small landowning or tenant farmers who faced ruin during the period of economic restructuring ushered in by the Meiji government. In their own minds they were sojourners, not immigrants; they went to Hawaii to earn sufficient money to pay off family debts, buy land in Japan, and return to their homeland. They called themselves *dekase-ginin*, people temporarily working away from home. In this they were like the Chinese who came before and the Filipinos who came after, and like immigrants from southern and eastern Europe who arrived on the eastern seaboard of the United States at about the same time.[8]

Although economic forces pushed the Issei to Hawaii, personal decisions led the emigrants to leave the lives they knew. An Issei woman recalled, "I was born in a very poor family. I was a young girl when I first heard about Hawaii and America. These strange countries were pictured to me as the lands of unlimited fortunes where money was plentiful." Wanting to escape her "extreme hard life," the woman agreed to marry a thirty-two-year-old man who was seeking a wife to accompany him to Hawaii. She was seventeen. "To tell the truth I did not intend to stay married to my husband for longer than three years," the woman remembered. "I thought then that . . . I could come home with plenty of money. Then I would be twenty-one, not altogether too old to consider remarriage." Similarly impoverished, Usaku Morihara, the fourth of five children, came to Hawaii from Yamaguchi prefecture in 1907. "I didn't see any future in being a farmer in Japan," he remembered later. "I thought no matter how hard I tried, I wouldn't be successful."[9]

Similar thoughts probably ran through the minds of many Issei in the first group of *kanyaku imin jidai*, or government-sponsored contract laborers, disembarking the *City of Tokio*. The Hawaii that greeted them was a land awash with green sugarcane fields. The 1876 Reciprocity Treaty between the Hawaiian kingdom and the United States, enabling Hawaiian sugar to enter the United States duty-free, had stimulated the growth of an already dominant industry.

Living and working conditions varied from plantation to plantation and gradually improved, especially after Hawaii became a territory of the United States. Still, early plantation life was generally harsh. Workers performed tedious, backbreaking labor in fields thick with knife-sharp leaves among buzzing yellow jackets and wasps. Laborers toiled for ten to twelve hours a day, breathing dusty air and enduring the scorching rays of the sun.[10]

Plantations provided free but minimal medical care. Japanese doctors were often unavailable, and language and cultural barriers between Caucasian doctors and Issei laborers often resulted in faulty diagnoses and even death. The plantations also provided free housing, usually in camps segregated by ethnic group, reflecting the different waves of labor recruitment. As new groups joined the work force, plantation managers constructed new camps for them. The segregated housing furthered the efforts of plantation managers to divide and control the work force, though laborers themselves preferred living among their own kind. Life was more comfortable when they could speak their native language and live among those who understood their ways.[11]

With some exceptions, living conditions during the first two decades of Issei plantation life were poor, especially where the overwhelming majority of residents were men. Toden Higa described his living quarters in 1905: "The camp had a long building and several people lived in each room of the building. The rooms were just huts with clothes in them. Nothing else. We hung things on nails in the walls. . . . Each person was allotted one mat space to sleep." Another Issei described similar conditions at the turn of the century on a Maui plantation, adding, "There was no kitchen in the house. Since the laborers were almost all young single men there was no need for such an arrangement. In this camp there were only two couples."[12]

The *Nippu Jiji* editor Yasutaro Soga wrote of early plantation life, "The Waianae Plantation was doing a profitable business, but the dwellings of the laborers were filthy and unsanitary. . . . It would be more proper to designate these dwellings as pig sties than to refer to them as human habitations." Soga continued, "Single men lodged together in the big rooms, whose bunks rose in tiers against the walls. But sometimes the single men had to live in the [smaller] rooms of the married couples." Soga noted that the "sewage overflowed within the camp. And a certain unbearably foul smell hung in the air." During this early period, laborers of other ethnic groups experienced similar working and living conditions.[13]

An Issei woman recalled, "I used to get up around two o'clock in the morning and start cooking and get our lunches ready. My husband and I left our home usually around four. I worked out in the field for eleven hours, and upon my return I had to cook, to wash, and to sew." "In those days," recalled Usaku Morihara, "they treated the workers as . . . slaves. . . . The workers slept like silkworm cocoons [on boards] in houses that were lined up row after row." Morihara continued, "The plantation workers used to drink *shoyu* [soy sauce] . . . to have a fever. But then the camp police found out about this practice," Morihara said. "[The police would] drag [the workers] into the sugar field and force [them] to work. They were so cruel. . . . Since those Japanese workers didn't think there was any future on the plantation, they were running away. . . . [My brother] ran away with two or three others, from Hilo to Kona."[14]

In 1890 as many as 5,706 runaways of all ethnic groups were arrested. This figure does not count the many others who were never caught. Minoru Inaba recalled that his father, a plantation laborer before the turn of the century, escaped at night. In Kona he found a job as a cook for a family, for whom he worked for seventeen years. Another Nisei said that his father took a fictitious name after running away, and worked in the rice fields for a while before finding a job as caretaker at Waimea Stables.[15]

In the first two decades of Issei plantation life, Japanese women were few and immigrants eked out their lives far away from family and community mores. Many Issei became frustrated and disheartened when they realized that they were earning much less than they had anticipated and would be unable to save enough to return to Japan in a few years. In this atmosphere, as among the earlier Chinese laborers, social discipline temporarily disintegrated, and heavy drinking, gambling, wife selling, and prostitution flourished. Moreover, it was not unusual for women to run away, or to leave their husbands for more attractive or prosperous men.[16]

Men frequented nearby saloons, and on payday each month gamblers and prostitutes swooped down on the plantations. In Hawaii as in California, the Issei's hard-earned money often fell into the bottomless pit of gambling.[17]

Some men sold their wives to pay off gambling debts. G. G. Hitchcock, sheriff of the island of Hawaii, reported in 1892 that wife selling was "more or less prevalent on this island." In 1901 the Protective League of Honolulu rescued Yoshi Nonogawa from pimps who threatened to take her to the red light district of Iwilei in Honolulu if her husband did not pay his $165 debt. At the turn of the century, Attorney General Henry E. Cooper identified 269 prostitutes in Honolulu, 226 of them Japanese. Government officials tried to contain the red light district within a section of Chinatown, and after the Chinatown fire of 1900, within Iwilei, a few blocks away. Yet in 1904 no fewer than 203 "separate houses of ill fame" were scattered in other parts of Honolulu. The West Coast also had its share of Japanese prostitutes in this early period of immigration. In fact, during the late nineteenth and early twentieth centuries, impoverished girls and young women in Japan, often tricked or forced into prostitution, were sent to China, India, Southeast Asia, and Australia, as well as California and Hawaii.[18]

As for runaway wives in Hawaii, an Issei recalled, "There were plenty of them. Kona was the land of refuge for those who left the plantations [on the island of Hawaii]. They would come to Kona to hide in the coffee fields. In many cases the former husband came looking for his wife, so the wife had to keep on moving. . . . She would often change husbands so it would be harder to trace her." A Nisei girl wrote, "Women were scarce then, and unchastity and vice were commonly and openly practiced by both men and women. Sheiks always won the love of the married women.

Mother was one of them." After several attempts, the girl's mother left her husband and young daughter for another man. The woman had been a "devoted wife" in Japan, but her "disposition changed" after she arrived in Hawaii. She complained of her husband's "meager earnings," while men "with jingles in [their] pockets" attracted her.[19]

During this period Issei sang melancholy folksongs called *holehole bushi* as they toiled in the fields. *Hole* is a Hawaiian word meaning to peel or strip. *Holehole* referred to the process of stripping the sugarcane leaves from their stalks, a job done primarily by women. *Bushi* is the Japanese word for tune.[20]

> Send us money, send us money!
> Is the usual note from home.
> But how can I do it
> In this plight?
>
> Two contract periods have gone by.
> We are still here.
> Destined to become fertilizer
> For sugarcane.
>
> My husband cuts the cane stalks.
> And I strip their leaves.
> With sweat and tears we both work
> For our means.
>
> Shall I go to America?
> Or shall I go home to Japan?
> I'm lost in thoughts
> Here in Hawaii.
>
> If I work at *holehole*
> All I'll earn is 35 cents.
> If I sleep with a Chinaman
> I'll make $1.00!
>
> Tomorrow is Sunday.
> Come and visit me.
> My husband will be out watering the fields.
> I'll be alone.

Despite the difficulties they experienced in these early years, Issei laborers knew their financial situation was vastly better than it would have been had they remained in Japan. Many of them were able to send money home, and many earned enough to return to Japan as they had originally plannned. Then, too, ameliorating influences existed, and conditions gradually improved, especially after Hawaii was annexed to the United States.

One of those ameliorating influences was religion. Managers understood religion's stabilizing effect. They therefore encouraged the spread of Christianity as well as Buddhism on the plantations by allowing laborers to hold services. They even gave land and other financial support for the building of churches and temples.[21]

Kanichi Miyama, an evangelist from the Methodist-Episcopal Church of San Francisco, arrived in Hawaii in 1885, beginning the effort to Christianize the Japanese. Others followed him, among them Takie Okumura.[22]

Okumura was indisputably the most visible, zealous, and outspoken Japanese Christian minister. He arrived from Japan in 1894, under a three-year contract with the Hawaiian Board of Missions. As part of his effort to spread his faith among the Japanese, he established a language school in Honolulu, built the Okumura Home, a Christian dormitory, organized Boys Clubs, and published two periodicals, *The Boy* (later the *New Americans*), and *Paradise Times.* The Makiki Christian Church, which he founded, grew from a membership of twenty-four in 1904 to over five hundred in ten years.[23]

In 1921 Okumura began a six-year campaign, financed by the Hawaiian Sugar Planters' Association (HSPA), to Americanize the Issei. While he publically stated that he sought only to "remove causes of friction" between Japanese and Americans, his actual motive was to Christianize the Issei and convince them and their children to remain on the plantations. Later, in 1927, he organized a series of annual New Americans Conferences for Nisei youths, ostensibly to make them better American citizens. But privately he talked of working "under cover" to convince the Nisei to remain on the plantations. In return for his efforts, he hoped the planters would give him moral and other kinds of support in combatting "the adverse alien influence of Buddhism."[24]

Christian ministers like Miyama and Okumura performed a number of services, among them writing letters for laborers, teaching night school, mediating plantation disputes and family quarrels, and sending birth, marriage, and death notifications to the Japanese consulate so they could be recorded in Japan. Unfortunately for the Christian ministers, most of the Japanese immigrants came from southwestern Japan, strongholds of the Shin sect (and to a lesser degree, the Jodo sect) of Buddhism, and converts to Christianity were therefore few.[25]

The arrival of Soryu Kagahi of the Hongwanji mission in 1889 marked the beginning of Buddhism in Hawaii. Kagahi traveled from plantation to plantation on the island of Hawaii to comfort the Japanese; with money he collected from them, he laid the foundation for a temple in Hilo. After seven months he returned to Japan to seek financial aid for his struggling mission, but because of an impolitic essay he had written equating the Christian God with the Buddha, the Hongwanji missionary association in Japan refused to support him, and he was never heard from again. In 1894, Gakuo Okabe of the Jodo sect established a second Buddhist mission, also on the island of Hawaii. Yemyo Imamura, bishop of the Honpa Hongwanji mission, arrived in 1902. He was undoubtedly the best-known Buddhist leader during the first three decades of the twentieth century, a man respected for his compassion and integrity.[26]

Like their Christian counterparts, Buddhist priests not only ministered to the spiritual needs of the Issei, but performed other needed services. They, too, wrote letters for laborers, acted as go-betweens in marriages, and helped settle family problems and disputes between management and labor.[27]

The U.S. commissioner of labor reported in 1903 that plantation managers in Hawaii "rather encourage[d] the building of temples," believing "the moral and social influence of the priests among the laborers . . . to be good." Buddhist priests advised laborers to endure pain and cooperate with their employers. Only a year after the commissioner made the above remarks, Bishop Imamura convinced a group of striking laborers to return to work. Planters also believed that their support of Buddhism would appease workers and prevent the loss of labor. In the seven years following annexation, some forty thousand Issei left Hawaii for higher wages on the mainland, and plantation managers came to the conclusion that freedom to practice Buddhism might encourage Issei workers to remain in Hawaii and on the plantations. Christian leaders were understandably angry at plantation managers for "aiding and abetting Buddhism." Christian ministers struggled to convert the Issei with little result, and the availability of Buddhist priests and temples made their task more difficult.[28]

Despite Christian opposition, plantation managers continued to encourage the spread of Buddhism. As noted earlier, miserable working and living conditions during the early period made drinking, gambling, and violence commonplace among the Issei. Buddhist priests helped bring order out of that chaos by preaching acceptance, nonviolence, and peaceful cooperation. Additionally, their stress on social harmony and on the idea that each person is accountable to the larger group helped to solidify the emerging Japanese community and to control behavior. Managers, who liked these calming effects, continued to subsidize Buddhist temples until 1920, when Japanese workers staged a massive sugar strike. The support of plantation managers was one reason for the greater success of Buddhism in Hawaii than on the West Coast.[29]

The Issei also brought Shintoism to Hawaii. Shintoism was the ancient religion of Japan, existing long before the arrival of Buddhism. It involved a set of rituals, celebrations, and pilgrimages to shrines housing deities called *kami*. The most important of the deities was the sungoddess, *Amaterasu-O-kami*, believed to be the ancestor of the emperors of Japan. The first Shinto shrines in Hawaii were built in 1898 on Kauai and the island of Hawaii. By the second decade of the twentieth century, Shintoism was well established in the Islands.[30]

Buddhism and Shintoism mitigated the trauma of living in a strange and foreign land. Their coming to Hawaii meant Japanese could practice traditional rituals during such milestones of life as birth, marriage, and death, celebrate *bon* festivals to honor their ancestors, and usher in the new year in the Japanese way. Having long ago incorporated the Confucian concept of filial piety, Buddhism gave Issei a feeling of spiritual contact with their ancestors and strengthened the immigrants' bonds to their families and their home villages.[31]

Because Buddhism kept alive immigrant ties to Japan, the religion would be accused of anti-Americanism during the Americanization campaign that erupted after World War I. Moreover, because Americanizers assumed Americanization meant Christianization, Buddhism was, by their definition, un-American.

That the Issei maintained ties with Japan was only natural. In fact, it was unrealistic to expect immigrants to discard all sentiment for their mother countries. The unfamiliar American environment, the language barrier, and lack of extended family support all fueled nostalgia for familiar, traditional ways.

Oftentimes immigrants looked back to the land of their birth to give them the dignity and respect they so often found missing in the United States. Irish Americans, for example, passionately supported Ireland's fight for independence in the late nineteenth and early twentieth centuries. Pride in Ireland translated to pride in themselves. The same happened with the Zionist movement to establish a Jewish homeland, a symbol of strength for Jews who felt that their people had for too long suffered from helplessness and oppression. Other groups like the Czechs, Poles, and Slovaks enthusiastically supported the struggles of their homeland peoples during World War I, and many German Americans actively promoted the German war effort. Similarly, Chinese and Koreans in Hawaii and on the mainland during the first half of the twentieth century supported political and nationalistic movements in their home countries.[32]

Japanese in Hawaii also rallied to the causes of their motherland. Bursting with pride at Japan's triumph in the 1894–95 Sino-Japanese war, Issei in Hawaii organized a day-long victory celebration. They closed their businesses, decorated their homes and stores with flags and lanterns, paraded down the streets in Japanese military uniforms, cheered for the emperor, sang the national anthem, and staged wrestling and fencing matches.[33]

In January 1905, when the Japanese captured Port Arthur, the center of Russia's military and naval power in East Asia, and again five months later when Japan emerged victorious in the Russo-Japanese war, Issei enthusiastically cheered their homeland by parading with floats and lanterns in Honolulu. At the June celebration, wrestling and fencing matches and Japanese geisha dancers entertained the crowd. The haole community looked at these festivities with raised eyebrows. The Issei took understandable pride in Japan's emerging strength, just as Americans took pride in America's military might. But this show of support to their mother country would haunt the Japanese during the impending Americanization crusade.

European Americans in Hawaii were stunned by Japan's victory over Russia. On 3 January 1905 the *Pacific Commercial Advertiser*, one of Honolulu's two English language dailies, soberly editorialized, "Port Arthur with its . . . fifty and more forts, its high powered modern guns, its auxiliary fleet and its resolute garrison, was a multiplied Gibraltar," and the results of its fall would be "far-reaching."[34]

Regular visits to Hawaii's ports by Japanese warships on training cruises continued to call attention to Japan's growing military strength. They also kept alive the Issei's enthusiastic support of their homeland and exacerbated the suspicions of Caucasians who believed that Japanese in Hawaii should be loyal to America only.[35]

The suspicions directed at the Japanese in Hawaii reflected a general sentiment growing in the rest of the country. As a result of increasing agitation against Japanese in California, the United States and Japan negotiated the 1907 to 1908 Gentlemen's Agreement, which stopped the flow of Issei men to America. Under terms of the agreement, the wording of which was made public only in 1939, Japan agreed to stop issuing passports to laborers bound for the continental United States. The only exceptions would be former residents, parents, wives and children of current residents, and nonlaborers. Japan extended the terms to include Hawaii. This agreement ushered in a new phase of Japanese immigration, discussed in the next chapter: the arrival of wives and picture brides.[36]

The agreement was part of an overall effort by the two governments to abate the climate of increasing discrimination Issei faced as resident aliens in America. California was the center of racist propaganda that succeeded in convincing several state legislatures as well as Congress to pass laws against Asians in general and Japanese in particular, some of which were challenged in the federal courts. As a territory of the United States, Hawaii was naturally affected by the sentiments that lay behind these laws. In fact, the campaign against the Japanese on the West Coast merged with related activities in Hawaii.[37]

Ironically, Japan's emergence as a regional power after the Russo-Japanese war helped as well as hurt the situation of the Japanese in Hawaii and on the mainland. On the one hand, the American government hesitated to take steps that offended the Japanese government. On the other hand, Caucasians who became increasingly suspicious of Japan's international intentions vented their antagonisms on Japanese immigrants and their families.

Even before Hawaii had become a territory, leaders of the Kingdom and then the Republic of Hawaii had refrained from issuing conditional permits to Japanese immigrants, as they did to those from China. Such permits allowed their holders to remain in Hawaii only as long as they worked on plantations or as domestic servants. This arrangement functioned to control laborers and servants, and reflected the inability of China—but not Japan—to protect its citizens in foreign countries. Government officials in Hawaii knew Japan would be offended by treatment that reduced Japanese subjects to the level of those of a country as weak as China. Not only did the officials want to avoid antagonizing a growing international power, they wanted to keep Japan as a source of plantation labor.[38]

Annexation opened the door for all Japanese in Hawaii to go to the mainland. When labor recruiters from California arrived immediately thereafter, the Issei hesitated. But as word came back that wages on the West Coast were higher than in Hawaii, more and more Issei put aside their hesitation. Between 1898 and 1907 thirty to forty thousand Japanese left Hawaii for the mainland, about 20 percent of all Issei in Hawaii.[39]

This response was not unique. The West Coast attracted immigrants of all ethnic groups in Hawaii. Spanish, Portuguese, and Russians departed for the mainland in large numbers. In fact, most of the 17,479 Europeans brought to Hawaii to work on plantations during the first two decades of the twentieth century left for the mainland within a few years of their arrival.[40]

Most Issei who moved to the West Coast were single men. Some of the married men who migrated took their wives with them, while others left them behind, intending to call for them later. One Nisei later recalled that when she was an infant, her father told her mother he was going to the mainland to earn more money. That was the last they heard of him.[41]

Plantation managers in Hawaii looked on in dismay as their work force thinned. They called upon the Japanese consul-general to stop the exodus. The consul-general responded in 1903 by forming the Central Japanese League to discourage Issei from leaving Hawaii for jobs on the mainland. The territorial legislature joined the effort in 1905 by passing a law requiring labor recruiters to pay a $500 licensing fee. But not until 1907 did the flow effectively end, and what ended it was a proclamation by President Theodore Roosevelt, authorized by an act of Congress, barring Japanese and Korean laborers from entering the continental United States by way of Hawaii, Mexico, or Canada.[42]

Ever since the Japanese had begun arriving on the West Coast before the turn of the century, anti-Japanese agitators in California had called for their exclusion, regularly petitioning Congress to that end. With the increasing flow of Japanese into California after Hawaii's annexation, that agitation increased. The precedent pointed to was the Chinese Exclusion Act, first passed in 1882. But Japan was not China, and American officials balked at taking such action against citizens of a powerful nation. Moreover, the rest of the country was generally unconcerned about the issue.[43]

Japan's victory in the Russo-Japanese war, however, surprised most Americans, who looked apprehensively at the triumph of an Asian nation over what they thought was one of the strongest European powers. American business leaders worried about Japan's economic strength; American military leaders worried about that Asian country's military might. Indifference turned to disfavor as Americans began to look suspiciously at Japan's foreign policy.[44]

Exclusionists, led after 1905 by the California-based Asiatic Exclusion League, profited from the increasing tensions between the two countries. In 1906 the San Francisco School Board mandated that all Japanese public school students join their Chinese counterparts in a segregated school in Chinatown. Strong protests from Japanese officials, who took the action as a national insult, forced President Theodore Roosevelt to intervene. In return for his promise to end Japanese immigration, the school board revoked its order. The outcome was the aforementioned Gentlemen's Agreement between the United States and Japan.[45]

These and other events occurring between 1885 and 1908 foreshadowed issues that later erupted during the Americanization crusade in Hawaii. Caucasian opposition to Buddhism and anxiety over Japan's growing military strength, latent during the earlier years of this period, would become active concerns among Americanizers. Specifically, European American discomfort at seeing the Issei celebrate Japan's military victories presaged the Americanizers' demand that the Japanese in Hawaii hold undivided loyalty to the United States, a demand that included discarding Buddhism, the "alien" religion, and breaking all ties with Japan. The Gentlemen's Agreement became only one of many acts of discrimination against the Japanese instituted at the national and local levels. On their part during the first twenty years of immigration, Hawaii's Japanese behaved in ways that also foreshadowed their later actions. Like other immigrants, they refused to sever all ties with their homeland or otherwise follow the demands of Americanizers. The stage was thus set for conflict between the Japanese and their Americanizers.

Chapter 2

Settlers

The experiences of the Japanese in Hawaii during the first four decades of the twentieth century should be seen in the larger context of their evolving community. Although the evolution of Japanese community life was ongoing and multifarious, it is possible to discern a series of discrete yet overlapping stages of development. The first stage, from 1885 to 1908, was that of the sojourner who expected to return to Japan. As such expectation was frustrated or displaced, a period of increasing community settlement and stabilization emerged, lasting until 1924, when the arrival of wives terminated. Meanwhile, between about 1910 and 1935, Nisei children attended elementary and secondary schools, and their consequent acculturation became a dominant theme of Japanese community life. Most Nisei came of age between 1920 and 1941, entering the job market or going on to higher education. During this period they began to have a major impact on life outside the Japanese community. Then, abruptly, came the war and its profound effects. As a result of the war experience and of the changes underway well before it, a number of Nisei after 1945 began the rise to prominence that became noticeable in many areas of Island life by the 1960s and thereafter.

As discussed in the previous chapter, the sojourner period began with the arrival of the first government-sponsored contract laborers and ended with the Gentlemen's Agreement. During this period the Issei, like other immigrant groups from Asia, Europe, and the Americas, regularly sent money to their families they had left behind. A Nisei summed up this frame of mind: "They think about Japan, talk about Japan. They send their money to Japan."[1]

The Gentlemen's Agreement ended the flow of Japanese male laborers. Moreover, because it was interpreted to mean that the Issei who returned to Japan and remained there three years or longer forfeited the right to return to Hawaii, many considered remaining in Hawaii longer. Those Issei who felt they had saved enough returned to their villages as they had originally planned. But the rising cost of living in Japan made it necessary for many to remain in Hawaii to save ever-increasing sums.

Gradually the latter group began to realize that they would not be able to return as quickly as they had once thought possible. They began to think in terms of long-term residence and took steps to improve their lives in Hawaii. Married men sent for their wives. Single men went home to find brides or, like their countrymen on the mainland, sent home for picture brides.[2]

Picture bride marriages evolved naturally from ongoing Japanese practices, in which marriage was a family, not an individual, affair. Family heads selected marriage mates through go-betweens who supplied information on the prospective mate's genealogy, family wealth, education, and health. Sometimes photographs were exchanged. Because few Issei could afford the time or expense of returning to Japan to find marriage partners, they asked their parents or other relatives to select brides for them. The men sent photographs of themselves and information about their lives in America. The only legal requirement was that the names of the brides be entered into the husbands' family registers. After a six-month wait required by Japanese law, the brides embarked on the voyage to join their husbands. Between 1907 and 1923, 14,275 picture brides arrived in Hawaii. During the peak years of 1912 to 1914, the annual average was more than 1,400.[3]

The arrival of picture brides caused quite a stir in Honolulu. Although the couple was already married according to the laws and customs of Japan, indignant Americans claimed that the marriages were invalid. Responding to the outcry, territorial officials repeatedly called Shinto priests to the immigration station to officiate at marriage ceremonies for large groups of couples at a time. This was an example of the type of cultural misunderstanding that surfaced time and again between Caucasians and Japanese.

Picture bride marriages enabled Issei men to establish and enjoy family life. By 1920, 72 percent of Japanese men over twenty-five years old in Hawaii were married, compared to 50 percent of Chinese men and 38 percent of Korean men.[4]

Because of anti-Japanese hostility on the West Coast, the Japanese government in February 1920 stopped issuing passports to picture brides bound for the mainland, but continued issuing them to those going to Hawaii. In 1922 Henry Butler Schwartz, later superintendent of foreign language schools in the Territorial Department of Public Instruction, called for a law to end picture bride marriages in Hawaii. He was joined by members of the American Legion, who denounced the practice as un-American. The territorial legislature took no action on the matter, but the practice ceased when Congress passed the 1924 Immigration Act that ended Japanese immigration to the United States.[5]

What motivated women to become picture brides? Many simply obeyed the wishes of parents, which was the accepted, filial practice. Others from poor families hoped to help their parents by sending them money from Hawaii. Still others sought a better life than their circumstances in Japan seemed to promise. A few sought to escape social stigma of one sort or another.

"I found out that I would be going to Hawaii when I had my picture taken," Tsuru Yamauchi recalled, describing the arrival of her husband at the immigration station. "Those who came as picture brides with me were holding me down; I was trembling so much, scared," she reminisced. "I never had much contact with boys, so I was afraid. . . . Well, Yamauchi-san claimed me when they brought him over. . . . When he took me to Waipahu where we would live in the middle of the canefield, I really felt homesick. The people there had a party for us." Yamauchi continued, "Everyone drank and sang, but I was scared and couldn't even look at people's faces. There were almost thirty people, but I wouldn't look up. I couldn't enjoy it at all or even answer when spoken to. Afterwards, the others said, 'Better not talk to her. If you talk too much, she'll cry.' I was really a scaredy-cat."[6]

Another woman became a picture bride when she was seventeen. Her mother had told her, "Look how easy it would be to please only one person, your husband. But if you marry here in this village, you have many worries. You have to work until your eyes become dark (dizzy) from overwork, just to please your in-laws." So the young woman went to Hawaii. "To work out in the field under the burning sun was very hard," she later recalled. "I remember very clearly how my back ached the first day I went to work." After a week of pain, the woman wrote her mother about her feelings of discouragement, but she forgot to mail the letter. Instead her husband found it and read it. That evening he told her "never to write such a letter" because it would only make her mother worry. "So I never told her how hard it was to work out in the fields. Now, in spite of hard work I am very happy," the woman said. "I am the mother of five children and my husband has been very considerate and nice to me."[7]

Osame Manago agreed to become a picture bride in order to escape the shame she felt she had caused her family. When she was sixteen, she was forced to marry her father's relative, whom she strongly disliked. "If I didn't marry him, my father would have lost face," she explained. But after three days with her new husband and his family, she could stand it no longer, and she ran home to her family. "I told my mother . . . I wanted to leave Japan and go somewhere far away from home. My mother tried to comfort me, saying that . . . there would be other chances to marry somebody nicer. But I insisted that I should go somewhere far away, somewhere like Hawaii. . . . I was ashamed for my father and I wanted to . . . work very hard in Hawaii [to repay my debts]." A few years later, in 1913, she became the picture bride of a man living in Kona, on the island of Hawaii.[8]

Some disappointed picture brides ran away from their new husbands. When she was about fourteen, Raku Morimoto, who lived at the Susannah Wesley Home, a Methodist center that assisted Japanese and Korean girls and women, recalled the picture bride who came knocking at the door in 1905. "[The bride] said the go-between in Japan told her a very nice story about her groom-to-be in Hawaii," said Morimoto, "[that] he has a very nice job." But upon arriving at her husband's plantation camp in Aiea, the bride was "so surprised" because her "house" was "slightly bigger than a big box." She was even more surprised to see that her husband was "such an old man." The photograph she had seen in Japan had been taken twenty years earlier. Then a woman who lived in the camp told her, "You know, your husband owes us some money, but he doesn't pay. . . . Not only us, you know. He owes [some other people] money, too. So we tried to get the hard-working woman for his wife." The bride was so distraught that she ran away into the cane fields and then into the mountains the first night. When she heard men looking for her on horseback, she climbed up a tree, where she stayed for two nights. Somehow she reached the Susannah Wesley Home in Honolulu. Morimoto recalled that other picture brides also sought refuge at the home.[9]

But most picture brides gradually came to accept their lives in Hawaii, and their arrival brought stability to the lives of Issei men, further postponing their return to Japan. Childbearing and rearing limited the earning capacity of women. Growing families meant more mouths to feed and increased living expenses, and returning to Japan slipped further and further from the Issei's reach. Kame Okano, who came with her husband, recalled, "When we got to Hawaii we intended to make money, and then after ten years—when we had made lots of money—we would go back home to Japan. But then the children [came]—one the first year, two the second year—until there were eight." When Misae Yano was asked if her parents ever visited or returned to Japan, she exclaimed, "My parents had seven kids! How could they go to Japan?"[10]

Wives and families soon created complex communities, which in turn encouraged the establishment of institutions such as Buddhist temples and Japanese language schools. Japanese customs took root. Birth, illness, and death meant gift-giving as demanded by the culture, depleting family income.[11]

By 1909, when Japanese sugar plantation laborers staged a major strike (discussed in chapter 10), the Issei had shifted the focus of their lives from Japan to Hawaii. The Higher Wages Association, the labor union representing the striking Japanese workers, wrote to the Hawaiian Sugar Planters' Association to request an increase in pay for laborers because of their rising cost of living. "The general tendency . . . among the laborers is to settle here rather than go back to Japan with a small savings," the union explained. "In the recent years the status of plantation laborers has undergone a complete change from a transient to a settled labor." One of the union's spokespeople was the attorney Motoyuki Negoro, an Issei who had left Japan at the age of seventeen, worked his way through high school and college in California, and earned a law degree at the University of California at Berkeley—impressive credentials for a Japanese in America at the time. Negoro argued, "The situation has changed since 1885. The contract laborers then had no other thought than to work as temporary migratory workers and were satisfied to put up with make-shift living conditions." He continued, "However, this is no longer the case. Statistics show that in 1908, there were 21,500 [Japanese] married women in Hawaii." There were also, Negoro noted, approximately 17,500 Japanese children between the ages of one and fifteen.[12]

The Congregationalist missionary Doremus Scudder, who visited many plantations in 1903 and 1904, found few Japanese at that time who planned to remain in Hawaii permanently. Many were sending their children to Japan to be educated. But in 1910, Scudder believed, the dominant sentiment was to "stay in America and make it [their] country," and increasingly the Issei were keeping their children in Hawaii. In 1915, Sidney L. Gulick, a former missionary and theologian at Kyoto's Doshisha University and an advocate of immigration reform and of better treatment of the Japanese in America, spoke with plantation managers and doctors, school principals, Christian ministers, and Buddhist priests on most of the islands. They told him that Japanese laborers no longer talked of returning to Japan or of sending their children there to be educated, and many expressed concern that they themselves could not become American citizens.[13]

After breaking the 1909 strike, plantation managers increased wages and improved housing and working conditions. Realizing that contented workers meant fewer strikes and greater productivity, and recognizing the desire of married couples to live in separate houses, managers replaced the barracks-type housing with cottages, subsidized the building of Buddhist temples, and organized recreational activities such as movies and baseball games. The Issei used the plots of land surrounding their cottages to grow vegetables and create Japanese-style gardens with "little rocky pools and goldfish." They raised chickens, rabbits, ducks, and pigs, made and sold tofu (soybean cakes), and built *furo* (traditional Japanese hot baths).[14]

The Issei also organized Buddhist and prefectural associations, held bon dances to honor their ancestors, celebrated the emperor's birthday with sumo (wrestling) matches, and welcomed the new year in the Japanese way. As among Japanese on the mainland, a strong sense of group solidarity enabled Hawaii's Issei to look to their ethnic community for social and economic support. One example of this was the practice of *tanomoshi*, or rotating credit associations, adapted in Japan from the Chinese *hui*. Like the Chinese hui and the Filipino *hulugan*, the tanomoshi helped immigrants finance expenses they could not otherwise afford, and its effectiveness depended on trust, honor, and community solidarity.[15]

Tanomoshi involved varying numbers of people and amounts of money. In a typical instance a group of perhaps ten people would agree to contribute a given amount each month, say, $10 each, for a total of $100 a month. Those who wanted to use the money in a given month would bid for the sum. The highest bidder would take the $100 and the others would divide the amount of the bid, or interest payment, among themselves. Each group member was allowed to take the sum once in the life of the group. Those who did so no longer received interest payments but continued to make monthly contributions. *Tamomu* means dependable; there was no legal way to compel someone to pay what was owed. Sometimes a member quietly returned to Japan after receiving the monthly sum, leaving those who had vouched for his honor to pay what he owed. But such instances were rare.[16]

While thousands of Issei streamed into Hawaii and settled there permanently, thousands returned to Japan after their sojourn. The net effect of the immigration was therefore much less than it would otherwise have been. About 180,000 Issei (a number of whom were counted twice when they returned after a visit to Japan) arrived in Hawaii between 1885 and 1924, but fewer than half of them settled there permanently. Most who left returned to Japan, while thirty to forty thousand migrated to the West Coast of the United States. But there, too, less than half of all Issei settled permanently.[17]

Other immigrant groups displayed similar patterns of mobility. Almost half of all Chinese and more than half of all Filipino immigrants to Hawaii returned to their homelands, over 40 percent of all Korean immigrants either moved to the mainland or returned to Korea, and more than 80 percent of the Portuguese and most of the Spaniards recruited by sugar planters eventually left for the mainland. Similarly, substantial proportions of the European immigrants who flocked to cities on

the mainland to work in the booming industries during the late nineteenth and early twentieth centuries also returned to their homelands.
Of 22,000 Turks who arrived in the United States during the first quarter
of the twentieth century, over 80 percent returned to Turkey. Conservative estimates for other groups, in percentages, are 66 for Rumanians, 53
for Greeks, and 33 for Poles. And many of those who remained kept alive
the possibility that they, too, might one day return to their homelands.[18]

The number of Japanese arrivals and departures illustrates the Issei
pattern: 13,975 Japanese arrived in Hawaii in 1907, while 3,488 departed
for Japan. Five years later 3,465 arrived and 3,440 departed, and in 1927,
1,591 arrived and 4,745 departed. These figures reflect visits to Japan as
well as permanent returns, and by themselves do not reveal all the details
of what happened. By 1909, for example, more men and children were
leaving Hawaii than entering, while more women were arriving than
departing. Eventually this made the sex ratio among the Issei less unbalanced.[19]Most of the men arriving after 1907 were returning from visits
to Japan. Others were sons over sixteen years old of immigrants already
in Hawaii, who as family members were permitted to enter the territory under terms of the Gentlemen's Agreement. Still others were Kibei,
children born in Hawaii but who spent a good part of their childhood
in Japan. These children were sent to Japan to be educated in "Japanese
fashion" by relatives. A Nisei recalled, "My father . . . [believed] that the
children born in Hawaii were not up to the standard in their manners
and conduct and I remember him saying that it would do any one of
us good to go back to Japan and learn something of the manners of the
people there."[20]

To further complicate this picture, a number of Japanese left Hawaii
intending to remain permanently in Japan, but changed their minds and
returned. Sueno Matsushita's parents returned to Japan in 1899 with
their three children after ten years in Hawaii. "When they first went
back, they had some money so they built a house," Matsushita recalled.
But their family back home was too large for them to survive with their
little plot of land. "My mother told me, thirteen in the family. They work
in the field, they have not enough to feed the family. No rice. . . . [They]
kept it up for five years, then they came back. They were all going to
starve, so they went back to Hawaii."[21]

Edward Fukunaga's parents also came to Hawaii with the intent of
returning to Japan once they had enough money to start their own business. After about fifteen years in Hawaii, they returned to their home
village. That was in 1921, when Fukunaga was twelve years old. Once
in Japan, however, they changed their minds. "My mother . . . decided
that at the rate they were going, they would never be able to send us two

kids to college," recalled Fukunaga. So the family returned to Hawaii. Fukunaga eventually attended the University of Hawaii and became a chemist.[22]

In his autobiography, Tom Ige recounted his family's aborted return to Okinawa. After moving off the plantation, his parents leased about thirty acres of pineapple land deep in Kahaluu Valley on Oahu. For a number of years they worked hard and saved their earnings, eventually achieving what they regarded as "spectacular" economic success. By 1924, when Ige was about seven years old, his parents succeeded in fulfilling "the ultimate dream of all early immigrants, to return to their homeland." But once the Iges were joyfully reunited with their relatives in Okinawa, things began to turn sour. "Relatives borrowed heavily from the 'rich one just returned from Hawaii,'" recalled Ige. "It must have been difficult for my parents to deny any request as all our relatives were poor and struggling. Because of all these loans, our remaining assets quickly evaporated." After a few years, with nothing left, the family returned to Hawaii.[23]

Some of those who returned to Japan found they had become too acculturated to adjust to Japanese life. Misako Yamamoto's father went to Hawaii at the turn of the century and returned to Japan four and a half years later. "The idea had never occurred to [my father] to settle in the islands—it was a foreign land," recalled Yamamoto. "In Japan, however, he found that he could not be comfortable. He could not stay on the farm without finding fault with the way his relatives and friends lived." So he returned to Hawaii, this time with his wife.[24]

A number of Issei who decided to settle in Hawaii returned to Japan for visits. Sometimes, as with Osame Manago's experience in 1929, the trip back caused great sorrow. Her father had written, asking her family to visit so he could see his grandchildren. "My father was so glad to see us," Manago remembered. "[He] said that seeing the children was worth more than a house filled with gold, and he cried, even though he was a man." Manago continued, "When the eight of us came, the house was full of people and became cheerful. My mother said . . . she wouldn't know what to do when we were gone, that it would be like a typhoon had gone by. She begged me to stay, asking if I really had to go." On the day of their departure, her sister took her aside. "My sister . . . said that [my seven-month-old baby] was so young that she couldn't tell who her mother was, that I should leave her with my mother. My sister said that my mother would feel so sad when we left that she would go crazy or become sick. . . . I felt I shouldn't have come back if I had known that I would have to leave my baby behind. I didn't know what to do." Manago finally decided to leave her daughter in Japan. "I was very sad, but I also thought of the time I left my mother to come to Hawaii. I owed her for that, and I had to pay her back. I thought I had to do that for her."[25]

Even some of those who remained in Japan preferred living in Hawaii. In the late 1920s, the University of Hawaii sociologist Romanzo Adams visited Oshima Gun, an island in Yamaguchi prefecture. Of a population of 58,000, over six thousand had left for Hawaii. "Probably no other part of Japan contributed so large a proportion of its population to Hawaii," wrote Adams. Many who returned to the area seemed relatively prosperous to Adams. They told him that the Issei wanted to return to Japan only if they saved enough to live better than average lives. This meant being able to buy a house and farmland, and still have a tidy sum to invest. The great majority of the men who returned that Adams interviewed said they preferred living in Hawaii because it was easier to earn a living there. One man spoke with feeling of the greater freedom he felt in Hawaii from exacting rules of social intercourse. Then why did these men remain in Japan? Family. Filial piety dictated that a son, especially an oldest son, be with his father during his old age. If the son was too poor, he was excused. But if he was prosperous, he could not evade his duty and keep the respect of his neighbors.[26]

Visits to Japan or stories from those who made such visits led many Issei to realize that their standard of living in Hawaii was better than it would be in Japan. Moreover, they had grown accustomed to a way of life different from that of their home villages. Gradually they lost their enthusiasm for returning to Japan permanently. The sociologist Jitsuichi Masuoka noted that a decrease in movement to and from Japan reflected increasing settlement in Hawaii. The proportion of Japanese traveling back and forth between the two countries dramatically decreased from 316 to 66 per 1,000 Japanese between 1905 and 1910, reflecting the loosening of ties to Japan and the deepening of roots in Hawaii.[27]

This change paralleled the influx of wives and brides, and the consequent appearance of children. In 1900, Nisei were only 8 percent of the Japanese population in Hawaii, but by 1910 the percentage was 25 and in 1920, 44.5. (In 1920, Nisei youths constituted 92 percent of all Japanese youths in the territory, the rest being Issei youths.)[28]

Because of this "baby boom," enrollment in the public schools grew dramatically, rising from 20,245 students in 1910 to 41,350 in 1920 and 70,316 in 1928. In those three years the Nisei accounted for 32, 47, and 52 percent of these students.[29]

On or off the plantation, work was part of the life of Nisei children. Because both parents often worked outside the home, Nisei had to help out at home by taking care of younger siblings, cleaning the house, and cooking. Others worked at part-time jobs. As late as the 1920s and

1930s, children of plantation laborers often worked in the fields. Richard Inouye, who began plantation work in 1921, when he was ten years old, recalled giving all his pay to his father: "I didn't care to have the money because I know he's having a hard time with all the children, eight of them. So I gotta help him, eh. That hard life I had." Quitting school and going to work to augment family income was common, especially in the first two decades of the century, and continued in the third decade as well. Ethel Kina, whose mother was a field laborer and whose father was a plantation carpenter, helped her parents do the laundry for unmarried plantation men. On weekends they soaped, scrubbed, beat, and boiled the clothes. After Kina dropped out of school at the end of the fifth grade in 1930, she patched and ironed clothes on weekdays while taking care of her younger brothers and sisters.[30]

Alcoholism, while not common among Japanese, brought hardships when it was part of family life. A young woman who was born in the first decade of the twentieth century said of her early life, "My mother, who was born in the islands, was very unfortunate when she was young because at the age of fourteen, she was forced to get married to my father (a Japan born) who was then thirty years old. Father was a lover of liquor. . . . Everyday he invited several friends to a saloon and there they all drank to their hearts' content." Sometimes her father came home drunk at midnight, other times at twilight. When drinking made him violent, he would chase his wife "with a loaded pistol."[31]

Nor did his children escape this man's drunken wrath. One evening his daughter accidently bumped her younger brother, making his nose bleed. Without asking for an explanation, her father switched her legs "with a horse whip." "I gave a loud yell and a big jump and ran straight for the canefield nearby," the young woman recalled. "I had no supper that night except a handful of *poha* berries, which I gathered from the bushes near the field. I was about four and one half years old and I felt that I was unjustly treated." She stayed in the cane fields until 4:30 the next morning. Feeling chilly, she decided to go home "when suddenly a big owl began to who oo oo oo overhead," causing her to scream in fright. Her mother heard her and brought her back into the house. "Father, who was still full of liquor, wanted to give me a good thrashing," the young woman reminisced, "but mother would not allow him to do so."[32]

Like alcoholism, the death of a parent could make life more difficult. "My mother died when I was five years old," wrote a high school Nisei girl who was born in 1910, "leaving a baby sister of two years. Being the third child in the family and still not attending school, it was up to me to care for my baby sister." Sueno Matsushita's father died in 1907 when she was four. To support her family, Matsushita's mother worked on the plantation and sewed *tabi* or cloth shoes. "The plantation people never used to wear shoes, you know," explained Matsushita. "My mother used to make tabi every night. . . . On Sunday, too, she sew. . . . Three layers, and they put together, and they sew, back and forth, back and forth. My mother used to sew with machine." Her mother also raised pigs, one at a time. "Every morning [and] nighttime, when she come home, she and I have to carry the slop to the pig. . . . And every Saturday, when I come home from Japanese school, I have to pick the *hono-hono* grass, cut it, for the pig. And if I didn't feed the pig, the pig yelling his head off," she chuckled as she recalled those days. Her mother raised pigs so she could send money to Japan, to support two children she had left behind.[33]

Living off the plantation and having both parents alive made life easier for the Nisei, but in those families, too, the children were kept busy. Edythe Yamamoto's parents, who arrived in Hawaii in 1906, worked for a wealthy bachelor, Mr. Banning, who owned four large houses in rural Oahu. Her father maintained the grounds and her mother cleaned the homes. Yamamoto and her siblings spent their afternoons and weekends helping their parents. Of course, they also played as they worked. Charles Sakai's parents left plantation work to open a store. Charles, who was born in 1910, worked at the store while attending Waialua Elementary and Leilehua High Schools. Since few of his customers had cars, young Charles took their orders and made deliveries all across the districts of Haleiwa, Waialua, Kawailoa, and Opaeula. "Our parents were . . . working all day, all night just to support the family," he recalled. "They had no time for their children."[34]

As these stories demonstrate, the Issei and their children strove, often under trying circumstances, to make a life for themselves in Hawaii. As they did so, they gradually adapted to their American environment. To appreciate this process of acculturation, it is necessary to have some understanding of the world view the Issei brought with them to Hawaii.[35]

A perspective that helped the Issei adjust to Hawaii's class-dominated life was their hierarchical view of society. At the top of the social structure from which they came was the *shi* (warrior, administrator, ruling class), followed by *no* (farmers), *ko* (artisans), *sho* (merchants), and lastly, outcasts. This sense of hierarchy was built into the language. How a person addressed another depended on the status and roles of the individuals involved. Japanese courtesy governed a wide range of behaviors, among them the ways people bowed upon meeting and departing, how and what they said on different occasions and to different people, how they offered and received a bowl of rice, and how they drank their tea. There was a correct way of doing everything, depending on one's role as husband, wife, son, daughter, leader, farmer, and so on.[36]

The system of values that became the national ideal during the Meiji era developed from the moral code of the warrior class, the samurai. The code was based on Confucianism and Buddhism. From Confucianism came the patriarchal family system, in which children demonstrated unquestioned obedience to fathers, wives to husbands, and younger siblings to older brothers, especially the oldest brother. From Buddhism and Confucianism came the concept of *on*, the sense of deep obligation to superiors. This translated into compliance with the social order, and to duty, obedience, loyalty, and filial piety. The entire system assumed reciprocal relationships in which superiors protected and assisted inferiors.[37]

The code of the samurai prescribed sobriety, restraint, and frugality: "Be sparing of speech. Where you would speak ten words, speak but one. . . . As with feasting so with everything else: know when and where to stop. . . . When you leave a festive place, take leave while you still desire to stay. When you feel satisfied, you have had more than enough. Enough is too much." The code also demanded control over emotions, because duty to lord and to warfare came first. According to the anthropologist Minako K. Maykovich, "Buddhism furnished a sense of calm trust in fate, a quiet submission to the inevitable, a stoic composure in the face of danger or hardship." Unlike Westerners, who valued spontaneity and individuality, the Japanese emphasized predictability, control, and selflessness. These differences in cultural values would cause conflict within individual Nisei as they encountered American ways.[38]

Confucianism and Buddhism stressed devotion to the group. According to the anthropologist Takie S. Lebra, the individual's pride and shame were interwoven with those of the group, so that the group took on the status of the individual and the individual that of the group. This sense of interdependence formed the basis of the concept of *amae*, "the need to be loved and cherished." As described by L. Takeo Doi, amae is basic to understanding the personality structure of the Japanese. Both it and its verb form *amaeru*—"to depend and presume upon another's benevolence"—stem from the same root, *amai*, sweet. The feeling of amae developed first between mother and infant, with the child later extending it to other relationships.[39]

The family, which included past, present, and future members, was the basic social unit; the individual was its representative. The welfare of the family came before the welfare of the individual. When a woman married, she became the wife not only of her husband, but of his family. She was expected to show respect and obedience, not love and affection, to her husband and his family.[40]

The patriarch controlled the family's property and the lives of its members; his word was law. Oftentimes he had but distant relationships with his children. The eldest son, the future patriarch, was the most important child. He learned family traditions and obligations, inherited family property, and cared for his parents in their old age. Among the siblings he received favored treatment. But if he failed to live up to expectations, he might be forced to give up his rights. Parents who had no sons might adopt a son-in-law, who then took on the family name and assumed the role of eldest son.[41]

Filial piety was at the core of Japanese morality. More than just obedience to parents, it formed the basis of an outlook on life that prescribed a wide range of behaviors. The central idea was that since parents sacrificed unstintingly for their children, children must do their utmost to make their parents happy. Children who quarreled among themselves, acted disrespectfully or disobediently, lied or stole, or did anything that caused parental worry or unhappiness, were violating their filial duty.[42]

Because achievement brought family honor, the Japanese prized diligence and discipline, including the ability to set and adhere to long-term goals; these values became assets in the Nisei's drive to achieve success in America. If children failed to achieve, they failed to fulfill their filial obligations. Their mothers would criticize themselves for having raised their children improperly, and the children would in turn feel a heavy sense of guilt for having let their mothers down.[43]

The *on* or obligations owed parents were so great that they could be only partially repaid. Since parents sacrificed for their children, children had to obey their parents' wishes, especially in such major decisions as choosing occupations and marriage mates. Preoccupation with one's own happiness was considered selfish. As the American value of individualism, which ran directly counter to these values, inevitably crept into the thinking of the Nisei, it became a major source of generational conflict.[44]

During the Tokugawa regime the samurai devoted themselves to a lifetime of learning. Although its two-century long rule was in many ways a time of social and technological stagnation, the regime nevertheless achieved remarkable growth in the schooling of its people. The samurai devotion to education permeated the entire society. Commoners developed a voluntary system of temple schools, the *terakoya*, which spread nationwide so that by 1818, 40 percent of all boys and 10 percent of all girls attended school. By 1870 the literacy rate in Japan, roughly 50 to 60 percent, compared favorably with that of contemporary western European countries.[45]

It should be stressed that commoners welcomed the spread of schools. Parents willingly sacrificed so their offspring could attend school, believing it would help their children enhance their prestige and self-respect as well as materially improve their lives. By the time of the Meiji Restoration in 1868, the desire for schooling so pervaded the population that, according to the anthropologist Ronald P. Dore, "when political and technological change created new opportunities in a more fluid Meiji society they were eagerly taken up." In fact, the development of literacy during the two and a half centuries of Tokugawa rule was a necessary precondition for Japan's successful modernization during the Meiji era.[46]

Issei men, the bulk of whom came to Hawaii between 1885 and 1907, had on average four to six years of schooling; Issei women, most of whom came between 1900 and 1924, had generally completed from two to five years of schooling. Thus most of the Issei were functionally literate, having at least rudimentary skills in reading and writing, and many had more than that. But more than literacy, the Issei brought with them the idea of the importance of schooling, an idea that played an important role in their children's drive to enter middle-class American society.[47]

Issei valued schooling because they believed it provided opportunities to improve their standard of living. But even those without schooling strove to improve their economic standing. On the plantations Japanese moved steadily into skilled jobs, learning trades that were later useful in the outside world. In 1902 they made up 56 percent of all skilled employees on the plantations, and by 1910, 63 percent. At the same time their percentage among unskilled plantation laborers decreased from 73 percent in 1902 to 64 percent in 1910. Carpentry was among the skilled trades in great demand on the plantations. Buildings needed constant repair, and new buildings had to be constructed. The Japanese filled this need. By 1915 Japanese were proportionately represented among skilled plantation workers. In comparison, Portuguese supplied almost twice their normal proportion of skilled plantation workers, Hawaiians and Part-Hawaiians over two-and-a-half times, and Caucasians about four-and-a-half times.[48]

Like the Chinese and Portuguese before them, Japanese regularly left the plantations for opportunities elsewhere. During and after a devastating strike in 1920 (see chapter 10), thousands of Japanese workers and their families left the plantations permanently. Only the stepped-up importation of Filipinos saved the sugar industry from disaster. The increase of Japanese plantation laborers during the 1930s, like parallel increases among Portuguese, Hawaiians, and Part-Hawaiians, was a temporary phenomenon brought on by the economic depression. By 1920, the period of the Japanese-as-plantation-laborer had ended. That is, they were no longer overrepresented as plantation laborers but had moved into other occupations in sufficient numbers to achieve proportional representation in the plantation work force.[49]

How long individual Issei remained on the plantation and the kinds of jobs they took when they left varied widely. Some, like Richard Inouye's father, never left plantation work. Arriving in Hawaii in 1902, Inouye's father worked on different plantations on the islands of Hawaii and Oahu, first as a field laborer and then, in his later years, as a grounds and bathhouse keeper.[50] Others moved off the plantation after three, ten, or twenty years. Shoichi Kurahashi's father left plantation work at the turn of the twentieth century as soon as his three-year contract expired. He then leased three acres of farm land in Kamuela on the island of Hawaii, where he grew cabbages, lettuce, burdock, cucumbers, and buckwheat. He and other Kamuela farmers shipped their vegetables to Honolulu. Kurahashi's mother, a picture bride, joined her husband in 1907. Misae Yano's parents also stayed the minimum three years of their contracts before moving to Hauula in rural Oahu in 1903 to work for a haole doctor. Her mother worked as a maid, while her father took care of the grounds and stable. After a few years they purchased a clothes cleaning shop in Honolulu, where they worked until retirement.[51]

Yoshiko Oda's parents worked on a Maui plantation from 1900 to 1906 before moving to Wailuku town. There her father became a carpenter, while her mother raised vegetables and sold them to railroad workers and stevedores in Kahului. After fifteen years they bought a grocery store, where they made and sold such Japanese confections as *senbei, manju,* and *mochi.* Kazuo Hosaka's father worked on a sugar plantation for ten years before moving with his wife to Honolulu in 1908, where they raised their family. Hosaka's father worked first as a stevedore, and then bought a liquor store and bar on Hotel Street. He later sold the store and became a salesman for Acme Beer. His mother took in laundry while she raised the children. Lowell Takahashi's parents worked on Waialua plantation from 1900 to 1912, after which they set up a small business in the neighboring village of Haleiwa, making and selling *shoyu* (soy sauce). They also raised pigs, chickens, and ducks. When they had saved up enough money, they bought a small store. Tetsuko Tamura's father worked from 1905 to 1925 as a plantation carpenter in Lahaina, Maui. After moving off the plantation, he farmed and took odd jobs as a carpenter.[52]

Why did Japanese workers move off the plantation? Primarily because "the plantation [did] not treat the Japanese people equally with the white people," according to a Kona storekeeper in the 1920s. "The Japanese are paid less and have no chance for advancement," he explained. This was also true for other Asians. The experience of a Chinese bookkeeper at McBryde Plantation on Kauai during the second decade of the twentieth century illustrates the point. "My father was . . . asked to give up his position, which he had held for nearly ten years, to a *haole* man from the states," his daughter wrote. "As soon as that man stepped into the office, his salary was raised from sixty to a hundred dollars, while my father had worked at the same position for years without a raise of his salary."[53]

Lack of respect was an important part of this treatment. "Nothing is so disagreeable as being driven by a luna who keeps crying, 'Go ahead, go ahead,' at our back," explained a coffee farmer in the 1920s. He had left the plantation some years earlier. Lack of freedom, closely related to lack of respect, was yet another aspect of this treatment. In the 1920s, a Kona coffee farmer who had left the plantation years earlier explained, "We cannot make money here [growing coffee], but we do not worry about time and the *luna*. If we oversleep in the morning ten minutes, we do not have to lose a day. If we take a day's rest, we regain it by working twice as hard next day. . . . Our children play about on the farm with us." As Charles Sakai, explaining why his father left the plantation in 1907 to open a store, observed, "You can't get ahead working as a laborer."[54]

Both on and off the plantation the Japanese eagerly sought to improve their economic condition. "The Japanese in Hawaii are alert to seize every opportunity to advance themselves in . . . the skilled trades and mechanical industries," reported the U.S. labor commissioner in 1906. "Wherever a Japanese is given a position as assistant to a skilled worker or in a mechanical position, he becomes a marvel of industry, disregarding hours, working early and late, and displaying a peculiarly farsighted willingness to be imposed upon and do the work which properly belongs to the workman he is assisting." According to the commissioner, Issei fathers took their sons to builders and mechanics to get instruction in the trades, even offering to have their sons work without pay while learning the skill. "When I was doing work on the Sanitary Laundry," an employer said in 1905, "a Jap offered me $50 to teach him to wipe a joint. Some white plumbers who came down here in 1900 and 1901 made a good deal of money teaching their trade to Japs." But many craftsmen rejected the idea of training potential competitors. As one of them said, "I won't teach men to cut my throat."[55]

By 1900, skilled Caucasian workers and petty shopkeepers began to feel competition from Japanese who had left the plantations. That year, 619 of 1,955 carpenters outside the plantations were Japanese. And while in 1898, 13 percent (452 out of 3,411) of all small businesses in Hawaii were run by Japanese, six years later they accounted for 30 percent (1,241 out of 4,158). It should be noted, however, that six haole firms in Honolulu had an inventory of goods equal in value to more than all the goods carried by Japanese businesses in the territory. In addition, some of the Japanese businesses were actually distributors of haole firms. Among the types of businesses Japanese engaged in were hack driving; peddling vegetables, cakes, and cigars; raising ducks and chickens and selling their eggs; and running small restaurants and lodging houses. Japanese, like the Chinese before them, often took over small farms Caucasians had given up. One Japanese farmer explained that the lower standard of living of the Japanese enabled them to succeed where Caucasians had failed.[56]

Plantation managers originally recruited Japanese laborers because they wanted a work force of people who were "accustomed to subordination, to permanency of abode, and who [had] modest expectations in regard to a livelihood." Managers hoped these laborers would return to Japan after their contracts ended. But many Japanese, like many immigrants of all ethnic groups, chose to remain in Hawaii, despite haole misgivings about the growing Japanese population in the territory.[57]

As long as the Issei were "content to hoe cane," the economic overlords of Hawaii praised them. In the words of one hotel keeper, things were "all right as long as the Japs [kept] on working [on the plantations]." But when they sought to make it outside the plantations, as the Chinese had done in the 1870s and 1880s, they, like the Chinese, met resentment and discrimination from Caucasians who felt their own livelihoods and social positions threatened.[58]

Echoing attempts made in the 1880s to prevent the Chinese from competing as small businesspeople and skilled craftspeople, haole merchants and mechanics convinced the territorial legislature in 1903 to pass a law that excluded Issei from government employment. The law stipulated that only citizens or people eligible to become citizens (Issei were not eligible) could be hired by the government. Two years later the legislature enacted additional laws that made it more difficult for Asians to compete in the building trades. That same year the U.S. attorney in Honolulu wrote an opinion calling the 1903 law an unconstitutional violation of an 1895 treaty between the United States and Japan.[59]

By 1920 Japanese men outside plantation work were numerous as coffee, rice, and general farmers, carpenters, retailers, chauffeurs, fishermen, gardeners, longshoremen, painters, tailors, blacksmiths, machinists, mechanics, and brick and stone masons. Japanese women who worked outside the plantations found ready employment as domestic servants, farmers, laundresses, saleswomen, retailers, barbers, dressmakers, and tailoresses.[60]

During the first two decades of the twentieth century, Japanese women, more than women of any other ethnic group in Hawaii, worked outside the home both on and off the plantations, demonstrating their drive for economic advancement. In 1910, 44 percent of all Japanese females ten years and older worked outside the home for wages, compared to 17 percent of Caucasian and 12 percent each of Chinese and Part-Hawaiian females. In 1920, the corresponding percentages were 30 for Japanese, 25 for Caucasian, 12 for Part-Hawaiian, and between 11 and 12 for Chinese, Korean, and Filipino females.[61]

Issei mothers struggled between caring for their homes and raising their children on the one hand and augmenting their family incomes on the other. In the second decade of the twentieth century Richard Inouye's mother cooked, laundered, ironed, and performed a myriad of housekeeping tasks for her family as well as for Filipino laborers who boarded at their house. She also worked alongside her husband on sugarcane land they leased. Miyo Asuka and her husband settled in Waikiki in 1914 in an all-Japanese section of "shabby" rowhouses having a common kitchen and bathhouse. The men who lived there worked in hotels, usually as waiters, which brought them in constant contact with more affluent Caucasians. Asuka's husband worked at the Halekulani Hotel and she herself was a laundress. "The women who did not have children did family work for Caucasian families," she later recalled. "After the children came, [the Japanese women] could not go out so usually they took in laundry at home. . . . They would take [the laundry] outside under a *kiawe* [mesquite] tree and set up a table in the shade and set their metal washtubs on it and wash everything by hand. They strung wire between the trees and hung the wash there. . . . When their children were small, they would also do the ironing with them on their backs." Other women in Waikiki worked in rice paddies, still others in small shops they operated with their husbands—general merchandise stores, clothes cleaning shops, barbershops, and restaurants.[62]

The diversification of Issei economic life thus proceeded apace. Japanese men and women were proportionately represented in coffee farming and fishing before 1910, and in rice farming, independent businesses, and sales by 1920. Caucasians began growing coffee in the mid-nineteenth century, followed in succession by the Hawaiians, Chinese, and Portuguese. Japanese entered coffee farming as they moved off the plantations. By 1910 they were overrepresented in the industry. They grew most of their coffee in Kona, a remote rural district on the island of Hawaii, where they either owned or leased the land. Although coffee farming was not financially lucrative, Japanese farmers were satisfied with their lives, and once settled, they rarely left the district. According to a Kona resident in the late 1920s, "Kona [was] a city of refuge for the Japanese unable to stand plantation life."[63]

Fishing afforded another attractive means of earning a livelihood for Japanese, who, along with native Hawaiians, provided the bulk of the fishermen in the 1910s. Rice growing was also an important economic activity until about 1910, when competition from California drove hundreds of farmers away. At first most rice farmers were Chinese, but by 1920, when the industry was in decline, Japanese farmers achieved proportional representation in it. By that time, Japanese had also made significant gains as sales people, reaching a normal proportion by 1920.[64]

The Issei also began small businesses as they moved off the plantations. In this they followed the Chinese. Between 1890 and 1920 the Chinese were overrepresented among retailers in Hawaii, having two- to three-and-a-half times the normal proportion. The Japanese slowly increased their representation in this arena, reaching a normal proportion before 1920. As the experiences of the Aoki family suggest, the route to store ownership was often circuitous. In 1908, after a few years of plantation work on the island of Hawaii, Niro Aoki moved to Waikiki, where he worked as a waiter and then as a cook's helper at the Moana Hotel. After he married, he told himself, "Working for somebody, you'll never go ahead." So, with a horse and buggy he began peddling vegetables to residents in Waikiki. Meanwhile his wife laundered the uniforms hotel waiters wore and raised some thirty to forty chickens and ducks for sale. His son recalled, "Every night [my mother] used to sleep two . . . sometimes three hours. . . . The mongoose used to come around. . . . She have to get up, look around with lantern. Those days, no more flashlight. . . . And chase 'em away." By this time the Aoki's had four growing children, and they needed a less taxing business. "[My father] made a lot of friends, you know, with these *Haole* people," their son continued. "That's why, when he opened his store, they know him when he used to ride horse and buggy. . . . So when he started the business, they started to buy from him." The little grocery store offered canned goods like pork and beans, coffee, pineapple, peaches, corned beef, and sardines, as well as kerosene, motor oil, and (● soline.[65]

Moving off the plantation meant, for some workers more than others, contact with Caucasians and other ethnic groups, and with such contact came increasing acculturation into American ways. Transactions with non-Japanese employers or customers meant that the Issei had to learn at least rudimentary levels of English. The experiences of Misae Yano's parents illustrate this pattern. During the first thirty years of the twentieth century they owned a clothes-cleaning shop in Honolulu. Their business brought them in constant contact with haole, Portuguese, Hawaiians, and Chinese customers. As a result they, like Niro Aoki and his wife, became more integrated with the larger community.[66]

As this occurred the Issei—like Misako Yamamoto's father, who found he preferred American to Japanese ways—came to see Hawaii instead of Japan as their permanent home. During the second decade of the century they began buying property, building homes, and saving their money in Hawaii rather than sending it to Japan. Their experiences told them that America, despite its European American power structure, offered economic opportunities they did not have in Japan. If particular avenues of mobility were closed to them, the Issei pursued other routes, often taking occupations other groups had left, such as farming, or jobs others did not care to enter, such as domestic and laundry services. With their savings many were able to open their own businesses and further improve their economic situation.

In their efforts to improve their lives in Hawaii, the Issei found that some of their values conflicted with those of middle-class Americans. On the other hand, other values such as diligence, commitment to long-term goals, and frugality, as well as respect for schooling and for social hierarchy, facilitated their adjustment to American society. Then, too, living for so many years away from the exacting rules of Japanese social intercourse led many Issei to grow accustomed to the looser American lifestyle they found in Hawaii.

Generally optimistic about their own future and that of their children in America, the Issei who remained in Hawaii did so because they believed their lives there were better than they would be in Japan. This they believed despite the racism they encountered during the Americanization crusade that surfaced during World War I.

Part Two

The Americanization Campaign

Chapter 3

Americanization Fever

Tatsue Fujita, born in 1917, grew up like many other Nisei girls in Hawaii during the 1920s and 1930s. Her family struggled to make ends meet. Her father was a chef, and her mother took in laundry. But Fujita also stood out among her peers. She had a quick mind, loved to read, and excelled in both Japanese and English schools. In those days girls who aspired to white-collar jobs usually chose teaching, nursing, or secretarial work. Fujita chose teaching.[1]

After graduating from high school, she attended the University of Hawaii Teachers College for five years. During her last year there she became embroiled in a controversy that shook the Japanese community in Hawaii, veered her off her chosen course, and shattered her dreams.

Tomizo Katsunuma, a columnist for *Nippu Jiji*, brought Fujita's story to public attention in June 1939. "Last year a University of Hawaii coed of Japanese descent, whom I know," wrote Katsunuma, "finished her four-year course and was graduated from the university as an 'honor student.' This year she was to have graduated from the Fifth Year of Teachers College, after spending six months in classroom studies at the college and six months in [probationary] teaching." But, according to Katsunuma, Fujita had been accused of having "undemocratic" and "pro-Japanese" ideas, and on that basis was denied a teaching certificate. "How, in particular, must her parents feel," Katsunuma continued, "after having sent her to school all these many years at great effort, awaiting the day when she would receive employment. This young lady has been not only proficient in her studies but extremely gentle in disposition. . . . She is, in fact, a model coed embodying the good points of both America and Japan." Unfortunately for Fujita, this very quality made her suspect to Americanizers. Troubled by what had happened, Katsunuma went to see Dean Benjamin O. Wist of Teachers College. "The dean said that he was truly very sorry," reported Katsunuma, "but that after various investigations it was learned that the girl was one-half devoted to American culture and institutions and one-half to Japanese culture and customs." Wist told Katsunuma, "This person was above reproach in her morals;

she was an honor student in her studies; in her practice-teaching she did not make an A but did get a B. At all events, (I) lament the fact that this is the first instance of the denial of a teacher's certificate on the grounds of [being] 'undemocratic' and 'pro-Japanese.' "[2]

Three days before Katsunuma's article appeared, Fujita sent a letter to Wist. "After returning home," she wrote, "I have given due deliberation to our discussion as you advised me to do. As I understand it, the charge of being pro-Japanese and hence undemocratic was brought against me by Mrs. McCleery as the chief reason why I should not be recommended to receive my fifth year certificate. After spending five years of earnest preparation in Teacher's College, it is no small matter to me to be denied my certificate on the grounds of such a charge." Fujita agreed that she was interested in Japanese culture, but said it was secondary to her "far greater interest and concern for the welfare of a democratic culture." What she wanted to do, Fujita said, was "to glean the best in both Oriental and Occidental cultures," as Nisei had "repeatedly been urged to do by outstanding people in the community." Fujita continued, "You asked me then whether I were in any position to say what was the best for me to do, enrolled as I was in a democratic educational institution. I recall your exact words, 'Who are you anyway to judge what is best for you or for a democracy?' And you pointed out the fact that although as an individual, you recognized the existence of certain worthwhile elements in Oriental culture, as head of a democratic educational institution, you could not, in justice to your position, send out public school teachers who were interested in alien cultures."[3]

Fujita then demonstrated her grasp of the democratic ideal and the considerable degree to which she had acculturated. "According to my understanding of democracy, every individual is entitled to his opinion," she told Wist. "Undeniably if the opinions held by an individual are subversive to the welfare of democracy, they should be discouraged. But my so called pro-Japanese propensities are purely of a cultural nature and free from any political prejudice. There is a difference between nationalistic interest of a political nature," she pointed out, "and purely cultural interest that should be clearly recognized. If a public school teacher must refrain from showing interest in foreign culture, that would indeed be undemocratic." Fujita found it unacceptable to take the easy way out. "You asked me to be intellectually frank with myself, and offered to give me another chance at probationary teaching if I could completely revise my attitude in a more democratic direction," she said. "But I cannot perceive the necessity for changing my attitude, for I have never been anything but democratic. I have taken the legal steps to expatriate and have never expressed concern in the political welfare of Japan."[4]

In response Wist denied that Fujita failed to receive her Fifth Year Diploma because of Mrs. McCleery's charge that Fujita was pro-Japanese. "Your failure to receive the diploma was based on the rating of you as a probationary teacher," Wist wrote. "[McCleery] rated you unsatisfactory in teaching effectiveness, unsatisfactory in personal equipment, and . . . passable in professional equipment and growth." Wist then quoted from McCleery's evaluation report. "Miss Fujita," McCleery had written, "is unaware of, indifferent to, or unable to cope with the problems which arise in the process of guiding pupil growth. There was no desirable response to constructive criticism, little growth as a result of the many suggestions for improvement of teaching procedures. Throughout her whole teaching experience, there was little evidence of enthusiasm, energy, resourcefulness, thoroughness or purpose—those qualities so necessary for effective teaching." Wist continued, "There is no direct charge of un-Americanism against you." Yet he revealed the underlying issue when he added, "I raised the issue with you, quite aside from your probationary teaching record, as a problem for our consideration before definitely assuring you of a second trial at probationary teaching. From various statements made by Mrs. McCleery, a question arose in my mind relative to your judgment in matters which might cast some reflection on an American public school teacher of American children. I did, in my conversation with you, ask you whether you are in [the] best position to judge what is best in terms of American democracy. In view of the circumstances, I shall continue to reserve judgment as to whether or not you should be permitted to repeat probationary teaching."[5]

Both Japanese language dailies, *Hawaii Hochi* and *Nippu Jiji*, gave extensive coverage to this incident, and news of it spread throughout the Japanese community. A concerned father wrote *Nippu Jiji* that he was "truly shocked" at this turn of events. "Someone has explained the term 'un-democratic' and 'un-American,'" he wrote, "but they are still not clear to me. If the problem arose from character, it could not have risen suddenly just before graduation. . . . It is most important to ascertain what sort of words were adjudged to be undemocratic." *Nippu Jiji* protested editorially that Dean Wist had "ignored the usual practice" of granting another try at probationary teaching.[6]

To complicate matters, a few days before commencement, Fujita's mother sent a gift to McCleery "as a token of goodwill according to Japanese etiquette." Unfortunately, this gift—a bed-sheet costing $4.25—tied another knot in this already tangled web, for McCleery interpreted it as an attempt to bribe her to change her evaluation of Fujita's probationary teaching. The gift was not a bribe; it was sent after McCleery had turned in her report to Wist. Nevertheless, to someone culturally unattuned to Japanese custom, as McCleery clearly was, it cast another shadow on the case.[7]

In late July, the *Hochi* publisher Fred Kinzaburo Makino wrote President David L. Crawford of the University of Hawaii, urging him to ask Wist to reconsider his decision. Crawford did so, and Wist replied that he was willing to meet with Fujita again.[8] But there the matter seems to have ended. Fujita may have decided to drop the issue, for it is not difficult to imagine how emotionally wrenching this experience must have been for her. That she never discussed the experience with the man she later married—he was on the mainland at the time of the incident and therefore unaware of it—or with her children suggests the extent of her emotional scars. At any rate, according to family and friends, she never received a teaching certificate. Instead, she entered the College of Arts and Sciences at the University of Hawaii and earned a degree in philosophy. Soon after, she met her husband-to-be, who had just returned from the mainland, and after they married, she operated a floral business from her home.

Her friends have described Fujita as brilliant, articulate, fluent in English and Japanese, unconventional in her thinking, and perhaps too bright for ordinary people to understand. *Hawaii Hochi* succinctly summed up the sorry episode. Official prejudice and discrimination, wrote editor George W. Wright, ruined the career of a young woman who was "honorable enough to admit that she love[d] the country from which her parents came" and "so honest . . . that she would not resort to the easy pretense of conformity to standardized opinions. She ha[d] a mind of her own and the courage to maintain her beliefs even in the face of outright persecution."[9]

Fujita was rejected by an American institution for demonstrating forthrightness and independence of mind, and for daring to stand up for what she believed in, personality traits admired in middle-class Americans, but criticized by Americanizers when displayed by Nisei. Ironically, her "American" qualities cost Fujita a career in teaching.

This paradigmatic episode reveals the kind of discrimination Japanese Americans faced during the interwar years, and raises a question that lay at the heart of the Americanization mania that swept across the United States and Hawaii during the second and third decades of the twentieth century. Must children of immigrants reject their cultural heritage in order to be good Americans? The Fujita case illustrates the contrasting perceptions of dual identities Americanizers and Japanese held. While Americanizers insisted that the Nisei purge themselves of all interest in their ancestral country, the Nisei wanted to keep the best of their

Japanese culture while acculturating into American society. The case also shows the autocratic ways in which "democracy" was used, and the fragile nature of the tolerance granted Japanese Americans. Acceptance came only on condition that they follow the dictates of Americanizers. Fujita's case was rare because most Nisei were unwilling to pay the price for speaking their minds. Yet while they avoided openly challenging the authority and thinking of Americanizers, Nisei rejected the Americanizers' vision of the future role of Japanese in America because it constricted their freedom and denied them rights they believed they had as Americans.

Fujita's story took place on the eve of World War II, but it exhibited the kind of anti-foreign sentiment that fueled the Americanization crusade of the 1910s and 1920s. That crusade began on the mainland and found considerable appeal among European Americans in Hawaii. How it affected Caucasians, Issei, and Nisei in the territory is an important part of the history of the Americanization campaign and the acculturation of Americans of Japanese ancestry.

The Fujita case highlights three concepts that constitute the core of this study: Americanization, acculturation, and ethnic identity. During the first three decades of the twentieth century the term *assimilation* was used rather than *acculturation*. Further, *assimilation* was used interchangeably with *Americanization* to refer to what historians and sociologists now call Anglo-conformity. The assumption was that immigrants from southern and eastern Europe would absorb the culture of the dominant, white middle class until all vestiges of their old cultures disappeared. The result would be cultural uniformity and homogenousness in the country. It should be kept in mind that underlying this thinking of older Americans was the idea that immigrants and their children would remain in their "places" at the bottom of the socioeconomic ladder, at least until they disappeared as recognizable cultural groups.[10]

The idea of cultural uniformity was embodied in the phrase "melting pot," coined by Israel Zangwill in his 1908 play by that name and popular during the first quarter of the twentieth century. Zangwill saw America as a crucible in which all European ethnic groups, including Anglo-Americans, would melt and fuse together into an indigenous American type. Although the phrase implied biological as well as cultural merging of older and newer Americans, it came to refer to a unidirectional process in which immigrants of European ancestry would "melt into the dominant Anglo-American character." Racist thinking excluded African Americans, native Americans, and Asian Americans from this definition.[11]

In the 1920s the sociologist Robert E. Park, a pioneer in the study of inter-ethnic relations, posited what became a much debated thesis that ethnic groups underwent a cycle of contact, competition, accommodation, and assimilation—the final stage being the point at which a group's ethnicity was no longer a major issue.[12]

Park was followed by another major theorist of ethnic group relations in the United States, Marcus Lee Hansen. In 1937 Hansen noted "the almost universal phenomenon that what the son wishes to forget the grandson wishes to remember." This became a classic formula for the American experience of immigration and acculturation. "Hansen's law," as the sociologist Will Herberg called it, saw acculturation progressing with each succeeding generation. While the first generation remained attached to the old country and its traditions, the second—in the push to acculturate—rejected the ways of their immigrant parents. Because they were often not fully accepted by older Americans, however, the second generation was marginal to both societies. (The term "marginal man" was first used by Park to describe this plight of the second generation.) It remained for members of the third generation, secure in their identity as acculturated Americans, to revive interest in their ethnic heritage. Hansen's thesis, taken suggestively rather than literally, offers a useful perspective on the Nisei experience in Hawaii.[13]

Milton M. Gordon was yet another seminal student of American ethnic groups. His *Assimilation in American Life,* published in 1964, analyzed the multidimensional nature of the acculturation process. Previous scholars had assumed that the process was unidimensional. Gordon acknowledged the groundwork laid by Park and others, and used the term *assimilation* instead of *acculturation.* According to Gordon, cultural assimilation referred to conformity to the host culture in behavior, values, and customs; structural assimilation was the large-scale entrance into the friendship circles, social clubs, and institutions of the core society at the primary group level; marital assimilation meant widespread intermarriage; and identificational assimilation occurred when the group identified exclusively with the host society and lost its separate identity. Gordon recognized that each of these subprocesses occurred in varying degrees for different groups. In addition, before homogenization occurred, intergroup conflict had to disappear and prejudice and discrimination on the part of the host society had to be eliminated.[14]

Gordon placed structural assimilation at the center of his model. He believed that once structural assimilation occurred, either during or after cultural assimilation, all other types of assimilation would follow. "If children of different ethnic backgrounds belong to the same play-group," he wrote, "later the same adolescent cliques, and at college the same fraternities and sororities; if the parents belong to the same country club and invite each other to their homes for dinner; it is completely unrealistic not to expect these children, now grown, to love and to marry each other, blithely oblivious to previous ethnic extraction." Many scholars, though, have rejected Gordon's model largely because it posits the "old" American society as normative and the United States as a monocultural country, and because it fails to account for the distinctive experiences of non-whites.[15]

The historian John Bodnar recently criticized Gordon's model for its linearity. According to Bodnar immigrant communities were not the harmonious and undifferentiated groups Gordon assumed them to be. Immigrants within the same group came to America with unequal resources, skills and attitudes, and the histories of all groups include intragroup rivalry and divisiveness, as well as commonality, cooperation, and solidarity.[16]

Some anthropologists have posited a nonlinear, bicultural model to describe the acculturation process. According to this model the host culture does not replace the immigrants' traditional culture but instead is added onto it. Bicultural people choose the appropriate behavior for given occasions from their bicultural repertoire.[17]

Closely associated with acculturation is the concept of ethnic identity, and with it cultural pluralism, first articulated in 1915 by Horace M. Kallen. Kallen argued that ethnic group identity would not disappear, but that in fact cultural diversity would persist. In the words of Harold J. Abramson, Kallen viewed the United States as a "fabric woven of different but persisting ethnic communities."[18]

Scholars who have written about the persistence of ethnicity, among them Nathan Glazer, Daniel P. Moynihan, Andrew M. Greeley, and Michael Novak, reject a static view of pluralism that limits it to the maintenance of traditional culture. They recognize that subcultures can and frequently do evolve into something new. Nicholas Appleton has argued that "groups change and develop in directions that cannot be explained solely on the basis of traits inherited from their past or from the characteristics of other groups." Greeley posited the concept of ethnogenesis to account for these dynamics. Others have explored the idea of "the invention of ethnicity." According to this view, groups continually adapt, construct, and recreate in response to changes in the host society and within the groups themselves.[19]

Acculturation appropriately accounts for part of the Nisei experience in Hawaii. Gordon's model, despite its flaws, provides a useful framework for understanding the varying degrees of Nisei acculturation—in terms of their behavior and values, friendship circles and clubs, intermarriage, and identity with the host society. At the same time, cultural persistence also describes what took place with the Nisei. In fact acculturation and the persistence of ethnic identity together characterize their experience. While the Nisei acculturated into American middle-class society, they also retained aspects of their Japanese cultural heritage. Many felt pressures and dilemmas coming from the conflicting forces of absorption and differentiation. Tatsue Fujita reaped the unfortunate consequences of that predicament.

Although Americans during the first half of the twentieth century used the terms *Americanization* and *assimilation* interchangeably to refer to Anglo-conformity, this study uses acculturation instead of assimilation to highlight the cultural adaptive processes, and distinguishes between the concepts of Americanization and acculturation. Acculturation refers to the adaptation of a group to American middle-class norms and assumes that the process entails the persistence of ethnic identity. Americanization, on the other hand, refers to the organized effort during and following World War I to compel immigrants and their children to adopt certain Anglo-American ways while remaining at the bottom socioeconomic strata of American society.

The national movement to Americanize immigrants and their children began at the turn of the twentieth century. It escalated into a feverish crusade even before America entered the First World War, producing a frenzy of xenophobia between 1915 and 1921. The movement reflected a felt need of older Americans, generally of north European, Protestant ancestry, for greater national unity behind what they regarded as traditional American values. It developed as a reaction to the millions of southern and eastern European immigrants who arrived in the United States from about 1880 to 1914, who seemed much more "foreign" and therefore threatening than had earlier immigrants. The threat was magnified by the crowding of the "new" immigrants into industrial cities in the northeast and midwest, where they often transformed established neighborhoods into overcrowded slums. Underlying the Americanization movement was what Barbara Miller Solomon has called "the Anglo-Saxon complex," the conviction that American traits derived from English forebears, a conviction that found intellectual credence in the nineteenth century.[20]

While the Americanization campaign was in many ways a product of its time, its characteristic push for Anglo-conformity echoed earlier attitudes of cultural arrogance in American history. During the colonial period the predominant English Americans were ambivalent at best toward other European but non-English Americans. Greatest prejudice focused on the two largest groups, the Irish and the Germans. Non-whites were the target of a more hostile racism in which all European Americans participated. Colonists branded native Americans as uncivilized, dispossessed them of their lands, and demanded that they strip themselves of their culture, convert to Christianity, and adopt other Anglo ways. Where it proved profitable, colonists imported enslaved Africans. While the experience of each ethnic group was unique due to cultural and historical differences, patterns of discrimination first developed against native Americans and African Americans during the colonial period laid the basis for later discrimination against Asian immigrants and their children.[21]

During the revolutionary and post-revolutionary era only about ten thousand immigrants arrived yearly, most of them Britons. A change in the immigrants' ethnic origins coupled with an increase in numbers during the decades after 1820 engendered increasing intolerance among Americans. Much of this immigration, which crested in the mid-1850s, came from Ireland and Germany, and many of the immigrants were Catholics.[22]

The historian John Higham has noted that nativism, "intense opposition to an internal minority on the ground of its foreign (i.e., 'un-American') connections," has been present throughout American history. It erupted during times of national uncertainty: during threat of war with France in the late 1790s, resulting in the Alien Acts; after a period of increased immigration, resulting in vicious anti-Catholicism of the 1850s; during the economic upheavals of the 1880s and 1890s coming from the industrial revolution; and during and after World War I.[23] Fueled by the same distrust of "foreign" ways that generated earlier nativist movements, the Americanization crusade of the late 1910s and early 1920s developed into a massive effort to imbue immigrants with "American" ways.

The primary impetus behind the crusade came from two contrasting groups. One group consisted chiefly of social workers who sought to alleviate the living conditions of impoverished immigrants and help them adjust to their new environment. The other was made up of nationalistic groups like the Daughters of the American Revolution (DAR) and the American Legion, who were committed to programs of education designed "to indoctrinate the adult foreigner with loyalty to America."

They hoped to accomplish this through lectures on American history and government and in preachments designed to inculcate obedience to the law and awareness of the dangers of European radicalism. Both groups were abetted by industrialists alarmed by labor unrest and union activity, and by city governments concerned about the impact of immigration on their communities. The combined efforts of these groups gathered momentum after 1910, when state and federal agencies concerned with education and naturalization joined them. Before World War I, however, most Americans remained indifferent to this cause.[24]

The war shattered that indifference. Enthusiastic Irish, Lithuanians, Czechs, Poles, Slovaks, and others in the United States spoke out for the independence of their homelands. More important, German Americans actively supported the German Empire in a cause other Americans considered immoral.

America's entry into World War I "gripped the nation like a fever," arousing "intense patriotism" and "a suspicion of all things alien." The resulting atmosphere fueled the efforts of Americanizers to "mould the immigrant into a full-fledged American with undivided loyalties." Amid calls for "100 percent Americanism," Americanization became a national crusade.[25]

After the war the Red Scare, coming on the heels of the Bolshevik Revolution, further propelled the crusade. The years 1919 and 1920 were marked by the so-called Palmer raids. Led by Attorney General A. Mitchell Palmer, agents of the Department of Justice arrested and deported thousands of aliens suspected of acting against the government. It should be noted that although Americanizers called for 100 percent Americanism, during the Red Scare the Americanization movement was the positive thrust. The negative thrust came from exclusionists who advocated immigration restrictions and deportation.[26]

While the focus of exclusionists differed from that of Americanizers, the restriction and deportation campaigns helped to fuel the Americanization crusade. Thus when Congress passed immigration restriction laws in 1921 and 1924, drastically cutting the immigrant flow from southeastern Europe and largely ending it from Asia, the excesses of the restriction campaign and of the Red Scare abated, and the Americanization movement on the mainland lost its steam. Nevertheless, educators and others, who saw public schools as major instruments for Americanization, maintained their interest in the cause.[27]

Americanizers freely tossed about such terms as patriotism, loyalty, American ideals, and the American way of life, but they did little to explain what these terms meant. They took for granted that "real" Americans understood them. *Webster's New International Dictionary of the*

English Language, unabridged and published in 1920, defined *Americanize* as "to render American; to assimilate to the Americans in customs, ideas, etc.; to stamp with American characteristics." Its 1935 edition softened its definition by substituting "bring into conformity" for "stamp with," and added "speech" as another area for Americanization. The 1935 edition defined *Americanization,* a term missing from its 1920 edition, as the "instruction of immigrants in English, civics, American history, and other studies designed to prepare them for life in the United States."[28]

Americanizers on the mainland, like those in Hawaii, sought to strip immigrants of their native customs. "What kind of American consciousness can grow in the atmosphere of sauerkraut and Limburger cheese?" asked a member of the DAR. "What can you expect of the Americanism of the man whose breath always reeks of garlic?"[29]

Community groups across the nation joined the effort to Americanize the immigrants. Ethnic societies, with the support of the foreign language press, attempted to ease the immigrants' adjustment to their new environment through clubs, libraries, lectures, kindergartens, and classes in English, civics, sewing, and cooking. City governments, churches, public libraries, and YWCAs sponsored similar programs. But the effort had limited success. Rates of attendance lagged far behind enrollment, probably because evening classes had little appeal for people who worked hard all day.[30]

While evening classes focused on adults, public schools concentrated on the more malleable children. Americanization bureaus appeared in state and local school systems across the nation. The New York City school superintendent William L. Ettinger, who called New York in 1918 "one of the largest Jewish cities, one of the largest Italian cities, and one of the largest Russian cities of the world," warned that Americanization would not happen automatically. Evening schools, neighborhood centers, industry, government, and especially public schools—"the chief instrument of Americanization"—must actively teach immigrants and their children the English language and American democratic ideals.[31]

The idea that public schools should teach newcomers the responsibilities of citizenship was not new. In the years before the Civil War citizens had called on schools to Americanize immigrants. What was new was the "heightened self-consciousness" and "greater sense of urgency" with which the calls were now made. In this context American history and civics courses took on crucial roles.[32]

Schools also attempted to instill patriotism in other ways, among them daily flag salutes, observation of national holidays, and English-only instruction. By 1923, primarily as a result of the war against Germany, thirty-four states required English as the language of instruction in public elementary schools.[33]

Hawaii's Americanization crusade mirrored its mainland counterpart, but with two differences. Its "new" immigrants were mostly Asians, not southern and eastern Europeans. Moreover the movement in Hawaii, which focused on the Japanese, the largest and most conspicuous Asian group, continued until World War II, well after the effort on the mainland had dissipated.

To most Americanizers on the mainland, Asians were undesirable racially and thus unpromising prospects for American citizenship. Reflecting this view was Edward P. Irwin, former editor of the Honolulu newspaper, the *Pacific Commercial Advertiser.* "The Oriental races are practically all of small stature, slight physique, yellow or brown color and, in the case of the Japanese, characterized by flat features, protruding teeth and short legs," he declared. "We have a right to ask ourselves if we want to incorporate such characteristics in the American body." To Irwin and his counterparts on the mainland, southern and eastern Europeans were at least Caucasians and therefore possibly salvageable, but Asians were not. "Ever since [the Japanese] began to arrive on the Pacific Coast in sufficient numbers to attract attention," wrote the sociologist Jesse F. Steiner in 1921, "they have been the subject of controversy at times so bitter that it has threatened to involve us in war with Japan." A professor at the University of North Carolina, Steiner criticized the prevailing view. "A decade or more ago we condemned [Japanese immigrants] as undesirable because they were willing to work for low wages and brought with them a low standard of living," he continued. "Today . . . the charges made against them are that they demand high wages, insist upon owning land, are successful in business competition, and desire to establish themselves as residents in white communities. The qualities that would ordinarily command respect become in their case a reproach." Steiner suggested that the "fundamental difference" between Asian and European immigrants was physique. "No matter, therefore, how responsive the Japanese may be to their American environment," he wrote, "their physical type marks them out as Orientals." Such thinking rejected the possibility of Asians ever being Americanized as that term was understood by Americanizers on the mainland. But Americanizers in Hawaii realized that many Japanese would remain in the Islands, and undertook to apply to them notions of Americanization that had been worked out on the mainland with southern and eastern Europeans in mind.[34]

The Americanization movement in Hawaii mushroomed at the end of World War I and continued unabated through the early 1920s. In those years editorials in both of the haole-controlled daily newspapers in Honolulu echoed mainland Red Scare rhetoric. R. A. McNally, editor of *Honolulu Star-Bulletin* warned in 1919, "The red flag must not be raised in America." The *Pacific Commercial Advertiser* more pointedly urged, "Wipe the Bolsheviki off the earth." As if to reinforce these sentiments, the United States Attorney in Honolulu, S. C. Huber, declared that "no remarks of an anarchistic or Bolshevik nature" would be "tolerated" in the territory.[35]

But the Americanization campaign in Hawaii was not primarily concerned with Bolshevism. Its main thrust grew from a subtler anxiety over the future of American control of the territory. The source of this anxiety was the presence of so many Japanese. Americanizers worried that the Japanese held on to their customs and language, encouraged racial pride of their own, and wanted to "Japanize" the territory. To be sure, these worries were never examined critically, but the rhetoric they inspired increased the anxieties that lay beneath them, and the resulting xenophobia pervaded the movement in Hawaii.[36]

Since the Japanese constituted the largest group of plantation laborers, anti-Japanese sentiment became fused with anti-unionism. Moreover, opponents of labor unions in Hawaii as on the mainland succeeded in drawing on the fears inspired by anti-Bolshevism and anti-radicalism. Following in the footsteps of mainland states, the territorial legislature passed a criminal syndicalism law in 1919 aimed at blocking effective union activity.[37]

Michael R. Olneck has interpreted the Americanization movement as "an effort to secure cultural and ideological hegemony through configuration of the symbolic order." By controlling rhetoric and ritual, Americanizers would determine social perceptions, thereby limiting "the field of legitimate action and choice." Olneck's analysis is especially useful for understanding the movement in Hawaii. By accusing the Japanese of attempting to "Japanize" the Islands, Americanizers framed the discourse on and public policy toward the Japanese, and brought to the surface latent fears of Japanese power in the territory.[38]

Anti-Japanese sentiment in Hawaii had existed before the Americanization campaign. It first emerged in the 1890s, as soon as the influx of Issei became substantial, continued intermittently thereafter, and increased dramatically prior to and during World War II. Sheer numbers made the Japanese conspicuous and therefore objects of anxiety. Between 1900 and 1940, Japanese constituted from 37.2 to 42.7 percent of the territory's population (see figure 1).[39]

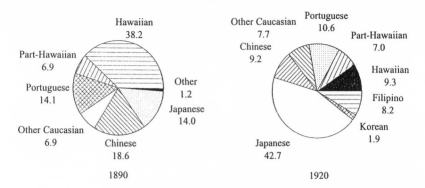

Figure 1. Population Percentages in Hawaii,
by Ethnic Group, 1890 and 1920.

Source: Lind, *Hawaii's People*, 28.

During the 1890s, leaders of the Republic of Hawaii attempted to stem
the tide of Japanese immigration even as they tried to use the fear of Japanese domination to encourage American annexation. Their effort was
unwittingly aided by Japan, who was just then demanding indemnities
for insults to its citizens in Hawaii. In this context the supposed threat
of Japan's territorial ambitions toward Hawaii emerged, and dire warn-
ings of a "Japanization" of the Islands commenced. Yet the hostility of
this early period had focused on politics and diplomacy. To the political
and diplomatic issues of the 1890s, the Americanization movement after
World War I added conflicts over religion, dual citizenship, the Japanese
language press, and Japanese language schools.[40]

As had been the case with Chinese immigrants earlier, attitudes
toward the Japanese depended on the size of their population. When
the Chinese had been proportionately more numerous in Hawaii in the
1880s, Caucasians had denounced them and praised the Japanese, but
once the Japanese became more numerous, they became objects of criticism while the Chinese were praised and their help sought in controlling
Issei rebelliousness. Thus in 1921, sugar planters made a concerted effort
to do something they once warned against, recruit more Chinese contract laborers. With the support of Governor Charles McCarthy, they
convinced the territorial legislature to create a Hawaii Emergency Labor
Commission to lobby Congress to relax restrictions against the immigration of Chinese laborers. In doing so, planters and government leaders
who joined them deliberately attempted to incite fears of a "Japanese

menace." While failing to convince federal officials of the need to import Chinese laborers, Hawaii's oligarchy did succeed in convincing them of a Japanese peril. The federal government's final report on this matter supported later military intelligence surveys during and after World War II that warned of Hawaii's Issei and Nisei as national security threats.[41]

Labor-management conflict, most notably manifested in strikes by sugarcane workers in 1909 and 1920, sustained tensions between Japanese and Caucasians. Moreover Japan's expansionist foreign policy increased the uneasiness among Caucasians, who read of the country's actions with the Hawaii situation in mind. Incendiary speeches in 1922 by the California exclusionist V. S. McClatchy, former publisher of the *Sacramento Bee*, and by former Senator James D. Phelan of California, who periodically visited Hawaii after World War I, added fuel to the anti-Japanese hostility.[42]

But by 1924, local, national, and international events lessened the fears of many Caucasians. Locally a 1920 sugar strike failed and the territorial legislature enacted laws to control foreign language schools and foreign language newspapers. Nationally the Supreme Court, in a case involving Takao Ozawa, ruled in 1922 that Japanese aliens could not become American citizens, and Congress in 1924 passed an immigration law that excluded Japanese immigrants. Internationally Japan accepted a ratio of naval tonnage, worked out at the Washington Conference, that seemed to make the country a secondary naval power. Yet anxieties about the Japanese never entirely disappeared, nor did efforts to Americanize the Nisei.[43]

How did Americanizers in Hawaii define Americanization? Albert W. Palmer, minister of the Congregationalist Central Union Church, the house of worship of many of Hawaii's haole elite, said in 1920 that to Americanize meant to inculcate the "ideals of democracy, representative government," and "religious freedom." Frank F. Bunker, excecutive secretary of the Pan Pacific Union, defined Americanization in 1922 as the process of acquiring "a love for . . . liberty, justice, tolerance, fairness, and a desire for an enriched life for others as well as oneself."[44]

But such definitions were in the minority. What Americanizers really wanted was for the Nisei to give undivided loyalty to the United States and discard all vestiges of Japanese culture. They also insisted that the Nisei read, write and speak Standard English, become Christians, obey the law, and be good plantation workers. Americanizers also had less clearly defined expectations of the Nisei, such as wanting them to get an American education, establish American homes, use American business methods, and maintain good moral character. Although the Nisei were their primary targets, Americanizers also expected the Issei to behave like Americans and regarded them with suspicion when they cheered Japan's military victories and otherwise behaved too much like Japanese.[45]

Schools, most agreed, had to play a major role in Americanization. Lorrin A. Thurston, publisher of the *Pacific Commercial Advertiser*, told Japanese language school teachers at an Americanization Institute in 1919 that public schools were the only hope to Americanize the Nisei. Similarly the *Honolulu Star-Bulletin* editor Riley H. Allen believed that public schools were the "chief agency" for developing citizenship, because they reached "impressionable children, quick to grasp a new language and new ideas."[46]

Indicative of the Anglo-conformity characteristic of the Americanization campaign was a statement made in 1920 by Edgar Wood, principal of the Territorial Normal and Training School. "In the elementary school, about 97 or 98 per cent of the school population are non-[Standard] English speaking," Wood wrote. "They come from homes slightly removed from alien standards; they do not know our language, or practice our activities, or enjoy our sports or wear our style of clothes, nor do they live in houses similar in design to ours, or under similar sanitary conditions; they are non-American in activities, in manners and customs, in ideals and standards, in hopes and ambitions. It is necessary then, to make of this polyglot group Americans with the hopes and ambitions of Anglo-Saxons." Accordingly Wood's Normal School stressed "home geography," American history, civics, and literature, as well as music, drawing, and vocational work. While mathematics and the sciences were "not neglected," they were not stressed "for the simple reason" that they did not inculcate patriotism. Clarence Kobayashi, a Nisei teacher in the 1930s, recalled the Americanization effort in the rural Oahu school in which he taught. "Up to the Second World War," he said, "we always had patriotic programs. In the morning the whole school assembled and we used to have the pledge to the flag, and we used to sing patriotic songs—everyday."[47]

Concern over Nisei patriotism continued with Japan's apparent militarism. In 1932, Rear Admiral Yates Stirling, commandant of the Fourteenth Naval District, which included Pearl Harbor, warned Washington of "an acute threat of sabotage" against military property by "hostile elements in the local population." He called "the large number of aliens" there "a matter of grave concern," and doubted the loyalty of "certain island-born orientals . . . in event of war with an oriental power." As tensions between Japan and the United States grew during the 1930s, the question of Nisei loyalty loomed larger and larger. Hawaii's Congressional Delegate Samuel W. King, a Republican, had to reassure a Washington audience in 1941 that the Issei, who were denied American citizenship, were "an elderly group, rapidly passing off the scene through natural causes." Their children, who were citizens, he added, were "without the shadow of doubt, as loyal as any other American."[48]

The Americanization campaign rested on a combination of ignorance, fear, xenophobia, and racism. Had Japan been a weak country, Americanizers' anxiety over the future control of the territory would have been completely unfounded. But Japan's visibly growing military strength and aggressive foreign policy, the large size of the Japanese population in Hawaii, the patriotism the Issei displayed so fervently on the occasions of Japan's victories, and the frequent visits by Japanese warships to Hawaii made the anxiety understandable, even if exaggerated. The limited reality behind the anxiety existed because the Issei, as subjects of Japan, did feel loyalty to their homeland, and some Nisei, too, felt strong attachment to Japan. According to the historian John Stephan, some Nisei showed enthusiastic support for Japan in her war against China during the late 1930s by joining the Imperial Army. Moreover, a sizable number of Nisei who went to Japan in the 1930s for education or other reasons remained there even after the American government in 1940 and 1941 advised its citizens to return to the United States.[49]

Ironically, while Americanizers called on the Nisei to show undivided loyalty to the United States, prejudice against the Japanese helped sustain Issei loyalty to Japan and encouraged some Nisei to view Japan as a place of refuge from racial and social discrimination to an extent that at least a few of them chose Japan over the United States when war between the two countries threatened. This points to an important element in the Americanization campaign, the degree to which it pushed Issei and Nisei away from rather than toward America.[50]

The Issei were aware of the suspicion against them, and as they put down roots in Hawaii, they became increasingly sensitive to it. In 1915 they took concerted action to mitigate this suspicion by forming the Hawaii Japanese Education Society, whose first activity was revising textbooks used in Japanese language schools. The revisions deleted sections encouraging emperor worship and Japanese nationalism, and adapted stories and lessons to the life and experiences of children born in Hawaii.[51]

Among the Issei, three men dominated the debate on Americanization. In their calls for accommodation and confrontation they were like leaders of other ethnic groups responding to pressures from the dominant American society. One Issei was a Congregationalist minister, the Reverend Takie Okumura, and the other two were newspapermen, the

Hawaii Hochi publisher Fred Kinzaburo Makino and the *Nippu Jiji* president and editor-in-chief Yasutaro Soga. All three were educated in Japan, and all three left Japan for Hawaii as young men at the turn of the twentieth century.[52]

Okumura, the oldest, was thirty when he arrived in 1894. He quickly accommodated himself to the haole elite, internalized their values and saw his fellow Japanese and their children through the eyes of Americanizers. In keeping with the Americanizers' social and economic agenda, Okumura zealously sought to Christianize the Japanese and convince them to remain on the plantation. As discussed earlier, with the covert financial backing of the Hawaiian Sugar Planters' Association (HSPA), he began a six-year campaign in 1921 to Americanize the Issei. A bitter sugar strike had just ended, and controversy over Japanese language schools raged. Okumura was convinced that the Japanese must "go more than halfway" to "dispel the thickening clouds" that had appeared. He held meetings with laborers on plantation after plantation, urging them to adopt American ways, become Christians, remain on the plantation and encourage their children to do likewise, and otherwise work to improve relations between themselves and Caucasians. In 1927 he began a series of New Americans Conferences. While he stated publicly that the chief purpose of the conferences was to make the Nisei good American citizens, he admitted privately that he actually sought to convince the Nisei to work on the plantations.[53]

In 1939, as war between Japan and the United States seemed inevitable, Okumura continued to urge the Nisei to be 100 percent Americans, "without even a string tying them to Japan." But even then, like most Issei, Okumura advised the Nisei to retain such Japanese values as duty, responsibility, and loyalty, which he believed were thoroughly compatible with Americanization. In his autobiography, written in 1940, Okumura said of the Nisei, "Just so long as Japanese blood flows in their veins, they should grasp the real spirit of Bushido [the way of the samurai], Americanize it, and carry it along with them."[54]

While urging the Japanese to "think and act from the viewpoint of American people," Okumura nevertheless opposed the legal challenges to territorial laws subjecting Japanese language schools to controls that would have effectively destroyed them. His vision of the future of the Japanese in Hawaii was as subordinate members of a society dominated by European Americans.[55]

In contrast, Fred Kinzaburo Makino, the most acculturated of the three Issei leaders, vehemently rejected the viewpoint of Americanizers and instead was an advocate for the rights of Japanese in Hawaii. He urged the Nisei to be Americans in the fullest sense of the term.

The third son of an English merchant and his Japanese wife, Makino was born twenty-one years before he arrived in Hawaii in 1899. His fun-loving, mischievous ways as a young man led an older brother, Eijiro, by then a Yokohama businessman, to send young Makino to Hawaii, where his eldest brother already lived, to "gain some real-life experience." Upon his arrival Makino lived with his brother, who operated a store in Naalehu on the island of Hawaii.[56]

Instinctively a champion of the underdog, the feisty Makino, who was fluent in English as well as Japanese, threw himself headlong into multiple causes of the Japanese as they encountered racial, social, and economic discrimination. He helped lead a massive sugar strike in 1909, fought for naturalization rights for Issei soldiers who served in the army during World War I, and led a court battle in the 1920s that success-fully challenged territorial laws aimed at destroying Japanese language schools. He also fought for a retrial when a Nisei, Myles Fukunaga, faced hanging in 1928 for the murder of the son of a prominent haole. When that fight was unsuccessful, Makino implored Governor Lawrence M. Judd for clemency (chapter 4 discusses Fukunaga's case). Such actions made the Japanese appreciate, and the Caucasians respect, Makino.[57]

Makino inverted Okumura's advice to Japanese. He agreed that the Nisei should retain those aspects of Japanese culture that helped them adapt to and succeed in America. But he stressed "justice and a square deal" rather than acquiescence. According to Makino "bowing down in humility and kow-towing to supervisors" were uncharacteristic of Americans. "Americans," he said, "bow to no master and cringe to no superior. They are straight shooters and are very apt to say exactly what they think, because they are not afraid of anyone. Frankness, sincerity, and self-respect are the cardinal virtues."[58]

Makino's attitude toward Okumura's New Americans Conferences demonstrated the contrasting approaches of the two men. In a trenchant critique in 1934, a *Hochi* editorial called the conferences an attempt at "mental grooming" of Nisei youths through speeches in which "selected 'pap' " that fell "from the lips of the big shots" planted the "right views." Such practices, according to *Hochi*, only produced "outward conformity" and did not teach people to "think for themselves," which was essential for responsible citizenship.[59]

Makino criticized what he regarded as obsequious behavior of many Nisei. "What, in the older generation," explained a *Hochi* editorial, "was the deference and courtesy of the stranger in the presence of his host, has become in the young Japanese an obsequiousness that is almost servile and that is wholly foreign to the American standards." Makino urged the Nisei to "attack and overcome opposition." Otherwise, why insist that one was an American? "When the young Japanese are able to look their white brothers squarely in the eye and tell them to 'get out of the way,' " he argued, "they will find out whether there is any race discrimination that can hinder them or keep them from success."[60]

Makino's views point to the ambiguity of what being American meant. While Americanizers urged Nisei to adopt particular "American" characteristics such as patriotism, Christianity, the work ethic, and Standard English, while remaining contented workers at the bottom of the socioeconomic ladder, Makino stressed assertiveness and independence. He also insisted on fair play, economic opportunity, social mobility, individual diligence, and group solidarity, all of which were compatible with Japanese values.

Yasutaro Soga, the third Issei leader, stood somewhere between the accommodationist Okumura and the confrontational Makino. Educated in Japan at the Tokyo Pharmacy School and the English Law Institute, Soga, a Christian, arrived in Hawaii in 1896 when he was twenty-three years old. He clerked in and then managed stores in rural Oahu and Molokai before becoming assistant editor of the Japanese language newspaper, *Hawaii Shimpo,* and then editor of *Yamato Shimbun,* the forerunner of *Nippu Jiji.*

In his editorials, the mild-mannered and soft-spoken Soga advised caution in dealing with Americanizers. Like Okumura, Soga urged accommodation with European Americans, advising his readers, for example, not to litigate during the Japanese language school controversy. But unlike Okumura, Soga publicly criticized the haole establishment when he thought it necessary, exposing, for example, the "wretched" conditions of work and life on plantations, and admonishing the *Pacific Commercial Advertiser* and *Star-Bulletin* for anti-Japanese statements. He used the pages of *Nippu Jiji* to explain America to the Japanese and the Japanese to Americans.[61]

In the heat of the Americanization crusade Soga cried prejudice when the American Legion sought to abolish Hawaii's foreign language schools and newspapers. "The Japanese are proud of their race," he wrote. "It is a serious mistake . . . to adopt an Americanization policy [that] treats them, in the face of their children, as . . . less than human beings." Such a policy challenged their self-respect and thereby increased antagonism. Indeed the Japanese bristled at the racism directed against them, for they were as sure of their own superiority as Caucasians were of theirs. Soga also argued that efforts to abolish foreign language newspapers were not expressions of genuine Americanism, but violations of American ideals of liberty, equality, and justice.[62]

Like Makino and Okumura, Soga believed that Nisei should be loyal Americans, obey the law, and learn English. And like them he insisted that being a good American was compatible with fluency in the Japanese language. He argued that the Nisei should learn Japanese as well as English, not only to be able to communicate with their parents, but also to be in a position to bridge the cultural gap between Japan and the United States. Like most Japanese, Soga maintained that the essentials of good Japanese citizenship and good American citizenship were compatible, and that therefore the Nisei should keep what was best in Japanese culture while learning what was best in American culture. He defended the practice of including Nisei in celebrations of the emperor's birthday, pointing out that other Americans of foreign ancestry celebrated the national holidays and honored the heroes of their cultural homelands. Soga saw no conflict between such observances and loyalty to the United States.[63]

Like Makino but unlike Okumura, Soga advocated acculturation rather than Americanization. He believed that becoming a good American was a lifetime process, and that education and decent wages were key elements in that process. On occasion Soga reprinted speeches by Caucasians as well as Japanese that expressed his point of view. Such was the case in March 1923 when he reprinted a statement by the Reverend Royal G. Hall of Koloa Protestant Church on Kauai. According to Hall, an American was not of a particular race, but a person with a certain set of values. Americans manifested these values by participating in "political, social, religious and individual activities" and by rising "up from the ranks of unskilled labor." For Hall, America meant equal rights and opportunities, and education at public expense. To him patriotism was not transmitted by reading textbooks and memorizing the Constitution. "Participation," he said, "rather than paternalism is the thing to be aimed at." Japanese who read Hall's comments were well aware of the gap between American ideals and the obstacles that blocked their access to the promise of those ideals. Soga spoke for them when he pointed to those obstacles—the denial of citizenship to the Issei, discrimination against Issei and Nisei in social and economic affairs, and "deplorable" working and living conditions on the plantations. If plantation managers wanted immigrants and their children to be good Americans as they said they did, Soga declared, they had to improve these conditions and work to eliminate discrimination. As talk of a strike loomed in 1920, Soga questioned the sincerity of plantation managers' calling on their workers to Americanize while at the same time attempting to import Chinese laborers to undercut the efforts of workers for better pay.[64]

The Americanization campaign and the advice from Issei leaders called the Nisei's attention to the gaps between what they were and what those around them thought they should be. In this sense the debate about the Nisei accelerated their acculturation by making them acutely conscious of their dual identities.

Student essays written in 1927 show that the Americanizers' emphasis on patriotism had reached many Nisei, who responded enthusiastically to their American identity. "I am proud that I am an American," wrote a Normal School student, "living freely and happily under the stars and stripes of the American flag." A classmate recalled that in 1920, in the sixth grade at Waialua School, she entered an Oahu-wide essay contest entitled, "What It Means to be an American." Although she did not win first place, her essay was printed in the *Pacific Commercial Advertiser*, and the recognition gave her "inspiration to study English harder than ever." One of the stated purposes of the Japanese Students' Association of Hawaii, organized by Nisei in 1920 for university and high school students, was to promote good citizenship and Americanization. Unfortunately for the historian, the organization left no explanation of what those terms meant to its members.[65]

As war with Japan grew imminent, Nisei felt it necessary to declare their loyalty to the United States. In June 1941, the Imua Club of Honolulu, composed of Nisei and some Issei, sent a resolution to the governor of Hawaii, the commanding general of the Hawaii Department of the U.S. Army, and the Hawaii director of the Federal Bureau of Investigation. The resolution expressed "devotion to American principles of democracy and loyalty to the United States," and offered the services of Imua members "in this time of international stress." Attached to the resolution were one-page profiles of Imua Club members, including lists of their skills. In the same month the Meisha Young Buddhists Association, likewise composed of citizens and noncitizens, sent a similar resolution to the three officials.[66]

A few days after the Pearl Harbor attack, Shunzo Sakamaki, a Nisei who earned a Ph.D. from Columbia University and was then a history professor at the University of Hawaii, wrote, "Japan's dastardly attack leaves us grim and resolute. Japan has chosen to fight us, and we'll fight. This is a bitter battle to the end, and to all loyal Americans and other lovers of democracy and human freedom that end is the complete destruction of the totalitarian governments that are blighting our world today." A month later the Hawaiian Japanese Civic Association, the largest organization of Nisei in the territory, sent a statement to

Lieutenant General Delos C. Emmons, the commanding general of the Hawaii Department of the U.S. Army, expressing similar views. "We assure you," the statement read, "that we will do our part as loyal Americans in avenging Japan's treacherous attack against our nation." These statements and the Nisei's overwhelming response to the call for volunteers to join the U.S. Army in the aftermath of Pearl Harbor underscored their realization that they could leave no doubt about their loyalty to the United States.[67]

As objects of the Americanization campaign, many Nisei pondered the meaning of American citizenship. To some being good Americans meant, in the words of a Honokaa High School boy, that "Hawaiian born Japanese should try to forget their mother country." But most Nisei disagreed. "Some of the young people," a Normal School student wrote, "in their wrong notion of accepting everything American, have taken into their lives many of the objectionable elements of American culture" and "have foolishly and needlessly thrown away the good characteristics of the Japanese race." One of her classmates pointed out that "knowing the Japanese language, customs, literature and background [did] not make one the less American." She asked, "How can we be . . . broad-minded American citizens if we are ashamed of the blood and traditions behind us? . . . It seems queer that people should ask us skeptically whether we love the American flag. Naturally we do; we have no other flag."[68]

Shigeo Soga, son of the *Nippu Jiji* editor Yasutaro Soga and one of the first Japanese graduates of Punahou, the exclusive haole-dominated private school, attempted to explain the Japanese culture in a 1924 essay that radiated ethnic pride. Japan, he wrote, was guided by the ethical code of *bushido*, which promoted values of justice, courage, benevolence, politeness, truthfulness, honor, loyalty, and self-control. That code, based on Buddhism, Shintoism, and Confucianism, continued Soga, enabled the Japanese to win the Russo-Japanese War and face with courage the recent tragedies of earthquake, fire, and tidal wave.[69]

Thus Nisei refused to repudiate their Japanese identity, partly because pride in their cultural heritage gave them the self-respect denied them in the American setting. A Normal School student wrote that she had once rejected her Japanese heritage only to change her mind later. Her second grade teacher in 1915, whom she had "loved" and for whom she had been "willing to do anything under the sun," had disapproved of Japanese language schools. "I wanted to please my teacher and yet I was afraid to go against the will of my parents," she recalled. "I did what seemed to me the best I could do. I neglected my language school work. I developed a hatred toward it." She explained: "I was dying to be a hundred percent American. . . . I felt . . . I had to discard everything that was not in accordance with what the haoles did." But when the student entered McKinley High School, she became aware of "racial prejudices." Although elected to the Citizenship Club, the National Honor Society, and the Science Club, haole members ignored her outside of club meetings. "It was then," she wrote, "that I realized how foolish I had been in attempting to be what I could never be. . . . Knowing that it was not too late, I began to study Japanese once again." The student then put her finger on the ambiguous position the Nisei found themselves in as marginal members of two societies. "We who are born in Hawaii are in a peculiar situation because we are Americans and not Americans; Japanese and not Japanese," she said. "We claim to be Americans through the American Constitution and yet we are denied some of the privileges that Americans of other ancestry have."[70]

In their effort to reconcile their dual identities, the Nisei sought to embody the best of both cultures. Earl Nishimura, president of the Japanese Students' Association in 1928, called Nisei "the pioneer generation" who was trying to "hybridize" American and Japanese cultures. A Hilo High School boy in 1927 put it this way, "I think freedom with restraint should be the keynote guiding us all—not the extreme limitations of the Orient nor the full freedom of the Haoles."[71]

Nippu Jiji sponsored an essay contest in 1928 on the question, "What can American citizens of Japanese descent do to serve Hawaii and contribute to her progress?" One theme, cultural amalgamation, emerged from the winning essays. K. Kawachi thought that the Nisei "should find the best characteristics of their Japanese heritage and combine them with the best of American ideals and institutions." Shunzo Sakamaki, later to become a history professor at the University of Hawaii, offered another formulation of the same idea. "While we are citizens of the United States," he wrote, "we must not lose sight of the fact that within our veins surges the blood of the noble Yamato race. . . . Bushido, the Way of the Samurai! We could make no finer contribution to the Philosophy and Ethics of Young America than by living in our own lives the spirit of the samurai."[72]

This attitude was the same among Nisei on the mainland and in Canada. Mainlander Hisashi J. Kobayashi declared, "Some . . . accuse [the Nisei] of hating himself and trying to forget his Asian heritage. Rubbish! I have never met a Japanese or Chinese who was not proud of his cultural heritage and character." Similarly, the sociologist Stanford M. Lyman stated that Nisei on the mainland took "quiet but deep and pervasive pride in their Nisei identity," believing that they brought together "a perfect balance of Japanese and American traits." The sociologist Evelyn N. Glenn, in interviewing mainland Nisei women in domestic service, found that they identified themselves midway between American and Japanese cultures, and liked what was Japanese and what was American about themselves. The anthropologist John W. Connor found that Nisei men and women in Sacramento, California, rated themselves midway on a ten-point scale between Japanese and American identities. And Tomoko Makabe, who interviewed Canadian Nisei in Toronto, found that a majority identified themselves as both Canadian and Japanese.[73]

It should be kept in mind that within the Japanese community in Hawaii most of the debate about the Nisei's place in America occurred among the more educated Issei and Nisei, who regularly interacted with the larger community. Many other Japanese had little or no awareness of the Americanization campaign, and their acculturation was slower and much less self-conscious than that of the individuals just described. Nevertheless it occurred. Issei who returned to Japan realized how different they had become. Many were uncomfortable in their home villages and returned to Hawaii. Nisei Shoichi Kurahashi was unaware of talk about his generation's loyalty to America. He "just figured [he] was an American citizen." Edythe Yamamoto, Tetsuko Tamura, and Yoshiko Oda did not wonder about their cultural identity. Similarly Marie, a Nisei who preferred to be otherwise anonymous, did not think about the subject at all, for she had always assumed she was an American. "I was born here and raised here," she said. "I didn't care what happened to Japan across the sea. . . . We were so different, anyway."[74]

So whether the Nisei became embroiled in controversy as did Tatsue Fujita, wrote essays proclaiming their loyalty to the United States, or gave little thought to the issue of dual identity, they gradually acculturated into American life while keeping elements of their Japanese heritage.

Chapter 4

Discrimination and Americanization

While urging the Nisei to be patriotic Americans, Caucasians in Hawaii and on the mainland undertook a number of actions that demonstrated white racism and engendered feelings of resentment among the Japanese. These actions included unsuccessful attempts to destroy the Japanese language press and abolish dual citizenship, and successful efforts to prevent Issei from becoming American citizens, exclude Japanese immigrants, and in what became a cause célèbre in Hawaii, deny leniency to Myles Fukunaga. While denying American citizenship to Issei and blocking Japanese immigration fell outside the Americanization agenda, many Americanizers supported these discriminatory actions, and thus they overlapped with attempts to Americanize the Japanese.

Events surrounding all of these efforts highlight the differences in world views between Caucasians and Japanese. They also reveal the determination of Caucasians to contain the aspirations of the Japanese, and the realities of American life, which often fell short of American ideals.

In the first of these efforts, that of abolishing the Japanese language press, Americanizers wittingly or unwittingly ignored the existence of non-English language publications that flourished throughout the nation's history. Indeed the foreign language press has always been popular among immigrants in America. "As long as there are people in this country who have common racial or nationalist interests," commented the sociologist Robert Park in 1922, "they will have papers to interpret events from their own peculiar point of view." Christopher Sauer, a German Quaker, began in 1739 the first non-English language publication in what later became the United States. At that time there were only five other publications in colonial North America. Sauer's paper was read by German-speaking settlers not only in Pennsylvania, where it was published, but also in New York, Virginia, the Carolinas, and Georgia.[1]

In 1900, twenty-eight groups of non-English language speakers circulated 1,199 publications in the United States and its territories. In 1920, during the heat of the Americanization campaign and a year before Hawaii's territorial legislature passed an anti-foreign language press law, 1,147 publications were written in thirty-nine languages.[2]

Most of the publications were in German: 748, or 62 percent, in 1900, with New York, Ohio, Wisconsin, and Illinois each having over eighty German language publications. Anti-German hostility during and after World War I reduced these numbers considerably, so that by 1920, although still the most numerous, German language publications had decreased to 276, or 24 percent of all publications. Dano-Norwegian, Spanish, and Swedish language groups each produced sixty or more publications in 1900, and in 1920 Spanish, Italian, and Polish groups published at least that many. In comparison there were five Japanese language publications in the nation in 1900, four of them in Hawaii, and twenty-eight in 1920, including thirteen in Hawaii.[3]

Like other non-English language speakers, Issei valued newspapers in their native tongue not only because they, like most other immigrants, could not read English, but also for the assurances these publications brought the Issei in their alien environment. Adjusting to a different way of life was a difficult process. The Japanese language press kept immigrants in contact with a familiar world and explained things in ways they comprehended.

By informing Issei of events in Japan and in the Japanese community in Hawaii, the Japanese language press preserved and strengthened ties with the old country and contributed to the cohesion of the Japanese in their new environment. In these ways the press retarded acculturation, but that was common to all non-English language publications.[4]

Issei response to calls to aid patriotic causes back home was like that of other immigrants. During the Sino-Japanese conflict in the late 1930s, the Japanese press (not including *Hawaii Hochi*) collected large sums of money for the relief of wounded soldiers and their families. Similarly, Chinese in Hawaii and on the mainland contributed to the revolutionary movement in China during the first through third decades of the twentieth century, and Koreans in Hawaii and on the mainland raised tens of thousands of dollars during the first half of the twentieth century to support Korean independence.[5]

At the same time, the non-English language press on the mainland and in Hawaii helped immigrants adjust to life in their new environment by informing them of American ways, interpreting events around them, and encouraging integration with the larger community. In these ways the press hastened acculturation. *Nippu Jiji* editorials, for example, regularly admonished Issei for keeping to themselves and urged them to sócialize with Americans.[6]

Japanese language newspapers in Hawaii, by no means speaking with one voice, editorialized about living and working conditions of plantation laborers, and supported or opposed plantation strikes. During World War I they supported the Liberty Bond campaign and the campaign to produce and conserve food. They unanimously urged the Nisei to end their dual citizenship by expatriating themselves from Japan. In the wrenching controversy over Japanese language schools, the newspapers, differing in their positions and often mercilessly attacking each other, spoke out, often eloquently, for what they believed was in the best interests of the Japanese community. In sum, the press spoke to issues that most concerned the Japanese.[7]

The first Japanese language newspaper in Hawaii, *Nippon Shuho* (Japanese Weekly), began circulation in 1892, only seven years after Japanese immigration had begun. A modest publication printed on a mimeograph machine, it nonetheless had the distinction of being the first to serve the growing Japanese community. By the time Hawaii was annexed to the United States in 1898, ten other Japanese language papers had begun publication, although most of them lasted only a short while.[8]

Of the eighty-six Japanese language publications that appeared in the territory between 1900 and 1941, nineteen survived ten or more years. The largest ethnic group throughout this period, the Japanese generally supported the largest number of non-English language publications. In 1920 there were thirteen Japanese language, five Hawaiian language, and four Chinese language publications. The two largest Japanese language dailies rivaled their English language counterparts in circulation figures.[9]

Of all the Japanese language newspapers in Hawaii before World War II, *Nippu Jiji* and *Hawaii Hochi* were the best known and most widely circulated. The older of the two, *Nippu Jiji*, began in 1895 as *Yamato*, and changed its name a year later to *Yamato Shinbun*. In 1905 Yasutaro Soga became president and editor-in-chief, and the following year renamed the paper *Nippu Jiji*. In Japanese *Nippu* is written in two characters, signifying "Japan" and "Hawaii." *Jiji*, also written in two characters, signifies "time" and "event." A rough translation is "News of Japan and Hawaii."[10]

Highly conscious of the growing suspicion of Japanese among Caucasians after World War I, *Nippu Jiji* inaugurated a daily English language section in January 1919, the first Japanese language newspaper in Hawaii to do so. The purpose was to "bring understanding between Americans and Japanese" by informing Americans of Japanese views of their situation in Hawaii. To this end editorials, written primarily by Soga in Japanese, were usually translated in the English section of the paper.[11]

Hawaii Hochi (Hawaii News) was founded in 1912 by Fred Kinzaburo Makino. Although he collaborated with Soga in supporting a sugar strike in 1909, Makino felt that his and Soga's conviction and subsequent imprisonment for "conspiracy" had intimidated Soga into his later support for the sugar companies. While Soga was not a turncoat, as Makino charged, he did soft-pedal his views after the strike. Believing that the Japanese needed a more outspoken voice than Soga's, Makino started his own paper on a shoestring budget.[12]

World War I made Americanizers distrustful of foreign language publications. "[It] taught us that . . . the German language press had been working against the interests of the United States," declared Edward P. Irwin in 1920, when he was editor of the *Pacific Commercial Advertiser.* "In many instances it had not actually been preaching disloyalty openly," wrote Irwin. "It did not preach anti-Americanism; rather it preached Germanism. So here in Hawaii today, there are Japanese papers that do not actively teach anti-Americanism, but they do teach Japanism, and that amounts to the same thing." This assumption, that interest and pride in Japan automatically meant disloyalty to the United States, emerged repeatedly during the Americanization campaign. Moreover, to Americanizers, any criticism from an "alien" group was un-American. John K. Butler, executive secretary of the Hawaiian Sugar Planters' Association and department commander of the American Legion, summed up the Legion's view in a 1921 memo to Governor Charles McCarthy. "The evil of the Japanese Press is not in any particular article which has been published, or in any particular line of attack that has been adopted," wrote Butler, "but it has been the cumulative effect of vicious doctrines, lying propaganda, misrepresentation, and the preaching of racial unity that has had the effect of binding the Japanese community as a unit in all its activities, making it practically impossible, especially when coupled up with the previously existing Japanese School, to make any impression on this racial integrity or to inculcate American ideals and the doctrine of individual action."[13]

In 1921, during the height of the Americanization campaign, this hostility turned into action. Republican territorial senator Lawrence M. Judd, later governor of Hawaii, introduced an American Legion-sponsored bill that mandated that all foreign language publications include English translations of their content. Calling *Nippu Jiji* an "ingrate" and an "enemy of the Japanese interests in Hawaii," the *Honolulu Advertiser*, formerly the *Pacific Commercial Advertiser*, declared that it supported the mandatory translation bill because Caucasians should know "what poisonous statements" were being made "under cover" of a foreign language. The effect of Judd's bill would have been to force foreign language publications in Hawaii to reduce their output, raise their prices, or go out of business regardless of their views, including religious and non-Japanese language publications, because of prohibitive increases in costs.[14]

Criticism of the bill came from both haole and Japanese leaders. The Reverend Albert W. Palmer of Central Union Church in Honolulu protested that behind the bill lay the desire to silence all voices that spoke in support of labor, and the result of its passage, he warned, would be a social explosion. A letter to the *Advertiser* editor signed by Archibald A. Yound declared, "If it is in the public interest to know what the Japanese papers are saying, let the public pay for translating them. Why should we treat the newspapers worse than we do our criminals?" Soga warned that the bill was intended to abolish the Japanese language press and would have the effect of closing all foreign language newspapers, since it was impossible to translate every article in the permitted time. The bill's purpose, he argued, was not to promote Americanism, as its supporters claimed, but to protect the interests of sugar planters. But the planters' problems, he continued, lay not in the support Japanese language papers had given laborers in a recent strike, but in the plantation system itself. Soga declared that Japanese wanted to cooperate with Caucasians, but that cooperation "should be mutual."[15]

Because of such criticism, Judd's bill was shelved and a new one substituted for it. The new bill required that pamphlets, brochures, and other such publications be translated only if they referred to the government or law of the United States or the territory, or to any racial, industrial, or class question. Newspapers and periodicals had to be translated only if their publishers had been previously convicted of inciting violence, intimidation or ostracism, or creating distrust between different groups of people. In this version the bill became law, but it seems not to have been enforced. "Having satisfied the American feeling that there ought to be a law," John E. Reinecke wrote of this anomaly, "the territory immediately allowed the new act to become a dead letter." Non-English language pamphlets on political and social conditions, such as one written by Takashi Tsutsumi supporting a 1920 strike, circulated with impunity, "untranslated and unhindered." Apparently to satisfy Americanizers calling for "one flag, one language," the legislature felt compelled to go through the motions of "controlling" the foreign press. The law as enacted did not mention Japanese language newspapers, the actual target of the effort. And in rejecting the attorney general's request for special funds to enforce the law, the legislature effectively rendered it toothless. Yet passage of the law could not help but disappoint the Japanese, who wanted to be accepted members of the American community.[16]

The historian John Stephan wrote that news of the Sino-Japanese war in the late 1930s was reported in a "comparatively detached" manner in the English language sections of *Nippu Jiji* and *Hawaii Hochi*, while the coverage "reverberated with patriotic rhetoric" in the Japanese language sections. This was because such articles came from radio news services in Japan, and in the process of translating the news for the English language sections, translators toned down the rhetoric. Regardless, it is understandable if Japanese publishers and editors were enthusiastic about Japan's military prowess. So were Japanese language school teachers. After all, they were Japanese nationals who owed their allegiance to the emperor. As Stephan himself noted, "The Issei quite naturally loved the land of their birth and were proud of Japan's emergence as a world power. At the same time, they felt a deep attachment toward the land where they had spent in many cases most of their lives, the land where they had built their careers and raised their families."[17]

While news of the war, originating from Japan, was reported differently in the Japanese and English language sections, this was not the case in regard to editorials on news originating from Hawaii such as the language schools, the 1920 strike, dual citizenship, and the Americanization campaign. Editorials in the English language section of *Nippu Jiji* were direct translations of editorials in the Japanese language section. Editorials in the English language section of *Hawaii Hochi* were written by George W. Wright and then usually translated for the Japanese language section. Wright's editorials were colorful and hard-hitting in their criticism of the haole elite, enough so as to arouse their anger repeatedly. Nevertheless, to find out what *Hochi*'s Japanese language editorials were saying, the Hawaiian Sugar Planters' Association paid for its own translations. These translations found the paper's Japanese language editorials similar in viewpoint to those published in its English section.[18]

The non-English language press law was one of several actions taken against Japanese in Hawaii during and after the Americanization campaign. Americanizers did not read Japanese and could only imagine the "evil" messages conveyed in the pages of Japanese language newspapers. Anything that promoted pride in Japan or "Japanism," as they called it, was to them automatically anti-American. They sought to silence everything that, in their eyes, ran counter to undivided loyalty to the United States. Japanese, on the other hand, saw no contradiction between pride in Japan and pride in America. These contrasting perspectives collided in the controversy over the Japanese language press.

Another issue that brought Japanese into conflict with Caucasians was the question of the naturalization of Japanese immigrants. In 1790 Congress had enacted the first naturalization law, which restricted the right of naturalization to "free white person[s]." The restriction was aimed at African Americans; no thought was given to Asian immigrants, of whom there were none at the time. The Fourteenth Amendment, ratified in 1868, also without thought of Asians, declared that anyone born in the United States was automatically a citizen. It was because of this amendment that Nisei were citizens. In 1870, during Radical Reconstruction, Congress extended the right of naturalization to aliens of African descent, but ignored the arguments of Senator Charles Sumner of Massachusetts that the right be extended to all, including the Chinese.[19]

As Asians began to apply for naturalization in the decades that followed, the courts interpreted the meaning of "white" in different ways. Some granted Asians citizenship, so that in 1910 the U.S. census reported 1,368 Chinese and 420 Japanese as naturalized citizens. In late 1918 Congress passed a law authorizing the naturalization of aliens who had served in the armed forces during World War I. As a result, in January 1919, the territorial District Court Judge Horace Vaughan granted citizenship to seventy-seven Issei. Edward P. Irwin, editor of the *Pacific Commercial Advertiser*, objected to this action, and William H. Ragsdale of the Board of Naturalization declared that the law did not apply to Asians. Their objections did not deter the judge. By the end of 1921, five hundred Asians in Hawaii were naturalized citizens.[20]

In 1922 the U.S. Supreme Court resolved the issue definitively in *Ozawa v. the United States*. Takao Ozawa had immigrated to the United States as a high school student and had lived in the country for twenty years. He attended schools in California and then moved to Hawaii, where he petitioned the U.S. District Court in 1914 for naturalization. Judge Charles Clemons denied his petition, and Ozawa appealed to the Ninth Circuit Court and then to the Supreme Court. Ozawa argued that naturalization laws did not exclude Asians from citizenship, that the word "free" in the original law was more important than the word "white." He called attention to his American lifestyle, and to the fact that his children went to an American church and school, did not speak Japanese, and were not registered with the Japanese consulate. Despite these arguments the *court* declared that Japanese aliens were non-whites and therefore ineligible for citizenship.[21]

This decision shook "the faith of a large number of Japanese." "They don't know whether to go or to stay," declared a *Nippu Jiji* editorial.

Pointing to the contradiction, the editorial continued, "It is not Americanism that denies naturalization on the one hand and compels Americanization on the other." A few years after the *Ozawa* decision, a Nisei wrote of his father, who worked as a plantation clerk and interpreter and who had given himself an English first name, something unusual among the Issei. "My father is not a college graduate," wrote the Nisei. "But he is an educated man. His library numbers thousands of volumes, in both English and Japanese. He reads both languages. . . . He subscribes to many American magazines, and all the bigger newspapers of the territory, both English and Japanese." The Nisei continued, "I remember that as a child I listened to my father expressing his wish that he could become an American citizen before his death. He does not say so any more. There is a spirit of disappointment and resignation in his smile now, as he says, 'I can never become a citizen.' He has lived on American soil for so long, and he is so much an American in his ways and attitude that it is a tragic injustice to deny him the citizenship he deserves."[22]

The effects of this rejection of the Issei became visible during the late 1930s, a time of mounting tension between the United States and Japan, when the Nisei found themselves in the peculiar position of owing allegiance to a country that denied citizenship to their parents. Rejected by America, the Issei naturally focused their loyalty on Japan. As war between Japan and China raged, Issei responded with nationalistic pride, as they had done previously in the earlier Sino-Japanese War and the Russo-Japanese War. Language school teachers, Japanese language newspapers, and women's groups collected large sums of money and care packages for the war effort. Many Issei celebrated the emperor's birthday, a practice they had earlier discontinued, and attended war memorial services at Shinto shrines.[23]

The Nisei did not generally support these endeavors. The differing reactions of Issei and Nisei to the war reflected different degrees of acculturation. "My parents asked me to contribute to a war fund," said one Nisei. "I refused. I know for a fact that quarreling about the war between the older and younger generations goes on in many Japanese homes. Most of the immigrant generation feel that Japan had no other course but to go into China. Many of the younger people feel that Japan was wrong to go in."[24]

In a study of the Japanese community in Kona on the island of Hawaii during the late 1930s, the anthropologist John F. Embree described the attitudes of the two generations to the war. The Issei tended to accept the war news from Japan published in Japanese language papers as "infallibly accurate," while calling news printed in the English language papers "Chinese propaganda." Older Nisei thought China was a troublemaker, but did not favor Japanese aggression. Younger Nisei tried to be neutral and avoided discussing the issue. Since Issei read Japanese language papers and Nisei read English language papers, the two groups frequently disagreed about the progress of the war. Issei contributed money to the war effort, while younger Nisei objected to that practice. Some older Nisei contributed, but felt uncomfortable in doing so. A Nisei gave his explantion of the attitude of the first generation: because they were barred from becoming U.S. citizens, he said, their loyalty focused on Japan. While not the sole reason for their actions, the denial of naturalization rights did serve to direct their loyalties toward their homeland.[25]

Another event indicating that Caucasians placed Japanese beneath them was passage of the 1924 immigration law, yet another slap in the face for the Japanese. American exclusionists were dissatisfied with the terms of the Gentlemen's Agreement, which banned the entry of Japanese laborers into the United States, but allowed parents, wives, and children of Issei to enter. In 1907 and 1909 California legislators introduced bills aimed at discouraging Issei from settling permanently in America. Legislators in Oregon, Montana, and Nevada followed suit in 1909, but none of the bills became law. Japan's annexation of Korea in 1910 and Japan's twenty-one demands on China in 1915 helped the exclusionist campaign by exacerbating tensions between the United States and Japan. Success for exclusionists first came in 1913, when the California legislature passed a bill prohibiting Issei, as aliens ineligible for citizenship, from owning land in the state. Japan issued a formal protest, calling the bill unfair and discriminatory, but California Governor Hiram Johnson nevertheless signed the bill into law.[26]

The Issei circumvented the law by leasing land up to three years as allowed, and working with European Americans who had an economic stake in seeing that the Japanese continue farming. Some Issei placed their land under the ownership of corporations, with Caucasians acting as trustees. A more stringent law in 1920 closed loopholes in the earlier enactment by forbidding Issei from leasing and corporations from owning agricultural land. A 1923 amendment closed another loophole by prohibiting Issei from sharecropping, that is, working farmland in return for fixed percentages of the profits. Washington, Oregon, Idaho, Arizona, Texas, and Nebraska passed similar land laws between 1912 and 1923.[27]

John K. Butler, the Hawaiian Sugar Planters' Association executive secretary and department commander of the American Legion, proposed such a law for Hawaii. Riley Allen, editor of *Star-Bulletin*, warned that

Butler's proposal served only to increase friction among the races and retard the progress of Americanization. "A Japanese or Chinese . . . who cannot expect to become naturalized, and who cannot buy real estate here," Allen said, "will not root himself and his family in the community." The legislature did not pursue the issue.[28]

Issei farmers on the mainland challenged the land laws in court. The test cases reached the U.S. Supreme Court, which in 1923 delivered a stunning blow to the Issei by declaring the land laws constitutional. Shocked and disillusioned by the decision, the Issei nevertheless found they could continue farming, because authorities failed to enforce the laws. White businessmen, it seems, had too much at stake financially in Japanese farming. Issei also found they could circumvent the laws by placing land ownership in the names of their American-born children.[29]

In 1917 Congress passed a law requiring all would-be immigrants to pass a literacy test and created a "barred zone" that excluded all Asians except Filipinos (who were American nationals) and Japanese (who fought on the same side as the Americans in World War I). President Woodrow Wilson had convinced Congress to honor the Gentlemen's Agreement. But in 1924 the anti-Japanese crusade finally succeeded in blocking all Japanese immigration. Congress used the phrase "aliens ineligible to citizenship" to avoid naming the Japanese, but the intent of the law was obvious, since other Asians, who were also ineligible for citizenship, had been excluded earlier.[30]

This law, the culmination of lobbying by veterans groups, patriotic societies, labor organizations, and congressmen from the West and the South, permitted substantial immigration of northern and western Europeans while it decreased to a trickle the flow of southern and eastern Europeans and prohibited the entry of Asians except Filipinos. Quotas for European nations were based on the proportion of Americans in 1890 who traced their ancestry to each nation, before large numbers of southern and eastern Europeans had arrived. As a result Germany, Great Britain, and other nations of northwestern Europe received much larger quotas than did Italy, Greece, and the Slavic countries. Congress ignored President Coolidge's request to allow Japan a quota based on the formula applied to European countries. Instead the law banned all immigrants not eligible to citizenship, a phrase applying only to Asians. The exceptions were ministers and professors and their wives and children, and students over fifteen years of age. Resident aliens ineligible for citizenship, including the Issei, were permitted to return to the United States only after visits abroad of less than a year's duration.[31]

As this bill wound its way through Congress, the Japanese ambassador in Washington, Masanao Hanihara protested against its obviously discriminatory provisions, while Japanese language newspapers on the mainland deplored this "manifestation of white supremacy." In Hawaii, Yasutaro Soga, editor of *Nippu Jiji*, called the bill an "insult" to the Japanese people. While the Gentlemen's Agreement had allowed Japan to restrict emigration to the United States voluntarily, he argued, the bill humiliated Japan by discriminating against Japanese subjects. Yet he counseled his readers to avoid making "wild assertions of rights" that resulted in disturbing the whole community. Lorrin A. Thurston, publisher of the *Honolulu Advertiser*, objected to the "affront" to "a friendly nation," and urged President Calvin Coolidge to veto the bill. The Honolulu Chamber of Commerce sent the Senate a recommendation that Japan be accorded the same treatment as other nations, and that further regulation of Japanese immigration, if necessary, be accomplished by treaty.[32]

After the bill became law, Ambassador Hanihara resigned in protest, as did the American ambassador in Tokyo. The Japanese government issued a formal protest against "discriminations based on race," and newspapers in Japan denounced the law as a "breach of international etiquette" and a "deliberate insult" to the "national honor of Japan." Protestors in Japan staged mass meetings for several days in major cities, calling July 1, the day the law became effective, "National Humiliation Day." In Japan at the time, Soga reported strong hostility toward the United States over passage of the law. On 31 May 1924, *Nippu Jiji* reported that a Japanese citizen had committed suicide in front of the U.S. embassy in Tokyo to protest the law. Four days later the paper reported five more suicides, including the deaths of two people who had thrown themselves in front of oncoming trains. Several of the suicide victims left notes decrying the immigration law. To the Japanese government and its people, Japan, unlike China and Korea, was a power Western nations should treat with respect. They asked only that Japan be accorded a quota like those of European countries. Such a quota would have permitted only one hundred immigrants from Japan annually.[33]

Before the July 1 deadline, some Issei bachelors returned to Japan to bring back brides. Other men sent to Japan for their wives and children. Still others who were then visiting Japan abruptly ended their visits. A scramble for tickets ensued as prospective passengers converged on the Japanese port cities of Kobe and Yokohama.[34]

The immigration law caught some families in the political tangle. Prior to passage of the law, K. Nakashima had traveled to Japan with his wife and their two American-born children. While in Japan his wife gave birth to another child. When his family prepared to return to the United States, they were told that the new law forbade their third child from accompanying them. Only after persistent appeals to the American consul-general in Tokyo were they successful in obtaining an exception to the letter of the law.[35]

Despite the discrimination against Japanese explicit in the immigration law, many Issei realized that America offered them an easier life than did Japan, and many chose to settle in their adopted country. Nevertheless the law sent a clear message of European American rejection. It therefore reinforced their natural tendency to keep to themselves, heightened their children's self-consciousness about their marginal status as Americans, and retarded Japanese acculturation.

Four years after the 1924 immigration law went into effect, an incident occurred in Hawaii that shook the Japanese community and demonstrated once again that the Japanese were unequal in haole eyes. In 1928 nineteen-year-old Myles Yutaka Fukunaga, a Nisei, kidnapped and murdered ten-year-old Gill Jamieson. Jamieson was the son of a prominent haole employee of the Hawaiian Trust Company, which was then demanding that the impoverished Fukunagas pay their overdue house rent. Frustrated that he could not help his parents meet this demand and angry at the financial pressure put on his destitute family, Fukunaga, the eldest of seven children, sought revenge. Within two weeks of his arrest, Fukunaga was tried, convicted, and sentenced to hang. This unseemly haste was a direct result of the uproar the crime created among Caucasians. Because of that uproar, justice was sacrificed to speed. Fukunaga's attorneys, Eugene Beebe and Seba Huber, called no witnesses in his defense, and Judge Alvah E. Steadman and Governor Wallace R. Farrington refused pleas to have Fukunaga examined by a psychiatrist, despite overwhelming evidence of his emotional instability.[36]

The Japanese community had actively cooperated in the search for young Jamieson's murderer, but the speed of Fukunaga's trial and the severity of his sentence angered them. They collected funds to send his parents to Japan so they could leave the "horrible shame they felt in Hawaii," and signed petitions demanding a psychological examination for Fukunaga and a retrial.[37]

The *Hochi* publisher Fred Kinzaburo Makino retained attorney Robert K. Murakami to appeal Fukunaga's conviction to the Ninth Circuit Court in San Francisco and then to the U.S. Supreme Court. Both appeals were dismissed. As a last resort Makino and others in the Japanese community gathered signatures from people of all ethnic groups asking for life imprisonment instead of death for Fukunaga, but to no avail, and

Fukunaga was hanged on November 19, 1929. Sixty years after the incident, Ralph Honda recalled, "[Murakami] told me that nobody would defend [Fukunaga] . . . because these were Republican days. [Murakami] was a Republican, slated to become the city and county attorney. But since no one defended [Fukunaga], he offered and that was the end for him. He was black-balled. . . . Murakami was a man of principal, you see."[38]

In his confession of the murder, Fukunaga revealed the competing tugs and tensions he had felt growing up between two cultures. The strain intensified derangements that might in other circumstances have been less tragically resolved. Wanting to escape the life of drudgery his parents experienced, Fukunaga had looked to education as an avenue of escape. His "biggest disappointment," he said, had come when he realized that his poverty-stricken parents could not continue to send him to school. As a result of his predicament he came to dislike everything Japanese. He had an "intense desire to be an American," only to find that he was not accepted by European Americans. The philosophy professor Lockwood Myrick, who studied the case, wrote an open letter to Governor Farrington in which he said, "[Fukunaga's] tragic life brings out with start[l]ing clearness the painfully difficult situation of our American-born children of Oriental descent." Fukunaga had no friends, Myrick noted, being "out of touch with the Japanese and not accepted by the whites." His family was destitute, and he gave most of his earnings to his parents. He had no pleasures, no vices, no intellectually stimulating work, and there was no prospect that he would be able to continue his education. Reflecting on these circumstances, the psychologist Stanley Porteus of the University of Hawaii said he had "never come across a life-history so painful."[39]

While Makino threw himself into the effort to save Fukunaga's life, Yasutaro Soga of *Nippu Jiji* was unsympathetic. Pointing out that poverty was no excuse for breaking the law, he criticized Fukunaga and others who turned to crime for lacking self-control and "will power." "Brought up in a land where livelihood is comparatively easy," Soga wrote, "they are easily led into the ways of the criminals once they get into difficulties." He opposed a new trial for Fukunaga, reasoning that to try to let him escape hanging on grounds of insanity would be to encourage crime. Soga concluded, "The time has come when Fukunaga must reap the harvest."[40]

In later years many Nisei recalled the mixed feelings they had concerning the case. They had felt ashamed for having "the Japanese name spoiled," yet sorry for the Fukunaga family. "They were not rich people, you know," noted Sueno Matsushita.[41]

Marie, a Nisei who later befriended Fukunaga's younger sister when the two women were training to become nurses, later recalled the incident as "a sad, sad case." Her parents had felt sorry for the family, she said, especially since Fukunaga had been a good boy before the kidnapping and had wanted, though in a deranged way, to help his family. Raku Morimoto, a Nisei who was thirty-eight years old at the time, recalled that Fukunaga's parents "were about to commit suicide to apologize publicly for what their son did," but were stopped by a Christian minister, the Reverend Mr. Komuro. He convinced them that they had young children to consider. Morimoto said, "The Japanese people all sympathize with Fukunaga because he said, *Oya-koko.* That means he was thinking not [of] himself but . . . of the parents." Japanese sympathy for Fukunaga revealed a cultural perspective that saw in the young man's deranged action a devotion to his family that was valued by the Japanese.[42]

The Fukunaga case points to flaws in the functioning of Hawaii's judicial system during the decades before World War II. Just before Fukunaga was convicted and sentenced, a haole with political influence who murdered a Japanese taxi driver was convicted of second degree murder, and a white mechanic on Puunene Plantation on Maui who poured gasoline over a Japanese laborer and burned him to death was acquitted. Raymond Coll, managing editor of the *Honolulu Advertiser,* said in 1930 that there were three kinds of justice in Hawaii, one for Caucasians, another for Hawaiians, and a third for Asians. Referring to minor crimes and traffic violations, he declared, "If we cannot be perfect, let us at least be honest with ourselves."[43]

Later commentators such as the historian Gavan Daws have contrasted the Fukunaga case with the sensational Massie case that took place three years later. In the latter incident, Thalia Massie, a Caucasian and the wife of a naval officer, claimed she was raped by seven men. Police arrested five non-white men for the alleged crime, but conflicting testimony at their trial and a medical report that found no evidence of rape caused the jury to deadlock. As a result the accused were released and the charges against them dismissed, causing an uproar in the European American community. About a month later the murdered body of one of the accused was found in a car driven by Thalia Massie's mother. Also in the car were Massie's husband and an enlisted man under his command. Mainland newspapers immediately sent reporters to Hawaii to cover the story, and the Hearst newspapers ran editorials calling Honolulu unsafe for white women. Clarence Darrow flew in for the defense. When the jury found the defendants guilty of manslaughter, Governor Lawrence M. Judd commuted their sentence to an hour spent in his office.[44]

In these episodes Japanese in Hawaii saw how American realities fell short of American ideals of equal justice. Such discriminatory acts encouraged the Japanese to band together for protection against the outside world and discouraged free and easy relationships with Caucasians, thereby retarding acculturation.

While Americanizers sometimes withheld equal justice, they demanded undivided loyalty to the United States. "I cannot see how anyone can be a clean 100 percent American if at the same time he has allegiance to another power existing," declared Judge Alvah E. Steadman, former vice-president of the Cooke Trust Company and the presiding judge at Fukunaga's trial. Steadman articulated a unanimous conviction among Americanizers, that the Nisei had to renounce their dual citizenship. "It is this dual citizenship," warned Steadman, "that has created more suspicion, more discussions in Congress than anything else."[45]

Indeed, congressmen at statehood hearings held in 1937 declared that they found it unsettling that so many Japanese Americans had not bothered to expatriate. Honolulu city and county attorney Wilfred C. Tsukiyama, who testified at the hearing, argued that failure to expatriate did not mean disloyalty to the United States. But his words fell on deaf ears. When it was (future associate justice of the Hawaii Supreme Court) Masaji Marumoto's turn to testify, he was asked, "Can you tell me whether or not in the evenings the people of Japanese extraction born in the islands hold secret meetings in which they uphold the teachings of the Japanese Government and the Mikado?"[46]

Americanizers asked which country the Nisei would choose should war break out between the United States and Japan. Some of them even went so far as to declare that the Nisei might one day vote to make Hawaii a Japanese colony. Americanizers targeted Japanese Americans while ignoring the hundreds of thousands of other Americans of Italian, German, Swiss, French and Chinese descent who were also dual citizens. The targeting clearly indicates that Americanizers believed that Japanese alone were of questionable loyalty.[47]

Educators joined the expatriation campaign. McKinley High School principal Miles Cary urged his Nisei students to renounce their dual citizenship. In 1925 he invited a representative from the Japanese consulate to explain the procedure for doing so to students. He even offered the consulate a room in the school in which to process the paperwork. The Territorial Board of Commissioners of Education, forerunner of the Territorial Board of Education, mandated that all public school teachers of Japanese descent show proof of expatriation. By 1933 all had done so.[48]

Issei leaders shared this view. During the 1920s Yasutaro Soga consistently urged the Nisei to renounce their Japanese citizenship. Takie

Okumura wrote in 1933, "It is the plain duty of every dual citizen to . . . cut off every tie that binds him to the country of his parents." Even Fred Kinzaburo Makino, who normally disagreed with Okumura and Soga, was unequivocal in agreeing with them on this issue. "Until the young Japanese of Hawaii have completely freed themselves from all ties that bind them to Japan," declared a 1926 *Hochi* editorial, "they cannot expect to be regarded in quite the same light as those who have no taint of a divided loyalty." As talk of war between Japan and the United States increased, Makino's paper endorsed an American Legion proposal to ban dual citizens from territorial and city and county employment. The *Hochi* did not question Nisei loyalty. "We believe that they regard themselves as real Americans and simply disregard the legal claims of Japan," explained a 1939 editorial. But "prohibiting dual citizens from holding jobs would focus attention on the problem and spur these laggards [on]." Shortly before the attack on Pearl Harbor, *Hochi* declared editorially, "In times like the present there can be no split allegiance, no half-in-half loyalties."[49]

Dual citizenship was a frequent topic at Okumura's annual New Americans Conferences. At the 1928 conference Nisei delegates agreed that dual citizenship was undesirable, but pointed out that many Nisei were ignorant of expatriation procedures. In 1939 and again in 1941 delegates passed resolutions endorsing expatriation. Masato Sugihara, a public school teacher, told 1939 conferees, "I firmly believe that the young people of Japanese ancestry should be expatriated." George Shimizu, a plantation worker on the island of Hawaii, responded by pointing to a contradiction in Americanizers' thinking: "I do not favor expatriation," he said, "because although we are considered Americans and have been born and raised here as citizens, yet we are not treated as equals by *haoles*."[50]

Dual citizenship occurred because of conflicting nationality laws, which made ethnic Japanese born in the United States before 1924 citizens of both the United States and Japan. The United States was one of the few countries that held to the concept of *jus soli* (right of the soil), according to which anyone born in the United States automatically became a citizen of the country. On the other hand Japan, like most nations, including the United States, went by the concept of *jus sanguinis* (right of blood), which automatically gave citizenship to children of the country's male citizens no matter where the children were born.[51]

In response to requests from Japanese Americans in Hawaii and on the mainland, Japan revised its nationality laws in 1916 to permit Nisei (except males seventeen to thirty-seven years old who were subject to military service) to renounce their Japanese citizenship. The Japanese

Diet further amended the laws in 1924 to permit any person of Japanese ancestry born in the United States to expatriate at any age. Furthermore, persons of Japanese ancestry born in the United States after 1924 were not subjects of Japan unless, within fourteen days of birth, parents or legal guardians registered their births at the Japanese consulate.[52]

In order to expatriate, Americans of Japanese ancestry had to produce a number of documents, among them a copy of the family register from Japan, an American birth certificate, written approval of a parent or guardian (for minor children), "statement of approval, whenever required," and an application written in Japanese requesting separation from Japan. Once expatriation was completed, the applicant's family head had to report the action to the registrar of the family's record in Japan.[53]

After Japan revised its nationality laws in 1924, the proportion of Issei parents who registered their children's births at the Japanese consulate declined. Yet a sizable number continued to do so, especially during the first few years after the laws were changed. Of 5,024 Japanese American births in 1925, 72.6 percent were registered with the Japanese consulate, but in 1939, only 799 births, or 25 percent of the total, were so registered.[54]

According to the University of Hawaii sociologist Romanzo Adams, Issei continued to register their children with the consulate because registration was a family, not a political matter. It was the duty of parents in Japan to have the births of children recorded in the family register. To fail to do so meant a denial of rights for their children. Many Issei never abandoned the idea of eventually returning to Japan, and were they to do so with their children, those who were registered would be able to claim their rights as members of the family.[55]

Despite the overwhelming consensus that expatriation was the right thing to do, Nisei were slow to expatriate, and the rate of dual citizenship remained high even after Japan liberalized its nationality law. Of 103,467 Nisei in Hawaii in 1933, about 69 percent were still dual citizens. Even those who were considered potential leaders of the second generation were slow to expatriate. Out of twenty-six delegates at the 1928 New Americans Conference, fourteen had expatriated and four were beginning the process. At the 1931 conference, only nine of twenty-nine delegates had expatriated.[56]

The rate of expatriation gained momentum as tension mounted between the United States and Japan. As a result of a territory-wide campaign in 1940, about four hundred Japanese American dual citizens were expatriating monthly. According to *Honolulu Star-Bulletin*, "more dual citizens expatriated during 1940 than any year previously." At the 1941

New Americans Conference, 75 percent of the delegates had expatriated.[57]

But in the years before international tensions forced Nisei to demonstrate their loyalty in concrete terms, Japanese Americans thought expatriation was not worth the time and trouble. In some cases, Nisei found they could not expatriate if their parents were dead and their marriage had not been registered in Japan. Difficulties also arose for those whose births had not been properly registered with the territory of Hawaii, and for those whose parents had not registered their births at the Japanese consulate. Names of the latter were not on the family registers in Japan. In addition many Nisei could not write Japanese properly, which meant they could not write to Japan themselves for the necessary documents. Others did not know whether or not they were dual citizens, and some wanted to keep their dual citizenship because of property they would inherit in Japan. Finally, some Nisei honored their parents' belief that "to erase the name from the family register was a disgrace to the ancestors."[58]

Delegates to the 1931 New Americans Conference noted some of the difficulties expatriation involved. "It is quite difficult to expatriate if you do not have the birth certificate," said one. "The applicant must appear before the Secretary with his parent and two witnesses. When you are living away from Honolulu, everything is very inconvenient." Another delegate said, "I have tried to expatriate but due to too much red tape I have given up the whole thing." Judge Masaji Marumoto, who expatriated in 1922 when he was a sophomore in high school, recalled the problems he encountered. "It was necessary to get a certificate of Hawaiian birth from the Secretary of the Territory of Hawaii," Marumoto remembered. "Because there weren't any Japanese lawyers, our parents relied on Japanese interpreters to get the certificates. The interpreters used to collect $100 to arrange to get your birth certificate. They didn't do a thing. . . . My father went to . . . at least two. He spent at least a couple of hundred dollars." Because Marumoto's name had not been registered, he had to bring witnesses to swear that he had been born in Hawaii. "The woman who knew about my birth was so timid, she couldn't give her testimony correctly. She got confused. She said she wasn't in Honolulu when I was born. I had an awful time getting the certificate."[59]

George Sakamaki, who was vocal in declaring his loyalty to the United States, believed that "double nationality and dual allegiance [were] not synonymous." "Take my case as an example," he wrote. "Born in Hawaii, I had always regarded myself *ipso facto* an American without any obligation to Japan. Only a day or two before I testified before the Congressional Statehood committee last fall [in 1937], I learned that all persons of Japanese antecedent born prior to December 1, 1924, were automatically citizens of Japan, according to Japanese law, regardless of whether their births were or were not registered with Japanese authorities. That left me technically a dual citizen. . . . A few weeks ago, however, another member of my family had the occasion to check on her status and found that I had been expatriated back in 1925." Sakamaki continued, "I mention this to point out that registration of births and even expatriation are frequently executed without the knowledge of the parties most concerned and in no way imply divided allegiance." If such Nisei leaders as Sakamaki were confused, and others such as Honolulu deputy city and county attorney Wilfred C. Tsukiyama and territorial representative Andrew Yamashiro had not expatriated until 1932, it is no wonder that most Nisei were slow to expatriate. Thus the campaign to end dual citizenship, yet another aspect of the Americanization drive, illustrates how differently Americanizers and Japanese viewed an issue of consuming importance to Americanizers.[60]

The Americanization campaign was thus fraught with contradictions. While Americanizers insisted on loyalty from the Japanese, they refused to treat them in ways that encouraged that loyalty. While Americanizers demanded that Nisei renounce their Japanese citizenship, they gave tacit approval to the denial of naturalization rights for Issei. And while Americanizers spoke of democracy, they attempted to destroy the Japanese language press and denied Japanese the kind of justice accorded Caucasians.

These contradictions resulted from deeply ingrained attitudes among European Americans that Japanese were inferiors and desirable only as docile and hardworking plantation laborers. On their part the Japanese saw themselves as equal if not superior to Caucasians, and were therefore determined to improve their lives in Hawaii. To this end they refused to accept Americanizers' perceptions of them, opposed the discrimination they encountered, strengthened group solidarity, and promoted ethnic pride.

Part Three

The
Schooling
of the Nisei

Chapter 5

Schools as Avenues to Middle-Class Life

While the Japanese opposed efforts to discriminate against them, they welcomed the opportunities they found in America. One such opportunity was schooling. Many Nisei sought to enter and graduate from high school and some even aspired to graduate from college because they saw schooling as an avenue into American middle-class life.[1]

Such was the case with a University of Hawaii student born in 1902 in rural Kauai. His parents had gone to the island as plantation laborers and after a few years left plantation work. They moved to Waimea, another part of the island, where they grew vegetables on leased land. "I started to go to school when I was eight years old," this student, one of eight children, wrote. "I found that the town folk were dressed better than I, and they knew better English and knew more about the world than I. So, in the class, the town children . . . progressed more rapidly in their studies. . . . I used to think that it was hopeless to go to school." But he persevered. "I attended both the Japanese language school and English school in Waimea. . . . While in the lower grades I liked Japanese school more than the English school, but when I was in the higher grades, my attitude changed completely," he recalled, revealing the acculturating influence of public education, "due to the magazines I read in the school library. I read about the highly paid positions open to trained men and women. After considering which profession to select, I decided to become a doctor." This decision reflected the high aspirations Issei parents frequently instilled in their children.[2]

"With the desire to become a doctor," the student continued, "I put my whole thought into my studies, and I was able to progress very rapidly. When I was in the seventh grade, I came to Honolulu to continue my education." In Honolulu he did what many Nisei who wanted to continue their schooling did. He "worked before and after school hours as a school-boy in a private family." In 1919 he graduated from the Royal School and entered McKinley High School. "To work part time while attending school was a hard thing to do," he remembered vividly, "but, when one really needs an education, he'll get it in any means that is possible. When I was going to high school, I had to wake up at four o'clock in the morning to do my work. I polished the car, watered the plants and then prepared breakfast. After the meal, the dishes were washed, wiped and put away in order; then I walked to school. In the afternoon, I started work at 2:30 P.M. I did yard work until 5:30 P.M. and after getting dressed up, I prepared the evening meal. I got through with my night's work, usually, between 8:00 and 9:30 P.M. So when I commenced to do my study, it was sometimes near 10:00 P.M. After which I studied till late in the night: 1:00 A.M. was the usual hour for me to get into bed." He added proudly, "In spite of the long hours of work, and the short hours of sleep and study, I did well in my subjects. I was for two consecutive years on the honor-roll at the McKinley High School."[3]

Despite such dedication the student's future was uncertain. "In the fall of 1923 I enrolled at the University of Hawaii to study for the medical profession," he wrote. "I spent almost four years at the University during which time I have come in contact with men of various ranks in life, and also acquired many new ideas. . . . There are six months more for me at the University. . . . At present, I am up in the air and don't know what to do. . . . I need several years of university training before I become a doctor. . . . It seems that I will never have the required four-year training due to the family conditions at home, but nevertheless I plan to finish my study in the near future and realize my desire—it may take five or six years but I will wait. My motto: PUSH TO THE FRONT."[4]

This young man's story illustrates a number of experiences familiar to many Nisei. He began school after the normal age, felt disadvantaged in English and in general knowledge because of his rural background, and preferred Japanese school to English school at first but changed that preference as he came to see the advantages of excelling in English school. He also worked his way through school in pursuit of a long-term goal that he established early in life and that sustained his commitment to schooling. His story illustrates the close interplay of cultural values, family circumstances, and individual characteristics that made every story of acculturation a highly personal one.[5]

At this point something must be said of the schools in which the Japanese placed so much faith. By national standards they were adequate but far from outstanding. In 1920 the Russell Sage Foundation ranked Hawaii's school system twenty-third among the systems of fifty-three states and territories—above all the southern states and some northern and midwestern states, such as Vermont and Wisconsin, but below California, New York, Massachusetts, and Connecticut. Hawaii compared favorably in average days of attendance, length of school year, teachers' salaries, and average annual expenditures per teacher. It compared unfavorably in high school enrollment, average annual expenditures per student, and in the proportion of girls attending high school. One of its greatest strengths was that "educational opportunities were more equitably distributed throughout the entire area of the Territory of Hawaii than in any mainland state," said the report, and "in this respect Hawaii [was] more democratic" than the rest of the country.[6]

The Hawaiian Organic Act, which created the framework for territorial governance after annexation, made only minor changes in the public school system already in place. The act provided for a superintendent of the Territorial Department of Public Instruction (DPI) to serve four-year terms, and a territorial school board, called the Board of Commissioners, both appointed by the governor with the consent of the territorial senate. The Organic Act continued the practice of centralized control of the schools developed during the days of the monarchy and the republic, a feature unique in the United States.[7]

The school system expanded rapidly after annexation. In 1900, 11,501 students attended Hawaii's public schools, and 4,036 attended private schools. Twenty years later the public schools enrolled almost four times as many students (41,350) and private schools almost twice as many (7,573). By 1940, totals had risen to 92,812 in public and 17,560 in private schools. With the increase in students came a dramatic rise in expenditures for public education, from $717,000 for the biennium ending in 1900 to $12,608,414 for that ending in 1940. This expansion was due chiefly to growing numbers of Nisei students, increasing from 1,352 in 1900, to 19,354 in 1920, and 45,930 in 1940.[8]

During the 1920s the growth was especially notable in secondary schools. In 1920 there were only four high schools, one on each of the major islands. McKinley High School on Oahu had been established in 1896, Hilo High School on the island of Hawaii in 1905, Maui High and Grammar School in 1913, and Kauai High and Grammar in 1914. By 1930 six additional high schools and seventeen junior high schools had opened their doors, and by 1940 came twelve more schools with senior high divisions.[9]

The superintendents who administered this system were like their mainland counterparts—native-born, white, Protestant men with strong ties to the local power structure. The first non-white superintendent, appointed in 1967, after Hawaii became a state, was the Japanese American Ralph Kiyosaki. The territorial school board, known as the Board of Commissioners until 1931, when it became the Board of Education, was also European American and male-dominated. No more than two out of seven (six in the earlier years) board members were women, also haole, during the first four decades of the twentieth century.[10]

Like the superintendents and school board members, many of the teachers in Hawaii's public schools were haole, but their proportion gradually decreased as the children of immigrants acquired the schooling needed to become teachers. Until the 1920s, when the University of Hawaii established a department of education, all public high school teachers were European Americans from the mainland, and before 1930, Caucasians constituted between 40 and 45 percent of all public grammar school teachers. To illustrate, in 1926, 45 percent of all teachers in the grammar and high schools were Caucasians, 20 percent Part-Hawaiians, and 13 percent Chinese. Japanese and Portuguese teachers each constituted 9 percent of all teachers. In contrast, Japanese students made up 53 percent of all public school students.[11]

Teachers varied in their rapport with Japanese students and in their ability to motivate them. Nisei recalled that some were mean-spirited and bigoted, while others were kind, helpful, and inspirational. Probably most were somewhere in between. Certainly many Nisei received their share of poor teaching. A 1927 Hilo High School student recalled his schooling in the 1910s. "I remember one of my boyhood friends was flogged so hard with a bamboo stick that it left purple marks on his legs," he wrote. "Then [the teacher] put the boy in a closet for several hours just because he wept loudly." A Normal School student who began school in 1913 in Lahaina, Maui, remembered experiences with "cruel" teachers who "always scolded him" and made him dislike school. For punishment they had students stick out their tongues, which they slapped with a yardstick. "At other times," this student continued, "they would ask us to stand for a whole day. Sometimes they would have us eat red hot peppers."[12]

Some teachers were bigoted. A young Chinese woman recalled a McKinley High School teacher in the 1920s who favored European American students. "In my class," she wrote, "we had quite a number of *haole* students who received all the good marks from the teacher. They had their own mother tongue and naturally it [was] quite easy for them to speak English. . . . The Japanese students had the hardest time in class." When they volunteered to speak, the woman continued, the teacher "simply ignored [them]." A high school Nisei in 1927 recalled her sixth grade teacher, newly arrived from the mainland, as equally unsympathetic. "Everything we did or said seemed to irritate her," the girl reminisced, "and I remember she used to call us Japs and Chinks in the class." Some Nisei complained of discrimination at the Normal School. A young man attending the school in 1927 wrote, "I have never known a school where there was so much favoritism. . . . Since I came to the Normal, I have wished numberless times that I were a haole so that I would have better chance at graduation."[13]

But other teachers were warm and caring. One Normal School student wrote of a teacher he had in 1913, "[It was] as if our mother was teaching us." Years later, when this student decided to become a teacher himself, this early teacher served as his model. As this suggests, some Nisei developed strong emotional attachments to favorite teachers.[14]

A teacher's encouragement could be all-important in motivating individual Nisei to learn and continue in school. An Issei woman, herself tied to the plantation, recalled in the 1930s how a teacher influenced her daughter's future. "One day," she said, "our daughter told me that one of her teachers had asked her what she was going to do when she finishes high school. She told her teacher that she would be very likely working to help the family. The teacher told our daughter that she thought it was a foolish thing to do, as there is every likelihood of an opening in the teaching field in the Territory by the time she completes her university course." Acceding to the teacher's suggestion, the girl's parents let her continue her schooling.[15]

Besides teachers, Nisei encountered students of different ethnic groups in school. But since the ethnic mix of the school population reflected the territory's population, Nisei constituted the largest group of students. In December 1920, 8 percent of 41,350 public school students were Hawaiians, 11 percent Part-Hawaiians, 13 percent Portuguese, 4 percent Caucasians, 10 percent Chinese, and 47 percent Japanese. The Japanese student population remained high—56 percent in 1930, and 50 and 46 percent in 1940 and 1947. Japanese students were rather evenly distributed throughout the Islands, making up slightly higher proportions in rural areas than in urban Honolulu.[16]

Although the ethnic composition of Hawaii's schools was unique in the American context, ethnic diversity was no stranger to American schools. Students of more than sixty ethnic groups attended schools in urban communities on the mainland in 1908, and 58 percent of them were immigrants or children of immigrants, a proportion that reached 72 percent in New York City, 67 percent in Chicago, 64 percent in Boston, 60 percent in Cleveland, and 58 percent in San Francisco.[17]

Especially during the first two decades of the twentieth century, many students in Hawaii were older than the normal ages for their grades, the proportion of such older students progressively decreasing during the next two decades. In rural areas where population was sparse and families lived far away from schools, many children, particularly during the early decades, began school when they were seven or older instead of the legal age of six. Raku Morimoto began school in Spreckelsville, Maui, in 1911, when she was ten years old. She and a number of her schoolmates completed grammar school when they were seventeen or eighteen. Others never went to school at all, since schools were too far from home. One Nisei recalled walking two hours each way when he entered school at the age of seven in 1908 on the island of Hawaii. Although Sueno Matsushita began school at the officially approved age of six, for her, as for others in rural areas, getting to school seemed like a journey. "We all had to walk, you know, barefooted," she recalled. "And we had to carry our *bento* [lunch]. And then school was so far. We started at seven o'clock and we reached school about eight." This was in 1909 in Koloa, Kauai.[18]

Family responsibilities also prevented students from beginning school at the legal age. One girl from a plantation camp on Kauai recalled that she began school two years late in 1915 because she had to care for her little sister. She later went on to high school and Normal School.[19]

Besides starting school late, students commonly repeated one or more grades. But as the idea emerged that "children develop best when placed in groups of about their own age and social maturity," the practice of holding students back gradually lessened. Thus the proportion of all public school students who were repeaters decreased from 18 percent in 1927 to 4 percent five years later. Fewer repeaters and increasing proportions of students entering school at the legal age meant increasing percentages of students at the normal ages for their grades. Third graders who were older than the normal age, for example, decreased from 76 percent in 1916 to 56 percent in 1926 and 21 percent in 1936.[20]

During the first two decades of the twentieth century but decreasingly so thereafter, children entered school in Hawaii with little or no knowledge of Standard English—that is, the English associated with professional, middle-class Americans. Rose Falconer, who began teaching first grade in 1910 in the rural district of Kona on the island of Hawaii, recalled that "the Portuguese would speak Portuguese. Hawaiians, Hawaiian. And Japanese, Japanese. So we had [pantomime] motions. Like 'Up, up in the sky, the little birds fly' and things like that." As late as 1920, only 2 or 3 percent of all students entering public school spoke Standard English. Most students, about one-third to one-half of whom were Japanese, spoke Hawaii Creole English, what Hawaii residents have popularly called "Pidgin English" (further discussed in chapter 9).[21]

Before World War II, eighth graders had to pass examinations to qualify for public high school or Normal School. Some who failed the examinations enrolled in private schools, thereby increasing private secondary school enrollment and adding to the prestige of public senior high schools. Before World War II, McKinley, the oldest of the public high schools, was considered to be more rigorous than most private high schools in the territory. In 1914, 52 percent of all students who took the public high school entrance examinations passed, a figure that increased to 70 in 1915 and 81 in 1916. In 1928 the DPI began a promotion policy that permitted no more than 80 percent of all eighth graders to enter senior high school, but abandoned this policy in 1936. Attending and graduating from high school, then, were significant accomplishments during this period, accomplishments that many Nisei valued.[22]

Indeed, teachers in Hawaii as well as on the mainland frequently remarked on the seriousness of purpose with which the Japanese approached schooling. A Hawaiian-Caucasian teacher during the 1920s and 1930s later remarked that it was practically unthinkable for Nisei students to "play hookey." Mark and Zelie Sutherland, who taught in all districts on the island of Hawaii in the 1930s, recalled similarly that Japanese parents "always appreciated anything the teachers did." They continued, "We did everything we could to build up the students academically. The Japanese parents saw that, and appreciated it. . . . They saw to it that their children did what was expected of them in school. Consequently, the Nisei worked harder than other children." Eileen Tam, a Chinese American who taught in Makawao, Maui, similarly distinguished Japanese parents from others. "They were more appreciative of what you were doing," she said. "I found the parents so thankful that you were there to help their youngsters."[23]

The Nisei made similar comments about their parents. A youth wrote in 1927, "Both of my parents are so interested in education that although my home condition is poor, they are eager to let me have higher education." Indeed many Issei were determined that their children would have the education they did not. "Some of us are poor," explained a parent in the 1930s, "but yet we send our children through schools—high school and even through college, because we don't want them to live the same kind of life we, first generation, lacking education, had to live in Hawaii."[24]

Although Japanese families were traditionally patriarchal, mothers could, with tenacity, have their way. A University of Hawaii student wrote that his father wanted him to go to work after he completed the eighth grade, but his mother insisted that he continue in school. She was determined that his and his brother's lives be better than hers had been. Working at a pineapple cannery in the summer of 1923 while he was still in high school, this student received further encouragement from older employees who urged him to go to college so he could be independent of the "big bosses." They too fed his desire to "get away from the soil."[25]

Issei parents had little money to spare, but they willingly bought books and school supplies for their children. In return they expected their children to do well in school. A Lahainaluna High School boy wrote in the 1920s, "My parents always told me to study hard and become a great man and not a canefield laborer, who has to go to work early in the morning, rain or sun, and work to late in the evening. They even said that they would buy anything for me if it was related to school." "We were compelled to report every test to my father," wrote another high school boy in the 1920s. "When anyone in the family showed good work in school, father used to praise and give reward, often school equipment or money for saving, but not for spending. If we satisfied him at the end of our school year with our grades, he would supply us with all new books in the early part of the year, but otherwise we were to use the second hand books." Then the student pointed to the strong bond between Issei mothers and their children. "My older brother failed one year," he recalled. "Father gave him a good long lecture. At first mother was listening to what father was saying, but a few minutes later I saw she was crying near the bedroom. Father's lecture did not affect us very much, but mother's [reaction] struck us very hard and we never failed in school work [again]."[26]

Sometimes actions supplemented verbal encouragement. A young woman recalled that in the early 1920s,

> we were made to work in the cane fields at a very early age. Every Saturday father would wait for us to return from the Japanese School and would take us to the field. We believed, at that time, that he was not very kind—our neighbors always did the hard work and the children the easiest part, while we had to go through the whole process. . . . After a day's work in the fields dad used to ask, "Are you tired? Would you want to work in the fields when you are old enough to leave school? You can earn about fifty cents for what you did today. Perhaps in years to come you will be earning one dollar a day." Sometimes he used to say, "Isn't Miss Kojima [one of the pioneers in the teaching profession] lucky? She works from nine to two and gets eighty dollars per month. Her Saturdays and Sundays are free. She needs never complain about soiled hands and scratched arms." He sent me to work as a housemaid one summer and this experience made me dislike such employment. In fact, my father did everything in his power to make us realize that going to school would be to our advantage.[27]

When such encouragement failed, some parents resorted to physical punishment. "I used to hate school and always ran away," a young man who later became an outstanding student reminisced of his early schooling in the 1920s. "My father was furious. He gave me a beating and after that I never missed school." Another Nisei recalled his early school years in the second decade of the twentieth century. "When I was a tot, I was not very fond of books," he said. "The lure of the brooks or the valley, where the varieties of tropical fruits grew had greater attraction for me than the weird monotony of the classroom. The occasions when I made myself conspicuous by being absent were not infrequent. Each truancy, however, was rewarded in a warm manner at the hands of my parents. At times the reward was so ample and so hot that I could not stand on my feet or resume my normal sitting position. I used to resent this sort of treatment and on a few occasions I actually could not be subdued by them." But in time he realized that beneath his parents' harsh treatment was a concern for his future. They got him a tutor who thrashed him with a ruler when he made a mistake and praised him when he did well. Such praise led his parents to buy something he wanted, a baseball glove or bat or a bicycle. Eventually he became a serious student and went to college.[28]

In the absence of a parent, an earnest older sibling might discipline a younger one. A teacher recalled an episode from the late 1920s: "One day, while I was working with a small group around me, I heard a little disturbance in the room, and looking around, I saw a seventeen-year-old boy administering an old-fashioned spanking to his brother, aged five, whom he had across his knee. When I took the older boy to task, he replied, 'But he won't study. He won't keep his eyes on his book, and mother told me I must make him do it.' "[29]

Some parents were not satisfied with the school in their area, and if they could afford it, sent their children to what they thought was a better school in Honolulu. One mother in the 1920s, believing that Lahainaluna High on Maui was inadequate, sent her son to Honolulu to attend McKinley High. While there, he lived at a Christian dormitory established for Japanese students by the Reverend Takie Okumura.[30]

These varied forms of parental encouragement helped Nisei children internalize the drive to succeed. In the 1920s Hideo Tamura commuted an hour and a half each way by train to attend Maui High School. When he was in the eighth grade, he decided he would become a dentist. His parents owned a store in Wailuku, where they made and sold *senbei*, *mochi*, and other Japanese confections. Behind their shop a haole dentist had an office. The boy observed the dentist's patients coming and going, and concluded that dentistry was a well-paying profession. After high school, he attended the University of Hawaii, and eventually graduated from Northwestern University Dental School.[31]

Kazuo Hosaka, a Kibei who went to Japan in 1909 when he was a year old and returned to Hawaii when he was twenty, overcame formidable odds to learn English, graduate from high school in Honolulu, and enter the University of Southern California Dental School. In dental school he borrowed his classmates' notes, since he could barely understand the professors' lectures. He "studied about three and four times more than the other students," but his hard work paid off when he graduated after seeing some of his English-speaking classmates drop out.[32]

Similarly, a determined girl who graduated from McKinley High in 1925 did so only after expending great effort to overcome a weakness in mathematics and thereby qualify for the Normal School. "One night I resolved that I would put all my time in algebra," she recalled, "so that I [could] pass the final examination with a good mark, even if I had to ruin my health from lack of sleep. After I made that resolution, I retired every night at 8:00 P.M. and from 1:00 A.M. until 5:30 A.M. I worked on my algebraic problems. At first it was hard to get right out of bed and do my work, but a little force and will power on my part certainly kept me going until I arrived at a place where the habit became automatic." Her hard work and determination paid off, for she was able to declare proudly, "I passed my course in algebra with a B, which I deserved."[33]

The death of a parent might strengthen a child's determination to complete school. "Since my father especially wished me to continue schooling until I trained myself thoroughly for my calling," wrote a Maui High School girl in 1927, "I have made up my mind never to quit school. . . . For me to quit school would be unfair to my dead father."[34]

Despite the pattern repeated so frequently in all these cases, the cases themselves were exceptional. Before 1929 fewer than 20 percent of all Nisei who had attended second grade ten years earlier continued on to the twelfth grade, a proportion that increased to only 28 percent by 1935. Fewer still of the second graders eventually graduated from college, possibly 3 percent in 1930.[35]

More undergraduates attending the University of Hawaii in 1929–30 were Nisei (301) than were Chinese (206) or Caucasian (185), making the Nisei highly visible there, but the Nisei were actually underrepresented at the time, while Chinese and Caucasians were overrepresented. Whereas the Nisei constituted the largest group of undergraduates at the university that year—35 percent of the total—they made up 54 percent of all students in the public schools. In contrast, Caucasians and Chinese constituted 22 and 24 percent of University of Hawaii undergraduates and only 4 and 9 percent of public school students. For Koreans the percentages were 2 and 2; for Part-Hawaiians, 12 and 10.[36]

When compared with other groups in 1929 and 1935, the Nisei rate of school persistence was somewhere in the middle. Forty-six percent of

Caucasians, 40 percent of Koreans, 35 percent of Chinese, 20 percent of Japanese, 13 percent of Part-Hawaiians, 7 percent of Portuguese, 5 percent of Filipinos, and 4 percent of Hawaiians who were in second grade in 1919–20 entered twelfth grade in 1929. For the second graders in 1925–26 who continued on to twelfth grade in 1935–36, the percentages were 75 for Caucasians, 63 for Koreans, 56 for Chinese, 32 for Part-Hawaiians, 28 for Japanese, 11 for Portuguese, 6 for Filipinos, and 4 for Hawaiians.[37]

These figures reflect historical, socioeconomic, and cultural influences. The Chinese, who arrived in Hawaii before the Japanese, reached higher levels of educational achievement sooner. Koreans, on the other hand, arrived after the Japanese but often outperformed them. Unlike the Issei, who were mostly Buddhists, Korean immigrants were Christians, which helped ease their transition into American society. Additionally, unlike most Issei, who were impoverished farmers, Korean immigrants were urban dwellers from all walks of life and social strata. As a result Koreans in Hawaii experienced more rapid upward mobility than the Japanese. The Filipinos, who arrived after the Japanese, were mostly rural men; Filipino children, therefore, remained a small proportion of the student population before the Second World War. The Portuguese, who arrived a little earlier than the Japanese, and the Hawaiians fell behind the Japanese in persistence rates for reasons that need further exploring.[38]

Despite the Japanese interest in education, continuing in school during the first three decades of the twentieth century was difficult because most Nisei youths had to help their families make ends meet. Eighty-year-old Sueno Matsushita, whose father died when she was a little girl, reflected on her past philosophically. "Some people went to school, some people stayed back," she recalled of her childhood. "Like us, my mother not making too much money. . . . If my father was living, it would be different."[39]

Besides losing their potential earnings, keeping older children in school meant incurring extra expenses. There were fees to pay, books to buy, and boarding costs for some. Clarence Kobayashi, who came from Honokaa on the island of Hawaii, recalled that "it was rather expensive for plantation laborers to send their children to high school." Until the 1920s each island had only one high school, which meant that students from rural areas had to board in dormitories, work in haole homes for room and board, or live with relatives or friends.[40]

There was, of course, another factor that limited Nisei schooling: many were not interested in education. Richard Inouye, who grew up on the island of Hawaii as one of eight children, stopped attending school in 1922 after completing the sixth grade because, he recalled, to go to "junior high school, you had to go to another town, to Laupahoehoe." To do that cost money. "You had to ride the train and go, see. So I didn't go. And I didn't care. I wasn't interested." Teiki Yoshimoto, who dropped out of McKinley High School in 1924, recalled, "I used to be crazy for movie. We play hookey. . . . The show start at ten [o'clock], see. Go into Hawai'i Theater till about twelve o'clock. Finish that, go across the street, Empire Theater. And then, finish about two o'clock. Then we start walking, going back." Masayuki Yoshimura, who grew up in Waikiki in the 1920s and 1930s, liked to surf and have a good time. He recalled, "Our parents was strict for school. . . . School was very important to them. So, after I graduate high school, my dad wanted to send me to USC [University of Southern California], see. But I wasn't interested."[41]

For others, school was not seen as necessary for success. Shoichi Kurahashi, who quit school in 1935 after completing the ninth grade and who was fluent in Japanese, wanted to make his fortune in Manchuria. "I read in the Japanese magazine that Japan was giving out acreage for farms in Manchuria to anybody going there. When I got out [of school] at sixteen . . . I thought I'd go to Japan to learn carpentry and then go to Manchuria to build homes there. . . . But then the war broke out."[42]

But many who wanted to continue their schooling could not. In cases like these, two Japanese values collided, and often loyalty to family took precedence over the desire for schooling. Older siblings put aside dreams of education to help the family. This was particularly common before 1920. William Ishida wanted to go on to high school in 1916, but his parents could not afford to send him. Instead Ishida worked to send his younger brother to Mid-Pacific Institute, a private boarding high school in Honolulu. Similarly, Minoru Kimura's older brothers worked while he attended school. The sixth of eight children, Kimura graduated from McKinley High and the University of Hawaii, and from Tulane Medical School in New Orleans in 1936. His older brother sent him money for tuition and room and board. A Hilo High student in the 1920s who likewise benefited from the sacrifices of older siblings expressed his gratitude. "To my parents and brothers I owe my high school education," he said. "My elder brothers did not have the opportunity to attend school. . . . This great sacrifice I will always hold nearest my heart, and repay in the years to come."[43]

This practice continued, although decreasingly so, through the 1920s and 1930s. Eleven years his senior, Shoichi Kurahashi's older sister quit school at the end of the eighth grade in the early 1920s to learn dressmaking. When she was nineteen, she opened a dressmaking shop in Honolulu and became the main breadwinner of the family. Ethel Kina quit school in 1930 when she was eleven to help in the family's laundry business. She and her family washed clothes on the weekends; during weekdays, while her parents worked in the cane fields, she ironed and mended clothes and took care of younger siblings. She wanted to continue in school, but "in those days," she later recalled, "you no can say nothing! No answer back. Anything the parents say, you say 'yes.'" Hideo, a Nisei for whom no other identity is known, excelled in high school in the 1930s and wanted to go to the university. But his parents told him, "We can't allow you to do it. It grieves us deeply to say no, but . . . you have four younger ones below you, and you, being the oldest, should think of helping them go through school." Hideo's fellow workers in the plantation camp praised him for doing well in school, but told him at the time, "Your parents have done splendidly in rearing you and now it is your turn to be dutiful and help them in their old age."[44]

Death of a parent could end a Nisei's school career. A McKinley High School boy wrote, "My father was very greatly interested in my education. He bought many sets of books for me, such as the Harvard Classics and the Encyclopedia. . . . He planned to make me go to college on the mainland. His aim was to make me a medical doctor, but since he died, I am not sure of going to college, because I must work for my family."[45]

If a father died, his oldest son might take the father's role, giving encouragement and financial support to younger siblings so that they could continue in school. In 1911, when an oldest son was twelve years old, his father died. The boy quit school to work. Sixteen years later, his youngest sibling, then a Hilo High School student, wrote, "My chief aim [is] to study hard and make something out of myself. My brother [is taking] a great interest in me and promised to send me to college, so this last year, I am studying extra hard." Thus many who attended high school and college were able to do so because of help from siblings.[46]

Others worked their way through school. Japanese students at Maui High School in 1930 earned much more of their school expenses than did students of other ethnic groups, and 42 percent of Japanese students compared to 27 percent of all other students earned all of their school expenses. Nisei students worked part-time on sugar and pineapple plantations or family coffee farms; in pineapple canneries, retail stores, small hotels, or laundries; at carpentry or mechanical work; and as maids, houseboys, or yardboys in the homes of wealthy Caucasians. Some worked during summers, while others worked all year round before or after school or on Saturdays.[47]

Students commonly began work at the age of ten or twelve. Richard Inouye recalled that in 1921, when he was ten, instead of attending Japanese language school on Saturdays, he began helping his father *hoe-hana* (pull weeds) on the plantation. He also worked full-time during the summers. From the same age of ten in 1922, Lowell Takahashi weeded and irrigated Waialua Plantation cane fields during the summers. Later, during his high school years, he worked in the pineapple fields.[48]

Minoru Inaba, who later became a school principal and legislator, worked on his family's coffee farm in 1916. "You know, when you in the seventh grade like that, to carry one bag of coffee was quite a chore," he recalled. "And load three bags on a donkey and come up the trail. When it rain, the donkey would slip on the trail, fall. Had to unload the coffee, get the donkey up, load it again. I know, many times, I used to cry." Later, as a Konawaena High School student on the island of Hawaii, Inaba drove a school bus before and after school, and worked nights at a telephone exchange and weekends at a post office. All the money he earned he gave to his parents.[49]

Girls, especially, did unpaid work at home. "I was only eleven years old," recalled a Normal School student in 1927, "when I had to do the family washing, cooking and keeping house because Father and Mother had to work."[50]

Many Nisei accepted these patterns of working while going to school as part of life. "It is a hard task for me to work in a cane field," wrote a Hilo High School boy in 1927 of his summer job, "but I do not care, for I am eager to gain an education. Early in the morning I go to the field to cut cane. We had to cut 120 bundles of 62 pounds each in order to earn a dollar."[51]

Other students, especially those who worked all year round, felt deprived and envied their more fortunate peers. A high school senior in 1927 whose father was dead wrote of her "struggl[e] to acquire a higher education" by working her way through school as a maid. "Life is filled with responsibilities," she philosophized, but then admitted, "I cannot recall how many times I wept, thinking of my unfortunate life and . . . of what will happen to me in the future." A schoolmate whose mother died when she was five and who also worked as a maid wrote, "Whenever I see a girl or girls of my age playing, I think of myself and wish that I could play, too. But I think of how father suffered when mother passed away, leaving four of us children." A Normal School student who began working when she was thirteen "in the plantation cane fields, cutting, piling and planting" and then as a maid, was similarly affected by her experience. "How hard it is to work and to learn at the same time," she wrote in 1927. "Many a night I cried myself to sleep because I found that I couldn't very well have what I wanted or enjoy and have a good time like other girls." Another Normal School student in 1927 who had been supporting himself since high school admitted, "There were many hard times when I felt like crying, but my determination was to graduate from McKinley without any help."[52]

This determination to persevere combined with the idea of duty to keep many working students in school. "Many, many times, I went with only two meals a day," wrote Joe Kurihara, who moved from Hawaii to California to attend college. "To work through school is not an easy task. It requires super-human determination. . . . My body trembled and I experienced fainting spells frequently during those trying days of 1920. I saw boys and girls heading for picture shows while I had to stay in and study. I saw people going to a picnic party while I had to work. It really was discouraging at times but I felt and knew, to succeed I must deny all pleasure however painful it may be. . . . It was unquestionably the greatest and the most glorious day of my life when I [donned] the cap and gown. . . . It was my motto: 'Duty before pleasure.' I will not rest until I succeed."[53]

When they were unable to combine work and school, some Nisei alternated between them. A Nisei who wanted to become a doctor worked full-time for three years after graduating from high school in the early 1920s to send his brother and sister to Normal School. Then with the encouragement of his parents, he entered the University of Hawaii and planned to go to medical school. Another high school graduate who wanted to enroll in Normal School in 1926 knew his family needed his financial help. He therefore dropped out of school for a year and worked as a fisherman because doing so would enable him to earn money quickly. During his first week on the job, he came very close to quitting because of the danger he was exposed to, but his long-term goal sustained him. "Each month like Silas Marner I counted each nickel and dollar," he said of the experience. "Never a night passed by without my asking God to give me an opportunity to go to school again. Sometimes my fishermen friends thought that I was insane because I prayed. It was a good thing that they didn't understand a word I said, for if they knew they would never have given me a position on their boat." After a year he had enough money to enter Normal School.[54]

A girl who wanted to become a teacher quit school in 1916 after completing the seventh grade. While her parents went out to work, she tended the family store, cleaned the house, and took care of her baby brother and sister. After four years, her oldest brother, who had been studying on the mainland, returned home, and with his help she returned to school. She entered the eighth grade when she was eighteen years old, and then went to Kauai High School. While she was there, her father died, and she feared she might be unable to remain in school, but her mother and brother supported her and her younger brother and sister through school. After completing high school, she moved to Honolulu to attend the Normal School.[55]

Some Nisei who had to work full-time found less conventional ways to continue their education. Yuzuru Morita began working full-time at Oahu Sugar Company after he completed the ninth grade in 1933. He took advantage of the company's policy of allowing workers to attend school on company time half a day each week. He also attended night classes, and after six years, at the age of twenty-two, he received a high school diploma from the Waipahu Continuation School.[56]

A Normal School student recalled the aftermath of her father's death in 1919 when she was eleven and her eldest brother sixteen. "Feeling the great responsiblity of looking after [five younger brothers and sisters]," she recounted, "my brother left school immediately and worked as a carpenter." But determined to continue his education, her brother took correspondence courses from LaSalle Extension University, and his "strong will power" and his "mother's encouragement" enabled him to get the education he would otherwise have missed. "At the age of nineteen," his sister continued, "he was already at the head of the bookkeeping department of a garage with four high school graduates working under him. Besides being the supporter of the whole family," she added, "he was a father and guide to me."[57]

In 1915, the father of a fourteen-year-old seventh grade Nisei boy had to go to a hospital in Honolulu. His mother accompanied his father, and the boy was left in Kohala, on the island of Hawaii, to take care of two younger brothers. When his father returned two months later, he told his son to quit school. The youth did not voice his disappointment, for his father was very strict. The boy went to work on the plantation, and with the help of his English teacher, who regretted his leaving school, he got a job as a clerk in a large store in the district, working from 5:00 A.M. to 8:00 P.M. After work, he often read magazines and newspapers, and one night he came across an advertisement for a correspondence high school course costing five dollars a month. His father gave him permission to apply for the course, and for the next two years he studied every night until midnight. He completed the course in 1919 when he was eighteen, at which time he decided to move to Honolulu to continue his schooling. To prevent his leaving, his employer offered to double his wage to fifty dollars a month in addition to room and board, but he rejected the offer. In Honolulu he worked days and attended evening classes at the YMCA while supporting his younger brother, who was also in Honolulu attending Royal School and the Japanese High School. The young man did this for two years, but dissatisfied with the education he was receiving, he decided to attend day school full-time and work afternoons and nights. At age twenty he enrolled at Iolani, a private school, from

which he graduated in two years. At Iolani he excelled not only academically but in extracurricular activities as well. He was a member of
the debate team, editor of the school paper, and president of the student
body. He then went to the University of Hawaii while continuing to
support himself and his younger brother. At the university he majored
in commerce and received his bachelor's degree in 1927, when he was
twenty-six years old.[58]

As the Issei became more financially secure, they were able to send
their children to school for longer times. At the same time the building
of junior and senior high schools in rural areas of the territory, which
began in the 1920s, brought secondary schools closer to many children.
Japanese students took advantage of this development and remained in
school progressively longer. While very few were able to attend high
school before 1920, more did so during the 1920s, although even in 1930
less than half of all Nisei students graduated from high school. By 1943,
however, attending high school was common among Japanese youths,
and more than half of all Nisei students graduated from high school.
While fewer than 28 percent of the Nisei children in the second grade
in 1925 were in the twelfth grade in 1935, 58 percent of those in the
second grade in 1933 were in the twelfth grade in 1943. By World War II
the Japanese had laid what was in their eyes the foundation for achieving
their goal of entering the American middle class (see figure 2).[59]

Overall the Japanese improved their relative standing in school persistence between the two world wars. During the early part of this period a
smaller percentage of Japanese students reached the twelfth grade than
did Caucasians, Chinese, and Part-Hawaiians. But by 1943, the Japanese were second only to the Chinese in the percentage of students who
became twelfth graders (see figures 3 and 4).[60]

This dramatic climb occurred in large part because the Nisei had incorporated into their identity old-world values instilled in them by their
parents. Adapted to the Hawaii environment, Japanese values of perseverence, duty, frugality, endurance, devotion to education, filial piety,
and family solidarity enabled many Nisei to acquire the schooling they
believed important in becoming middle-class Americans.

As the Nisei acquired their education, a change occurred in the composition of Hawaii's European American population that had a major
impact on the public school system and on the schooling of the Nisei.
Until the first decade of the twentieth century, the haole population

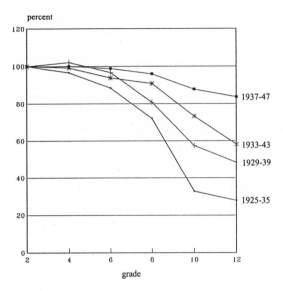

Figure 2. Persistence of Japanese Students in
Public and Private School in Hawaii, 1925–47.
Source: Tamura, "Americanization Campaign," 440–46.

had been quite small and primarily upper class. They had the means to
send their children to private schools, in particular to Punahou School in
Honolulu. But after annexation, middle-class Caucasians began migrat-
ing to Hawaii. Unable to send their children to Punahou, these parents
faced the prospect of having to send them to public schools where Hawaii
Creole English was the spoken language, and where, among "swarms
of Orientals," their children would "unconsciously pick up and adopt
Oriental manners and mannerisms."[61]

Under pressure to do something to avert this prospect, the Commissioners of Public Instruction designated Central Grammar School in
Honolulu at the close of World War I as an experimental school. Henceforth students had to pass an examination in oral English to enter. A
Nisei boy, then a student at the school, recalled his reactions to the
change. "Not until I was in the seventh grade," he said, "have I been
made to feel that I was a Japanese and not an American. . . . The principal
told us one day that beginning from a certain day the school would be
opened for . . . selected students only. When the day came and as we were
about to enter our classroom the principal who was standing at the door
proceeded to choose. 'You go in. You go out!' It was a big shock when I

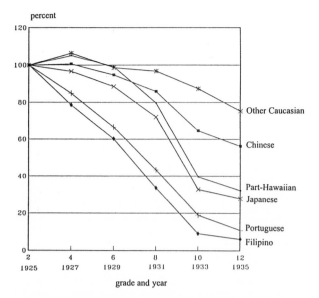

percent

2 4 6 8 10 12
1925 1927 1929 1931 1933 1935

grade and year

Other Caucasian

Chinese

Part-Hawaiian
Japanese

Portuguese
Filipino

**Figure 3. Persistence of Public and Private School
Students in Hawaii, 1925–35.**

Source: Tamura, "Americanization Campaign," 440.

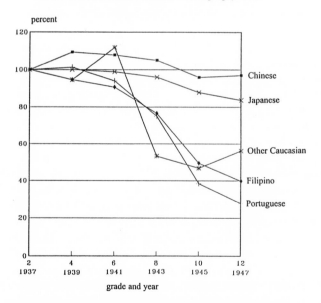

percent

2 4 6 8 10 12
1937 1939 1941 1943 1945 1947

grade and year

Chinese

Japanese

Other Caucasian

Filipino

Portuguese

**Figure 4. Persistence of Public and Private School
Students in Hawaii, 1937–47.**

Source: Tamura, "Americanization Campaign," 446.

discovered that . . . not one of the Haoles was excluded, however most of the Orientals were excluded. I felt extremely keen even at that time that a selection was not made on the basis of scholarship but on race."[62]

In 1920, when Caucasian parents petitioned the Commissioners of Public Instruction for more schools like Central Grammar, Superintendent Vaughan MacCaughey responded by endorsing the idea. The recently completed 1920 federal survey of Hawaii's school system had recommended that students within the same high school be grouped according to their proficiency in English, and MacCaughey cited that recommendation to buttress his endorsement. The commissioners took no immediate action, but by the early 1920s there was "growing agitation" for more schools like Central Grammar. "Children from English-speaking homes" were being "submerged" in Hawaii's public schools, wrote an advocate of such schools in *Friend,* a publication of the Hawaiian Evangelical Association. Central Grammar was a "success" in this author's view, "a genuine American public school."[63]

Meanwhile, in response to the program at Central Grammar School, a group of Japanese organized a kindergarten that emphasized the teaching of Standard English. To the dismay of European Americans who wanted to exclude "little Orientals" from the schools of white children, a year after the kindergarten was organized a number of Japanese first graders passed the qualifying language examination and were admitted to Central Grammar.[64]

Partly because of this, in 1922 administrators at the school began to segregate students by ethnicity. In response to this change an irate Portuguese parent protested to Superintendent MacCaughey. "Ever since the opening of school," the parent wrote, "I have witnessed such unjust treatment given the children of Portuguese blood that all my American ideals and ideas have been shattered. . . . The children at the Central Grammar School have been segregated—the Portuguese, Hawaiians and Orientals being put together and the AngloSaxons have been placed in rooms all by themselves—the others being considered unfit to mingle with them. Mrs. Overend, who is strictly *prejudiced,* and Vaughan MacCaughey did that on their own hook. . . . Those who preach Americanization the loudest are the worse *snobs* out. They *preach* but don't *practice.*" Such complaints caused MacCaughey to appoint a committee to investigate the situation, and the segregation apparently ended.[65]

In 1924 the DPI began designating a set of schools as "English Standard." That fall Lincoln Grammar School in Honolulu became the first such school, followed the next year by Aliiolani, another Honolulu grammar school, and in 1926 by Leilehua in rural Oahu and Maui Standard and Hilo Standard Schools on other islands. Also in 1926 the DPI created an English Standard division at Lihue Grammar School on Kauai called the Annex. By 1937, and for the next twelve years, there were ten English Standard schools, most of them in Honolulu where most European Americans lived. In 1949, the territorial legislature passed a measure phasing out the Standard schools. Beginning in the fall of that year no new students were enrolled as English Standard students; the last class of such students graduated from Roosevelt High School in 1960.[66]

Like the effort to channel the Nisei onto the plantation, the disagreement among supporters and opponents of English Standard schools reflected two different views of what America was. Americanizers, who supported Standard schools, saw America as a society that gave preferential treatment to particular groups. Japanese and other opponents of the system, on the other hand, saw America as a land of equal opportunity and called Standard schools discriminatory.

Supporters of English Standard schools insisted that these schools promoted Americanism by protecting the English language and encouraging good speech habits. Caucasian parents said they did not want their children to pick up Hawaii Creole English. A man who testified at a hearing in 1925 complained that his grandchildren's Hawaii Creole English prevented him from communicating with them. If Asian students could not pass the oral English examinations required for entrance into Standard schools, he declared, a large part of the blame fell on their parents, who sent the children to foreign language schools.[67]

Superintendent Will C. Crawford said in 1926 that the idea behind Standard schools was "to encourage the speaking of good English by promoting proficient scholars to a special school." "I firmly believe," he stated, "that the time is past for parents to feel that their children must be sent to private schools in order to safeguard their spoken English." Crawford's predecessor, Willard E. Givens, similarly defended Standard schools. "It is not fair," Givens said in 1925, "to have pupils who are so unevenly equipped [in English] to gather the fundamentals in the same room." Supporting this view was Emma Lyons Doyle, a descendant of the early missionaries to Hawaii and also a former teacher. In a letter she wrote to *Honolulu Star-Bulletin* in 1925, she argued that separating non-Standard English speakers was to their benefit. She explained that the teacher could not devote the time and attention necessary to help them "improve" their English when there were other students in the room who needed to move on.[68]

Critics called the Standard schools un-American because they were discriminatory. Dai Yen Chang, president of the Hawaiian Chinese Civic Association, said that the "select schools" encouraged "race prejudice" and were "a step backward" in the process of acculturation. Testifying at a legislative hearing, Chang asked, "Why is it that pupils permitted to enter are examined only in English and not in mathematics, geography, and other subjects?" Similarly, *Nippu Jiji* editorials argued that it was unfair to expect children whose first language was not English to speak perfect English when they entered school. Although advocates claimed otherwise, *Nippu Jiji* insisted that "select schools" were discriminating by race. A *Hawaii Hochi* editorial likewise criticized Standard schools as examples of a "Nordic caste system" that was "utterly at variance with the ideals for which America stands." Another critic described the schools as "Jim Crow" institutions. Against such accusations of elitism, Superintendent Givens protested in 1925 that the DPI never referred to Lincoln, the first English Standard school, as a "select" institution.[69]

Issues of race intersected with those of class in the development of English Standard schools. Arthur L. Dean, former president of the University of Hawaii and then vice-president of Alexander and Baldwin and chairman of the Territorial Board of Education, said in 1936 that the schools did what many communities on the mainland did—separate children of different cultural and economic groups. If that was the goal of the system, it was successful, for European Americans predominated in Standard schools. At the same time, segregating more privileged students in select schools while ignoring the needs of the vast majority assured Americanizers that they would remain above the masses. Children of the elite Japanese attended private schools and were not part of the bulk of Nisei in public schools.[70]

Dean conceded that Standard schools retarded acculturation of the children of immigrants, but in his opinion this was more than compensated for by the schools' success in preserving "good" speech habits. His comments point to contradictions in Americanizers' thinking about education. While they proclaimed that public schools should produce a common citizenry, they sought to maintain race and class segregation through the English Standard school system.

At statehood hearings held in 1936, Superintendent Oren E. Long admitted that Standard schools encouraged snobbishness among their students and violated the "ideal of the American public school system." This was an important admission coming from so high a school official, since the preservation of Americanism had been the main argument used to create the Standard schools. Long explained that the prevalence of Hawaii Creole English among the mass of public school students and the inability of middle-class Caucasians to afford private schools had brought about the Standard school system. Long added that he hoped the system would eventually end.[71]

The system did eventually end after World War II, when Standard schools became more controversial than they had been when Long spoke. Numerous articles and letters to the editor criticizing them appeared in Honolulu papers. By this time the issue of class predominated over that of race. In a 1945 survey of university students, school officials, teachers, and parents, the University of Hawaii sociologist Bernard Hormann found that attendance at Standard schools had become a mark of social status, that parents of all ethnic groups hoped to send their children to the schools, and that students attending the schools tended to look down on students in other public schools.[72]

English Standard schools encouraged such elitism, since only a small portion of all public school students—ranging from a low of 2 percent in 1925 to a high of 9 percent in 1947—were able to attend these schools. Until World War II, Caucasians constituted about half of all Standard school students, while they made up no more than 2.5 percent of the students in non-Standard public schools. Conversely, only 3 to 8.5 percent of Standard school students were Japanese, compared to about 55 percent of the students in non-Standard public schools. The representation of other groups in Standard schools was more balanced. Hawaiians and Part-Hawaiians, Portuguese, and Chinese constituted no more than 20, 11, and 7 percent, respectively, of Standard school students and no more than 16, 10, and 10 percent of non-Standard school students.[73]

The percentage of non-haole students in Standard schools increased notably over the years; by 1947 there were actually more Japanese than haole students enrolled in them. But this excess of Japanese students totaled only 91, while there were over 34,560 more Japanese than Caucasian students in non-Standard public schools. In addition the proportional rate of increase of Japanese students in Standard schools was lower than that of the Chinese and Koreans. And while there were numerically more Japanese than Chinese or Korean students in English Standard schools in 1945, the vastly larger number of Japanese students in all public schools meant that Japanese were still underrepresented in the Standard schools that year (see figure 5).[74]

Part of the reason for the underrepresentation of Japanese students in Standard schools may have been lack of space. Superintendent Long noted in 1936 that more students were qualified to attend Standard schools than could be admitted. In his study of education in Hawaii, Ralph Stueber argued that the failure to open more Standard schools showed that the DPI did not consider the speech of non-haole children a priority. Once haole parents had been satisfed, Stueber maintained, the pressure to expand the system ended. Either Japanese parents felt no

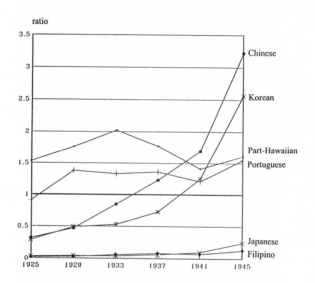

Figure 5. Ratio of Ethnic Occupancy in English
Standard Schools by Ethnic Group, 1925–45.

Source: Tamura, "Americanization Campaign," 449.
Note: A ratio of more than 1 indicates overrepresentation; a ratio of less than 1 indicates underrepresentation. See Tamura, "Americanization Campaign," 426–
29, for an explanation of how the ratio is derived.

need to push for more English Standard schools or, being noncitizens, did not feel it was their right to do so.[75]

Although the Standard schools generated a fair amount of dispute, the dispute never erupted into full-scale controversy as did the foreign language school issue (see chapter 7). No group took the issue of separate schools based on English language proficiency to court, as Mexican American parents did in Orange County, California, in the 1940s. Perhaps no such challenge developed in Hawaii because Japanese parents realized that the ability to speak Standard English was one of the keys to upward mobility for their children, and opponents of Standard schools offered no viable alternative for promoting the use of Standard English.[76]

The DPI's low-key approach to the issue also helped mute the controversy. Biennial reports of the superintendents included extensive discussions of vocational education, the Normal School, foreign language schools, and even private schools, but never mentioned English Standard schools. Nor did DPI directories indicate which schools were English Standard, and no official study was made of Standard schools until 1948, when the legislature prepared to phase them out. It seems as if the department sought by purposeful omission to divert attention from these schools. In 1949 the legislature began phasing out Standard schools. Public sentiment by that time had shifted against them. Middle-class Nisei and other Asians who were then gaining political influence probably felt uncomfortable about the schools, even when their children could pass the entrance examinations. By this time opponents of Standard schools did not need to use the courts to advance their cause because they could effect the change they wanted at the legislature.[77]

The legacy of the Standard schools is ambiguous. They did perpetuate the status-conscious mentality of many people in Hawaii, but they also accelerated the acculturation of Nisei and other non-haole youths who attended them by bringing the students in closer contact with middle-class Caucasians. On the other hand, they may have had some retarding effect on the acculturation of the vast majority of Nisei and other students by limiting their exposure to Standard English speakers. Yet, had there been no Standard school system, the small proportion of Standard English speaking students would have had little noticeable effect on the speech patterns of Hawaii Creole English speakers, who made up the vast majority of students. Overall, the effect of Standard schools on Nisei acculturation was negligible, since most Nisei did not attend them. Many Nisei who tried to learn Standard English did so outside Standard schools. And so pervasive was the use of Hawaii Creole English in Hawaii that it was less of a handicap there than it would have been on the mainland.

Private schools offered another alternative for haole parents who wanted to segregate their children from "the mass of children of aliens." Between 1925 and 1947, about 40 percent of all haole students in the territory attended private schools.[78]

In this same period increasing numbers of Japanese students also attended private schools. Between 1925 and 1947 Japanese enrollment in private schools in grades two through twelve increased from 561 in 1925 to 2,465 in 1947, and from 10 percent of all private school students to 16 percent. These increases seem meaningful at first glance, but of all

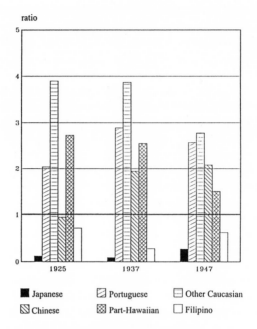

Figure 6. Ratio of Ethnic Occupancy in Private
Schools by Year and Ethnic Group.

Source: Tamura, "Americanization Campaign," 454.
Note: A ratio of more than 1 indicates overrepresentation;
a ratio of less than 1 indicates underrepresentation.

Japanese students in the territory only 2 percent in 1925 and 7 percent
in 1947 enrolled in private schools, and Japanese remained the most
underrepresented group in these schools. Haole students were the most
overrepresented, followed by Part-Hawaiian and Portuguese students.
The number of Chinese students grew from proportional to overrepresented, and Filipinos remained underrepresented, though less so than
the Japanese (see figure 6).[79]

Punahou, the most prestigious and ethnically exclusive of the private
schools, stood as the symbol of Americanizers' perception of themselves
as above the masses of Asians. Until the 1950s, it limited Asians to
no more than 10 percent of its student body, which was predominantly
haole. Japanese constituted 2.8 percent of the students at Punahou in
1925, 3.2 percent in 1937, and 4.2 percent in 1947. The few Japanese who
attended the school during this period were children of professionals and
businessmen, as for example, the son of the Reverend Takie Okumura,

the daughter of Professor Tasuku Harada of the University of Hawaii, and the son of the *Nippu Jiji* editor Yasutaro Soga.[80]

Occasionally, insensitive Caucasians could devastate a child unaware of ethnic and class barriers at the school. A Normal School student in 1927 wrote of a plantation manager who had offered a scholarship to Punahou for the eighth grader in her school having the highest grades. "There was only one pure American in our class," she recalled. "I did my best that last year and asked all my teachers [for help] in correcting where I failed and at the end of that year I found that I had the highest marks. But when the announcement of the winner was made, I was disappointed. The announcer was reading that Punahou School admitted children of the white race only. Naturally the other girl was the winner. If I ever did cry from sheer disappointment, I did then. . . . Since then there hasn't been anything but bitterness in my heart."[81]

But other private schools in the territory, like Mid-Pacific Institute, Iolani, St. Andrews Priory, Hawaiian Mission Academy, and the Catholic schools welcomed the Nisei. More than half of the students at Mid-Pacific Institute during the 1920s through the 1940s were Japanese. Parents or older siblings sent the Nisei there because they considered it a good school. Lowell Takahashi said he attended Mid-Pacific in the early 1930s at great sacrifice to his parents. A girl who grew up on Kauai wrote in the late 1920s, "When [my older sister] heard that Mid-Pacific was one of the best English speaking schools on this island, she immediately sent me to this school. I am now here to try my best."[82]

Boarding facilities made the school especially attractive. Aiko Tokimasa Reinecke's parents sent her and her younger sisters to Mid-Pacific during the 1920s, "which they could hardly afford." Her older sister had worked as a maid in a private home for room and board while attending McKinley High School, and as a result had no social life. So when young Aiko reached high school age, her parents, who lived in rural Oahu, decided to send her to a boarding school. Hajime Warashima, who attended Mid-Pacific during the early 1930s, recalled that costs for tuition, room, and board were a financial burden for many parents, but they considered the money well spent. All boarders helped with morning chores before school began, and those on scholarship worked in the school yard after classes and on Saturdays. Everyone was required to attend a Christian church on Sundays, a practice that probably influenced some Nisei in converting to Christianity.[83]

A number of the Nisei who attended Hawaiian Mission Academy were *kibei*, American-born youths who grew up in Japan. Kazuo Hosaka, a *kibei* who returned to Hawaii when he was twenty years old, attended a special English class for one year at the academy in 1930 before enrolling in its high school. In addition to regular elementary and secondary programs, the school offered special classes focused solely on teaching oral and written English.[84]

Catholic schools were surprisingly important in the education of Nisei youths. Although only 7 to 13 percent of the students at Catholic schools were Japanese in the years 1925 to 1947, this was from 30 to over 50 percent of all Japanese students attending private schools in the territory. The quality of the Catholic schools seems to explain why Issei parents sent their children there. "By the time my sister was five years old and ready for school [in the 1930s]," wrote a University of Hawaii student,

> my mother and father had made up their minds that since nothing was more important than education, they would send her to the best school possible, even if they had to skimp and save. After conferences with a Portuguese neighbor and after visiting various schools, mother and father decided on a private Catholic school. When [they] found out that Catholic students were given first priority in being accepted, they decided that nothing must stand in the way of a good education. Sister was baptized a Catholic and accepted at the school. Brother underwent the same thing. When it was my turn to enter school, however, the school no longer accepted children on the basis of religion and so I was accepted as a non-Catholic.[85]

St. Louis, a Catholic high school for boys, excelled in commercial courses. Masakazu Shimoda enrolled there in the late 1920s because his father wanted him to learn how to manage their family store. Shimoda felt out of place at St. Louis because there were only about ten Japanese students at the time, but he stuck it out. Ralph Honda, a Buddhist who graduated from St. Louis in 1927, went there "strictly for education, to get a good job." Of his teachers, he recalled, "The . . . Brothers . . . were dedicated, very much dedicated." Non-Catholics like Honda attended ethics classes while Catholics went to religious classes. "In our [graduating] class," Honda said, "there were seven Japanese. Six of them intended to become Catholics. I was an active Buddhist, so naturally we didn't become too friendly." Honda learned to speak Standard English at St. Louis, since the Brothers "got after [him]" when he spoke Hawaii Creole English. While few non-Catholics were admitted to St. Louis at the time, Honda was able to enroll through the help of a trustee of the school, who "was an important official of Oahu Railway," where Honda's father worked.[86]

Private schools were an attractive alternative to public schools for some Nisei seeking a high school education. Nisei attended private schools because of their academic benefits, special classes in English, and boarding facilities. Since only a small proportion of Nisei actually attended private schools during the interwar years, most were unaffected by these schools. Yet private schools played a key role in helping Nisei youths enrolled at these schools to acculturate into American society. By offering boarding facilities, especially important for rural youths, and admitting some who for one reason or another could not attend public high schools, private schools provided some Nisei with the schooling they would not have otherwise received.

While the Japanese valued schooling, they stressed it for boys rather than for girls. Like other old-world countries, the Japan the Issei knew was a patriarchal society, and the Issei brought that tradition with them to Hawaii. The lack of financial resources reinforced those values, especially when it came to the question of high school and especially college education for daughters.[87]

Before World War II, it was therefore unusual for Nisei women to have college degrees, and rarer for them to have degrees in medicine. One who did was Shizue Komu, who became one of the earliest Japanese American female physicians in Hawaii when she graduated from Tufts Medical School in 1935.

A number of circumstances explain Komu's unusual achievement. For one thing, she grew up in a medical environment. Although her father had been a plantation laborer, he was an extremely bright, self-educated man who learned English and Spanish on his own and devoured medical books. By the time his daughter was born, he was the plantation hospital's pharmacist. Then, too, there were no sons in the family; Komu was the eldest of three daughters. Additionally, Komu excelled in science at the University of Hawaii, which made it possible for her to attend medical school. The fact that she did not need to work part-time while going to school, since her family was financially more secure than most Japanese families, enabled her to concentrate on her studies. Moreover, her forceful personality and independence of mind enabled her to pursue a career in medicine at a time when few women did so.[88]

Even attending high school was unusual for Nisei girls when Komu was a student at McKinley High in the 1920s. In 1925, for example, girls made up only 35 percent of all Japanese students in territorial high schools. Most Nisei girls, like Misae Yano, acquired only a grammar school education. Yano recalled her seventh grade year in 1916:

"My father said girls don't need education. He said, 'You quit. Let your brothers go.' " Although she enjoyed going to school, like most Nisei, she did as she was told. In 1917, another girl so impressed her grammar school principal that the principal personally asked the girl's father to permit his daughter to attend high school. The principal even offered to provide room and board and pay for school expenses in return for help in cooking and cleaning. But the father refused, and as a result the girl's school career ended. Marie, too, "really liked school," but dropped out in 1929 when her father told her to do so. He believed that it was unnecessary for girls to go beyond the eighth grade. She gave it little thought at the time, but later she regretted her unquestioned obedience. "How foolish. Why didn't I go to school?" she asked herself. After quitting school, she worked first for a dressmaker for room and board, and then as a maid for a haole family. It was then that she made up her mind to become a nurse. By that time she had been on her own for a number of years and felt no need to ask her father's permission. She entered a work-study program at the Japanese Hospital (later renamed Kuakini Hospital), so she needed no financial assistance from her parents.[89]

Sometimes it was possible to change parents' minds. "[My parents] told me that girls must not go to school too long," recalled a Hilo High School girl in 1927. "They said that grammar school education was enough. They had the old Japanese idea. Mother did not force me to quit school, but Father insisted. . . . For two days I cried and begged Father to send me." Her pleading worked, for her father changed his mind. The same year, a student at Mid-Pacific Institute wrote, "My father is very old fashioned and doesn't believe in educating the girls. . . . I resented this and we had a miserable time [when he told me to quit school]. . . . In the end father won and I went to work." The student worked for a Dr. Strode for three years, and then decided she wanted to become a nurse. Realizing the importance of a high school education, she "begged" her father to let her return to school. He finally consented, on the condition that she finance her own way.[90]

Most girls obeyed their parents, but the more independent-minded ones rebelled, reflecting the erosion of old ways and the influence of the American environment. "My father thought that eighth grade was enough for girls," Tetsuko Tamura recalled of the 1920s. "He didn't want us to continue after that. He wanted us to work. For boys, he wanted at least a high school education. . . . My oldest sister didn't go to high school, but my second sister . . . insisted on going. . . . So . . . she worked as a maid and went to [Lahainaluna] high school on her own."[91]

That the American environment influenced some Nisei girls to reject patriarchal authority can also be seen in the case of a Normal School student from Lahaina, Maui. In 1919, at the end of her sixth grade year, her father sent her to a Japanese Girls' House in Wailuku to study Japanese language and etiquette. Her mother had died, and her father, who planned to return to Japan, wanted his daughter to learn to be a proper Japanese girl. While living at the Girls' House, the girl attended seventh and eighth grades at the public school. Contrary to her father's intention, her experience away from him brought out a "live-wire spirit that had been almost dead." She excelled in school and returned to Lahaina a changed person. "My little sister had evidently been working very hard while I was away," she recalled. "When I returned, Father told me that my school days were over and that I must begin earning. I tried to reason with him, but he would not listen. I even had a certain nurse come and speak to my father, but he remained obstinate." Determined to realize her dream of continuing her education, the girl declared that she would continue her education "even if [she] had to shift for [herself]." "Then in a sudden burst of anger," the girl continued, "[my father] cried out, 'If you want to go, get out!'" She did just that. She moved to Wailuku where for four years she worked her way through Maui High School. "It was not easy," she reminisced. "I had absolutely no financial backing, my pay was meager, but somehow I managed to get through high school." Her father returned to Japan with her two younger sisters, and with the help of a teacher, she moved to Honolulu to attend the Normal School. "Although my life has been full of hardships, I have had happy moments," she said while still enrolled there. "My friends were kind."[92]

Another Normal School student from Lahaina showed a similar independence of spirit. The fifth of seven children, she, too, was told when her mother died that she had to quit school. But she refused. "Since I was the first daughter," she recalled, "the whole family burden and responsibility fell on my shoulders. Being only a child of twelve, I was not very capable of managing home and at the same time looking after my baby brother. However, I learned to cook and wash and take care of the house. I continued with my schooling and studied every night with a kerosene lamp at my side. My carefree childhood life had been taken away from me so soon, and I faced the problems of life without the guidance of a dear mother." In spite of her difficulties, she graduated from grammar school in 1920 with honors. When she expressed interest in attending the Normal School, "everyone objected strenuously because it was out of the question to send a daughter away from home." So with the help of a brother, she "deserted home." "I was then only sixteen years old without any knowledge of city life," she recalled, "but with my faith in God and my deceased mother, I determined to work my way through school. . . . There was a turmoil back home when it was found that I left Lahaina at night on the S.S. Claudine without anyone knowing except my brother. But when it was learned that the purpose of leaving home was for education . . . everything went well. Nevertheless I dared not return to my hometown until a year and a half later."[93]

Deciding whether girls should continue beyond grammar school often involved friends and neighbors who frequently voiced strong opposition. A Nisei girl who graduated from grammar school with the "second highest honor" in 1922 "begged her parents every day" to let her continue her education. With her brother's help she finally convinced them to let her attend high school. "Some people still believe that girls do not need to be educated," she wrote five years later as a Normal School student, "that a grammar school education is more than sufficient. Most of the girls leave school when they are about twelve and then work in the fields. . . . So far I am the only girl [from my plantation camp] who is receiving a college education. When I go back to the camp for my vacation, the people are always talking about me. They say that my parents are crazy to send a girl to school. I think these people are crazy."[94]

Another Normal School student who grew up on the island of Hawaii and whose father died during an influenza epidemic finished seventh grade and made plans to continue her schooling in Honolulu. "The neighbors tried to discourage [my mother from] sending me to Honolulu," she wrote. "I heard it so I made up my mind all the more. I said that I'll show them what I can do and what the Japanese girls can do." Misao Kawakami recalled that family friends and neighbors criticized her parents for sending their three daughters to high school and Normal School. Neighbors insisted instead that the girls go to work and learn to cook and sew in preparation for marriage. But her mother felt that "girls needed an education even more than boys" did, for "in times of crisis, men can dig ditches and work in the fields, but it would be more difficult for women to find jobs."[95]

Some Nisei girls spoke out openly against community pressure. "I have hurt the feelings of some of the older generation when I said that boys and girls are equal," wrote a fifteen-year-old Lahainaluna High student in 1927. She reflected the views of Caucasian women who criticized American gender inequalities when she declared that "girls should have as much education" as boys.[96]

Yet, although women in America before World War II were striving for educational equity, their focus was on colleges and universities; since the late nineteenth century, their enrollment had exceeded that of men in high schools. In 1900, for example, 60 percent of all high school students in the United States were girls, and almost twice as many girls

ratio

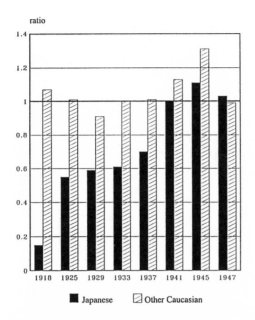

Figure 7. Ratio of Girls to Boys in Hawaii's Public High Schools, Japanese and Other Caucasians, 1918–47.

Source: Tamura, "Americanization Campaign," 460–61.

as boys graduated from high school. The higher enrollment of girls reflected their aspirations in seeking clerical and teaching jobs. Boys, on the other hand, had greater access to occupations that did not require a high school education.[97]

As Japanese families acculturated, they gradually moved toward these national norms. Whereas 6.5 times as many Japanese boys as girls attended high school in 1918, the proportion of girls gradually increased so that by 1941 their numbers were even (see figure 7).[98]

Caucasian, Part-Hawaiian, and Portuguese students in Hawaii reflected American norms, in that more girls than boys attended high school. Other Asian groups showed the same pattern as the Japanese, but at rates that reflected their first arrival to Hawaii as well as group characteristics. By 1925, just as many Chinese girls as Chinese boys attended high school; Korean girls reached equality with Korean boys as early as

1933, reflecting (as discussed earlier) their greater rate of acculturation when compared with the Japanese; and Filipino girls reached equality with Filipino boys by 1941.[99]

In their quest to pursue their education, Nisei girls used American middle-class values such as independence of mind and individual freedom, together with old-world values such as perseverence, frugality, and endurance, to break down old-world barriers that stood in the way of their gaining the schooling they wanted.

Schools were thus barometers of Nisei acculturation. But schools also provided an environment that brought Nisei in contact with American ways. There, away from direct parental supervision, the youths naturally acquired American attitudes and behaviors. There they learned Standard English, interacted with teachers and fellow students, and read about American values and practices. There they began to think about individual desires and began to voice those desires.

Schools also placed the Nisei beyond the control of Americanizers. In attending school regularly, obeying school rules, and minding their teachers, the Nisei behaved as Americanizers hoped they would. But the Nisei pursued schooling with a seriousness that went beyond the wishes of Americanizers, who, as we shall see in the next chapter, learned that they were ineffective in curbing Nisei aspirations, and therefore, Nisei achievement. Ironically schools, seen by Americanizers as key instruments for Americanization, undermined their efforts to keep the mass of Nisei on the plantations.

Chapter 6

Schools as Channels for Plantation Work

Like the Japanese, Americanizers attempted to use the schools for their purposes. But unlike the Japanese, who viewed schools as avenues for upward mobility, Americanizers saw schools as channels through which the Nisei would remain in "their place" as docile and productive plantation workers.

The efforts of Americanizers to channel the Nisei into plantation work demonstrate the validity of the "social control" thesis put forth by revisionist historians of American education. According to these revisionists, "old" Americans of the middle and upper classes who trace their ancestry to northwestern Europe have had power, wealth, and status, and have used public schools as instruments of social control of workers, minorities, and immigrants. Others not considered revisionists have also argued that fear of losing "the American way of life" led progressives and other Americans to push for social control, immigrant restriction, and the Americanization of immigrants and their children.[1]

Notwithstanding its significant contribution to the field of educational history, the revisionist thesis is inadequate for understanding the impact of public education on the Nisei in Hawaii. While useful in examining the intentions of Hawaii's leaders during the 1920s and 1930s, the thesis fails to explain the other side of the coin, the response of Nisei youths to the effort to shape their educational ideals and channel their employment. In fact, the opposing perspectives of Americanizers and Japanese collided in the 1920s and 1930s, when Americanizers made a concerted effort to achieve their goal.[2]

With Congress threatening to cut off the influx of Filipino laborers in the late 1920s, sugar planters realized that they would have to turn to domestic sources of labor. According to the sociologist Romanzo Adams, 1927 was the first year since the sugar industry expanded in which the number of native-born youths entering the labor force in Hawaii was sufficient to supply the needs of the industry. Forty-five percent of those youths were Nisei.[3]

Territorial leaders supported the use of native-born labor and saw the schools as vehicles for achieving that purpose. As early as 1920, Wallace R. Farrington, then business manager of *Honolulu Star-Bulletin* and soon to be territorial governor, favored shifting the emphasis in the public school curriculum from academic to vocational education. Anticipating the findings of a 1920 federal survey of education in Hawaii, Farrington said, "It is expected that the Federal Survey Commission . . . will recommend in its report that academic and classical courses be thrown overboard and replaced by domestic science, agriculture and manual training. We hope that this recommendation will be made." While the federal survey did not call for the elimination of academic courses, it did recommend that a full-scale vocational education curriculum be developed in the elementary and secondary grades, including programs in homemaking, industrial arts, and agriculture. As territorial governor from 1921 to 1929, Farrington made that recommendation his goal for the public schools. "As mental engineers your task is to find the angle at which the minds of the children respond favorably to . . . growing things," he told teachers in 1921. "The message . . . I wish to impress upon you," is the importance of "dignifying agriculture." By doing that, he continued, teachers would be "fulfilling the expectations of the watchful and interested taxpayer." In 1928 he expanded this theme by extolling the opportunities available on homestead lands for those who cultivated sugarcane or pineapple. A year later he was similarly enthusiastic about opportunities on the plantations. "A young man from my college [University of Maine] came down several years ago," he said, "and without any pull or any connections or friends secured employment as engineer on a plantation. He had no better education than graduates of our University of Hawaii, but he did the work that was given him to do, and eventually became the manager of the plantation. He came into the territory where some are saying there are no opportunities, but he found the opportunity and improved it. . . . It is a question of whether opportunitites are seen and taken advantage of."[4]

What Farrington and others who agreed with him ignored was that the opportunities he described were closed to Nisei. "The system of race discrimination in plantation employment is as old as the industry" and "firmly established," wrote the University of Hawaii sociologist Romanzo Adams in 1928. "Plantation advertisements for men for superior positions," he noted, ended with the words " 'must be white.' " The children of plantation laborers would continue to look elsewhere for employment, he added, until they saw "a fair opportunity to win the preferred jobs on the basis of ability and character."[5]

Educational leaders supported Farrington's effort to fill the labor needs of King Sugar. Anticipating the growing pool of native-born labor, Department of Public Instruction (DPI) Superintendent Henry W. Kinney addressed the "opportunity" that prospect offered. "The Department believes it should . . . educate the rising generation so as to equip it for the work which will come to its hands when it leaves school," Kinney wrote in 1918, "rather than to train it to measure up to certain arbitrary academic standards." According to Kinney, "one of the most serious tasks placed upon the schools [was] that of developing in their graduates a tendency towards agriculture and mechanical employment."[6]

A year later Kinney's successor, Vaughan MacCaughey, who agreed with this assessment, protested cuts in legislative appropriations for the industrial education program. "The fifth, sixth, and seventh grades are of strategic importance in industrial education," he argued:

> It is during this formative period that pupils gain a respect for, or a distaste for, hand work. . . . One of the most persistent criticisms . . . directed against Hawaii's public schools in recent decades has been . . . that the schools were educating children away from the country and from hand work, into the city and into "white collar jobs." Just at this critical time, when the industrial program has been partially developed throughout the schools, is an exceedingly inopportune time to make drastic retrenchments in industrial training. . . . We cannot dignify manual work unless we do it in the schools. We cannot do it in the schools unless we have an adequate program of industrial education.

On another occasion MacCaughey said, "Hawaii is preeminently a rural country. . . . Her basic industries are agricultural. Her country schools must be developed to serve the country, and not to drive children into the city."[7]

Benjamin O. Wist, whose views were equally important because he was principal of the Territorial Normal and Training School, agreed with MacCaughey that the public school curriculum must be reoriented toward vocational education. "We recognize the fact that Hawaii will always be an agricultural country," Wist wrote in 1921, "and that our special duty in the education of Hawaii's youth is to educate for, rather than away from, the plantations." Expressing similar sentiments, DPI Superintendent Will C. Crawford assured members of the Hawaiian Sugar Planters' Association (HSPA) in 1928 that he and his staff were working on programs to prepare more workers for plantation employment.[8]

Three years later George M. Collins, chairman of the newly created Territorial Board of Education, told the Hawaii Congress of Parents and Teachers that school programs had to fit the needs of "an agricultural community." Otherwise schooling would be "valueless and a waste of the taxpapers' money and the students' time." Teachers, Collins said, had to "emphasize occupations in agriculture," "guiding the youth toward, and not away from, the only occupations open to the big majority." In his view, the schools were "overcrowded with youth preparing for professional and technical employments" already "filled to overflowing." To correct this imbalance, schools must prepare "our local youth" to "supplant the Filipino worker on the plantations."[9]

Collins and like-minded haole leaders were reacting to the steady movement among laborers away from plantation work. The Chinese and Portuguese, who constituted 25 and 17 percent of the sugar plantation work force in 1890, each decreased their proportion to less than 7 percent by 1910. Similarly, Japanese workers were 64 percent of the total in 1910 but only 44 percent in 1920 and 18 percent in 1930. Meanwhile, laborers from the Philippines increased from 29 percent of sugar workers in 1920 to 70 percent in 1930. Persuading local youths to return to the plantations would be essential, reasoned Collins and others, when and if the influx of Filipinos ended.[10]

The ties among industry, government, and schools, so apparent in the comments of Hawaii's community leaders, reflected a nationwide trend that began decades earlier. As America's industrial revolution reached full swing in the late nineteenth century, multitudes from southern and eastern Europe as well as rural America filled the cities, and their children filled city schools. When students from the bottom strata of society began enrolling in the high schools in the 1890s, business leaders pressured educators to teach "useful trades" and "appropriate industrial skills and habits." As a result, high schools became places to train youths for existing jobs in industry.[11]

Support for vocational education grew, becoming an important part of the progressive impulse among educators. In 1917, after years of lobbying, Congress passed the National Vocational Education Act, popularly known as the Smith-Hughes Act, which made federal funds available for vocational education programs in all states. This "triumph of vocationalism," as the historian David J. Hogan has noted, was "not so much a victory of businessmen over educators as a partnership" between the two.[12]

In Hawaii, vocational education became part of a concerted effort by industrial, governmental, and educational leaders to use public schools to channel youths to plantation work. Toward this end territorial leaders organized a multi-pronged effort that included Takie Okumura's New Americans Conferences, a Governor's Advisory Committee on Education, a campaign to limit high school enrollment by charging tuition, and programs in vocational education in the public schools. Implicit in these efforts was the message that Americanization excluded academic education and occupational mobility.

The New Americans Conference, an annual event from 1927 to 1941, was, as discussed previously, the brainchild of the Reverend Takie Okumura. Its origins extended back to 1920, a time of growing tensions between Caucasians and Japanese. A bitter sugar strike had just ended and the Japanese school controversy raged. In this context Okumura began a six-year campaign ostensibly to Americanize Issei plantation workers. During the campaign, he met many Nisei, and from these meetings the idea of a series of conferences germinated. According to Okumura, the Nisei he met lacked an interest in politics, felt inferior to European Americans, and sought to leave the plantations. To reverse these attitudes, Okumura shifted his attention from the Issei to the Nisei, who were just then reaching adulthood.[13]

Okumura, then sixty-three years old, formed an executive committee to serve in an advisory capacity. He persuaded John P. Erdman, superintendent of the Japanese Department of the Hawaiian Board of Missions, and three prominent Issei—sixty-four-year-old Tasuku Harada, professor of Japanese History and Culture at the University of Hawaii; fifty-four-year-old Yasutaro Soga of *Nippu Jiji*; and sixty-three-year-old Iga Mori, a prominent physician—to join him on the committee. He also formed an associate committee to plan and organize the conferences.

About fifty to eighty Japanese American delegates attended the conferences each year, three-fourths of them men. They were a well-educated group for the time. More than 80 percent had graduated from high school and 30 percent had graduated from Normal School or college. Practically all were employed.[14]

In Honolulu the associate committee selected the delegates, in plantation communities the plantation manager chose them, and in nonplantation areas outside Honolulu the task fell to civic associations. Plantations and other businesses and community organizations paid the expenses of the delegates, while government, business, and civic leaders addressed the delegates and led "round table" discussions. Delegates discussed economic, social, and civic issues, and heard, met, and socialized with territorial leaders. Conference supporters, among them, the consul-general of Japan, the Sumitomo, Pacific, and Yokohama Specie Banks, and *Honolulu Star-Bulletin* and *Nippu Jiji*, feted participants at receptions and banquets.[15]

Okumura called these gatherings the "New Americans Conferences" after his monthly publication (established in 1916 and continuing until the 1930s) for Nisei youths, the *New Americans*. A *Hawaii Hochi* editorial criticized the name in 1928, pointing out that Nisei, born "under the American flag," were "just as full-fledged American citizens as any of the fair-skinned sons and daughters of the Nordic races." It maintained that conference leaders were creating the false impression that Nisei needed "a special education in citizenship." It pointed to the irony that among those instructing the Nisei in good American citizenship were Okumura, Mori, and Soga, all noncitizens, as well as Acting Consul-General Takeuchi. Others also protested the name of the conferences, but the name remained unchanged and only Japanese Americans were invited as delegates.[16]

During the span of fifteen years, conferees listened to speeches and participated in discussions on a variety of issues, including the value of speaking "correct" English, the question of which Japanese customs to retain and which to discard, the importance of participating in politics, and the evils of bootlegging whiskey. An issue that surfaced repeatedly was the need to expatriate and thus end dual citizenship. But dominating the agenda during the lifetime of the conferences was employment, specifically jobs in sugar and pineapple. "The cat is out of the bag," announced a *Hochi* editorial during the second conference, "and the real purpose underlying the calling of the conference . . . stands revealed in all its nakedness. . . . [T]he scheme is merely a cleverly disguised vehicle for a 'Back to the Plantations' campaign."[17]

Conference speeches confirmed the *Hochi* assessment. David L. Crawford, president of the University of Hawaii and older brother of the territorial school superintendent, told delegates to the first conference that "too many young people of Japanese and Chinese ancestry [sought] white collar jobs" when it was "obvious" that they had to "go into the agricultural industry—sugar, pineapple, coffee, and general farming." In 1930 he repeated this message. "Do not count on education to do too much for you, do not take it too seriously," he told delegates. "Do not expect a college degree, an A.B. or a Ph.D., to get you ahead unduly in this world." "Don't be afraid or ashamed of hard work," he lectured conferees a year later. "I know from experience. I was a farm boy. My son began at fourteen doing farm work in his summer vacations—he is today, at sixteen years, on a cattle ranch hired out as a common laborer. If he can do that, you can."[18]

One can only speculate at the delegates' reactions to these words. Crawford seemed unaware that as a matter of course Nisei students worked summers as "common laborers." In the summer of 1928, for example, more than 7,400 of them worked in the sugar and pineapple industries, while 4,600 did housework, yardwork, and other menial labor. Nor was it unusual for Nisei to work during the school year. Crawford's unspoken message was that, unlike his son who would leave his laborer's job when summer vacation was over, Nisei had to look forward to being laborers for life. Although Crawford claimed they could move up in the plantation world, there were very few positions in the upper levels of plantation management, and those few were closed to Nisei.[19]

Instead of inspiring Nisei to greater horizons, speaker after speaker at the conferences tried to temper their ambitions. Kamehameha Schools President Frank E. Midkiff told delegates that white collar jobs were limited, and advised them to go into agriculture. Superintendent Will C. Crawford warned of the "danger" of too many Nisei of inferior ability attending the University of Hawaii. Edward Towse, president of the Mercantile Printing Company, spoke of the worldwide "overproduction" of "high-brows," and told Nisei there were profitable opportunities to be found in such nonacademic work as farming and fishing; in streetcar, railroad, bus, and restaurant employment; and in the domestic services. George M. Collins, chairman of the Board of Education, likened the availability of plantation work to having "diamonds in our own yards." A parade of other speakers, such as Victor S. K. Houston, Hawaii's delegate to Congress, and Frank C. Atherton, president of Castle and Cooke, echoed the same thinking. So, too, did John H. Midkiff, younger brother of Frank E. Midkiff and manager of the Waialua Agricultural Company, who spoke in 1937 of the benefits of plantation life, including economic security, free housing, and low-cost medical care.[20]

Japanese speakers repeated these messages. The Reverend Hiro Higuchi of Waipahu and a group of young Nisei workers from the Ewa Plantation spoke at the 1936 conference of the advantages of plantation employment. One worker, Richard Hata, called sugar "the most stable industry" in Hawaii, and told delegates that his plantation "provided attractive homes for its employees." Richard Sato and Hideo Mansho said their wages and promotion opportunities were reasonable, and that recreational facilities made life on the plantation attractive.[21]

Frederick G. Krauss, director of the Agricultural Extension Service at the University of Hawaii, told conferees that the Japanese were "ideally suited for intensive farming." Okumura agreed. "I believe farming is inborn in every Japanese," he said. "Our second generation Japanese here in Hawaii have inherited that talent. The best and safest way for them is to depend on this talent. Select a plantation on which you want to work, and go there." Significantly, neither Okumura nor his sons chose plantation work, nor did any of the European Americans who were offering the same advice.[22]

The only haole speaker who challenged these views was Miles E. Cary, who had come to the territory in 1921 as a twenty-six-year-old teacher. Within a few years he was principal of McKinley High School, a position he held for twenty-three years. Former students remembered him as Hawaii's most inspiring educator in the 1920s and 1930s, a man who urged them to "think for themselves," "stand on their own feet," and "solve new problems." Because he was outspoken in encouraging the Nisei to strive for better lives, he became a thorn in the side of Americanizers. At the 1928 New Americans Conference, he said, "Instead of criticizing our young people for looking for the so-called 'white collar' jobs, we should compliment them for wanting to improve their present state." His speech ended his "career" as a conference speaker, and was one more instance of his refusal to bow to territorial authorities. This refusal cost him a faculty position at the University of Hawaii, which he had hoped for after receiving his doctorate from Ohio State University. In 1948 he left the territory to join the University of Minnesota faculty.[23]

The purpose of Okumura's conferences, which ended with America's entry into World War II, was clearly evident. Despite the rhetoric in which it was so often buried, the goal was to convince Nisei to work on the plantation. "True," Okumura told conferees in 1937, "we must encourage the education of those who have special talents; but that accounts for only one or two in a hundred. The majority must depend on the fruits of manual labor."[24]

While Okumura thus busied himself, haole leaders made a corresponding attempt to keep Hawaii's youths on the plantation. In November 1929 Lawrence M. Judd, who had been named territorial governor four months earlier, announced that he had just appointed a Governor's Advisory Committee on Education. "One of the most pressing problems of education today," he said, explaining the mission of the committee, "is the adaptation of teaching to fit the local industrial and social needs of this territory so that our young people may be properly trained to take their rightful places in their own home communities." In other words, the committee would look for ways in which schools could entice Hawaii's youths to turn to plantation work.[25]

Judd's committee was composed of business and economic leaders, several of whom were invited speakers at the New Americans Conferences: F. C. Atherton, president of Castle and Cooke; R. A. Cooke, president of C. Brewer and Company; A. L. Dean, former president of the University of Hawaii and then with Alexander and Baldwin; Walter F.

Dillingham, president of Oahu Railway and Land Company; J. D. Dole, president of Hawaiian Pineapple Company; and E. W. Greene, manager of Oahu Sugar Company. Other members were H. E. Gregory, director of the Bishop Museum and R. B. Wiley, director of the Division of Research of the DPI. The committee chairperson was George M. Collins, a civil engineer who later became chairperson of the Territorial Board of Education. At its first meeting, on 13 February 1930, the committee created twenty-one subcommittees to survey Hawaii's educational and industrial situation.[26]

With the approval of the committee and the territorial legislature, the Chamber of Commerce, through its Hawaii Bureau of Governmental Research, paid Charles A. Prosser, director of the William Hood Dunwoody Industrial Institute of Minneapolis, Minnesota, to study the Hawaii school system and advise the committee. Prosser, a leading proponent of vocational education in the public schools, was expected to endorse the committee's views on vocational education.[27]

Like supporters of the New Americans Conferences, the Governor's Committee began with the assumption that schools should give students the "proper attitude toward agriculture and manual labor." In February 1931 the committee and Prosser issued a joint report of their findings and recommendations. The report stated that Hawaii's public high schools and industries were "out of gear" with each other. The schools were training students for white collar jobs, which were limited, while industry needed workers. The problem, the report stated, was that students wrongly assumed that academic schooling would lead to white collar jobs when in fact such jobs were not available. Stressing the financial limitations of the territory, Prosser and the committee recommended that the DPI limit the number of students admitted to tenth grade in future years to the number admitted in September 1930, and that henceforth expenditures for senior high schools be limited to the amount spent in 1931. Similarly, they recommended that enrollment and expenditures for the University of Hawaii be frozen at the 1930–31 levels. To provide for students excluded from further schooling by these changes, they further recommended that public schools substantially expand their progams in vocational agriculture.[28]

These recommendations coincided with yet another effort to discourage the education of Nisei youths. This was the push to charge tuition at public high schools. This effort began in 1920 when the Chamber of Commerce Committee on Public Schools and Vocational Education passed a resolution urging a tuition charge for all high school students who were not American citizens or who were citizens but could not give satisfactory proof that their sole allegiance was to the United States. The rationale for this proposal was that high school education had become too great a burden on taxpayers, but its real purpose was obvious in the categories of students it singled out.[29]

The issue remained alive through the 1920s. In 1925 John Hind, president of the Hawaiian Sugar Planters' Association, indicted the public school system for being too idealistic and costly, and for failing to meet the needs of Hawaii's agricultural interests. He urged the DPI to eliminate students who should not be in school. "Why allow the students to parade around town with books tucked securely under their arms?" Hind asked. "Why try and mislead them with the idea that more education works for progress?" Taxpayers, he argued, should not have to pay for schooling beyond the eighth grade. He noted that in 1917, the territory spent $1,043,000 on public education, which was 23 percent of all taxes collected; in 1925 this total was $4,104,000, which amounted to 35 percent of all taxes collected. Such increases were unjustifiable, Hind said, for education, like everything else, had to be "considered from the business standpoint."[30]

Former University of Hawaii President Arthur L. Dean agreed. "I submit," he told teachers in 1931, "that it is not unreasonable for the people who pay the bills [he meant businesspeople] to have something to say about the way in which the money is spent." Complaining that most parents paid little of the cost of educating their children, he said, "It seems to me that our school system is drifting into the communist theory that it is the business of the public to take care of everyone."[31]

A haole parent echoed these sentiments in a letter to the editor of *Honolulu Star-Bulletin*. He favored high school tuition to "alleviate the burdens of the taxpayer" and "eliminate the growing army of office or 'white collar' job aspirants." "A look over the grounds of these public places of learning—McKinley high school, for instance, on a morning before [the] school hour is on," he continued, in an obvious reference to Japanese students, "will immediately show that there is a preponderance of a certain nationality (way in the majority) in attendance." "Our 'white' or Caucasian employers are employing this class of people in their offices," the writer complained, "in preference to our own boys and girls. It is no wonder, then, that the latter are losing interest and ambition at their school work, for they know that there is nothing in store for them when they leave school outside of ordinary common labor." For this father, "common labor" was fine for others but not for his and other haole children.[32]

The Territorial Board of Education joined the cost-cutting effort in 1931, when reduced revenues caused by the depression made economizing urgent. Going beyond Superintendent Crawford's proposal to cut operating expenses by 10 percent for the 1932–33 school year, the board reduced total expenditures by almost two and a half million dollars. To accomplish this the board among other things voted to drop four hundred teaching positions. Commissioner Elsie Wilcox, who opposed such drastic reductions, feared that this would wreck the school system.[33]

Territorial Senator Ernest A. K. Akina also objected to the board's drastic action. He introduced a resolution, passed by the Senate, demanding an explanation from the board. Another senator, James K. Jarrett, called the board's act "un-American." "They are trying to turn out half-baked students," Jarrett said of the board. "All [the graduates] will be able to do is pick pineapples and cut sugarcane." Senator Charles A. Rice, on the other hand, reminded his colleagues that the board's action was consistent with the recommendations of Prosser and the Governor's Advisory Committee. Characterizing Prosser as "the best salesman that ever came to Hawaii," Rice said "Prosser knew what [the business leaders who hired him] wanted him to say and he said it."[34]

Despite these objections, support for reducing the cost of education grew, and in 1933 the territorial legislature passed a bill requiring high school students to pay a ten-dollar tuition charge. The charge was added on to book rental costs and fees for elective subjects. When the school year opened that fall, Robert M. Faulkner, principal of Kawananakoa School, reported turning away students who lacked the required fee. Superintendent Will C. Crawford noted in his Biennial Report that the tuition was a charge for services that "in many States [were] furnished at public expense." Four years later, as a result of growing opposition from educators and Parent-Teacher Associations, the legislature repealed the tuition law.[35]

Public school officials contributed to the effort to channel youths into plantation work by developing programs in vocational education. Federal funds became available to Hawaii in 1924, when Congress extended provisions of the Smith-Hughes Act to the territory. The funds totaled about $30,000 a year, and were contingent on a territorial appropriation of an equal sum.[36]

According to the Congressional enactment, "vocational education" was "any form of education . . . planned to give definite training for a specific occupation." Previous courses in shop work, gardening, and homemaking, like earlier manual education on the mainland, had been part of the general educational program, designed to teach all students the "dignity of manual labor." In contrast, vocational education meant training specific students for specific kinds of employment.[37]

Except for the Territorial Trade School, which opened in 1920, little vocational education of this sort had existed in Hawaii before 1925. That year the DPI organized, according to federal guidelines, courses of study in three areas of employment: the industrial trades, homemaking, and agriculture.[38]

Industrial trades and homemaking education were taught at the Honolulu Vocational School, which in 1927 replaced the Territorial Trade School. The Vocational School offered courses in auto mechanics, machine shop, carpentry, and electrical work for boys, and dressmaking, cafeteria and restaurant service, and lauhala weaving for girls. All students were over fourteen years of age and attended school seven hours a day, eleven months a year. While students spent part of their time in classroom instruction in English, civics, and mathematics, they devoted most of their time to vocational training. Similar programs soon appeared at some high schools and grade schools across the territory.[39]

The homemaking program at Washington Junior High School in Honolulu, introduced in 1931, showed how far vocational education could be removed from academic work. The goal of this program was to train girls as maids, the rationale being that many students worked as maids while attending school and would continue to do so after graduation. Girls in the program began their school day with English and Social Studies classes. Then from 10:00 A.M. until the school day ended in the afternoon they devoted their time to homemaking, learning among other things "to cook on gas and electric ranges, to operate a washing machine, and to set a table artistically and [to] serve well."[40]

Programs in vocational agriculture were of two types. Type A, found mainly in grade schools, enrolled boys over fourteen years old. They spent half the school day studying English, mathematics, hygiene, geography, and agriculture and the other half in sugarcane fields. For their work in the fields the boys received payment once—at the end of their two-year apprenticeship, when the harvest was in. By 1928 eleven schools offered this Type A program. Type B programs, found mainly in high schools, enrolled boys in courses of study in coffee production, poultry and hog raising, and gardening. Boys in the program attended classes in agriculture at school and carried on their projects outside of school. By 1928 eight schools offered these programs.[41]

Although vocational education in the territory included programs in the industrial trades, the emphasis was on learning agricultural work.

The 1920 census reported that about half (50.3 percent) of all those employed in Hawaii worked in agriculture, while a sixth (16.3 percent) were in the mechanical and manufacturing trades. These figures declined somewhat in subsequent years, but agriculture remained predominant. With this in mind DPI officials focused their efforts on vocational agricultural programs, specifically programs that trained youths for work in the territory's major industries of sugarcane, pineapple, and coffee. As part of this effort, schools formed chapters of Future Farmers of America in 1930, within two years of the establishment of the national organization on the mainland.[42]

The Nisei rejected the idea that their future lay in plantation work. They had a contrasting vision, one in which they would advance educationally and occupationally. It was this desire to improve their social and economic standing that led some delegates to the New Americans Conferences to speak up in defense of academic education and in opposition to plantation work. They did so despite the fact that conference organizers created an atmosphere in which many delegates were "afraid to give negative ideas." At a round table discussion at the first conference, one delegate challenged Superintendent Crawford's assertion that Japanese parents pushed their children in school beyond their capacities. Declaring that education never injured anyone, the delegate asked, "How do we know when the limits of the child have been reached?" Another delegate warned of the "danger" of predetermining a child's capacity.[43]

Delegates to the next conference, in 1928, complained that plantation wages were too low to afford an American standard of living. "If we are needed on sugar plantations," declared one delegate, "conditions [there] . . . should be made attractive enough for us to [want to] go back." Another said, "We cannot live in the same way as early immigrants and cheap laborers now live." Pointing to the lack of advancement opportunities on the plantation, the delegate added, "We are willing to start to work from the very bottom, but plantations keep us there, that's the trouble."[44]

Delegate Walter Mihata remarked in 1929 that "all what plantations want is cheap labor," while delegate George Betsui objected to plantation paternalism. "Hawaiian Sugar Company is not playing fair with the laborers," Betsui said. "No visitors are allowed in the Japanese camps or Filipino camps after 7:30 P.M., although in the haole districts people can go and come as they desire." Two years later other delegates repeated these complaints. "When we see some of our boys working patiently at one steady position, never getting a promotion," said one of the delegates, "it is hard to convince the majority that there are opportunities back on the soil." A delegate in 1932 blurted out what was surely a widespread view. "I am a plantation hater," he said. "The plantations are not square shooters. They want ignorant laborers; educated laborers are like ptomaine poison to them." The reality behind this outburst was illustrated in the experience of Etsuo Sayama, who told fellow conferees in 1941 that he left the Waialua Plantation because his degree in sugar technology from the University of Hawaii earned him only half as much as haole workers without a degree.[45]

One of the speakers at the 1928 conference so infuriated Harry Kurisaki, a Nisei dentist, that he wrote an angry response. When the *Honolulu Advertiser* refused to print it, Kurisaki sent it to *Hawaii Hochi.* "The speaker implied," wrote Kurisaki, "that the younger generation of Japanese should be content to work on the plantations, as their fathers had worked, and that any effort to raise their status to that of the professional class was a mistaken effort, because they are incapable of making good as dentists, doctors or in similar lines of work." "Deeply resent[ing] the unjust and insulting charge," Kurisaki refuted it. "There are hundreds of well-trained, keen, ambitious young professional men in Honolulu who are of Japanese ancestry," he noted. "Their parents worked hard on the plantations in order to save up money for their proper education, just as my father worked and denied himself most of the good things of life in order that I might learn my profession." Kurisaki was pointing out what should have been obvious to Americanizers: that Japanese, no less than Caucasians, aspired to the promise of American life. "Caucasians . . . themselves have the same regard for their children," Kurisaki continued, "sending them to universities . . . to complete their education, expecting them to carry on and to improve upon the work of their fathers. How can they then have the heart to discourage the young Orientals, who are trying their best to live up to their responsibilities as American citizens and to be worthy of the trust placed in them by their parents?"[46]

Kurisaki concluded by criticizing the main flaw in the Americanizers' campaign to keep Nisei on the plantations. "The plantations cannot expect to attract the young people," he said, "until they can offer them as great advantages as are now offered in the professions and in commercial lines. If they had a gold mine of opportunities there, as some of the enthusiastic propagandists would lead us to believe, they would not have to launch an intensive advertising campaign."[47]

Like Kurisaki, George W. Wright, editorial writer for *Hawaii Hochi*, argued that the Japanese were behaving like good Americans in emphasizing the value of schooling. Wright chastised the University of Hawaii sociologist Romanzo Adams for proposing to survey Japanese to find out why they valued school so much. Instead of seeing them as strange for wanting an education, Wright declared that Adams and other Caucasians should be applauding them. After all, wasn't the desire for schooling an American value? Acknowledging Adams as a "sincere student of human problems," Wright nevertheless wondered why Adams was singling out Japanese. "Why," asked Wright, "does not Professor Adams conduct a survey among white Americans to find out why they educate their children? Why . . . does he not ask that question of himself? . . . He has been at considerable pains and expense to send his daughter away to the mainland to finish her education. The overcrowding . . . of white collar jobs did not discourage him from giving his child the very best education that she could assimilate!"[48]

Nisei delegates to the New Americans Conferences expressed the prevailing Japanese view of plantation work. Despite the efforts of managers to make plantation life more attractive through increased paternalism and physical improvements—including in the late 1920s, not only free housing and medical care, but also improved sanitation, inexpensive milk, free garden plots, infant care for working mothers, supervised playgrounds for children, baseball leagues, and English classes—Japanese continued to reject plantation life.[49]

Plantation managers were well aware of that rejection. While admitting that it was natural for parents to want better lives for their offspring, one manager spoke of working against parents and of having some success in getting "boys to quit high school and work on the plantation." But it was an uphill campaign. "[The Issei] will half-starve himself, if necessary, to send his children to high school or technical school and frequently to college," wrote Lillian Symes in *Harper's Magazine* in 1922. "He does not want them to come back to the plantation; for he knows from observation that Americans do not perform hard and dirty labor."[50]

Like the Issei, the Nisei rejected plantation work. Wright spoke for them when he wrote in a *Hochi* editorial, "Mr. Crawford and [others] . . . may preach about the 'dignity of labor' till they are black in the face and they will make no impression on the youths of the Territory, who, themselves, have first hand information that refutes all such beautiful fairy stories."[51]

The grueling work under the hot sun was enough to turn anyone away. Richard Inouye, who worked on the plantation for a number of years in his teens, was "real happy" to move to Honolulu in 1927. "That kind of job is a man-killer," he said. Another boy who "worked in cane fields, sugar mills, and pineapple canneries" during his summer vacations began thinking of a better future in 1920, when he was fourteen years old.

Whenever he saw a well-dressed businessman, he thought of himself in the cane fields. "Jealous of those who had high positions," he decided to study so that he could be like them. Because of his experience, he had "no interest in agriculture." A girl from the island of Hawaii who worked in the cane fields from the age of fourteen reached a similar conclusion. "I shed my tears secretly," she wrote when she was a Normal School student in 1927. "I thought if I only had the chance, I'll never come back to the fields."[52]

Nisei experiences refuted the claims of educators and business leaders that the sugar plantations offered "every chance to advance" for anyone "worthy of promotion." One Nisei youth who worked in the cane fields in the 1920s concluded at once that plantation work was a dead end with "not much chance to get promoted or get better wages." A University of Hawaii student drew the same conclusion, noting that "the Scotch people, whether they know about sugar cane or not," received the "good jobs on the plantations and were well paid," while "the dirty work was left to the Japanese, Filipino, and other laborers." Even those whose circumstances forced them to remain on the plantations shared these sentiments. "You can't go very high up and get big money unless your skin is white," said a twenty-three-year-old plantation worker who had to abandon his dream of attending the University of Hawaii in the 1930s. "You can work here [on the plantation] all your life and yet a *haole* who doesn't know a thing about the work can be ahead of you in no time."[53]

One reason for discrimination was social segregation at the higher levels of plantation employment. One plantation manager admitted candidly in the 1920s that he could not promote Asians to certain skilled positions because they would have to live in the residential area set aside for such employees. "Then I'll have to invite him to my home on Sunday afternoons to play tennis with the other upper-grade employees," the manager explained. "But the chemist's wife may object to this and dissensions may arise. The upshot of it all is that I cannot promote him." Sometimes Asians were promoted but not permitted to move into the kind of housing normally assigned to employees in their position. This happened to a Nisei graduate of the University of Hawaii who lived with his wife in housing far poorer than that of his haole counterparts on the same plantation. Asians might also be promoted but excluded from social activities available to Caucasians of equal positions, as was a Nisei civil engineer whose bid for membership in a "white man's tennis club" in the 1920s was blocked by club members.[54]

Besides racial discrimination, Nisei objected to poor treatment and low wages. A boy who worked in a sugar mill after graduation from high school in 1923 wrote, "I shall never again work in such a place." What he found especially objectionable was "the autocratic bossing." A University of Hawaii student likewise complained in 1927 that plantation laborers were not only "greatly underpaid" but "treated like animals."[55]

Also objectionable to these youths were the restrictions on freedom of movement. "Plantations have a gentlemen's agreement," explained an Issei in the 1920s. "A young man from one plantation cannot get a job on an neighboring plantation unless he gets a release from his home plantation," but a young man with a trade was free to work wherever he wished.[56]

While agreeing that white-collar jobs were limited and that many youths would have to look to agriculture for jobs, many Nisei nevertheless rejected such employment for themselves. Indeed, many Nisei came to see schooling as the only sure way out of the plantations. A University of Hawaii student wrote in 1927 that at first he disliked "English school" because the teacher scolded and hit students whenever they displeased her. But when he realized that school provided a way out of plantation work, he changed his mind. A Mid-Pacific High School boy recalled in 1927, "I did not like studies at all, and my father knew it. He wanted me to at least graduate from a high school, so for my eighth grade year, he told me to go to Mid-Pacific Grammar School and after that, to continue there for high school." The boy continued, "I hated to think of leaving Ewa [his hometown in rural Oahu] . . . [so] my father started to scare me and tell me of the future. He told me that if I graduated from Ewa School, I was going out with a pick and shovel in the fields to work, but if I graduated from Mid-Pacific Grammar School, I was going to the high school and after [that] . . . to college and be numbered among the great men. . . . If he had mentioned any other job than pick and shovel, I would have chosen that, but I [preferred going] to school rather than working under the hot sun with pick and shovel, so I [went to Mid-Pacific]." A University of Hawaii student wrote in 1927 that his parents' constant complaint of working for low wages under a hated boss convinced him that he should "go to college to get away from manual labor." An Issei summed up these views metaphorically: "A Hawaii born young man is like a cockroach in a bathtub," he said. "If he tries to crawl out he falls in again and again. The wise cockroach will fly up and away instead of crawling."[57]

The Nisei attitude toward plantation work reflected the general view of all young people in Hawaii at the time. To learn the occupational preferences of territorial youths in 1922, Governor Farrington appointed a Committee on Industrial and Manual Training. At the committee's request, school principals questioned boys in grades seven to twelve about the kinds of work they hoped or expected to do as adults. In his report to the governor, committee chair Arthur L. Dean, president of the University of Hawaii, pointed to "a large discrepancy between expectations of the boys and the employment requirements of Hawaii." While 5 percent of the 1,901 boys who responded expected to work in agriculture, half of all male workers at the time were in agriculture. In contrast, half of the boys intended to enter the skilled trades, but only 12 percent of all male workers were in those occupations. And 15 percent of the boys wanted to be professionals, but only 2 percent of all men at the time were professionals.[58]

In view of these attitudes, it is not surprising that the DPI's programs in vocational agriculture fell short of their goal. In June 1929, *Star-Bulletin* reported on a Smith-Hughes class at Hakalau School that had just ended its two-year project. DPI officials calculated that each of the ten boys in the program earned $3.56 a day for his labor. Principal Eugene S. Capellas called the project a success, but *Hawaii Hochi* sharply criticized the DPI for using the Smith-Hughes program to create a false impression of the earnings of plantation workers. "Surely the labor of a hardened adult worker should be more effective than that of a callow school boy," it declared. "Why, then, is the minimum basic wage for adult laborers on the plantations kept at $1.00 per day?" But *Hochi* need not have worried about false impressions. Plantation parents and children were aware of plantation conditions. Despite the upbeat article on the Hakalau School project, plantation managers admitted that the Smith-Hughes program had "little success." One noted that the "biggest difficulty" of the program was the parents' "strong desire to have their children educated away from plantation work." Another complained that those enrolled were "students who were not particularly bright," which stigmatized the program. A manager who had twenty-two acres under cultivation by students of a nearby school reported that "the presence of Japanese students on this contract was conspicuous by their absence," reflecting the attitude of parents who were "willing to educate their children at considerable hardship to themselves."[59]

Japanese language newspapers ran editorials on programs in agriculture. *Hochi* criticized the DPI in 1927 for operating the public schools "as a labor recruiting agency" for Hawaii's major industries. "[Superintendent Crawford] admits without the slightest blush of shame," declared *Hochi*, "that under his guidance 'the educational system is being molded . . . to teach *familiarity with the tools of Hawaii's industries.'* This is a fine program for one who calls himself an educator to sponsor." *Hochi* continued, "He would make our schools training shops in the gentle art of manipulating the end of a plantation hoe, and drill the pupils in the most approved technique of walking up a narrow plank with one hundred pounds of loose cane on their shoulders!" The paper concluded that Crawford had "shifted Hawaii's educational machine in *reverse gear*" and was "stepping on the gas!" During the economic depression of the 1930s, *Hochi* softened these views, as many Nisei, like everyone else, faced the prospect of having to return to the plantations.[60]

Nippu Jiji looked more favorably at agricultural employment, reasoning that Hawaii's economy was based on agriculture and that white-collar jobs were limited. Yet it hoped that the DPI would "not train pupils merely for work on the plantation." It urged Nisei to consider dairy farming or raising fruits, nuts, or vegetables, but the lack of good farm land was a problem in the 1920s. Planters held the most fertile land and discouraged diversified farming. After the depression hit and the federal Agricultural Adjustment Administration limited sugar production in 1933, however, plantation managers began recommending that their surplus lands be used for diversified farming.[61]

Yasutaro Soga, editor of *Nippu Jiji*, blamed plantation managers for Nisei flight from the plantations. He said that the manager was "like a feudal lord" who held "absolute power." He advised Nisei to work to "break the wall of inequality of opportunity lying in their path." He also urged that planters give Nisei greater independence by dividing plantations into "small farms." This was an extension of the contract system that developed during the 1920s. Instead of working under close supervision for wages, a man or group of men in the contract system leased or otherwise took responsibiltiy for growing cane on designated fields. There were different variations of this system, but generally plantations advanced the cost of the fertilizer and other materials while workers cultivated the fields for minimum wages. The final payment workers received depended on the size of the harvest and the price of sugar.[62]

During the depression years, Soga, too, looked more favorably at the plantations, noting that they had eliminated wage discrimination and had made "marked improvements" in living and working conditions. He therefore encouraged Nisei to seek plantation employment.[63]

Since programs in vocational agriculture operated in the public schools, teachers became caught up in the campaign to convince the Nisei to work on the plantations. Plantation managers complained that teachers looked down on plantation work and discouraged students from entering it. Both Superintendent Will C. Crawford and his brother, David L. Crawford, president of the University of Hawaii, urged teachers to display more positive attitudes. President Crawford told Normal School graduates in 1931 that teachers must inculcate in their students "a better respect for rural and plantation life, and for the dignity of the labour that is done without a white collar."[64]

Some teachers accepted this advice, in part because they believed it "inevitable" that most Nisei would work on the plantations, but others did not. "It does not appear psychologically possible," members of the Hawaii Education Association observed, "to teach that a certain kind of labor is dignified when it is engaged in only by the people at the lower end of the economic scale."[65]

McKinley High School principal Miles Cary recognized the contradiction between encouraging youths to be plantation laborers and preparing them for "full, intelligent and open-eyed citizenship." Some segments of the community, he said, feared that children of plantation laborers were becoming too acculturated, filled with ideas of equality of opportunity and posing challenges to others in the job market. Gladys Feirer, who taught at McKinley when Cary was principal, recalled that some people did not like him because he encouraged students to investigate issues that concerned them. "He told kids," she recalled, " 'If you want to find out about something, you find out about it. If you think your parents are paying too much [in] taxes, go and find out, see what's going on.' In the core studies program, we had a unit on crime or housing or statehood. It made students do a lot of thinking. Members of the Board of Education were against the program," Feirer added. "We teachers had to go down every once in a while to defend the program."[66]

Even teachers who taught vocational agriculture often did not proselytize for the plantations. Clarence Kobayashi, himself a Nisei who taught in the 1930s, recalled that he encouraged his bright students to continue their schooling. Yet, if teachers generally were not enthusiastic supporters of the work-on-the-plantation campaign, neither did they make a systematic effort to subvert it.[67]

Yet it was not so much the views of teachers and Issei leaders, but those of the Nisei and their parents that determined the outcome of vocational programs in agriculture. Except for the depression years of the 1930s, enrollment in these programs was low. In the late 1920s a high school principal reported that of sixty boys invited to enroll in his school's agricultural program, "only a few" expressed interest. Indeed parents of fifteen of the invited boys removed them from the school and enrolled them instead in a private Catholic school to avoid the program.[68]

In 1928, Superintendent Crawford reported that only 6 percent of boys over fourteen years old in the public schools were enrolled in vocational agricultural programs. While this meant a 400 percent increase in three years, Crawford was disappointed. A year later and again in 1931 he lamented that among the obstacles to successful programs in agriculture were parents and Japanese language newspapers who saw the DPI as a "propaganda agent for the plantations." He noted that it was easier to "recruit students for shop classes . . . than for agriculture."[69]

In assessing the program, Crawford did not mention the evident success of high school graduates in finding non-agricultural employment in Hawaii. That was unlike the experience of California Nisei, who found it difficult to find white-collar jobs outside the Japanese community, and unlike the oft-repeated claims that in Hawaii few jobs existed outside agriculture. That at least is one way to read the results of a 1931 survey. That year DPI officials sent questionnaires to 5,418 public high school alumni, of whom about half were Nisei. Of the 86 percent who responded and were able-bodied, 98 percent were employed or attending institutions of higher learning. Of the 3,126 who were employed, 94 percent were living in Hawaii, and only 3 percent were in agriculture. A majority were clerks and teachers.[70]

As with the English Standard school controversy, the differing views of the future of the Nisei in Hawaii pointed to the age-old conflict between aristocratic and democratic tendencies. *Hawaii Hochi* expressed the Japanese view when it called the Governor's Committee a "Jim Crow commission." "If the object is to intensify the gulf between an educated aristocracy and an ignorant peasantry," said *Hochi*, "then they have found an excellent way to help the movement along. But we cannot agree with the theory that assumes a certain privileged class to be ordained for supremacy and that would sacrifice the great mass of the people for the sake of a spectacular civilization built upon the labor of exploited millions." Nisei M. Nakamoto expressed the same view when he asserted that the tuition charges for public high schools were "contrary to the spirit of this country" and that "both the rich and the poor [were] entitled equally to higher education."[71]

In any case, the effort to limit high school enrollment by charging tuition, like the parallel effort to channel Nisei youths into plantation work, failed. In the 1930s twelve schools in the territory added senior high divisions, and enrollment in grades ten through twelve increased from 4,905 in 1930 to 12,716 in 1938. Ironically, this growth was partly due to an about-face on the part of sugar industry leaders concerning secondary education. The depression caused a temporary surplus of plantation laborers, while demographic changes halted the rapid increase in school expenditures. At the same time, industry leaders came to believe that secondary schools in rural areas were more apt than urban schools to train workers for the plantations and would in any case help keep youths away from the city.[72]

This change in thinking accelerated educational trends already underway. By 1941, more and more Nisei were remaining in school longer and longer, thereby increasing the likelihood that they would find employment outside the plantations. This was the Nisei version of the fulfilment of the American dream.

Chapter 7

Japanese Language Schools

In the early years of Japanese immigration, when the Issei believed they would soon return to Japan, they sent their children to Japanese language schools so they could receive a Japanese education and be able to continue their schooling when the family resettled in Japan. Seiji Fukuda opened the first such school in Kula, Maui, in 1892, seven years after the first *kanyaku imin jidai,* government-sponsored immigrant contract laborers, arrived from Japan. By 1900, there were ten Japanese language schools in Hawaii enrolling about fifteen hundred students. Within ten years the number of schools had mushroomed to 140, with about seven thousand students. Some of the schools were sponsored by Christians and some by Buddhists, while others were run by groups of parents. Plantation managers considered the schools a positive, stabilizing influence, and provided them with rent-free land and financial help. The schools charged a small tuition and received donations from Issei who had no children attending them.[1]

In 1920, at the beginning of the controversy over these schools, 98 percent of the 20,651 Japanese students attending English schools also attended the Japanese schools. During the height of the controversy in the 1920s, that percentage dipped to 70, but then rebounded to 87 in the early 1930s. In 1934 more than 41,000 students attended the schools. Thereafter, as the Nisei became more acculturated and tension mounted between Japan and the United States, the percentage dropped somewhat. Still, until the United States entered World War II, the vast majority of Nisei in Hawaii attended Japanese language schools.[2]

Especially before 1915, language schools served as centers where Issei celebrated Japanese holidays. On such occasions parents kept their children from school, and entire families spent the day in celebration. Because Japanese children made up such a large percentage of public school students, their absence on these days was conspicuous, and public school officials began to wonder if the children were learning loyalty to Japan instead of the United States.[3]

But no concerted opposition to the schools developed until World War I, when a wave of exaggerated patriotism swept the nation. In the face of such xenophobic slogans as "one nation, one flag, one language," German and other foreign languages on the mainland became targets of suspicion. In Hawaii as in California, hostility focused on the Japanese language, and continued after the war ended.[4]

By 1919 the threat to Japanese language schools was serious. After several unsuccessful attempts, the territorial legislature passed a series of measures—beginning with Act 30 enacted in November 1920—whose supporters hoped would effectively abolish language schools. Language school teachers' open support of a bitter five-month strike by Japanese plantation workers in 1920 intensified sentiment against the schools and helped promote laws "controlling" them.[5]

Instead of abolishing the schools, as recommended by a 1920 federal survey of education in Hawaii and as urged by many Americanizers, Act 30 was a compromise. Territorial leaders realized that outright abolition would arouse strong opposition from the Japanese community, but a compromise, they hoped, was something many Japanese would accept, while the restrictions placed on the schools would ultimately destroy them. Issei leaders who proposed the compromise, on the other hand, hoped it would satisfy Americanizers while preserving the schools.[6]

Act 30, which took effect in July 1921, required foreign language school administrators and teachers to obtain permits from the Department of Public Instruction (DPI); such permits were to be granted only to applicants who demonstrated that they "possessed" the "ideals of democracy, knowledge of American history and institutions," and the ability "to read, write and speak the English language." The act also limited language schools to one hour's instruction each day after the public schools had closed and to no more than six hours a week, and directed the DPI to prescribe the courses of study and textbooks to be used in the schools.[7]

In November 1922, pursuant to Act 30, the DPI adopted a set of regulations recommended by a joint Caucasian-Issei committee and endorsed by Governor Farrington. The regulations required that students complete the first two grades of English school before attending language school, and that textbooks be written for students whose first language was English.[8] The regulations ignored the fact that the Nisei's first language was either a localized version of Japanese, or more likely, Hawaii Creole English.

The Issei had been upset with Act 30, but they were alarmed at the DPI's sweeping regulations. Prohibiting kindergartners and first and second graders from attending language school—what contemporaries called "curtailing the course of study"—presented major problems for families having mothers who worked outside the home. Sending children to language schools had been a way to keep youngsters productively occupied while their parents worked. "Everybody went [to Japanese school]," recalled Aiko Tokimasa Reinecke. "It was a good setup for the parents who worked. . . . At least the children were not left alone with nothing to do."[9]

Moreover, prohibiting these youngsters from attending language schools meant a huge loss in tuition for the schools, resulting in "financial disaster" and closure. In fact, over eight thousand students would be excluded from foreign language schools in the territory, 98 percent of them Japanese. (A small number of children attended Korean and Chinese language schools.)[10]

Because of such draconian measures, Palama Japanese Language School, soon joined by three other schools, took the lead in challenging the constitutionality of Act 30 and the DPI regulations based on it. The suit was filed in the Territorial Circuit Court in Honolulu on 27 December 1922.

The chief counsel for the language schools was Joseph Lightfoot, an Englishman who came to Hawaii in 1886 when he was twenty-three. He first taught on the island of Hawaii and then in Honolulu, became a naturalized citizen in 1900, and then studied law. He was forty-one when he passed the bar in 1905. Four years later he represented the Japanese in court during a sugar strike and became favorably known in the Japanese community. His son, Bert, became his partner in the 1920s, and Lightfoot and Lightfoot, in association with Joseph P. Poindexter, who became governor of the territory in 1934, represented the language schools.[11]

On 2 February 1923, Judge James J. Banks found Act 30 constitutional, but the DPI regulations "curtailing the course of study" invalid. The territory appealed this decision to the Territorial Supreme Court, which sat on the case for almost two-and-a-half years.[12]

Meanwhile the legislature passed two more laws aimed at dismantling language schools. Act 171, passed in 1923, required language schools to pay annual fees to the territory at the rate of one dollar per pupil. For larger schools this amounted to fees of hundreds of dollars each year, and for the system as a whole—based on 1922 enrollments—a total of more than $21,000 annually. Act 152, enacted in 1925, attempted intimidation by giving the territorial government the power to file civil and criminal proceedings against teachers and governing board members of schools that refused to pay their fees. In response, litigants filed for and were granted court injunctions against these two laws.[13]

As the territory tightened the screws with Act 171, Japanese who had cooperated with previous laws and regulations felt betrayed, and as a result more language schools joined the suit. By the end of August 1923, eighty-four schools, about 62 percent of all Japanese language schools, had done so.[14]

In June 1925, both sides agreed to discontinue the case pending before the Territorial Supreme Court. By this time Lightfoot had decided to change his strategy. In a surprise move he filed for an injunction in federal district court against the territory, naming Governor Farrington as the defendant. Judge John T. DeBolt granted the injunction and advised that the case be appealed to the Ninth Circuit Court in San Francisco "for a decision on the constitutionality of the Territorial laws." Judge DeBolt also granted litigating schools a temporary injunction against the payment of fees after they agreed to submit a $12,500 bond.[15]

The case reached the Ninth Circuit Court on 15 September 1925, and on 22 March 1926, the court declared Act 30 unconstitutional. Writing for the three-man court, Judge Frank H. Rudkin noted that "the right of a parent to educate his own child in his own way" was beyond the police powers of the state. "The children . . . do attend the public schools," he pointed out, "and when they have done this we take it for granted that they have an undoubted right to acquire a knowledge of foreign language, music, painting, drawing, and such other accomplishments, not inimical to good order and good morals, as their parents or guardians see fit." He continued, "You cannot make a good citizen by oppression, or by a denial of constitutional rights." The court based its decision on three Supreme Court precedents, *Meyer v. Nebraska*, *Bartels v. Iowa*, and *Pierce v. Society of Sisters*. Judge Rudkin quoted from the *Meyer* decision: "The protection of the Constitution extends to all, to those who speak other languages, as well as to those born with English on the tongue."[16]

As these court cases suggest, the effort to abolish Japanese language schools in Hawaii was part of a much larger nativist agenda to stamp out cultural and ideological diversity. Nativists convinced state governments to rein in the forces of pluralism by legislating against foreign language schools and newspapers as well as against Catholics, evolutionists, and Bolsheviks. Opponents of such laws sought relief in the federal courts. In *Meyer v. Nebraska*, a German language teacher successfully challenged a state law forbidding the teaching of any language other than English to a child who had not completed the eighth grade. With *Meyer* as precedent, the Supreme Court in *Bartels v. Iowa* declared similar laws in Iowa, Ohio, and Nebraska unconstitutional. Aimed primarily at the large German American populations in those states, those laws prohibited the use and teaching of all non-English languages below the eighth grade in public and private schools. In *Pierce v. Society of Sisters*, private schools successfully nullified an Oregon law—aimed at Catholic schools—that required parents to send their children to public schools up to the eighth grade.[17]

Undaunted by these rulings, the territory appealed the Ninth Circuit Court decision validating Japanese language schools, but on 21 February 1927, the Supreme Court upheld that decision without a dissenting opinion. That ruling, in conjunction with its previous decisions in *Meyer*, *Bartels*, and *Pierce*, negated laws against schools teaching foreign languages and laws against parochial schools in at least twenty-two states.[18]

The turmoil aroused by the language school controversy in Hawaii split some Japanese communities apart. After Act 171 passed the legislature, for example, supporters of the Kakaako Japanese Language School broke into two factions, one urging compliance with the new law and the other supporting the challenge to it. The dispute itself ended up in court when one faction took physical possession of the school building and excluded the other from it. In Kona a similar rift occurred; in 1937, ten years after the Supreme Court had settled the issue, the Japanese there continued to maintain two language schools, although residents agreed the duplication was wasteful. This inability to reunite underscores the depth of the emotions involved in the original split.[19]

Such incidents exemplify the contrasting approaches of accommodation and confrontation Issei and their leaders took in reacting to discrimination. The two reactions reflected two interpretations of what America was for Japanese in Hawaii—a place where they lived in the shadow of the haole, or a place where they lived as equals.

Led by the Reverend Takie Okumura, Yasutaro Soga of *Nippu Jiji*, Professor Tasuku Harada of the University of Hawaii, and Dr. Iga Mori, a physician, the accomodationists called for cooperation and restraint in dealing with Americanizers. After the Caucasian-Issei joint committee recommended that students below the third grade be excluded from language school, Soga advised the Japanese to "weep into silence and drop the entire matter." Despite the hardships the proposal entailed and his own opposition to it, Soga in Japanese fashion "urged" his readers "to be silent" because he believed opposition would make matters worse. Soga reasoned that too many agents of power—the DPI, the Republican party, the American Legion, the governor, and "influential American papers"—were behind the recommendation so that overturning it was impossible, and there was nothing the weak could do but submit to the strong. "People might not understand my attitude," Soga wrote. "But when I think about the future of the Japanese people, how delicate the situation is, I must take this attitude. The fact that I must do so is sad." Such accommodationism did Soga and the Japanese little good. After the bombing of Pearl Harbor, American soldiers and officials took Soga, Iga Mori, and other Issei leaders from their homes, incarcerated them, threatened them with bayonets and guns, and otherwise treated them with contempt.[20]

In contrast to the accommodationists, Fred Kinzaburo Makino not only advised Issei to stand up for their rights, but led the effort to take the language school issue to court. "Though there were many who counseled the Japanese to bear their wrongs in patience and to weep in silence," observed a *Hochi* editorial after the Ninth Circuit Court had decided in favor of the language schools, "this paper was the outstanding champion of the real AMERICAN WAY, and advised the language schools to fight for their rights in the courts." After the Supreme Court affirmed the appellate court decision, Makino told a crowd of five thousand people who came from near and far to hear him speak, "It is the right of a people living in a free democracy to advocate their rights guaranteed under the Constitution. . . . It behooves us, who live in this country, to understand the characteristics of the Americans. Individuals and organizations alike must never forget to stand up for their rights and freedom."[21]

Makino was not interned during World War II. Perhaps officials believed he would have challenged his internment in court. On the other hand, he had always refused to visit Japanese training ships in Hawaii's ports or to entertain Japanese dignitaries visiting the territory. Such behavior, so unlike that of other Issei leaders, may have kept his name off the list of those suspected of disloyalty to America.[22]

Issei who agreed with Makino's position in the controversy showed just how far they had acculturated. Many, however, were more ambivalent. They wrestled with the idea of challenging the language school laws, and over the course of the seven-year litigation, many of them changed their minds regarding accommodation and confrontration. In debating whether to join the litigants, they became more and more educated about American ways. In this sense the controversy was itself an acculturating force.

Differing cultural perceptions lay at the root of the controversy over Japanese language schools. Japanese no less than Americanizers believed that the Nisei should become good American citizens. But while Americanizers thought language schools impeded that process, Japanese insisted that the schools promoted it. The resulting dispute was thus a classic instance of two groups of people talking past each other.

To Americanizers good citizenship meant that the Nisei should discard all traces of Japanese ways. Japanese language schools impeded good citizenship, Americanizers said, because the schools promoted loyalty to Japan by fostering Japanese nationalism, Japanese culture, and Buddhism. Moreover, according to Americanizers, learning Japanese interfered with learning English, the language of America.

To Japanese, good American citizenship meant that the Nisei should incorporate the best of Japanese culture with the best of American culture. Language schools promoted good citizenship, Japanese said, because the schools taught Japanese moral values compatible with American values that made good American citizens. While a number of language schools were Buddhist-sponsored, most were not, and in any case, Japanese said, Buddhism helped its followers become better American citizens. Learning Japanese did not interfere with learning English, Japanese argued, but it did expand job opportunities and promote family harmony by improving communication between parents and children, and having jobs and good family relations made for productive and contributing members of society.

Americanizers called Japanese schools "un-American" because, as argued by the 1920 survey report, the schools retarded the Nisei "in accepting American customs, manners, ideals, principles, and standards." Governor Farrington claimed that the schools represented "a daily effort to keep the children as fully alien as the teaching of an alien language in an alien atmosphere and under alien ideals can make them." The schools also represented, according to Farrington, "a desire to hold our children who are our future citizens, under a control that is not American."[23]

Many public school teachers concurred. In response to a questionnaire the DPI sent in 1922 to forty-nine teachers, most of "alien parentage," a majority said language schools hindered or did not help Americanization efforts. Some Nisei students also agreed. One such student at the University of Hawaii opposed language schools because, he wrote in 1922, "Hawaii should stand first for Americanism and do away with all the foreign elements which are tending to go against the real American Spirit."[24]

But most Japanese disagreed with accusations that language schools were un-American. When attempts were made in 1919 to pass legislation against language schools, thousands of Issei from all over the territory sent petitions to Governor Charles J. McCarthy, insisting that they "never attempted to educate [the Nisei] against American principles."

Similarly, a Hilo High School student who attended language school during the controversy recalled in 1927, "I was shocked to hear that the government was trying to abolish foreign language schools. My opinion was that it was an outrage since the language schools were not doing any harm." A schoolmate declared, "The white race is going too far if it wipes out these schools." A Normal School student who was "not in any way ashamed of the customs, ideas, or practices of the Japanese people," called the language school controversy a "disagreement of the broad-minded against the narrow-minded."[25]

Americanizers accused the schools of encouraging Japanese nationalism through patriotic celebrations, the employment of "alien" teachers who knew little or nothing about American traditions, and the use of textbooks that encouraged loyalty to Japan. These accusations pointed to practices that had once been common, but by the 1920s, were no longer so.[26]

Opposition to language schools abated after 1927, but re-emerged in the mid-1930s with Japan's aggression in Asia. In October 1935 the *Honolulu Advertiser* accused the schools of fostering "loyalty to the Imperial Government of Japan." As war between Japan and China raged and tension between Japan and the United States mounted, talk of eliminating the schools resurfaced. To alleviate the persisting suspicion and demonstrate their loyalty to the United States, the language schools in 1940 began a daily ritual of having their students recite the pledge of allegiance before an American flag. That year the *Advertiser* carried a photograph of children at the Moiliili Language School bowing in Japanese fashion before an American flag and a picture of George Washington.[27]

As this suggests, promoting Japanese nationalism at the language schools declined over the decades. As the Japanese put down roots in Hawaii, they reassessed the role of language schools and thus the textbooks used in them. Teachers had complained that the textbooks from Japan were inappropriate for Hawaii-born children who could not relate to stories of places unfamiliar to them and could not keep up with books meant for children attending all-day classes. They were also uncomfortable with books encouraging emperor worship and Japanese nationalism.[28]

In February 1915, the Hawaii Japanese Education Society was formed, and with the help of Professor Yaichi Haga from Japan, adapted the textbooks for use in Hawaii. The schools began using the revised textbooks in September 1916, and a subsequently revised set in 1924. In 1927, after the Supreme Court decision and again in 1937, still newer revisions were used, before World War II closed all Japanese language schools.[29]

The textbooks used after 1915 were progressively less nationalistic, and Japanese school teachers after 1915 also progressively decreased their nationalistic references to Japan. With Japan's war with China in the 1930s, however, "bolder schools plastered their bulletin boards with clippings of Japanese military successes."[30]

Despite the controversy over language schools, the extent to which they actually influenced Nisei attitudes toward Japan remains open. Some Nisei did not recall references to Japanese nationalism. "The belief of some people that a foreign language school influences the children to be loyal to their mother country is not founded on facts," wrote a Normal School student who attended language school before 1920. "Nothing was said to me to that effect when I attended school." Others recalled celebrations in honor of the emperor, but their reactions were probably not what adults at the time expected. In his autobiography, Tom Ige, who later became an economics professor at the University of Hawaii, wrote of his childhood in the 1920s: "New Year's Day in the valley began with ceremonies at the Japanese school. We would sing the Japanese National Anthem and bow very reverently before the picture of the Japanese emperor and empress hanging on the front wall." Ige's reaction to such rituals would probably have surprised his teachers. "Even at an early age," he recalled, "I resented this very much, but I couldn't excuse myself since ours was the closest house to the Japanese school and we were the closest neighbor of the school principal." Edith Yonenaka recalled how she and her classmates celebrated the emperor's birthday at her language school during the 1920s. "We'd have some kind of ceremony and everybody would stand up, and there would be his picture and we'd all bow down, way down to our knees!" she said. "And they'd sing songs and then they would give us soda and *manju* [a Japanese confection]!" The celebration, she added, had no real meaning for her. When Timmy Hirata was about sixteen, his language school class went to the Japanese consulate to honor Japan's ambassador to the League of Nations. "We were asked to give three banzai for the occasion. We did it. It didn't mean anthing to me about loyalty to the emperor. But I saw nothing wrong with saying banzai. . . . This was in 1931 or 1932. . . . We used to sing the Japanese national anthem. It didn't mean anything to me, although I thought the song was beautiful."[31]

While Americanizers believed that language schools retarded Nisei "in accepting American customs, manners, ideals, principles, and standards," Japanese believed the schools advanced acculturation by teaching moral education, or *shushin*, one of the most important subjects of study in Meiji Japan. Moral values taught at language schools, Japanese correctly believed, were compatible with American values and helped Nisei become better citizens. To that end, all revised textbooks continued to advocate filial piety, duty, honesty, perseverence, industry, courtesy, cooperation, and courage. The only value that may have conflicted with American thinking was filial piety, since it subordinated the individual to the family and thereby discouraged individualism. On the other hand, respect for parents and siblings and honoring family obligations, all part of filial piety, were certainly compatible with American values.[32]

Some Nisei valued the moral education they received in Japanese school. "I shall never forget . . . the lessons I learned in the Japanese language school about a 'Child's Duty to His Parents,' " wrote a Normal School student in 1927. "Lessons were taught with a moral purpose, but the characters were human beings and they appealed to me so much that I learned them thoroughly. These lessons will stay with me." A schoolmate wrote similarly, "It was the moral education which I had at the Japanese school that formed my character, that made me see the right and wrong and to uphold the high ideals." Shoichi Kurahashi, who attended Japanese school during the late 1920s and early 1930s, recalled that his lessons included *shushin,* or ethics. "That's the one where they teach you not to talk back to the elders," he explained. "Because of that I think I was really nice to my parents." These were students who took their schooling seriously and who understood enough Japanese to benefit from stories on morality. But most, less serious about learning the language and less fluent in it, were less affected.[33]

Americanizers were suspicious of Buddhist-sponsored language schools because they believed that Buddhism was un-American. Christian Japanese like Takie Okumura tried to use this suspicion to lessen the influence of Buddhism. Okumura and other Christians blamed Buddhists for the language school controversy and for using the schools to spread their religion, and urged the separation of language schools from any religious affiliation.[34]

At the beginning of the controversy in 1920, about 39 percent of the 163 language schools were Buddhist-sponsored, most of them affiliated with the Hongwanji sect. In contrast, only 6 percent of the schools were Christian-sponsored, while most had no religious affiliation. Once language schools became an issue, affiliation with Buddhism diminished. As a result the percentage of independent schools increased from 55 in 1920 to 76 in 1934, due in large measure to Okumura's efforts. During those years Buddhist-sponsored schools decreased to 18 percent and Christian-sponsored schools to 1 percent. Yet many Japanese continued to believe that Buddhism was fully compatible with American citizenship.[35]

Americanizers argued that language schools interfered with learning

English, and a number of researchers sought to find out if, in fact, that was so. Results were inconclusive. Language school might have made some students more aware of differences in language structure, and in that way might have improved their ability to speak English. The problem with studies on the effects of language schools was, as Percival M. Symonds pointed out, the difficulty in finding an adequate number of Nisei who never attended such schools.[36]

Although Nisei in Hawaii as in California generally performed inadequately on verbal tests in English, this did not necessarily mean that Japanese language school attendance was the cause. A more likely reason was the Nisei's bilingualism or trilingualism, which was independent of their attendance at language schools. That is, even those in Hawaii who did not attend language schools spoke Hawaii Creole English and some levels of Japanese and Standard English. Ironically, Henry Butler Schwartz, the DPI supervisor of foreign language schools whose goal was to eliminate the schools, concluded in 1925, "Badly as the pupils in the first and second grades of the Public Schools are handicapped by their ignorance of English, the handicap arises not so much from their attendance at Language School as from their whole environment, which is not changed even though they do not attend language school." Of students he studied at Hilo Junior High School, Schwartz wrote that "the relation of language school attendance and scholarship [was] practically *nil.*"[37]

Japanese argued that learning Japanese improved family relations by increasing communication between parents and children. Immigrant parents in Hawaii as on the mainland were understandably concerned about language barriers between themselves and their children. "I can't talk too much to my mother," explained a high school Nisei, "because . . . I don't know the language too good. Sometimes I'm trying to tell her something but she misunderstands. And sometimes she tells me something and I don't get the right idea." Although this student attended high school in the 1940s, she spoke for many Nisei growing up in the 1920s and 1930s. One of her schoolmates described a misunderstanding with her father. "I was cooking meat and threw away the fat part," she said. "He told me to keep it for stew and I asked when we were going to have stew. My father thought I said, 'For what are we going to have stew?' and he got angry with me because he felt I was being sassy to him. I think he often doesn't understand me."[38]

In addition to these instances of miscommunication, Nisei often failed to use the proper honorific expressions appropriate to different occasions. When this occurred, their Issei parents called them disrespectful, but in reality the culprit was ignorance.[39]

Unfortunately for both generations, language schools were generally unsuccessful in producing students who were fluent in Japanese. (Even had the schools been successful, they might not have improved communication between the generations, since language schools taught standard Japanese, not the dialects spoken by the Issei.) "In the English school, I was always among the first five highest in the class," recalled a Normal School student, "but in the Japanese school, I was at the tail end." He attended the Japanese High School, a language school in Honolulu, and said of his experience, "Imagine a student who went so far as the third year in the High School and who cannot even read or write simple Japanese characters." Similarly, his classmate, who attended language school for eight years, said in 1927, "I can speak [Japanese] quite fluently, but I have difficulty in reading character words. That language is so complicated and it is easily forgotten." Another Nisei wrote in 1922, "I went to the Japanese language school for eight years on Maui, but I cannot write a letter in Japanese to my parents in Japan. . . . Nearly all of the boys of Japanese parentage cannot speak correctly the Japanese language after attending that school for more than eight years."[40]

Like this youth, most Nisei were bilingual in that they could converse rudimentarily with their parents and other Issei, but they were not fluent in speaking and writing the language. This pattern is common to most immigrant groups. While immigrants themselves continued to speak their native languages, knowledge of those languages diminished notably with the second generation and practically disappeared with the third. As a result, without the constant arrival of new immigrants, ethnic communities have been generally unsuccessful in keeping their native languages alive.[41]

Despite the reality, Americanizers, like Issei community leaders, assumed that language schools taught their students more effectively than they actually did. It was this assumption that led Americanizers to try to eliminate the schools and caused Japanese to want to preserve them. Americanizers believed that abolishing the schools would arrest so-called un-American behaviors, while Issei believed that abolition would exterminate their language and cultural heritage. Like other immigrant groups the Issei looked to these schools to bridge the language and cultural gaps separating themselves and their children.[42]

Opponents of the language schools were not necessarily against the teaching of the Japanese language. Much more important to them was the question of who would control this teaching, the territorial government or "alien" groups like Buddhist organizations and immigrant associations that might encourage loyalty to Japan. The Ad Club, highly critical of language schools, proposed that they be abolished and foreign languages be taught in public schools. As this suggests, all the rhetoric about not teaching Japanese to young children because doing so interfered with learning English was a smokescreen to hide the real goal of eliminating schools under "alien" control. "Abolish all foreign language schools," Superintendent MacCaughey recommended to Governor Farrington in 1922, and "simultaneously" "organize in any school where there is sufficient demand, a class or classes in any foreign language desired" to be taught after school in public school buildings by public school teachers. He suggested they begin with the first grade if there was a demand. As the language school suit wound its way through the courts, the DPI thus began offering Japanese language classes of its own.[43]

Despite the assumptions and efforts of Americanizers and Issei alike, the language schools were ineffective agents of cultural transmission because the Nisei, on whom all the attention was directed, were generally indifferent to the schools. Many, including a University of Hawaii student who attended the Japanese High School in the early 1920s, thought language school instructors "uninteresting and difficult" to understand, for he had "never seen Japan" and had "little intention of going there." Most Nisei were much more interested in their English language schooling, and as a result, they learned little at Japanese school. This suggests that the bonds tying the Issei to Japan loosened considerably with their children.[44]

There were of course exceptions to this generalization. Some Nisei liked Japanese school and learned much there. One Normal School student recalled in 1927 that she had done well in language school, and could read Japanese novels, magazines, and newspapers. Shoichi Kurahashi, who was always at the top of his class in Japanese school, recalled his experience in the 1930s. "I never did rest one day of school," he said. "Even though I was sick and I didn't go [to] English school, I was going to Japanese school. . . . I liked Japanese school. When I was nine or ten years old I used to read all kinds of Japanese magazines."[45]

Some Nisei liked Japanese school at first, but later lost interest. A girl who enjoyed Japanese school in the second decade of the twentieth century stopped attending after she began working as a maid for a Caucasian family, because she "wished to specialize in American customs and the English language." A Normal School student who attended language school during the same period recalled, "I was very interested in Japanese during my early years, but I despised it as I grew older." Similarly, one of her classmates recalled that when she was about twelve years old she began frequenting the public library in Hilo, on the island of Hawaii. She began spending more and more of her spare hours with library books, reading "by candle-light after all the house had retired." "Up to this time, I had liked going to the language school," she reminisced, "[but then]

I began to neglect the Japanese school work." She began going to the library instead of attending language school. Punishment by her father when he learned of her truancy did not deter her, so he finally let her quit language school.[46]

Indeed, most Nisei were more interested in English school. A Normal school student said that she felt "freedom" when she dropped out of language school in the early 1920s when she was in the eighth grade. "There was no worry about memorizing the hard written characters in Japanese," she explained, and she had "more time to study and do [her] recreational reading of books and magazines." A student at Hilo High School in the early 1920s also recalled, "I hated the [Japanese] school, so I learned almost nothing. . . . I did not come in close contact with American boys and girls [in English school], yet I loved their language, their customs, ideals, and manners of living." One of this student's schoolmates, who did well in Japanese school, also preferred English school. "I attended the Japanese School for seven years," this student recalled, "and during that time I have always ranked first and second in my classes. Nevertheless I prefer English School better than the language school, so at night I used to study only the English books." Ethel Kina, who grew up during the 1920s and 1930s, said similarly, "We were forced to go [to Japanese language school]. We wasn't that interested in Japanese." She was more interested in English school because she "was born here." A Hilo High School girl summed up this view in 1927: "I think it is of some use to learn the foreign language . . . but it is of greater benefit to learn the English language . . . for we are all Americans."[47]

In contrast to the seriousness of purpose Nisei typically exhibited toward English school, their attitude toward Japanese school was one of indifference. Tetsuko Tamura, who attended language school in the 1920s, said, "We were forced to go because our parents wanted us to learn Japanese. At the beginning it wasn't too bad, but later I didn't care to go. . . . I wanted to play." Aiko Tokimasa Reinecke attended Japanese school during the 1910s. "There were some kids, boys particularly, who horsed around," she recalled. "When we did calligraphy, the boys would splash ink on some of the kids and when you got it on your dress it was hard to wash it off." About herself she said, "We didn't take Japanese school very seriously." Similarly, a Honokaa Junior High School boy said in 1927, "During [language] class we used to play and talk instead of studying." A Japanese language teacher said of his students in the 1930s, "They don't study, you know. . . . They don't listen too much."[48]

Truancy among Nisei students, infrequent at English school, was not unusual in Japanese school. A Normal School student recalled living in the 1910s on the island of Kauai, where she and her friends walked directly to Japanese school from English school. "It was so far," she said, "that we always reached the Japanese school at about 4 o'clock in the afternoon. I used to be [so] tired and uninterested in the Japanese school that I often stayed away from it." Minoru Inaba, who became a public school principal and territorial legislator, also recalled that he often "played hooky" from the Japanese school he attended during the 1920s. Similarly, Tetsuko Tamura recalled that during the early 1920s she and her friends occasionally "cut [language] class" to go to the movies, and their parents never found out. Likewise in the late 1920s and early 1930s, Tokio Okudara and his friends skipped Japanese school to attend Kalakaua Intermediate School football games. When the Japanese school principal reported their truancy to their parents, the boys flattened his automobile tires.[49]

This refusal to take language school seriously echoed the conduct of mainland Nisei, who also lacked the motivation needed to gain fluency in Japanese. With these attitudes, it was no wonder that most Nisei learned little in Japanese school. A Normal School student who attended language school for ten years before and during the 1920s, said, "One must devote much time to the study of [the Japanese language] to fully appreciate [its] beauty. . . . I can read and write very little and I am very much ashamed of myself. I did not take much interest in the Japanese school while attending, so now I find the conversation with the older generation very hard." Thus in Hawaii as on the mainland, Japanese schools failed to teach the Japanese language just as they failed to teach Japanese nationalism.[50]

With the outbreak of war between the United States and Japan, all Japanese language schools were closed, and community leaders believed they had seen the last of the schools. In 1943, the territorial legislature once again passed a bill, this time prohibiting students up to grade five from attending foreign language schools. In turn the Chinese challenged the law in federal court in Honolulu. The court declared the law invalid in June 1947. Within months of that decision, Japanese language schools began to reopen. Most Issei and many Nisei, now adults, supported their reopening, believing the schools would keep children "out of trouble" and improve unity in families where parents or grandparents spoke Japanese. But some Nisei, especially war veterans, feared that hostile reactions from Caucasians would nullify all their efforts to be accepted as full-fledged Americans.[51]

Ironically, Americanizers who demanded that Americans speak only

English were trying to stamp out knowledge that became extremely valuable during World War II. Nisei volunteers assigned to U.S. military intelligence played a vital role in translating captured documents and interrogating Japanese prisoners. Some Nisei, like interviewee Shoichi Kurahashi, learned to read Japanese at language school. "At McCully Japanese School, we had one thousand Chinese characters [to learn]," he said. "Out of one thousand, I had about 960 or 970 correct. That was a real accomplishment. . . . Because of that I was able to translate and interrogate . . . the [Japanese] prisoners [during the war]. We picked up a lot of captured documents."[52]

Japanese immigrants arriving with their belongings in Honolulu, 1893. Courtesy of the Hawaii State Archives.

Loading sugarcane by hand, c. 1885. Although machines gradually replaced humans, using human power to load cane continued on many plantations through the 1930s. Courtesy of the Hawaii State Archives.

Japanese plantation children with their mother on the porch of their plantation company house at Naalehu on the island of Hawaii, c. 1910. Living conditions varied from plantation to plantation. Courtesy of the Bishop Museum.

The Reverend Takie Okumura, in his mid-forties, along with his wife and their children, c. 1908. This photograph was taken fourteen years after Okumura arrived in Hawaii. Courtesy of the Bishop Museum.

Yasutaro Soga, editor-in-chief of the *Nippu Jiji*, in his late forties, c. 1910. Courtesy of Helen Sato.

Fred Kinzaburo Makino (seated), publisher of the *Hawaii Hochi*, in his thirties, with unidentified men, c. 1915. Courtesy of Paul Yempuku.

Women washing clothes in a stream in rural Oahu, c. 1920. The baby in the foreground is a girl. The front of female infants' heads was shaved regularly to make the hair thick and coarse so that when these girls grew up they could sweep back their hair in the traditional Japanese bouffant style. Courtesy of the Hawaii State Archives.

Japanese woman offering vegetables for sale in a plantation camp in Waimanalo, Oahu, c. 1925. A sugarcane field is behind her. Courtesy of the Hawaii State Archives.

Students saluting the American flag at Ewa School in rural Oahu, 1914. Rural children did not usually wear shoes to school. Courtesy of the Bishop Museum.

Elementary school students in rural Anahole, on the island of Kauai, 1936. The students are walking toward their classroom. Courtesy of the Hawaii State Archives.

Students from the Nuuanu Girls Japanese (Language) High School attending a Buddhist service conducted by Bishop Zenkyo Komagata of the Soto Mission, 1939. Courtesy of the Reverend Shugen Komogata.

First graders at the Moiliili Japanese Language School in Honolulu bow in Japanese fashion to the U.S. flag and a portrait of George Washington, 1940. After bowing, the students recited the pledge of allegiance to the United States. This practice became a daily ritual that year in most Japanese language schools in the Territory. Photographer unknown.

Japanese women (plus a Caucasian woman, on the far right in the back row) standing in front of the Nuuanu YMCA, 1933. The women were taking an English class at the Y; this photograph was taken at a farewell party for the woman in the center wearing a lei. Most of the women are in Western-style dresses and hats, while others are wearing the Japanese kimono. Courtesy of the Hawaii State Archives.

Casual and apparently acculturated young adult Nisei sitting along a rock wall, c. 1920s. Courtesy of the Bishop Museum.

Part Four

Nisei
Acculturation

Chapter 8

Social Changes

As the Issei decided to remain in Hawaii permanently, they became more receptive to American values and customs. Yet even from the outset of their sojourn they were acculturating however involuntarily into American society, and the longer they stayed the more they acculturated. This process was naturally accelerated with their American-born children.

By the 1920s the oldest Nisei were entering adulthood and many Issei had concluded that Hawaii and not Japan was their home. They had already begun to buy property, build homes of their own, and save their money in Hawaii instead of sending it to Japan. Japanese per capita investment in real estate in the territory grew from $2.61 in 1911 to $9.17 in 1920 and $92.31 in 1930. Similarly their per capita savings in local banks rose from $2.40 in 1910 to $17.91 in 1920 and $64.83 in 1930. As their savings grew, their remittances to Japan decreased dramatically. The Honolulu post office reported a drop in international money orders from Hawaii to Japan, from over one million dollars in 1921 to less than $300,000 in 1930. The largest single-year decrease, almost $444,000, occurred in 1922.[1]

To be sure, not all Issei who lived out their lives in Hawaii decided unequivocally to remain permanently. Even as their children grew up and became unalterably acculturated, some Issei clung to the idea that someday they would return to their homeland, and some died still hoping to realize that dream. Others returned to Japan after ten, twenty, or even thirty years. They took their young children with them, but children who had grown up, more likely than not, remained in Hawaii.

Those Issei who decided consciously to remain in Hawaii did so because Hawaii afforded them a better life than they could hope for in Japan. The plantations offered opportunity, however limited, for upward mobility. They could also leave the plantation, as many did. Yoshiko Oda recalled that her parents, who worked on a plantation for six years and then peddled vegetables and ran a small confectionary shop, remained in Hawaii because their standard of living there was much better than it would have been in Japan. Having lived in Japan for several years in the 1930s, Oda understood that fact. "I worked hard [in Hawaii]," she explained, "but compared with Japan . . . it was easier." Ties to Japan further loosened as the Issei's children grew up with little or no knowledge of life in Japan. In his novel *No-No Boy,* John Okada aptly described the transition many Issei experienced during the early decades of the twentieth century. In the novel Kenji's father looked back after World War II on his life and realized that

> he had long forgotten when it was that he had discarded the notion of a return to Japan but remembered only that it was the time when this country which he had no intention of loving had suddenly begun to become part of him because it was a part of his children and he saw and felt it in their speech and joys and sorrows and hopes and he was a part of them. And in the dying of the foolish dreams which he had brought to America, the richness of the life that was possible in this foreign country destroyed the longing for a past that really must not have been as precious as he imagined or else he would surely not have left it.[2]

As the Issei adapted themselves to American life, they developed tightly knit communities that served to cushion the impact of the changes their immigration entailed. At the same time these communities retarded acculturation by reducing contacts with the larger community and ostracizing those who deviated from Japanese norms. On the plantations Japanese lived in segregated camps, and off the plantations they continued to live largely among themselves. Even in urban Honolulu they congregated in enclaves in Moiliili, Kalihi-uka, and Manoa. In these and other communities—with the support of *kenjin-kai* (prefectural associations), Buddhist temples, and language schools—the Japanese retained much of their customs.[3]

In Moiliili they raised pigs and cultivated rice on land they leased from large estates. Many worked in the stone quarry, one of the area's best known landmarks. By 1920, Moiliili was a small Japanese town of camp-style houses, flower shops, and meat and produce markets fronted by dirt roads.[4]

Also in the 1920s, Manoa Valley provided fertile soil for Japanese farmers, who leased the land from companies or individuals. (Chinese farmers also worked the land, growing wetland taro.) The Japanese grew vegetables—Japanese taro, burdock, radishes, sweet potatoes, and carrots—and flowers—asters, gardenias, marigolds, African daisies, Easter lilies, and carnations. They sold the flowers to florists in Honolulu, and took the vegetables downtown to the River Street market, where they sold them to green grocers and street hawkers who peddled them door to door. But by 1930 this pattern was in decline, as homes owned mainly by European Americans came to replace agriculture in the valley.[5]

This tendency to live among themselves, also characteristic of West Coast Japanese, was hardly distinctive. In the 1920s Honolulu abounded not only with "little Tokyos" but also with "new Cantons" and "Azores of the Pacific." Because of their numbers, Japanese, Chinese, and Portuguese were the most noticeable groups maintaining ethnic enclaves, but Puerto Ricans, Spanish, and Filipinos also lived in smaller settlements in the city.[6]

This pattern was equally characteristic of Europeans who moved to America's growing industrial cities. "To the foreigner, ignorant of the English language, bewildered by his new surroundings, and homesick for his native environment," wrote the historian Edward Hartmann of the Europeans, "association with his own kind offered a sense of security in the midst of confusion, a kind of haven from the new, vigorous, competitive environment which he found all about him. Here in these growing colonies, he heard the friendly sound of mother tongue, saw many of the old familiar customs, and obtained the advice and friendship of those who had arrived before him." The sociologist Emily G. Balch observed that the tendency of those who spoke the same language to exhibit "a sort of clannishness . . . [was] not peculiar to any class" or group. "They go to those whom they know," wrote Balch, "to those whose speech they can understand, to those from whose experience they may draw large drafts of suggestion and help."[7]

In Hawaii as on the mainland tightly knit Japanese communities became reference points for individuals and families, who received social pressure to behave in ways favorable to the community's reputation. In turn the community provided psychological security from the hostile world outside and helped ease the transition to American society.[8]

In a survey of Sacramento Japanese Americans conducted during the early 1970s, 75 percent of the males and 66 percent of the females said that they were taught not to do anything that would bring shame to the Japanese community. "You didn't dare step out of line," said one youth. "The first time you did, your parents would be sure to hear about it." Another study, of Japanese American youths in Los Angeles in the early 1970s, found that delinquents, unlike non-delinquents, failed to identify with their families, neighborhoods, or schools.[9]

This community cohesion helped keep down the incidence of juvenile delinquency, which was noticeably low among Nisei. From 1917 to

1928, the number per 10,000 population of boys ten to seventeen years old declared delinquent by the courts in Hawaii was 135 for Japanese and 468 for all groups except Japanese; for girls, it was 23 for Japanese and 132 for non-Japanese. During the same years the number of boys per 10,000 charged with larceny was 53 for Japanese and 215 for non-Japanese.[10]

In a study of two impoverished Honolulu neighborhoods in the late 1920s, the sociologist Andrew W. Lind found that the community having a high concentration of Japanese had no cases of Nisei juvenile delinquency, while the ethnically mixed neighborhood had several cases of Nisei deliquency. In the first neighborhood gossip was prevalent, and the threat of disgrace served to control Nisei behavior. Residents whispered about everything everyone in the neighborhood did. Those who moved out, either because they found this intolerable or because their occupation forced them to, found it more difficult to keep their children in line. A Honolulu teacher described a Nisei girl whose behavior changed after her mother moved from a Japanese community to a mixed neighborhood to run a lodging house. "The girl had been in every sense of the word a model daughter and student previous to her mother's taking over this lodging house," said the teacher. But after they moved, the girl "began going out with a gang and on one occasion remained out all night with a group of boys who had stolen an auto."[11]

This relationship between closely-knit communities and social stability also characterized other ethnic groups. With them, too, Lind found a "rough inverse correlation between social disorganization, measured in terms of juvenile delinquency and dependency" on public welfare, and the "degree of segregation and concentration" of the group.[12]

Because crime among Nisei was rare, Myles Yutaka Fukunaga's 1928 kidnapping and murder of Gill Jamieson shocked Hawaii's residents. Believing that Fukunaga was mentally ill, the Japanese community rallied in support of Fukunaga and his family. In writing about this episode, Dennis Ogawa argued that belief among Japanese that Fukunaga was insane helped them accept his deed. If Fukunaga were sane, Ogawa suggested, the "implication was that any Japanese could commit such a brutal crime. If he were insane, however, the community's strained image and responsibility for the boy's criminal nature would be absolved. What was at stake wasn't only the fate of Myles Fukunaga, but the [self-] image of the Japanese American community."[13]

Fukunaga's case revealed the pressures many Japanese bore, and the extreme effects those pressures could yield when family and community proved insufficient to control the anger and frustration of a deranged person. Yet Fukunaga's case was the exception. For most Japanese the influence of family and community kept individual behavior in check.

Community cohesion also enabled the Nisei to keep the Japanese first names they received at birth. Conversely, increased contact with the American community encouraged the Nisei to acquire American names. Taking American names reflected a desire to fit into the dominant society, and was thus one indicator of acculturation. Calling oneself "Robert" or "Mary" created a different self-identity from "Chotoku" or "Shizuko."[14]

Issei parents almost universally gave their children Japanese first names, indicating their substantial and continued ties to the old country. While growing up, most Nisei kept those Japanese names. Of 985 Japanese eighth graders in 1924, 91 percent were known to their schools by their Japanese first names. In urban Honolulu, where exposure to American ways was greater than in rural Oahu and the neighbor islands, Nisei acquired English names earlier and more often. Thus 20 percent of Honolulu eighth graders had English names, compared to 5 percent of those in rural areas. Two schools, Paia School on Maui and Kuhio School in Honolulu, recorded English first names for all their Japanese students. In those cases school officials probably gave English names to all who did not already have them.[15]

Ten years later little changed in rural districts, where only 9 percent of all Japanese eighth graders were listed with English names. Among adults that year, of four hundred Japanese having family names beginning with Matsu, only 1 percent had an English name alone and 12 percent had an English name with a middle initial indicating a Japanese name. In contrast 56 percent of four hundred Nisei public school teachers that year had English given names.[16]

The much larger percentage among teachers demonstrated their greater awareness of and sensitivity to the Americanization efforts of educational and other territorial leaders. A Nisei who in 1939 became the first Japanese American principal of a high school was listed as Masaichi Miyamoto in school directories from 1926 until 1932, and then as Stanley M. Miyamoto from 1933 on. Another teacher who became principal was listed as Sanae Kanda from 1925 until 1942, and then as Stephen S. Kanda from 1943, an example of the war accelerating the acculturation process.[17]

Increased schooling brought greater contact with American culture and thereby encouraged Nisei to acquire English names. Thus 19 percent of all Japanese students who graduated from the University of Hawaii in 1926 had English given names. With time and the influence of World War II, the percentage was even greater—31 in 1936 and 61 in 1946.[18]

Many Nisei kept their Japanese names in childhood, but adopted English names after reaching adulthood, demonstrating that acculturation was a lifetime process. In a random sample of 276 Nisei residents in Honolulu in 1971, the political scientist Yasumasa Kuroda found that 45 percent used Japanese, 44 percent used English, and 11 percent used both Japanese and English given names. Comparing these percentages with those of the Honolulu eighth graders in 1924 revealed a 24 percentage point increase in the use of English names after half a century. Although not necessarily the same individuals, both groups were Nisei urban dwellers, the first being youths and the second adults.[19]

Nisei youths sometimes acquired English names from their teachers. "I used to go to the Episcopalian Church [in the 1920s] across my house, and my friends used to call me 'T' for Teichiro," recalled former state superintendent Timmy T. Hirata. "One of the Sunday school teachers said, 'From now on your name is going to be Timmy.' The guys in the block started calling me Timmy. . . . It was so simple compared to my Japanese name." He legalized his American name in the 1960s. Richard Inouye's fourth grade teacher, who could not pronounce Kazuo, also gave him his English name. Thomas Ige, former economics professor at the University of Hawaii, recalled a similar experience. "Our second grade teacher," he reminisced of the 1920s, "decided our given Japanese names were too cumbersome and un-American, so one day she went right down the aisle and gave us all English names: 'You are John, you are William, you are Mary, you are Sheppard.' When she came to me she said, 'You are Thomas.'. . . I must agree that my Japanese name, Heihachiro, is indeed very cumbersome; ironically, the teacher's name was Miss Kamakawiwaole, even more cumbersome than my own name."[20]

Others chose American names for themselves or asked siblings to do so. Edythe Yamamoto picked her name while in high school in the early 1920s because she "liked it." Her parents continued to call her Masako, and her sisters and brothers continued to call her *nesan* (older sister). She did not legalize her English name, but used it throughout her adulthood. A Honokaa Junior High School boy chose the name Edgar when he was baptized. Another Nisei at the age of twelve asked his older sister to give him an American name because teachers had difficulty pronouncing his Japanese name. After thinking about it carefully, she named him Ralph and it stuck.[21]

Some chose their American names after reaching adulthood. Marie picked her name in the 1930s, when she was in her twenties and in nursing school. Vivian Nakamura, a Kibei, took her American name in 1939 when she was twenty-one and working for a haole family who had a friend named Vivian. Ethel Kina, whose Japanese name was Yoshiko, chose her American name in 1954, when she was thirty-five. She and her husband Theodore legalized their new names, she said, "because [it] was good to be modern, you know."[22]

Friends sometimes gave Nisei colorful nicknames that stayed with them as adults. Boys, especially, were inventive in naming their buddies. Yukito Izumi's nickname was Dyke for *daikon* (turnip). He continued to use the name as an adult. Tokio Okudara recalled that some nicknames derived from the boys' Japanese names: "Sub," for example, came from Kosaburo. Other names came from the boys' physical features or personality. Rabbit Arakaki, whose first name was Takezo, had pointed ears. Mullet Arakaki, whose first name was Takemitsu, might have been elusive, like his aquatic namesake. Other nicknames Okudara remembered were "Donkey" and "Pluto." "In fact some of them we don't know their first name, even to this day," he noted. "We never heard their first name."[23]

As illustrated by the foregoing examples, Nisei took to American ways more easily than their parents. Once outside the confines of their families, Nisei youths came in contact with American manners and mores. The extent of their exposure, of course, depended on where they lived. Rural areas usually provided fewer acculturating influences, and urban enclaves like Moiliili in Honolulu were relatively insulated. Yet the outside world touched even those places. Schools, clubs, churches, and jobs, as well as books, magazines, and movies, brought all Japanese and especially the Nisei in contact with Western ideas and customs.

In school Nisei learned English, interacted with teachers and fellow students, and read about American ways. "We are educated in the American public schools and there we learn the Occidental mannerisms and customs," wrote a Normal School student who grew up in Lahaina, Maui, during the first two decades of the twentieth century. "When we return to our own homes we are not like our parents in customs and traditions." Increased education often drove a wedge between the two generations. A University of Hawaii student from Kauai wrote that beginning in high school in the early 1920s, he felt himself drifting away from his parents.[24]

Teachers, almost half of whom were haole, served as models of Western behavior and thinking. A Normal School student recalled that as a first grader in 1913, she observed her teacher's hair arrangement, dress, and shoes, and tried to imitate her. A University of Hawaii student wrote that his "broad-minded, unbiased, and friendly" public school teachers in the 1910s and 1920s helped shape his attitudes. Aiko Tokimasa Reinecke recalled Maude Sisson, her eighth grade teacher in 1920 at Kahuku School in rural Oahu, as "truly wonderful." Sisson often invited her students to her home in the evenings to read the works of Shakespeare and other English writers. Besides being a principal and teacher, she was a friend.[25]

Teachers sometimes introduced Nisei youths to Christianity. "Five years ago I was a 'heathen,'" wrote a high school boy in 1927, "but I came in contact with a teacher and a minister who gave me a fine foundation of the Christian religion." That same year a Normal School student wrote that she had just converted to Christianity due to the influence of her fifth grade teacher, Florence Whitton.[26]

Teachers often encouraged Nisei to pursue their education and sometimes gave needed help at crucial moments. One teacher in the 1920s helped a Maui High School graduate find a job as a maid in Honolulu so she could attend the Normal School. Another encouraged a twenty-year-old Nisei who had dropped out of Konawaena High School for financial reasons to return to school. He did so, and later continued on to the University of Hawaii.[27]

Perhaps the most widely influential public school teacher and principal during the 1920s and 1930s was Miles E. Cary of McKinley High School, whose political and social attitudes were noted earlier. An enthusiastic, dedicated educator, Cary had a genuine interest in his students' welfare. "Every time he went to the auditorium," recalled former state legislator Akira Sakima, "he used to walk up and down and give his talk. He was always preaching democracy. Think for yourself." Cary developed programs that encouraged students to investigate political, social, and economic issues. Andrew In, a Chinese student at McKinley in the 1930s who later became dean of the University of Hawaii's College of Education, recalled that Cary wanted students to learn to be active, contributing members of society. Similarly, former state superintendent Timmy Hirata characterized Cary as "remarkable," "a pioneer in developing student activities—student government, club work, extracurricular activities."[28]

Peers also exposed Nisei to Western ideas. A young man recalled in 1927 that a classmate stimulated his interest in Western literature during his last two years of high school. But more often peer influence led to changes in dress and social activities, which often clashed with parents' ideas of what was proper. "There was a time when I was looked upon as the disturbing element in the family," recalled a university student in 1938. "I was radical, always dazzling my parents with something new. They said that I imitated the American boys and girls, that I was trying to be 'haolefied.' At first my parents insisted on my accepting Japanese customs, but they have gradually yielded to my desires to be like the other girls of the neighborhood." Because her friends "were wearing bobbed hair," the girl begged her parents until they let her do the same. "On another occasion," she continued, "I shocked my parents by nonchalantly walking down the lane into my home in a pair of slacks. Imagine what a step I was taking! I had borrowed this pair from a friend of mine whose parents were lenient. My parents ordered me to take them off, but I defied them. After much pleading, I finally prevailed upon them to let me dress like the other girls and by the time I began wearing shorts, my parents were well acquainted with my desire to be like other girls."[29]

As on the mainland, social functions became issues of conflict between Issei and Nisei. An honor student attending Maui High in 1927 wrote that his parents "violently" objected to his learning how to dance. That same year a university student explained her parents' viewpoint: "They believe that many temptations will arise from the dancing pleasures." Another Nisei, a high school girl in the 1920s, wrote, "It is instinctive in every young person to want to go out with friends to parties or picnics . . . but I hardly went because I was forbidden to do so by my father." Then, illustrating the influence of American ideas, she continued, "I didn't mind it very much then, but now if he tries to stop me from going I stand for my rights, as I do believe that young people should be allowed a certain amount of liberty to get together and have a good time in a decent manner." Issei who thought their children unmanageable sometimes took them to probation officers, as did the parents of a fourteen-year-old in the late 1930s. "Sachan [a friend whose parents were born in Hawaii] is lucky," protested the girl. "Her mother let her do what she wants. She even let her go to the school dance. I wish my mother had been born here." Another girl brought to probation officers at about the same time complained that her parents refused to let her go to dances, football games, and American movies.[30]

Besides teachers and peers, school libraries exposed Nisei youths to American ways. A University of Hawaii student recalled spending a lot of time in the 1920s at his high school library poring over magazines such as *American Boy, Boy's Life,* and *Popular Mechanics.* Similarly a Lahainaluna High School student wrote in 1927 that she learned about "Haole Americans" through books, newspapers, magazines, and movies.[31]

Clubs also helped acculturate the Nisei. A Hilo High School girl wrote that she joined a club "to learn to be at ease among people and learn American ways." Schools sponsored a number of clubs, and in 1920 the Nisei themselves organized the Japanese Students' Association. Open to high school and college Nisei, the association was formed "to help make the Hawaiian-born citizens of Japanese ancestry better Americans." Calling their characteristic "shyness" a weakness that Nisei had to overcome in order to be active members of the larger community, the association sponsored events like picnics and dances in addition to monthly association meetings. The intent was not only to "promote closer friendship and unity," but also to "help [Nisei] mix more readily . . . with students of other races." To expose its members to new ideas, the association also invited speakers and held conferences and debates.[32]

This strategy of banding together to solve mutual problems was not unique to the Japanese. The Chinese Students' Alliance of Hawaii had been organized several years earlier, and in 1932 the Korean Students' Alliance of Hawaii was formed, patterned after the other two groups.[33]

Sometimes jobs were agents of acculturation. Richard Inouye learned to speak English only after he moved to Honolulu in 1927 when he was sixteen. "I didn't speak English on the [island of Hawaii]," he said, "because there were mostly Japanese around. When I came to Honolulu, I had to talk to the boss. . . . That's how I learned to speak English."[34]

Some Nisei learned American ways as a result of their parents' jobs. One whose parents worked as domestic servants for "a religious and well to do American family" recalled the 1910s. "I came to be regarded almost as one of the American family," wrote the Nisei. "I played with the children; had the same food; ate together with the children; and came to look upon them almost as brothers and sisters." Similarly a McKinley High School girl grew up among Caucasians in the second decade of the twentieth century because her parents worked for a haole. "We lived in a small house in the back yard," the girl reminisced. "[The woman] loved me as she would her own child. She took me everywhere with her. It was she who taught me to speak English correctly before I attended school. As my playmates were all white children, I spoke more English than Japanese."[35]

Many Nisei themselves also worked as domestic servants. While the job was menial, it afforded a glimpse into American practices. They observed Caucasians cooking and eating their meals and interacting with each other. Undoubtedly the Nisei also improved their English through such close contact. Ethel Kina worked for a professor and his family during the 1930s as a live-in maid when she was about sixteen. There she cleaned the house, washed and ironed the laundry, helped care for the children, and learned to cook American meals. At first she ate by herself in the kitchen, but after the family came to know her, they invited her to eat with them in the dining room. She developed a friendship with them that continued long after she left the job.[36]

Some Nisei who admired the family interaction they saw began to question Japanese family life. "For the last four years I have been working for a prominent American family in Manoa," explained a young woman in the 1930s. "One thing which impresses me most is the way in which an American man treats his wife." The young woman continued, "An American man is very affectionate and kind to his wife. Unlike a Japanese man, who regards his wife as a mere tool for making money and for gratification of his physical desires, an American man looks at his wife as if she were a living human being and treats her accordingly. . . . [He] never tells his wife, 'You, a foolish wife, should never forget your place in the family. Be quiet and be gone!' but brings every-day affairs frankly before his wife and asks her opinion." The woman concluded, "When I am married I want my husband to treat me just like an American man treats his wife."[37]

Some Nisei intentionally took jobs as domestic servants in order to learn American ways. "Even though I have mingled freely with Americans," a girl wrote in the 1920s, "I do not feel perfectly at ease at times, and to get rid of this awkwardness I am at present working in an American home just to learn their ways and their etiquette." The girl chose this menial job over the objections of her mother. "At times [working as a maid] hurts my pride," she admitted, "but I want to learn." Another girl attending Hilo High School in 1927 developed the ease so desired by the other. "For four years I have lived in American families," she wrote, "and I began to act as if I was among them. The white people considered me as a girl of their race and was [*sic*] fond of me. Evidently, I have more American acquaintances than my own racial group."[38]

The extent of Nisei acculturation can be appreciated when their experiences are compared to those of the Kibei, Nisei who were sent to Japan in their youth to receive a Japanese education. Often these children left Hawaii or the mainland before reaching school age and returned in their late teens or early adulthood. Many found it difficult to adjust to life in America, for they spoke no English, had few emotional ties to parents and siblings in America, and knew very little of American culture. Adjustment was difficult even for those who remained in Japan for only a few years. A Kibei who was born in 1909 left Hawaii with his parents two years later. In 1915 the whole family returned to the territory. Although only six, the boy was already an outcast. "My sister and I were teased," he later recalled, "just because we . . . did not understand [American] ways. Many a time, I recollect, I have sat in the corner of the yard and cried." He called those days "long" and "cruel."[39]

While Kibei difficulties pointed to the extent of Nisei acculturation, the Nisei, too, encountered problems. William Caudill among others hypothesized "a significant compatibility," not to be confused with identity, between the value systems of the Japanese and the American middle-class. What the two cultures shared in common, according to Caudill, were respect for authority and parental wishes, diligent work habits, and self-discipline, including commitment to behavior necessary to achieve long-range goals. But Caudill also noted that there were great differences in social structure, customs, religion, material culture, and basic person-ality and character structure of the two societies. Such differences, he said, generated conflict for individuals adjusting to American society.[40]

In some individuals the conflict was pronounced enough to make the "marginal man" concept particularly apt. Coined by the sociologist Robert E. Park in 1928 and further developed by the sociologist Everett V. Stonequist, the term referred to those who were simultaneously bound to two cultures. Park said such people developed wider horizons, but Stonequist said they suffered anxiety, ambivalence, and hypersensitivity, since they stood on the edge of two cultural worlds without fully being a member of either.[41]

Miya Harada Soga, daughter of Professor Tasuku Harada of the Univer-sity of Hawaii, attended the predominantly Caucasian private Punahou School in the 1920s, as well as Central Union Church, also predomi-nantly Caucasian at that time. Yet she did not have close Caucasian friends. "I did not have Japanese friends [either]," she recalled, "because the few at Punahou were not in my grade. Until I got to the University [of Hawaii] I did not have any Japanese friends." Although she identi-fied with American culture and associated with Caucasians, she was not quite one of them. "I was Japanese in my ways, too," she pointed out. After she married, she stopped attending church on Sundays because she felt she could not leave her parents-in-law at home by themselves. "My father-in-law [Yasutaro Soga, the editor-in-chief of *Nippu Jiji*] worked everyday, and Sunday was his only day at home. I felt my place was at home. . . . I felt I had to do what my parents-in-law wanted me to do."[42]

Nisei learned American ways in the larger community and returned home to families strongly influenced by Japanese practices. "At home we try to act and speak like typical Japanese," explained a University of Hawaii student in 1927. "Outside the home we try to act and speak like Americans." Another University of Hawaii Nisei characterized her generation as "neither wholly Japanese nor wholly American," and "fully accepted by neither." Walter Y. Mihata, a university student in 1928, de-scribed the Nisei predicament. "Our parents and elders are bewildered with our American ways and manners," he wrote. "They complain that we are too readily forgetting the language and customs that are so dear to them." At the same time, he continued, Caucasians criticized Nisei for not "speak[ing] English so well" and questioned their sincerity in "be-com[ing] true Americans." "We live a dual life," Mihata said, "for on the streets we try to be 'Regular Americans,' but at home in order to please our parents we try to be as Japanese as possible."[43]

Part of the difficulties Nisei experienced came from fundamental differences in the personality and character structures of Japanese and Americans. While both Japanese and Americans valued perseverance and commitment to long-term goals, Japanese also emphasized restraint, control of emotions, composure in the face of hardship, deference, reticence, and nonverbal communication. The Nisei exhibited personality traits that reflected the Japanese ideal, and in this way Japanese culture persisted. But these traits conflicted with American ideals of spontaneity, confrontation, and verbal assertiveness.[44]

Nisei found distasteful emotional expressions that were boisterous, passionate, and excessive. In turn Caucasians criticized the Nisei as unemotional. Critics misinterpreted the "unwrinkled brow or the dry eye as a sign of lack of feeling or of an unperturbed, impenetrable nature." L. Takeo Doi has used the terms *omote* (outside) and *ura* (reverse) to describe the Japanese outside-inside dichotomy. The *omote*, or surface, was the public manner used with guests and respected outsiders. *Ura*, its complement, referred to the private side revealed only to the most intimate. These distinctions of outside and inside were exemplified in Japansese behaviors, vocabulary, and grammar. Thus the Nisei might be highly controlled in public, but in private "tempers [were] allowed to fly and tears flow[ed] quite freely."[45]

Nisei also avoided aggressive and conspicuous behavior, voicing contrary opinions, and speaking out in the classroom and at work. European Americans who criticized the Nisei as inarticulate and nonverbal were unaware that unlike them, the Nisei grew up in families that discouraged verbal communication and considered talkative people to be show-offs. Instead Japanese families encouraged communication through attitude, action, and feeling.[46]

A mainland Nisei woman in the 1970s expressed the problem well. "At home we were taught to shut-up and listen," she recalled of her childhood. "But with *haku-jin* [Caucasians] you've got to learn how to speak up loud and clear or never be heard. What we had to learn was how to switch styles of communication from group to group so that with *nihon-jin* [Japanese] you use a more subtle, group consensus approach, making sure you're not too loud and pushy, and with *haku-jin* you use a more aggressive, individualistic approach, putting yourself out in front so you can be seen and heard."[47]

In the 1950s, Evelyn Y. Kimura and Margaret Z. Freeman interviewed well-educated business and professional Nisei men who had lived on the mainland, either during their college days or during World War II. Kimura and Freeman found that these men, who valued schooling, spoke Standard English, held high status jobs, and maintained business contacts with Caucasians and occasionally socialized with them, nevertheless fraternized mainly with people of Japanese descent, with whom they felt more comfortable. Sometimes decisions on socializing came from hypersensitivity to possible rejection by Caucasians. "I went to school in New Haven," one Nisei recalled. "When the Japanese bombed Pearl Harbor, we Hawaii boys got together. Some of them were of the big Haole families, Big Five, you know, and we talked together just like we were old friends. Even now we still talk when we see each other on the street," the Nisei continued, "but we never go beyond that and visit in each other's homes." He added, "I'm always careful to ignore the alumni club notices and meetings here because I know they wouldn't feel comfortable if I were there."[48]

Nevertheless the Nisei were much more acculturated than their parents, and it was often Nisei children who introduced the Issei to American ideas and practices. "My folks are changing because I advise and show them the ways of American living," wrote a Hilo High School boy in 1927. "One thing good with my mother is that she listens to me and takes my part in advising dad." A schoolmate told of learning to prepare cakes, cookies, and American-style meals in her homemaking class and then introducing them to her parents, who at first thought the dishes strange but then grew accustomed to them. A Normal School student that year wrote that her older sister, who had lived in Honolulu for a while, returned to their plantation home and taught the family "what food Americans ate and how Americans furnished . . . their homes." As a result her parents bought "spring beds, chairs, tables, dressers, curtains, American dishes," and even replaced their "old stone fire cooker with a fine, new oil stove."[49]

Many Issei tried to be open to the new ways. "I know that [my children] know and understand about America better than we who come from Japan," said a father in the late 1930s. "My children tell their mother what foods are good for our health." The father continued, "They learn this in school—American school, I mean. I believe that their teachers are better informed along this line so I don't interfere nor ignore their suggestions." Yet he realized that a large gap existed between the two cultures. "Judging from what my children tell me," he mused, "nearly all the ideas that we have are greatly different from what they learn in the school."[50]

Even adjusting to the outer trappings of American life could be difficult. "At home, we have beds as well as *futon,* or Japanese mattresses for use on the floor," wrote Misako Yamamoto in the late 1930s. "No one in the family, except mother, uses the *futon*. . . . Whenever we insist that she sleep on the bed she concedes, but it is not uncommon on such occasions to see mother wake up in the middle of the night to lay out the *futon* and sleep on the floor."[51]

Indeed, adopting American ways and learning English were difficult for Issei, who had grown up in Japan. For many it was easier to continue speaking Japanese and remain among other Japanese than to learn English and venture into the wider community. One man put it this way in the late 1930s: "We have 'old heads.'" He placed his hope in his children. "They know how to talk the American language," he said, "and associate more freely with the members of other races."[52]

Because the Issei's ties to the old country were stronger than those of the Nisei, conflict sometimes arose between the two generations. In these instances, the common generational conflict was compounded by cultural conflict. Probably conflict was stronger in Japanese families in which parents held on to the idea of returning to the old country with their children. In such cases parents made greater efforts to raise their children as they would have in Japan. Then, too, movement off the plantations added to the strain between Issei and Nisei. When Misako Yamamoto's family moved to Honolulu in the early 1920s after about fifteen years on a plantation, her parents found it more difficult to keep to Japanese ways as their children developed "thoughts and actions which deviated from the conventional patterns."[53]

To be sure, not all Nisei experienced distinct cultural clashes with their parents. Many who grew up in Honolulu's Japanese communities seldom ventured outside their neighborhoods. Others who grew up in rural Oahu or on neighbor islands had limited contact with European Americans. Nisei who could not recall cultural conflicts with parents said they did not question what their parents told them to do.[54]

Still, for many in Hawaii as on the mainland, friction was real. Both Issei and Nisei spoke grandly of bringing together the best of both cultures, but in fact the process was rocky and difficult for both generations. The Issei saw with dismay that their children were becoming strangers to them, behaving poorly, filling their heads with appalling ideas, and becoming increasingly difficult to control. The Nisei, on the other hand, found their parents constricting and old-fashioned.[55]

Japanese leaders sought to understand and alleviate the problem. In February 1921, Issei leaders invited selected Nisei to a dinner to improve communication between the two generations. Referring to the dinner, an editorial in *Nippu Jiji* said the relationship had been distant, that the older generation worried that the Nisei were disregarding valuable aspects of their parents' civilization while embracing the "bad points of the new civilization." Three years later the Thursday Luncheon Club, composed of Issei business and professional men, invited an equal number of Nisei to a luncheon. The group discussed issues separating the generations and agreed that "closer contact" would "aid to bridge the gap." They agreed to hold monthly meetings to discuss mutual problems.[56]

One subject that caused considerable disagreement between the generations was the roles of husbands and wives. The Nisei rejected their parents' view that the father was the "lord of the house." Reversing that outlook, one Nisei declared that the "woman should be the boss of the family," since she "stay[ed] at home and [knew] all about home affairs." American notions of assertiveness sometimes led Nisei to disagree openly with their parents. "Once I stayed for about one month with my parents and this was a most heart-breaking time for my mother," recalled a University of Hawaii student. "She tried to make me happy, but my father and I were always quarreling over some matter. . . . We came to blows over many questions, especially over the place of women. As a result my mother got the worst of these clashes with my father for she was blamed for bringing up such a naughty boy."[57]

While other Nisei avoided open clashes with their parents, they nevertheless sought to influence changes at home. One Nisei told of the role she and her siblings played in bringing about these changes. "In a Japanese home," wrote Misako Yamamoto in 1938, "the mother . . . is considered a servant to her husband. . . . [But] more and more, mother is considered on an equal level with father. That is the position we children have given her and in most instances she seems to have the last word, just like an American woman!" Sometimes Issei men objected angrily to the erosion of patriarchal authority. "Everything is upside down and inside out in Hawaii," an indignant man declared in the late 1930s. "Here in Hawaii women tell their husbands what to do and not to do; they 'boss' their husbands. . . . In Japan a wife waits for her husband's return no matter how late it might be. But here in Hawaii when he comes home late he finds his wife sound asleep. It's disgusting!" Other Issei men acquiesced to their changing roles. "My father is no longer a 'commander' or a 'dictator,'" noted a Nisei in the late 1930s. "My mother has influenced him a great deal. For example, in the past my father used to invite his friends regardless of whether mother liked them or not. But now whenever he makes a list of guests he submits it for mother's approval, and he is quite apt to leave out those whom my mother dislikes." The Nisei added, "[My father] used to say that he and his wife were to choose my brothers' wives. But today . . . he has discarded such an idea and says that it is up to my brothers."[58]

The disintegration of patriarchal authority was part of a larger breakdown of Issei ideas of family life and its cornerstone, filial piety. The concepts of ancestor worship and *sosen* (forefathers) carried slight significance for Nisei who knew little about their families' genealogies. "My parents talk about our family, our family's pride, and our family's name," explained a Nisei in the late 1930s. "They say that we must study hard and do good work in school, otherwise we disgrace our family name; they say, too, that we must be very careful to whom we get married, otherwise we smear dirt on our forefathers' faces. But, we second generation know that what they say is all bunk."[59]

The Issei believed that parents should sacrifice for their children, and the children in turn were expected to appreciate that sacrifice, obey their parents, and make them happy. But the Nisei rejected absolute adherence to the implications of this concept. A high school girl in the late 1940s said, "Once in a while I talk to my mother, but we always argue. . . . She always telling me that she wants me to be just like the girls in Japan." "Sometimes I wonder why I work," mused a son, also in the late 1940s. "All I do is bring home the pay envelope and leave it with my father. . . . I don't know what's going to happen when I want to get married and can't afford to give them everything. When I say something like this I feel bad because I know I should support my parents. But I can't help wondering how the haoles manage so that their children don't have to be tied down to the family all the time."[60]

An editorial in *Nippu Jiji* deplored the "serious domestic problem" of two generations living in the same household. While the daughter-in-law wanted to run the household in the American way, the mother-in-law wanted it run in the Japanese way. An Issei woman described her situation in the 1930s. "My eldest son," she lamented, "is not at all like the young men born in Japan. He lets his wife run our house very much to her own liking. . . . Instead of my being the important person in the management of our home, his wife is the boss. Although I am in the early fifties I still go out in the field and earn money to meet the family expenses," complained the woman. "This sort of thing is not done in Japan. As soon as a son marries, his mother retires, and the young wife does most of the hard work in and out of the home."[61]

"The children of Hawaii don't seem to show any respect for age, especially toward us parents," protested a father in the late 1930s. "We tell them that to the older people, to their teachers, and to their own parents they must show respect by bowing, by using proper honorifics and by being always obedient and humble before them. But they think everybody is the same and equal." Instead of children obeying parents, the man continued, the opposite occurred. "Our children ought to know how much we really sacrificed for them," he said. "But yet, they are frequently disobedient and rebellious."[62]

"It is so very hard to make my children understand what I mean by 'duty,' 'respect,' and 'obedience,'" lamented a mother in the late 1930s. "It is just like talking to horse's ears. I cannot talk to my daughter heart-to-heart. There is some barrier which stops us from being mutually sympathetic." When the woman wanted to talk to her daughter about the "duty of woman as a wife to her husband and in-laws," her daughter refused to listen. Another mother in the late 1930s described her predicament: "I feel like a chicken that has hatched duck's eggs."[63]

Although the Japanese were eager to see the Nisei combine the best of Japanese and American cultures, they often found the process strained. Seeing their lives naturally affected by their children's American behaviors, Issei realized they were losing cultural practices they once held dear. At the same time Nisei often found their role of bridging the two cultures painful.

One Japanese practice that clearly conflicted with American custom was the way in which marriage partners were selected. In the Issei view of marriage, love was unimportant. According to this view, marriage was a family affair, not an individual one; therefore parents chose marriage partners for their children.[64]

Some Nisei accepted this arrangement. Tsuruyo Kimura did not know the man she agreed to marry. When the go-between approached her in 1925, she was seventeen years old. At first she said she was not interested, but she finally agreed "to please [her] father." Similarly, Yosoto Egami had planned to get a job in Honolulu in 1934, but his parents convinced him instead to marry and remain in Kona on the island of Hawaii to farm coffee on land they owned. Egami did not know his bride before the wedding; his parents and the go-between handled all arrangements. Mrs. C's parents also arranged, with the help of a go-between, the marriages of their ten children. Her father insisted on marriage-mates whose parents came from Fukuoka, Japan. Having come from that prefecture, he could more easily investigate their families' histories.[65]

Other Nisei, high school and college educated and writing in the late 1920s, demonstrated exposure to American ways when they rejected this practice. "My idea of marriage is to marry whom I love and choose by myself," declared a Hilo High School boy. A university student wrote that she found "the Japanese method of match-making . . . extremely unattractive." She vowed she would never submit to her parents' wishes if they tried to force a marriage partner on her. "I sometimes feel like crying, at other times like laughing, and still at other times . . . like giving [my parents] a piece of my mind," wrote a Kauai boy attending

McKinley High School. "I tell them that they have no right in deciding my future but they insist that these marriages has [*sic*] in most cases been successful." Another boy was more forceful. "Will I . . . accept my parents' choice of my life mate? Categorically, no!" he wrote. "I cannot afford to sacrifice my happiness at the expense of upholding traditional customs. . . . I hold my liberty, my independence, more sacred."[66]

Besides wanting to choose marriage partners for their children, Issei from the main islands of Japan had a hierarchy of preferences in potential mates. Those whose family came from the same home village or neighboring villages took first preference, followed by those from the same prefecture, and then by those from the main islands of Japan. The Nisei were not as particular, but generally did agree that it was best to marry someone of Japanese descent. In this way they showed how culture persisted.[67]

Japanese were much less likely to 'marry out' than other groups in Hawaii. Even in the territory's multicultural setting the Issei's propensity to 'marry in' was extraordinarily high. Between 1912 and 1916, Issei men and women outmarried at the rate of 0.5 and 0.2 percent. In contrast, outmarriage percentages for men and women of other groups during that same period were 19 and 40 for Hawaiians, 52 and 66 for Part-Hawaiians, 17 and 12 for Caucasians, 42 and 6 for Chinese, 26 and 0 for Koreans, and 22 and 3 for Filipinos. While Japanese immigrant men, like the Chinese who came earlier and the Koreans and Filipinos who came later, far outnumbered women of their ethnic group, Japanese men tended to reject the idea of marrying women of other ethnic groups. Instead they arranged to marry women back home through the system of picture bride marriages.[68]

Exogamous rates in Hawaii for Nisei men and women were eight and thirty times higher than for Issei men and women. Yet compared to other groups these rates were low. In the 1930s, only 4.3 percent of Nisei grooms and 6.3 percent of Nisei brides outmarried. In contrast, outmarriage percentages in that decade were 55 and 63 for Hawaiian men and women, 28 for Chinese men and women, 24 and 39 for Korean men and women, and 38 and 4 for Filipino men and women.[69]

Although Hawaii's racial climate was more relaxed and intermarriage more common than on the mainland, outmarriage rates of Hawaii's Japanese were slightly lower than those of mainland Japanese. The historian Paul R. Spickard has suggested that the Japanese in Hawaii maintained more cohesive communities that enforced marital customs more effectively.[70]

Several hypotheses have been proposed to explain differences in intermarriage rates. According to one, the larger the group the lower the rate of outmarriage. This thesis seems to explain the low outmarriage rates of the Issei and Nisei, but as Akemi Kikumura and Harry H. L. Kitano point out, it does not explain the higher outmarriage rates of the Sansei (third generation Japanese Americans). Hawaii, with a Japanese population of 217,307 in 1970, and Fresno, California, with a much smaller population of 6,207 that year, had similar outmarriage rates. Another hypothesis states that an unbalanced sex ratio leads to outmarriage. While this seems to explain the outmarriage rates of several groups, it fails to explain the Japanese pattern. The Issei had an unbalanced sex ratio but chose picture bride marriages over intermarriage. On the other hand both Nisei and Sansei had balanced sex ratios but the Sansei outmarried at considerably higher rates than the Nisei. According to a third hypothesis, held by Kikumura and Kitano, outmarriage increases with each succeeding generation because of increased acculturation. The Sansei, more acculturated than the Nisei, intermarried more frequently. Combining these elements, Spickard has argued that "the images that one group has of another and of itself" interacted with generation, ethnic concentration, class, and individual choice to shape intermarriage patterns.[71]

Clearly the Issei more than the Nisei held strong views against outmarriage. One irate father took his seventeen-year-old daughter to the Detention Home in Honolulu in the late 1930s because she told him she was going to marry a Portuguese man. Another seventeen-year-old girl, noted in court records, was pregnant by her twenty-one-year-old Chinese boyfriend, but her parents refused to let her marry because the boy was not Japanese.[72]

Why did the Issei oppose intermarriage? One reason was simply racism, the Japanese belief in their inherent superiority. "We do not favor intermarriage," wrote *Nippu Jiji* editor Yasutaro Soga in 1926, "with those whose racial stock does not measure up with that of the Japanese." Two years later he softened his words, but he still assumed all Nisei preferred marrying their own kind. "We are not opposed to intermarriage," he wrote. "As a matter of fact, we sympathize with those [Nisei] who intermarry because they cannot find spouses of their own race."[73]

Some Issei felt it important to maintain the Japanese family system. "My son is not going to marry a Haole, a Chinese or a member of any other race," declared an Issei father in the 1920s. "He is the only son in the family and it is expected that he should take our family name. Can a 'happa' (a person of mixed blood) take the name Tokunaga and be the head of the Tokunaga family? 'Happa' is not worthy of such an honourable position in a Japanese family." Another Issei in the 1920s explained,

"We Japanese expect lots from our children even after our children are married. Japanese parents expect to live with their children after they grow old. Every worthy child of a good Japanese family know [*sic*] that they must be loyal to their parents, as long as they live. But how can such an ideal be kept should my children marry other races?"[74]

Some Issei believed cultural affinity made for better marriages. "I am well convinced that marriage with members of other races always ends in divorce," said an Issei parent in the 1920s. "See, Mr. A, a dentist, Mr. B, a doctor, returned from the mainland with Haole wives. How long do you think they lived together? Everyone of them had separated after a year or two," declared the Issei. "You can't expect to be happy with a Haole woman or a Portugese woman because our culture, our modes of living, our philosophy are not the same as theirs."[75]

Japanese communities used powerful social pressure to prevent deviation. "My parents were strongly against my marriage," recalled a young woman in the 1940s. "Especially my father. He had always been somewhat of a leader among the Japanese in the community, and felt I had disgraced the family by marrying a soldier." A high school student in the 1940s recalled his sister's marriage to a Hawaiian-Puerto Rican man. "She ask my father if she could marry," related the boy, "and my father said, 'No.'. . . My father was shame because he neva like his old friends to say funny kind things," the boy explained. "I think he find it hard, for the neighbors going do plenty talking."[76]

Community pressure was especially strong in rural areas. During the war a young Nisei woman married a haole soldier in Honolulu. Her parents' farming neighbors in rural Kauai criticized them endlessly "for letting such a marriage take place." After the war the young couple and their child visited her family, who lived in a dilapidated house. When the neighbors learned of the visit, they wondered, "How is he going to regard his wife after learning that she comes from such surroundings?" But the haole husband did not react as expected. Instead he helped on the farm and got along well with his in-laws. This surprised the neighbors, who then said, "How lucky his wife is, her husband is so nice."[77]

Because of parental and social pressures, as well as belief in cultural compatibility, the Nisei preferred marrying "Hawaiian-born member[s] of [their] own race." "I prefer Japanese because . . . our tastes and ways of living would be similar," wrote a University of Hawaii student in 1940. Another said, "I want to marry a Japanese girl, not because I really want to, but because of filial piety." Still another: "It would be unwise to marry outside of my group since neither my parents, their friends, many of my own Japanese friends, nor the people of the community where I live, are ready for it." The tendency to marry within their own group set the Nisei apart from the rest of the population and showed how they were bound to their culture.[78]

Sometimes the Nisei could be the strongest critics of intermarriage. When one of Emi Yoshizawa's sisters wanted to marry a non-Japanese man in the 1930s, her oldest sister remarked, "I never saw such a thing in my life. She's always been the sneaky type anyway. You would never think this would happen in our family, of all the families! I bet those people are making fun of us. Imagine father's position when he has been trying to prevent intermarriages in other families; why they'll snicker and say 'How about your own daughter?' " Her eldest brother surprisingly broke down in sobs, saying, "The fool, I am not going to work tomorrow. I can't face my friends." A young woman who married a Caucasian during the war recalled, "My mother objected very much. My father was not living. She was concerned for my happiness, but the strongest argument was the shame that would come to the family." The young woman continued, "Even the night before the wedding, my older sister tried to talk me out of taking the step. My older brother, taking the role of the head of the family, told me, 'You need not expect to come home if you marry him.' . . . My younger brother who was seventeen then, was the most violent in opposing the marriage. He even struck me." For several months after the woman's marriage she had no contact with her family, until one day her mother came to visit. "My husband couldn't speak Japanese and my mother couldn't speak English, so the first meeting was strained for all three of us," the woman said:

> But it broke the ice and since then our relations became gradually better and better and we now visit our family and they visit us. My younger brother is now in the Army on the mainland and our relations haven't had a chance to improve but I sent him a Christmas present this year after I asked my husband about it. My older brother's attitude has changed for the better, but my sister is still cool to us. Whenever we visit my mother's home and my sister and her husband and their children are there, they would leave right away. My sister speaks to me but is usually cool. We used to be very close.[79]

The degree to which individual Issei had acculturated was crucial in the extent of their openness to their children's marriage to Caucasians. Christian Issei, having had good relationships with missionaries in Japan and being more familiar with Western ways, were more open. Aiko Tokimasa Reinecke's father, a Methodist minister, did not object when a Caucasian began courting his daughter in the late 1920s. "My parents suspected his motive," she recalled, "since he was coming to see me so often." She explained their attitude: "Having been Christians, they had had broader contacts, so they did not object to my *haole* suitor." Her brother also married a Caucasian. Another Nisei woman, a librarian who married a Caucasian in 1948, said, "I think [my mother] is different from the typical Japanese parent in Hawaii. You might say she is more Americanized and she could see that decisions are up to the individual concerned." As ties to old-world practices loosened and as American ideas entered their world view, the Japanese in Hawaii became more open to intermarriage.[80]

But ties to the old world loosened slowly. In aspects of Nisei life in which Japanese and American values concurred, as in the schooling of males, Nisei acculturation was substantial. On the other hand, where there was cultural incompatiblity, as in their personality structure, conflict within Nisei individuals resulted. In such instances Nisei found themselves marginal members of two worlds that tugged at them.

The Japanese sense of themselves as a people and their cohesive communities helped sustain old-world practices, to the displeasure of Americanizers. Thus Nisei tended to keep their Japanese given names, especially in their youth, and tended to reject intermarriage. At the same time, the Nisei maintained low rates of juvenile delinquency, which accorded well with the Americanization agenda.

That acculturation was clearly taking place, more easily among the Nisei than among their Issei parents, could be seen in conflicts between the two generations over the social lives of the Nisei, the selection of their marriage partners, and the roles of fathers, mothers, and children. Although painful, these conflicts were an inevitable part of the acculturation process and demonstrated the extent to which the Nisei were becoming integrated into American life. By 1940 these children of immigrants had achieved moderate but significant social acculturation.

Chapter 9

Cultural Changes

The Japanese in Hawaii came from a heritage that exalted them as a people superior to all others. Even when Japan encountered the technologically more advanced West, the Japanese still believed themselves better because of their spiritual culture. This sentiment was illustrated by a *Nippu Jiji* editorial, written when two Nisei won first and second places in a 1927 territory-wide essay contest for public and private high school students. "We are proud," declared the editorial. "Other recent contests of a similar nature have shown Japanese students superior to students of other races."[1]

Part of this self-perception derived from ideas of skin color, ideas the Japanese had formed long before contact with Westerners. Japanese saw themselves as white-skinned, which they considered beautiful; they viewed black skin as ugly. Interestingly, upon meeting Westerners, Japanese took little notice of the foreigners' skin color, but were more impressed with their height, hair color, hairiness, big eyes, and big noses.[2]

In a 1930 study of racial attitudes among Japanese in Hawaii, the sociologist Jitsuichi Masuoka found that the Issei felt friendliest toward Caucasians, followed by Chinese, and then Hawaiians. Negative feelings were expressed toward Portuguese, Filipinos, and Puerto Ricans. Nisei, on the other hand, felt friendliest toward Chinese, followed by Caucasians. Masuoka speculated that this difference signaled a reduced "hero-worshipping" attitude toward those holding the highest socioeconomic status. Nisei attending the University of Hawaii responded similarly in 1940. After Japanese they ranked Chinese and then Caucasians as desirable marriage mates. Last on the list were Portuguese, Filipinos, and Puerto Ricans. In this regard ideas from the Nisei's cultural heritage merged with views rooted in the Islands' class-based society. Caucasians and Chinese had lighter skins and were at the top of the socioeconomic ladder. Portuguese, on the other hand, although light-skinned, were less economically successful.[3]

Like their parents and befitting their plantation environment, Nisei generally rejected individuals of poor, dark-skinned groups. "I hate the

Filipinos," wrote a Lahainaluna High School girl, "because they cannot be trusted and they sometimes are very untidy in their habits." A McKinley High School student admitted that her negative feelings toward Filipinos were based on "gossips." "Whenever I see a Filipino," she wrote, "I always hasten my steps. This I do unconsciously. However, there have been one or two Filipino classmates. Toward them, I do not feel as I do toward the others. Somehow, working and striving together, besides enjoying and cooperating, have made them different." During the late 1960s Frederick Samuels found continued sensitivity among Nisei toward darker out-groups such as Hawaiians, Filipinos, Puerto Ricans, and blacks. "I have one son in Germany," said a Nisei housewife living in the upper-middle-class district of Manoa. "I don't care if he brings home a Haole girl as long as she is a good girl. My husband said: 'It's okay if you marry a redhead, but not colored.' "[4]

Personal experiences helped shape racial attitudes, which sometimes became a defense against goading. A McKinley High School boy wrote in 1927 that he became aware of "racial groups" and began to dislike the Portuguese during baseball season the year before when Portuguese students from St. Louis College (a Catholic high school) called his school "Tokio High," its band the "Japanese Navy," and made fun of his team because it was composed mostly of Japanese players. Another Nisei in 1927 reacted to being called "Yellow Belly" and "Jap" by telling himself, "Most of the ones that did call me names were Portuguese or Spanish and I classed them as inferior to us mentally, morally, and spiritually." Obviously, dislike of out-groups was not a one-sided affair.[5]

Indeed, Japanese prejudice toward others mirrored the prejudice they encountered in Hawaii, prejudice often nurtured at an early age. "Sometimes when I saw these Japanese children playing," wrote a Portuguese girl recalling the early 1920s, "I longed to play with them but was afraid to be seen playing with Japanese children. And I knew that my mother would scold me if I played with these children." By the time she was a student at Maui High School, her racial views had hardened. She "despised" Hawaiians because "they were so dark." "I despise Filipinos and Porto [sic] Ricans," she added, "and I feel rather proud for I have not spoken to any yet. I have always associated with people of the white race."[6]

"The Jap (that is all the respect I have for them) is essentially a copier," wrote a haole boy attending St. Louis College in 1927. Reflecting his parents' views, he continued, "He will work with you till he learns your trade. He then goes into business for himself and cuts his prices so low that a white man has to work at a loss. A Jap can live much cheaper than a white man. And besides this, a Jap can never equal a white man in quality of work." A haole girl attending McKinley High School that year complained of the preponderance of Japanese students at her school. "The consequence of this is that Japanese run our student body government," she wrote. "The majority of these officers are not capable of holding such offices because they cannot talk good English." "I think I should like to go to a college on the American mainland," wrote a haole girl at Hilo High School, "because if I went there I wouldn't have to mingle with the kind of people (Orientals) like here. I don't mind going around with the part-Hawaiians and a few exceptional Portuguese," the girl continued, "but with the Oriental—I cannot hear it. No experience led me to dislike the Japs and Chinks, but I think all the Whites had a tendency to dislike them." Obviously she did not like being in the minority. In 1927, 7 percent of 536 students attending Hilo High were Caucasians, while 58 percent were Japanese.[7]

Despite this prejudice, Caucasians in Hawaii were less overtly hostile to the Japanese than Caucasians on the West Coast. Visitors from California to Hawaii remarked at the contrast in racial atmospheres between the two places. Hawaii Nisei related bitter experiences on the mainland, experiences they had not known in Hawaii. Joseph Y. Kurihara, who moved from Hawaii to Sacramento, California, in 1915 to pursue his education, recalled being constantly called a "Jap," being kicked, and having rocks thrown at him, in contrast to his experiences in Hawaii. Another college student from Hawaii recalled an experience in San Francisco in the late 1920s. "I went to a barber to get my hair trimmed," the young man said, "and on entering the shop, one of the barbers approached me and asked my nationality. I answered that I was Japanese. As soon as he heard that I was of the yellow race, he drove me out of the place as if he were driving away a cat or a dog. I never felt so cheap as when I was treated this way by this animal who wore the face of a man." Common to West Coast Japanese was the experience of a California Nisei girl in the 1930s. "Oftentimes I would be greeted by such complimentary appellations as 'Jap,' 'skibee,' 'Chink,' and 'yellow dog,' and some bold rascal would even fling stones at me," she said. "These thoughtless cruelties, which were like knife stabs into my heart, especially painful because of my extreme timidity and sensitiveness, made me shrink from walking along the street alone. At times, I would be filled with hatred against America and Americans."[8]

Hawaii maintained a more tolerant racial atmosphere than the West Coast for a number of reasons. For one thing the size and composition of the European American population differed in the two places. While Caucasians constituted only 6 to 8 percent of Hawaii's population during the first quarter of the century, they made up as much as 95 percent of the population on the West Coast. And while most West Coast European Americans were of the middle or working class, a large portion of the haole population in Hawaii was in the upper socioeconomic strata. The Japanese did not pose an economic threat to them. Those Hawaii Caucasians—carpenters, mechanics, shopkeepers, and clerks—who did encounter Japanese competitors were too few to oppose them effectively. Also, due to Hawaii's limited land area, Japanese in Hawaii lived much closer geographically to European Americans and other groups than did Japanese on the West Coast. This made Hawaii's residents more aware of the necessity of getting along with each other. Then, too, the larger percentage of Japanese in Hawaii made interacting with them almost inevitable, and frequent interaction probably increased understanding and tolerance.[9]

Yet the difference in racial climate between Hawaii and the West Coast was one of degree rather than kind. White supremacy was assumed among European Americans in both places. Even Joseph Lightfoot, the brilliant lawyer in Hawaii who represented the Japanese in a number of court cases—including those involving a sugar strike in 1909 and the language schools in the 1920s—harbored such an attitude. He objected vociferously in 1911 when he found out that his daughter's seventh grade public school teacher was of Japanese descent. "One of the most damnable outrages I have ever heard of in Hawaii," he declared. "A Japanese teaching white children in the schools! . . . I don't care how qualified the girl may be, she is a Jap, and no Jap can be properly qualified to teach white children. The Japanese fifty years ago were barbarians, and our civilization is the growth of a thousand years."[10]

Yet Hawaii's prevailing racial atmosphere was more tolerant than such an outburst suggests. As mentioned earlier, increased contact helped soften racial attitudes. A Hawaiian-Chinese boy in 1927 said he hated the Japanese until he entered Mid-Pacific Institute. "I came in contact with the nation I once hated," the boy wrote. "The Japanese are nice people and I began to love them and treat them like my Hawaiian brothers." A Normal School girl whose father was Scotch-English and whose mother was English-Hawaiian said she grew up in the 1910s with the idea that she was "superior" to all who "were not haole, Hawaiian, or Hawaiian-haole." "Especially did I look down on Orientals," she recalled. "I believed that they were brought here as plantation laborers and should stay where they belonged. . . . I am afraid I showed all too plainly my attitude because all of the Oriental girls detested me." During this girl's senior year in high school, her grandmother, who had been taking care of her, died, forcing her to find work in order to make ends meet. She found a summer job in a pineapple cannery, where her fellow workers were "mostly Korean and Japanese women who could hardly speak English."

"I had plenty of time to think," she said. "One night as we were working overtime, I caught myself thinking of my past life. All of the mean things the girls had said of me in boarding school came back. I began to see myself in a different light, in the way the Oriental girls must have seen me. These were very upsetting thoughts." After much thinking, the girl decided to change her behavior. "Here in the cannery would be an ideal place to solve a few things for myself," she decided. "The next morning I began to talk to my neighbors. I don't blame them for being surprised. It was hard work talking to one another but with 'pidgin' English and many gestures we managed to exchange ideas. They began to teach me little tricks of packing so that I did better work. I began to like these women." As the girl was placed in a variety of jobs at the cannery, she came in contact with different people. "Many could speak fairly good English and from these I got a good deal," she reminisced. "I questioned them on many of their queer customs and ways of thinking and after they had explained some of these things to me I had to admit that seen from their point of view these queer ideas were really logical." At the end of summer she left the cannery to enter Normal School where she befriended and came to respect and admire students "of many nationalities."[11]

Ironically, Japanese racism served to counter the racism they faced in Hawaii. The Japanese sense of superiority helped them maintain pride in themselves in the face of discrimination and intolerance and helped them overcome many difficulties. Japanese prejudice was directed not only at out-groups but also at minorities within their own group. As previously noted, traditional Japanese society was hierarchical. At the bottom were the *eta*, Japan's hereditary outcasts, whose occupations dealt with animal slaughter and disposal of the dead. Physically indistinguishable from other Japanese, they nevertheless suffered visceral rejection from them. As part of its modernizing efforts, the Meiji government in 1871 abolished the eta classification, but de facto discrimination continued. Hiding one's origins was difficult in a society with scrupulously maintained family records, which go-betweens carefully checked when undertaking marriage arrangements.

Even in Hawaii and on the mainland, it was difficult for eta or *burakumin*, as they were later called, to pass undetected. As late as 1938 a young Nisei couple from Kauai committed suicide by jumping from a steamer in passage from Kauai to Honolulu. The girl was of eta descent, although she did not know it until the subject of marriage came up. *Shinju*, double suicide for love, was traditional in Japan when parents forbade a couple's marriage. Three other cases of shinju are known to have occurred earlier in Hawaii, in 1908, 1913, and 1919. One wonders how many other marriages never took place because one party was found to be of eta descent.[12]

Discrimination against the eta was strong enough for some Nisei to protest actively against it. In 1930 Mamoru Okamura of Kauai wrote a pamphlet, "Let Us Eradicate Traditional Evils," in which he declared himself an eta and urged other Japanese to end their prejudice and discrimination against this group. One of Okamura's friends, Kijiro Ogata, joined his effort after Ogata's younger brother was accidently electrocuted at work. Ogata decided that the only way he could console himself after that tragedy was to work wholeheartedly for an important cause. Using volunteer contributions, he had fifteen thousand copies of Okamura's pamphlet printed, and took a six-month leave from his job to travel through the territory to distribute the pamphlets and speak against social prejudice. "On Kauai, discrimination against eta families seems to be exceedingly strong," Ogata said. "Parents will not consent to the marriage of their sons or daughters with those of Eta families. And it has been the cause of much unhappiness for years." Yasutaro Soga of *Nippu Jiji* pointed out the dimensions of the problems Ogata addressed. "As a rule the Japanese are a haughty people," Soga wrote in 1930. "When discriminated against racially . . . they consider it a lasting disgrace, and yet there are many among them who themselves discriminate against the Eta class."[13]

Also discriminated against by fellow Japanese in Hawaii, though to a lesser degree, were Okinawans. The first shipload of Okinawans arrived in Hawaii in 1900, fifteen years after the first *Naichi,* those from Japan proper.[14]

Geographically distant from the rest of Japan, the islands of Okinawa had maintained stronger or weaker ties to the main islands over the centuries, depending on the strength of the Japanese central government. During the Meiji era Okinawa was incorporated as a prefecture of Japan. Although Okinawans were ethnically Japanese, differences in language and culture led the dominant Naichi to relegate Okinawans to a position as second-class citizens. Moreover, the Meiji government taxed the people of Okinawa more heavily than it did those of other prefectures, without compensating benefits.[15]

In Hawaii, Okinawan immigrants, who used the term *Uchinanchu* to distinguish themselves from the Naichi, constituted about 14 percent of all Issei. Like their counterparts in Japan, the Naichi in Hawaii discriminated against the Uchinanchu. Naichi parents strongly objected to their children's marriage to Uchinanchu, and Nisei Uchinanchu were the brunt of name-calling, teasing, and unkind remarks by Nisei Naichi.

Just as Caucasians looked down on Japanese, so Naichi looked down on Okinawans. Few Naichi reflected on the irony of their behavior, behavior they resented when directed at them.[16]

Thoughtless remarks could be hurtful. "One day in elementary school," said a Naichi student recalling the 1930s, "a group of girls got together and somehow, someone introduced a subject related to the Okinawans. I wasn't familiar with the term so naturally I inquired, 'What is Okinawan?' Most of the girls suddenly turned to me with surprised expressions on their faces. 'Don't you know? They're the lowest class of Japanese,' one of the girls replied. During this little 'shock' I observed that one of the girls was extremely quiet. She seemed as though she wanted to avoid everyone and fixed her attention on some other subject. Later I learned that she was an Okinawan." Such incidents made Okinawans hypersensitive to criticism. "When mother played native records on the phonograph," a Nisei Uchinanchu said of the late 1930s, "the rest of the family would be concerned over whether they could be heard by nearby Naichi families. My sister would close the lid of the phonograph and adjust the volume to be heard only in our home."[17]

Because some Okinawans raised pigs, Naichi children teased them, "Okinawa *ken ken, buta kau kau.*" (*Ken* means prefecture; *buta* means pig; *kau kau* means food.) The Naichi rarely ate pork, which they thought unclean. And the work of collecting "pigslop" from homes was dirty and smelly. So the tease meant that since Okinawans raised pigs and ate pork, they were unclean. Philip K. Ige, who later became an administrator at the Hawaii Department of Education and the University of Hawaii, recalled that although he got along with the Naichi and was not teased, he "couldn't get rid of a feeling of shame deep inside" because his family raised pigs and he collected pigslop in the neighborhoods of Honolulu. "I knew that at any time in the classroom, on the playground, or anywhere in Honolulu," he said, "someone knowing who we were and what we did could make some nasty or embarrassing comment about us." Such incidents happened from time to time. When he was a ninth grader in the late 1930s, Ige happened to overhear two classmates snicker about Okinawans. One of them was his friend, an outstanding student, who became embarrassed when he realized that Ige had heard them. "I admired this classmate for his brains, good looks, sense of humor, popularity, and speaking and writing abilities," recalled Ige. "He wrote an essay on 'What America Means to Me,' which won a Territory of Hawaii award and a national commendation. I could not believe that anyone who wrote so eloquently about the meaning of America and democracy, about freedom and individual rights, about racial equality and the dignity of man, about white discrimination against black people in America could look down upon Okinawans in Hawaii."[18]

The Uchinanchu's own sense of pride in themselves helped them succeed in school and at work. In time, especially as they experienced success in their business enterprises during and after World War II, they saw Naichi attitudes soften.[19]

As the foregoing shows, the Japanese came from a status-conscious culture. This background enabled them to adapt rather easily to the class-driven society they encountered in Hawaii. Moreover, their sense of superiority motivated them to seek a place at the upper levels of this society. In this context Japanese attitudes toward the haole were more ambivalent than their views of any other group in Hawaii.

Some Nisei felt hurt by haole rejection of them. "Most of my Haole friends are friends in school only," wrote a Hilo High School boy in 1927. "They hardly know me once I leave the school grounds." A young woman recalled a remark made in the early 1920s by a Caucasian classmate whom she had admired. "That remark," said the Nisei, "trifling though it may have been to her, was so cruel that I cried over it that night and hated her for one whole year. We were having sewing in our class. It happened that the pupils . . . were all English-speaking except three Japanese girls, one of whom was I. While we were sewing this certain American girl flung her head back and said, 'I wouldn't know what I'd do if I were a Japanese. I hate them!' Those words stung me, especially because I thought she was a very sweet and decent girl. . . . For a moment, how I wished I was a Haole. I was both very angry and sad, but I was helpless."[20]

Some Nisei resented haole feelings of superiority. "People living in the country districts usually do not have a kindly feeling toward the haoles represented in those districts by the Plantation officials, lunas, and office workers," explained a young man who grew up on the plantation during the first two decades of the twentieth century. "These Haoles live in a 'clique' apart from the peoples of other races." "The *haoles* feel their skins are white and that they are superior to the Japanese," wrote a high school girl in 1927. "Why harbor such ideas? God created us equal."[21]

Sometimes meeting other Caucasians turned negative attitudes to positive ones. "Up to a few years ago I hated Haoles," wrote a planation youth in 1927. "The cause was the way in which Haoles at the plantation acted. They treated the laborers like a machine." Once he left the plantation, however, he found that Caucasians were "just as human as any other race." In fact, after "mingling with many Haole boys," he considered them "the most sociable group."[22]

As late as the 1960s, a Nisei described a common reaction among Japanese. He said that many were "afraid to associate with Haoles. It [was] not so much being clannish, but being afraid of Haoles." A Japanese language school principal in the 1920s explained, "I go away whenever I see a white man approaching me, because I don't speak good English."[23]

Others welcomed the friendship of haoles. A high school Nisei wrote in 1927 of a haole friend he had in Hilo. "He is the only white boy who is so close a friend of mine. In [Honokaa]," the Nisei explained, "there is no chance of associating with Haole boys for the idea out here is that they think they are far superior." A sensitive young man said in the 1920s, "I like to get acquainted with Haoles but I am not at all sure that they would want a Japanese for their friend." Some Issei parents went to extremes to have their children socialize with Caucasians. A McKinley High School Nisei who grew up in Honolulu recalled playing solely with haole children in the neighborhood. "I do not know why," she said, "but my parents did not wish me to play and mingle with the Japanese children of our immediate neighborhood."[24]

Some Nisei saw Caucasians as human beings, no better or worse than others. "So far I can say that they are just like us," observed a young woman who worked as a maid for haole families. "They have certain petty feelings toward other nationalities at times and consider them as inferior people."[25]

Some Nisei remembered pleasant experiences with Caucasians. A McKinley High School girl described her fourth grade teacher in 1910 as a "white friend who became very dear" to her. An honor student recalled with pride that the haole principal of Royal Grammar School called her into his office when she graduated in 1925 to encourage her to keep up her good work. A Hilo High School student who worked as a maid in the 1920s developed a warm relationship with her employers. "Captain Reid . . . and his wife were very nice and good to me," she said. "I took them as my parents while they took me as their daughter even though I was of different nationality." The captain "urged" her to attend Normal School, so during her junior year in high school she decided to become "a teacher instead of a stenographer." A Normal School student in 1927 credited a Caucasian family for her continued education. Being the oldest child, she had quit school to work after the seventh grade, but the family, who lived nearby, convinced her parents to let her continue school. "The mistress of that family was then the principal of the Kilauea School in the neighboring town," the student explained. "She took me to that school in her automobile, together with her four children. . . . After graduating from the eighth grade at Kilauea School, I was very anxious to go to the high school but I was afraid to ask my parents because I knew that they could not afford to send me. . . . Fortunately the same English people were so interested in me that they asked my parents to send me to school." She worked as a maid for room and board while attending Kauai High School. After her junior year "the same English people" offered to take her to Honolulu if she agreed to work for them. In Honolulu she attended McKinley High School and then the Normal School.[26]

Despite these positive experiences, the Nisei realized that Caucasians received preferential treatment. "Since America is a country of freedom and equal rights," complained a Hilo High School girl in 1927, "I should think that all people, regardless of races, should be treated equally and fairly. But no! Others have the first chances and privileges."[27]

Such discrimination led some Nisei to wish they were Caucasians. "I used to wonder why some teachers picked on Orientals and praised . . . Caucasians," wrote a Normal School student in 1927, "because I thought Orientals usually did better work. . . . Because of such partiality I wished many a time that I were born Haole." A schoolmate said, "There are more chances and opportunities for a white man than any other. I wish that my physical body be that of a white man but . . . my spirit be Oriental." Another schoolmate said he wanted to be Caucasian so that he would receive better treatment, hold a better job, and "not be called a Jap."[28]

Indeed some Nisei believed Caucasians enjoyed a better life. In the 1920s and 1930s, recalled Marie, "the Caucasians [in Hawaii] were big-shot kind, not the ordinary kind, you know. So they had a better . . . house. And they seemed to have more money." Then she added with a laugh, "To me they were better looking." Others were attracted to the Caucasians' greater freedom from self-restraint. A University of Hawaii student attended a camp in the 1920s in Washington where he frater- nized with "regular American students." Before this trip his contact with Caucasians had been almost nil. In Washington he worked with them, ate with them, and slept under the same roof. He found they "express[ed] themselves rather freely," and were "very easy to get along with." If given the choice, he would choose to be Caucasian, because, he explained, "I think and feel American and not Japanese."[29]

Other Nisei envied the Caucasians' fluency in English. "When I en- tered High School," wrote a girl attending McKinley High in 1926, "I could not speak half as well as the Haoles and I had to study hard to im- prove my English. I sometimes wished that I were a Haole so that I would not have difficulty in speaking English." Many Nisei who envied Cau- casians and wished they were haole were expressing a desire for greater status in the American community. Many used that desire to motivate themselves to persist in school and find jobs that would enable them to enter the middle class.[30]

Although some Nisei said they wished they were haole, they were not necessarily saying they wanted to be carbon copies of the haole. Rather they meant that they wanted the rights and privileges due them as Americans without having to reject their identity as children of Japanese plantation workers. This attitude of the Nisei was reflected in their use of Hawaii Creole English, which Americanizers attempted to eradicate.

Superintendent Willard E. Givens in 1924 called the "English problem" the "most baffling of the academic difficulties" in Hawaii's schools. Agreeing with him, Superintendent Will C. Crawford said in 1927 that the need for "better English" was the schools' most pressing problem. He complained, "The bane of pidgin English [Hawaii Creole English] has eaten deeply into the vitals of our language." As an example, Crawford reported, "A child asks a grocery clerk for 'ten pounds lice, pliss.' "[31]

Americanizers attempted with difficulty to have public school teachers serve as Standard English speaking models for their students. "Hawaii's English problem is unique," noted Benjamin O. Wist, president of the Territorial Normal and Training School. "Inability to hear English sounds correctly, faulty enunciation, a peculiar inflection and the use of certain local idioms are its chief characteristics." Wist continued, "Language is, after all, largely a matter of habit. The high school during its four-year program cannot break down the faulty habits acquired during the previous eight years, nor can the Normal School in two years do what the high school has failed to do in four years, in spite of its greater selection and its efforts during the period of training. The result is elementary teachers who are incapable of developing the proper English habits of our children."[32]

To remedy the situation Wist began a systematic effort in the mid-1920s to test the oral English of aspiring teachers. He required them to give five-minute extemporaneous speeches before a seven member board. Those who passed had no further language examination, but those who failed had to work on their oral English and repeat the examination. Wist reported that in 1925 twenty-four students failed to graduate from the Normal School because of their inability to express themselves in Standard English, and courses in "corrective speech, public speaking, dramatics and parliamentary procedure" were added to the curriculum. The Normal School also developed a test to "measure the speech" of entering students and "eliminate those whose speech habits" were such that the school could not correct them.[33]

Despite these efforts Wist reported little success in 1928. "Students of Japanese ancestry had, as a group, more difficulty with English speech than did others," he wrote. But singling them out sometimes produced negative reactions. A University of Hawaii student who had attended the Normal School in the late 1920s wrote that she had never been aware of her "race" until she attended the school. "Then like a thunderbolt I realized that we were different and that the teachers treated us differently," she said. "We were constantly reminded of our language handicap. . . . Many of us cultivated the inferiority complex." She concluded, "I suppose that was why life at that school was so distasteful."[34]

Hawaii residents have commonly used the term "Pidgin" to refer to the entire spectrum of languages spoken by plantation workers and their descendants. John E. Reinecke, whose seminal study of language use in Hawaii continues to be widely consulted, observed important distinctions within this spectrum. He distinguished between the Pidgin English spoken on the plantation and what linguists today call Hawaii Creole English, an English-based creole influenced by plantation Pidgin and developed by the children of Pidgin-speaking parents. It was this creole language that plantation children brought with them to the public schools.[35]

Pidgin English was "makeshift speech" that evolved on the plantation "as a language of command for the employing Haoles and as a lingua franca among the immigrant nationalities." It was based on the Pidgin Hawaiian that had developed earlier between English-speaking foreigners and native Hawaiians. Partly from this Pidgin English, children of immigrants and native Hawaiians developed an English creole "more adequate and more refined than the makeshift speech of the immigrants." While Pidgin English eventually declined in use, Hawaii Creole English flourished.[36]

According to the 1920 federal survey report, only 2 to 3 percent of all students entering Hawaii's public school at ages six and seven, about one-third to one-half of whom were Japanese, spoke Standard English. Reinecke estimated that in the 1930s, about 15 percent of Hawaii's population, chiefly Caucasians, spoke Standard English; about 45 percent, mainly immigrants, spoke Pidgin English; and about 40 percent, largely descendants of immigrants, spoke Hawaii Creole English. Reinecke observed that the English of plantation children varied according to "their home language, schooling, associations, and ambitions."[37]

Because the Nisei's first language was not Standard English, their first year of school could be traumatic and confusing. "It was not until I went to the haole kindergarten [in 1910]," wrote a Normal School student, "that I found that differences in language existed." The student continued, "I liked my teacher because she was a pretty lady. She smiled and spoke to me. I smiled back at her but I could not understand what she said. I was miserable."[38]

Nisei communicated with their parents in Japanese or a mixture of

Japanese and Pidgin English. Of the 271 Japanese students attending Maui High School in 1930, 97 percent said their parents spoke some form of Japanese to them. Of the 1,837 Japanese youths attending a Honolulu language school in 1937, 95.5 percent said they spoke Japanese or a mixture of Japanese and English to their parents. "Because [my parents] were born in Japan, and do not understand English so well," explained a Honokaa eighth grader in 1933, "I often talk mixed language to them. When I tell them anything that happened in school, or is [sic] making a long speech to them I use half Japanese and half English. When you speak you hardly know that you are talking half English and half Japanese. That is because you are more interested on the thing you are talking about than the kind of English you are speaking. I'd like to talk all Japanese to them, but I am not so good in Japanese." She added, "We have a hard time speaking good English because we do not use them [sic] carefully at home."[39]

Among their peers the Nisei either spoke some level of Japanese or Hawaii Creole English. In the first decade of the twentieth century Japanese was the common language among playmates, but by 1920, Hawaii Creole English dominated. By learning Standard English at school, many became bilingual or trilingual—speaking various levels of Japanese, Hawaii Creole English, and Standard English.[40]

One boy who started school around 1910 recalled that he spoke Japanese with his playmates and read stories in Japanese during his spare time. Yoshitake Takashiba, who began school around 1919 in Kona on the island of Hawaii, grew up speaking a mixture of different Japanese dialects and Hawaii Creole English. Misako Yamamoto recalled the 1920s: "I tried to speak English at home because my teacher told me that if I wanted to be 'smart' in English I had to use it at home." But her parents "put a stop to this" because they could not understand English. So Yamamoto spoke Japanese in their presence and English at other times.[41]

The fact that Standard English was the Nisei's second or third language affected their proficiency in it. Hawaii's junior high school Nisei in 1934 scored over two years below national norms in verbal tests but over two years above those norms in nonverbal tests. In 1937, public high school graduates entering the University of Hawaii, of whom about half were Japanese, took written and oral English tests. The results illustrated dramatically the handicap posed by the students' language backgrounds. While most scored well on the written test, over 40 percent scored poorly in diction and enunciation on the oral test. Reinecke suggested that bilingualism combined with the "students' lack of acquaintance with American culture" to produce such test results.[42]

Students in rural districts had even less exposure to Standard English and American cultural norms than those in urban Honolulu and consequently had greater difficulty with Standard English. Richard Inouye, who grew up on the island of Hawaii, spoke Japanese with his parents and friends. He quit school in 1925 when he finished the sixth grade partly because he spoke little English and "school was hard" for him. Yoshitaka Takashiba, who grew up in the coffee district of Kona in the 1920s, recalled that he "was very poor in speaking English," and as a result his "English schooling was almost . . . zero." A McKinley High School girl who grew up speaking Hawaii Creole English in Koloa, Kauai, was sent by her parents to Kaahumanu School in Honolulu in 1921 to continue her schooling. "I found out that Koloa School was lower in standard than Kaahumanu," she recalled. "I felt as though I didn't know any grammar. I did not read much during my seven years in Koloa School. [After moving to Honolulu] I had to force myself to read newspapers and books. I hated reading because I was not used to it and I could not read fast." In Honolulu she became aware of differences between Hawaii Creole English and Standard English. "Even now when I go home for summer vacation," she said, "my sisters and brothers say 'I been go' [I went] or 'you was.' "[43]

California Nisei also had difficulty mastering English. As in Hawaii, housing patterns among California's Japanese meant de facto segregation for many, and as a result Nisei failed to develop facility in English. At the same time, like their counterparts in Hawaii, few Nisei in California became fluent in Japanese. A 1927 study found that their lack of fluency in English negatively affected their IQ test scores. Like the Nisei in Hawaii, those in California did better in nonlinguistic tests.[44]

Teachers played a major role in the Nisei's language development. Sometimes their influence was negative. One young man attending the Normal School recalled that his eighth grade teacher in 1921 used "sarcasm and made the situation worse." "I was criticized severely," he said, "and this discouraged me in my work. . . . Instead of remedying our defects, which we were well aware of, she made us hate her." But more often teachers encouraged students to improve their Standard English skills. "I would say my first consciousness of Pidgin [Hawaii Creole English] was in the seventh grade [in 1927]," recalled Timmy Hirata, former state superintendent of schools. "We had a teacher who was born in England. One day she told us, 'I hear some of you people speaking in a . . . foreign tongue. I talked with some boys and they said, "You wen stay go?" [Had you gone?] and "I no like" [I don't want it/to]. I can't understand this. Will you teach me?' So we had to explain, and I'm telling you we had the hardest time translating Pidgin to proper English. I could write at grade level but the vocabulary wouldn't come when I had to speak. That teacher put me on the right track." Yoshitaka Takashiba recalled that in the 1920s, his teacher used visual aids to help students speak Standard

English. "We used to draw a tombstone," said Takashiba, "and on the tombstone we write, 'Here lies Ivan Go' and pasted it to the wall. Then when I said 'I been go' . . . [my classmates] said, 'There's the tombstone saying that Ivan Go is dead.' "[45]

Some Nisei demonstrated their intent to adapt to American middle-class norms by consciously attempting to learn Standard English and urging their younger siblings to do likewise. "We were forced to speak English by my brother," a Hilo High School student remembered. "He never answered us if we talked in Japanese." A young woman recalled that as a high school student in the early 1920s she came "in contact with English speaking people." This helped her "immensely," for it was her "utmost desire to be able to speak as fluently as any American." One Nisei recalled in 1927 that he was very conscious of "being poor in English," so that as a ninth grader two years earlier he regularly practiced enunciating English words. A Normal School student boarding at Okumura Girls' Dormitory in the 1920s said, "The girls correct each other's mistakes [in English]." Another Nisei said her teachers and sisters impressed upon her the idea that English was important "in a person's future life as a citizen of the United States." As a result of an older sister's prodding, this Nisei's parents sent her to a private school in the 1920s "to improve in both speaking and writing [English]."[46]

Nevertheless, despite these efforts, Hawaii Creole English remained the primary language of most Nisei. Why did it persist, when lack of fluency in Standard English limited educational and economic success? For most Nisei, Hawaii Creole English functioned as their mother tongue language, "impressed" on them in their "tenderest years" and "most intimate associations." Learning and speaking Standard English with fluency was thus for Nisei no less a challenge than learning a second language would have been for native speakers of English. Yet, as Reinecke suggested, even those Nisei who learned to speak Standard English with ease readily felt "the warmth and intimacy" that came from "using one's childhood dialect within one's own circle, and the stiffness which would result from an attempt to talk 'Haole English' there." "I tried to talk good English," said a girl in the 1930s. "I felt as if I were not a Japanese, but a 'haole,' and felt out of place." A Honokaa Intermediate School girl said in 1934, "Sometimes when I used good English some people say I act as if I know everything or acting fresh." "If we speak good English," explained her classmate, "our friends usually say, 'Oh you're trying to be hybolic [high and mighty], yeah!' " Thus Nisei were ambivalent about speaking Standard English. As Reinecke has argued, to speak Standard English was to proclaim oneself an American and to associate oneself with the dominant haole culture. At the same time it meant "dissociating one's self from one's class and racial group." So Hawaii Creole English, a badge of identity for the Nisei, continued to flourish. It has continued to develop and persist to the present day among Islanders of all ethnic groups, more so in rural areas than in Honolulu.[47]

Buddhism was another source of identity. Its persistence, like the persistence of Hawaii Creole English, demonstrated that the Nisei intended to keep their ethnic identity as they acculturated.

Because Japanese immigrants to Hawaii were Buddhists, Buddhism rather than Christianity spread throughout the Japanese communities dotting the islands of the territory. Unfortunately for Japanese, Americanizers found this unacceptable. In 1917, an article in *Friend*, a publication of the Hawaiian Evangelical Association, accused Buddhists of being "strongly anti-Christian" and therefore "strongly anti-American." Two years later Edward P. Irwin, editor of the *Pacific Commercial Advertiser*, called Buddhism "a religion hostile to our principles," "certain tenets" being "incompatible with the Constitution of the United States." The Congregationalist Reverend Henry P. Judd in 1920 urged his fellow Christians to stop the "repaganization" of Hawaii. "We cannot be complacent and say it is none of our business," he wrote, "for it is our business, this matter of a pagan religion encroaching upon our Christian civilization." Judd concluded, "The only way to Americanize Hawaii is to Christianize her."[48]

Americanizers blamed Buddhist priests for inciting unrest among laborers. Just before Japanese sugar workers went on strike in 1920, *Honolulu Star-Bulletin* declared that the "cloven hoof of Japanese paganism" was "responsible for agitation among the Japanese." Americanizers also accused Buddhist leaders of using language schools to spread their religion. The historian Louise Hunter, whose *Buddhism in Hawaii* is the standard work on the subject, argued that the campaign to dismantle language schools was in reality an effort to end Buddhist influence in the territory.[49]

Americanizers charged that Buddhism "allied itself too closely with the Japanese national life"; "an American Buddhist" was therefore in their eyes "a practical impossibility." While it is true that Honolulu Hongwanji members sent money to Japan during the Russo-Japanese war, and Buddhist temples sponsored victory celebrations and held memorial services for Japanese soldiers at the end of the war in 1905, what they did was typical of other immigrant groups. English, German, Greek, Irish, and other immigrants and their descendants also identified with and rallied to support their motherlands. But while Americanizers criticized support of Japan among Japanese in Hawaii, they accepted Anglo-American admiration and support of England.[50]

Unable to differentiate between Buddhism and the state religion of Shintoism, Americanizers like Superintendent Vaughan MacCaughey accused Buddhism of "Mikado-worship." Buddhist Bishop Yemyo Imamura responded in exasperation to such statements. "It is really a regretful fact to hear such statements so often among the highly educated Americans," he said. "This is the time when people should do away with prejudices so that the community and the nation at large shall have peaceful, harmonious relations." Imamura constantly found himself on the defensive against Americanizers accusing Buddhists of "autocratic or anti-American" tendencies. He repeatedly pointed out how the Hongwanji participated in YMCA citizenship drives, published American documents to encourage Nisei loyalty to the United States, supported Red Cross drives and War Savings Stamp campaigns.[51]

Yet when Bishop Imamura tried to clarify the Buddhist view of autocracy and democracy, his philosophical explanation confused more than enlightened Americanizers. In a pamphlet published in 1918, Imamura said that "if autocracy has no absolute value, neither has democracy," and "autocracy does not unconditionally exclude democracy." Imamura was clearer in a letter to the editor of *Honolulu Star-Bulletin*, in which he said that the definition of democracy given in an April 1918 article in a publication called *Outlook* reflected his views. Democracy, according to the article, was more than a form of government. It was "mutual regard for each other's opinion," and "liberty, equality, fraternity, in the institutions of religion, industry and education as well as in the government." In sum, said the article, democracy was "human brotherhood." To Imamura, Buddhism was therefore compatible with democracy.[52]

As Buddhism spread in Hawaii, it adapted to its new environment. It kept some of its traditional practices, discarded others, and embraced customs it found in its American setting. A Japanese priest explained that when Buddhism penetrated China it adapted to the Chinese civilization, in Japan it changed to fit into Japanese culture, and in America it would become American. Indeed it was Buddhism's innate flexibility that accounted for its spread into various countries and allowed its successful adaptation to the American environment.[53]

In Japan Buddhists performed daily rituals, observed monthly and special religious days, and participated in religious community activities. Because the main function of the temple in Japan was to look after ancestors' souls, an important role of the Buddhist priest was to officiate at funerals and memorial services conducted at regular intervals after a family member's death.[54]

In Hawaii Bishop Imamura took the lead in adapting Buddhism to its American setting, and largely as a result of his efforts, Buddhism saw greater success in Hawaii than on the mainland. Buddhists in the territory referred to their temples as churches and their priests as reverends. Their leaders installed pews and organs as in Christian churches, and initiated Sunday services, Sunday schools, and the singing of *gatha* (religious songs) patterned after Christian hymns. Buddhists sponsored Young Men's and Young Women's Buddhist Associations (YMBA and YWBA) modeled after the Young Men's and Young Women's Christian Associations (YMCA and YWCA). The YMBA and YWBA later merged into the Young Buddhists Association and became popular with Nisei by sponsoring lectures in Buddhism and dramatics; classes in arts and crafts and Japanese martial arts; oratorical contests; and social events. Although in Japan the Shinto priest officiated at weddings and the Buddhist priest at funerals, in Hawaii, to conform to the role of American ministers, Buddhist priests did both.[55]

Despite these changes, some Nisei still found Buddhist services strange. "I used to accompany mother on her missions to her Buddhist temple," said a University of Hawaii coed recalling the years around 1920, "but the mysterious prayers and ceremonies, although fascinating, never appealed to me as the simple straight-forward Sunday afternoon meetings conducted by my Christian leaders." "Last summer I attended a Buddhist ceremony back home," related another university student. "I had no intention of going, but just to satisfy my dear mother I went. My two younger sisters, both in high school, were with me. When the ceremony began I could hardly keep myself from laughing, since the priest's chanting sounded so funny. I saw my two sisters giggling with their handkerchiefs against their mouths to avoid any distraction. I had better sense than to laugh, but I laughed within. I couldn't stand it. This shows how much we American-born Japanese are losing the customs of our forefathers."[56]

Bishop Imamura realized that it would take more than outward trappings to attract the Nisei to Buddhism. In an effort to make Buddhism more meaningful to them without changing fundamental Buddhist beliefs, Imamura called on priests to emphasize the teachings of the historical Buddha and the ethical elements of Buddhism rather than its more philosophical and metaphysical aspects. Aware of the Nisei's limited command of Japanese, Imamura also established an English department at the Honpa Hongwanji mission in 1921, an act that proved to be instrumental in attracting the Nisei to Buddhism. While the man he first appointed to head the department, M. T. Kirby, a Canadian who converted to Buddhism, was unsuited to the task, his successor, Ernest Shinkaku Hunt, also a convert to Buddhism, an Englishman of dignity and forbearance, won wide respect among Buddhists and successfully spread the religion among Nisei. (Hunt took the name Shinkaku—"true-light bearer"—upon his ordination to the Buddhist ministry.) "As a senior [in 1925] I became interested in the Buddhist movement in Hawaii," recalled a Normal School student who grew up on Kauai. "My parents were staunch Buddhist believers and I had attended countless Sunday evening services, conducted by Buddhist priests. The teachings of our Lord were hard to understand. More so, because they were brought to me in the Japanese language. Then Reverend Hunt and Dr. Kirby, both Buddhist teachers, made a lecturing tour on Kauai. I then awoke to the great significance of my belief. I began reading books on philosophy and teachings of our Lord." Her classmate recounted a similar experience. "It was during my high school years that I came in close contact with Buddhism," he said. "Heretofore, I was afraid to profess that I was a Buddhist, because I thought I might be thought of as a pagan. Truly, at this time many of my friends were turning to Christianity, because Buddhism was incomprehensible. At the [Buddhist] church, where the dormitory boys attended on Sundays, an Englishman gave a series of talks on Buddhism. Somehow I got more out of his talks than I got from anybody else. I am not afraid of being called a Buddhist," the student concluded, "because there is nothing in Buddhism that I should be ashamed of."[57]

In spite of these efforts to adapt Buddhism to America, Americanizers continued to reject the "alien religion," insisting that Buddhism was incompatible with American ideals. In turn Buddhist leaders continued to defend their religion as compatible with Americanism. In 1928 Hunt wrote an article in *Dobo*, a Buddhist publication, in which he said that both Americans and Buddhists believed in religious freedom and equal opportunity for all. For Hunt and other Buddhists, religious freedom meant that Americans were free to choose any religion, including Buddhism. For Americanizers, America was a Christian country and therefore religious freedom meant freedom to choose among the varieties of Christianity.[58]

Many Christian leaders, who were otherwise sympathetic toward the Japanese, were antagonistic on this subject. An interdenominational meeting of ministers illustrated the depth of their animosity. In 1924 the Reverend Henry P. Judd, secretary of the (Congregational) Hawaiian Board of Missions, invited priests and ministers to the Alexander Young Hotel in Honolulu to discuss ways to increase religious participation among youths. Hunt was invited to the meeting. During the introductions Bishop Stephen Alencastre of the Roman Catholic diocese glared at the Buddhist priest, refused to shake his hand, and declared, "I love Protestants, but I hate Buddhists!" An Anglican dean then announced that he, too, hated Buddhists. As the two men marched toward the door, Hunt told them, "Do not go. You are of greater importance at this meeting than I. I am the one who will leave." He then quietly left the other men to discuss the topic at hand in the spirit of "Christian fellowship."[59]

In this context many Nisei became uncertain as to which religion to choose, and many lost interest in religion altogether. In 1923 C. N. Kurokawa, secretary of the YMCA, reported that of 6,500 Nisei boys twelve years and older, 62 percent said they had no religious affiliation. Other Nisei took the attitude that "any religion [was] good." "I think that all religions are the same," remarked a high school girl in 1927. "They all teach you to do the right things. The only difference is the way they teach this principle."[60]

Some Nisei believed they would "get more of the American ideas" from haole churches. But others disagreed. "Unfortunately, many students of the Oriental parentage think that in order to be an American, one must be a Christian," said a Normal School student in 1927. "They condemn the Buddhist religion and ridicule the customs. Our parents believe in Buddha, just as much as the Christians believe in Jesus. . . . I should think that ridiculing other religions is one of the most degrading things a man can say."[61]

Nisei who began attending Christian churches sometimes returned to Buddhism when their parents objected, while others refused to do so. "I used to be rebuked when I said that I wanted to be a Christian," wrote a Hilo High School sophomore recalling the early 1920s. "For several weeks I attended the Buddhism Sunday School but it did not satisfy me. When father died, I got a little bolder and I went to the Christian Sunday School without mother's or brother's permission." They scolded her but she persisted and finally got her way.[62]

A number of Issei who were Buddhists allowed their children to attend Christian churches, and some even actively encouraged it. "My mother says whether I go to Buddhist or Christian church, doesn't make any difference," recalled Sueno Matsushita. The parents of a Normal School student who grew up in the 1910s sent him to a Christian church to keep him "away from bad company." Misao Kawakami's parents encouraged her to attend the Lihue Congregational Church on Kauai in the 1920s because "she was in America."[63]

Siblings sometimes introduced Nisei to Christianity. "One of my sisters who returned from Honolulu [in the 1920s] started a Christian Sunday School right in our house," recalled a Normal School student. "My parents objected at first since they were Buddhists themselves, but later they consented. Many people began to talk about the 'conduct' of my sister. But still, many young people attended the Sunday School and even today I can hear them singing the song, 'Jesus Loves Me' from the bottom of their hearts."[64]

Living away from home, in Christian dormitories or in haole homes, also exposed Nisei to Christianity. "We had Bible study in the mornings and evenings," remembered a Normal School student who had boarded "at a Christian Home" as a high school student. "At first I did not like it but later I was so interested that I was baptized." A Hilo High School student who worked as a "housemaid" wrote in 1927, "The home is a Christian home where the members of the family love one another and have good manners. It is an ideal home. Since I came to this home, I go to the church regularly on Sundays and learn about the ideal living that I had never learned before."[65]

Sometimes school introduced the Nisei to Christianity. A young man from Kauai who grew up as a Buddhist converted to Christianity in the 1920s, after he joined the Christian Hi-Y club in high school and studied the "teachings of Jesus Christ." A Normal School student recalled the second decade of the twentieth century, when he and his sister were sent at an early age to boarding school on the island of Hawaii. "For miles around this boarding school there wasn't any church," he said, "and on Sundays my teacher, who was a devoted Christian woman, was accustomed to spend a great portion of the day in reading Biblical stories to both my sister and me. I remember I used to listen with delight to the stories she read me." But not all teachers were successful. A Nisei recalled that teachers in her "earlier school days" in the years before 1920 repeatedly told her and her classmates that Christianity was "the best religion." She attended services but they "did not satisfy" her.[66]

While a number of Nisei did convert to Christianity, the percentage of Japanese Christians remained small throughout the decades before World War II. Only rough estimates on the numbers of Japanese Christians and Buddhists exist, but they all point to the conclusion that the overwhelming majority of Issei and Nisei in Hawaii who professed a religion claimed to be Buddhists rather than Christians. By 1917, only 1,714 Japanese, or less than 3 percent, had converted to Christianity. Ten years later the situation was similar: the *Honolulu Advertiser* reported that 2,464 or less than 2 percent of Japanese in Hawaii were Protestant, while most were Buddhists. In 1937 there were 107 Buddhist temples divided among twelve sects, with over 39,719 registered members. The largest sect was the Hongwanji, with 45 temples and 18,164 members. In 1941 about 50,000 or 35 percent of the entire Japanese population in Hawaii were registered members of Buddhist churches. Many Japanese who were not registered nevertheless still identified themselves as Buddhists. As late as 1971, among the 80 percent of Honolulu Nisei who professed having a religion, 60 percent said they were Buddhists, while 29 and 5 percent identified themselves as Protestants and Catholics.[67]

Like the Japanese in Hawaii, a large percentage of the Japanese on the mainland continued to identify themselves as Buddhists. But with a smaller concentration of Japanese living together, which made it more difficult to maintain traditional institutions, proportionately more of the Japanese on the mainland than in Hawaii converted to Christianity. Similarly, it seems that the Japanese in Brazil embraced Christianity somewhat more readily than Japanese in Hawaii. And when Japanese Brazilians converted to Christianity, they naturally chose Catholicism, Brazil's dominant religion, over Protestantism.[68]

Despite the slight variation in conversion rates, a large proportion of Japanese immigrants and their children in the three settlement areas just discussed remained Buddhists. In a sociological study of Japanese in Hawaii, M. Hilo and Emma K. Himeno argued that a major reason for this was Christianity's call to forsake all other gods in the name of the one Christian God. Buddhism did not make the same demand; it never replaced Shintoism or Confucianism but coexisted with them, even incorporating the concept of filial piety into its dogma. On the other hand, converting to Christianity meant that the Japanese had to leave their ancestors' and families' religion. But filial piety was integral to Japanese culture, and loyalty to the family a core value. This sacrifice was too much for many Japanese to make.[69]

In 1940, at the fiftieth anniversary of the Koloa Japanese Christian Church on Kauai, church member Ichizo Tao reminisced about the early years of the church. "We had to walk many miles to carry the Gospel message to people living in [plantation] camps," said Tao. "Our work did not go on without persecution. In those days," he continued, "Christians among the Japanese community were thought of as queer people and were treated as outcasts. We were objects of ridicule and scorn. We were even stoned at times." Even in 1940, when he spoke, membership in his church was small. The Reverend T. Watanabe of Olaa Japanese Church spoke the same year of the constant struggle to Christianize the Japanese on the island of Hawaii. "Our churches are working hard and earnestly," he said, "but the results are not very conspicuous because other religious forces are strong."[70]

Since a large proportion of Nisei continued throughout their adulthood to identify themselves as Buddhists, the question arises as to the role of Buddhism in the acculturation process. In strengthening ties to their ancestors and in enabling Japanese to practice traditional customs, Buddhism retarded acculturation. At the same time it aided the acculturation process by easing the transition from one cultural environment to another by integrating American customs into its overall framework and bringing together the familiar with the unfamiliar. Probably Buddhism did as much as Christianity to acculturate its Japanese adherents. Because Christian churches were ethnically segregated, the sociologist William Petersen has questioned the extent of their acculturating influence. He interviewed both Buddhist and Christian clergymen in the 1960s, and found that Japanese Christians were like Japanese Buddhists in moral values, and unlike other Christians in their deeper attachment to family and greater respect for authority.[71]

The preference among Hawaii's Nisei for Buddhism rather than Christianity and their reluctance to abandon Hawaii Creole English, both denounced by Americanizers, as well as the Nisei sense of superiority, all point to the persistence of culture. But while the Japanese were proud of their cultural heritage, they were also highly cognizant of their low socioeconomic status in the territory. These two contradictory self-images generated a tension within the Nisei self-identity. The Nisei attempted to reduce this tension by moving up the social hierarchy while at the same time embracing their past. That is, in acculturating into American society, the Nisei sought to improve their status within the American community without rejecting their identity as children of Japanese plantation workers.

Chapter 10

Occupational Changes

Japanese dominated the plantation work force between 1890 and 1910, but by 1920 so many had found other occupations that their proportion in jobs off the plantations equaled their proportion on them. Japanese continued to leave plantation work in the 1920s and 1930s, chiefly because of inadequate pay. The experience of Nisei Sam Uyehara shows the difference in wages on and off the plantation. Uyehara worked as a carpenter's apprentice at Pepeekeo Plantation on the island of Hawaii in the 1920s. "After working about couple years," he said, "I decide to myself, well, no sense go ahead and stay in plantation making only one dollar one day. Work so hard, eh? (Laughs) If you work twenty-five days, you get ten cents one day, bonus [of $2.50 for the month]," he said. "But if you work twenty-four days [and get sick], you don't get the ten cents. Well, those days was big money. So I decide . . . I better quit and go Honolulu." He moved to Honolulu in 1928 and found a job with a Japanese contractor for $2.75 a day.[1]

Others less skilled also found jobs in Honolulu offering better pay. Richard Inouye labored on the plantation in what he called "a man-killer" job before moving to Honolulu in 1927 when he was seventeen. At first he worked as a laundry boy at the Alexander Young Hotel, and then found a job as an oiler with Oahu Railway. Not only was the job much easier than plantation fieldwork, but the pay was better.[2]

Ill-treatment on plantations lessened over the years, but worker complaints continued to be heard even in the 1920s. "We can stand the long hours of work in the hot sun," a Nisei said, "but it burns us up to have an ignorant *luna* [foreman] stand around and holler and swear at us all the time for not working fast enough. Every so often, just to show how good he is, he'll come up and grab a hoe or whatever we are working with and work like —— for about two minutes and then say sarcastically, 'Why you no work like that?' He knows and we know he couldn't work for ten minutes at that pace." The Nisei added, "Another thing that gripes me is to have the [luna] walk right into my house without knocking and waiting till I say 'come.' "[3]

It is important to keep in mind that despite the steady reduction of Japanese workers on sugar plantations, many Japanese continued to work there. In 1919, 55 percent of all plantation workers were Japanese. By 1925 the percentage had decreased to 29, but that figure represented over 12,700 workers. Many older Nisei who reached maturity in the 1910s and 1920s worked on the plantations. In doing so they infused the plantation work force with American ideas, as the 1920 strike showed.[4]

But well before that strike and even before Hawaii was annexed by the United States, low wages, overwork, and luna brutality led Japanese and other plantation laborers to protest, refuse to work, and sometimes to "riot." When Hawaii became a territory, voluntary labor replaced the system that had bound workers to their contracts. Laborers rejoiced at their liberation, and an epidemic of strikes, twenty in 1900 alone, spread among the plantations. These strikes were spontaneous, unorganized, short-lived, confined to individual plantations, and only occasionally effective in achieving needed changes.[5]

Gradually Japanese workers realized they needed to organize. In 1909 they staged the "Great Strike," the territory's longest and largest labor conflict to date. The strike lasted from May to August and involved Japanese workers from practically all plantations on Oahu. Unlike previous work stoppages that had been isolated and largely spontaneous, the 1909 strike came after eight months of meetings and fierce debate. The major issue was the meager wages paid Japanese workers at a time of rising prices, wages lower than those paid to laborers of other ethnic groups. The strikers demanded a raise, an end to ethnic pay scales, a reduction of the workday to ten hours, better housing, and improved sanitation. "Japanese laborers in Hawaii are assigned pigsty like homes and receive only $18.00 per month," argued Motoyuki Negoro, one of the strike leaders, "while Portuguese and Puerto Rican workers doing the same type of work are paid $22.50 and given single family cottages to live in." Although the strikers lost, improvements in wages, working conditions, and housing soon followed the strike's end.[6]

Why did the Issei, who respected authority and hierarchy, valued harmony and cordiality, and normally avoided confrontations, walk off the job in defiance of their employers? Part of the answer lies in the social context in which they found themselves in Hawaii, which contrasted sharply with what they had known in Japan. In Japan farmers were a respected class, but in Hawaii agricultural workers were demeaned. In Japan a system of reciprocal obligations meant that superiors protected and assisted inferiors in a mutually interdependent system; in Hawaii the relationship between luna and laborers was confrontational and often antagonistic. Events outside Hawaii also played a part in the Issei's growing resistance to maltreatment. Japan's defeat of China in 1895 and, especially, Russia in 1905 boosted the immigrants' pride and increased their indignation over the treatment they were receiving. Moreover, militancy was not foreign to Japanese farmers. Riots were common in Japan in times of major famines during the Tokugawa regime, and riots and strikes occurred repeatedly during the economic upheavals resulting from the Meiji government's modernization program. In fact rural militancy was probably a major factor in convincing the Meiji government to allow the emigration that began in 1885.[7]

The next massive sugar strike in Hawaii occurred in 1920. Lasting from mid-January to July 1 and involving workers on all Oahu plantations (laborers on the other islands continued to work so that they could contribute to the strike fund), the strike ignited the latent hostility that had been building against Japanese immigrants since the beginning of the century. The increasing numbers of Japanese in the territory made the group more and more conspicuous, and Japan's growing military might made Caucasians uneasy. The strike triggered an eruption of anti-Japanese sentiment. In the wake of the strike, Buddhist temples, Japanese language schools and newspapers, and dual citizenship, all irritants to Americanizers, became major targets of discrimination.[8]

The issues surrounding these targets, which brought ethnic animosities to the surface and pitted Japanese against Caucasians, gave the 1920 strike a distinctive dimension. Nevertheless the strike was not unique in the context of the American labor movement, which had reached Hawaii. Wartime inflation coupled with labor scarcity inspired increased union activity. In 1916 Hawaiians, Filipinos, and Japanese in the International Longshoremen's Association went on strike, and three years later other groups in Honolulu did the same, among them fishermen, telephone operators, and ironworkers and molders. It was in this atmosphere that plantation workers began to organize in 1919.[9]

Higher wages to meet the rising cost of living ranked at the top of the workers' list of demands; inflation from 1914 to 1920 had cut the purchasing power of the dollar in half. Honolulu Mayor Joseph J. Fern, Chinese consul Tan Hsia Hsu, and other community leaders who opposed the strike acknowledged the sugar workers' need for better pay.[10]

In fact most Hawaii residents agreed that plantation conditions as a whole needed improvement. The *Pacific Commercial Advertiser* ran fifteen of the "best" articles submitted by community leaders and the general public in 1919 on the question of how to solve the labor problem in Hawaii. The articles pointed to "low wages, long hours, the uncertainty of the bonus system, racial discrimination in pay, lack of a pension system, labor by pregnant women, wretched and often unsanitary living quarters, lack of recreational facilities, lack of grievance machinery, and what [Wallace R.] Farrington [then vice president and general business manager of *Honolulu Star-Bulletin*] called the 'Prussianistic methods' of [the sugar] industry."[11]

Unlike the 1909 strike, in which the Japanese union made no effort to join with laborers of other ethnic groups, the 1920 strike was notable for the efforts made to achive intergroup solidarity. The well-organized Federation of Japanese Labor gave substantial financial support to the more loosely organized Filipino Labor Union, whose fruitless attempts to bring planters into negotiation led Filipino workers to walk off the job on January 19. The Filipinos were soon joined by Puerto Ricans, Spanish, Portuguese, Hawaiians, and Chinese, and on February 1 by Japanese workers. Practically all workers of all ethnic groups walked out.[12]

The Hawaiian Sugar Planters' Association (HSPA) attempted to force strikers back to work in mid-February by issuing an ultimatum that gave them only a few days to return to work or be evicted from their homes. To make matters worse, the announcement came during an influenza epidemic in which fifty-five Japanese and ninety-five Filipinos died. In all, 10,538 Japanese and 1,472 Filipino men, women, and children moved off the plantations.[13]

The Reverend Takie Okumura "vigorously" opposed the strike. He believed the strikers had "no chance of victory," and because Japanese nationals were involved, the dispute would turn into a "racial clash." In his autobiography, written two decades after the strike, Okumura said, "I feared that it would surely become the chief cause of all friction between American people and Japanese."[14]

Indeed, the HSPA and the two English language dailies, the *Pacific Commercial Advertiser* and *Honolulu Star-Bulletin*, ignored the Filipinos and other ethnic groups and focused on the Japanese, by far the most numerous of the strikers. Articles in both newspapers warned that Japan used "peaceful penetration" to colonize Mongolia, Formosa, and Shantung, and the same was happening in Hawaii. They accused "unscrupulous Japanese agitators"—meaning Japanese language teachers and newspapers and Buddhist ministers—of enticing "ignorant" laborers to strike to achieve Japanese control of the sugar industry and then of the whole territory. "If the alien agitators could establish their pretensions to the control of labor," editorialized *Honolulu Star-Bulletin*, "Hawaii would be as thoroughly Japanized so far as its industrial life is concerned, as if the Mikado had the power to name our governor and direct our political destiny." *Star-Bulletin* then went on to ask, "Is control of the industrialism of Hawaii to remain in the hands of Anglo-Saxons or is it to pass into those of alien Japanese agitators? . . . Is Hawaii to remain American or become Japanese?" The paper concluded, "The American citizen who advocates anything less than resistance to the bitter end against arrogant ambition of the Japanese agitators is a traitor to his own people." During the strike, articles appeared weekly attacking some aspect of Japanese life in the Islands, including the language press, language schools, Buddhism, picture brides, and dual citizenship. The *Pacific Commercial Advertiser* accused the Japanese language press of "daily preaching sedition." In fact—considering the bitter feelings aroused during the strike, especially during the mass evictions, and the extreme language of the English language press—the Japanese language press showed restraint. Acting Governor Curtis P. Iaukea, a part-Hawaiian, warned that "the racial issue [was being] deliberately emphasized to cloud the economic issue."[15]

The haole elite used the strike to warn of an alleged threat of the "Japanization" of Hawaii, but the strike actually illustrated the contrary, the increasing acculturation of the Japanese in Hawaii. The strike showed that the Japanese were discarding more and more of their old-world ways and embracing American attitudes and methods.

While outsiders, intellectuals and newspapermen, had led the 1909 strike, rank-and-file workers generated their own leaders in the second great Oahu strike. Yasutaro Soga and Fred Kinzaburo Makino, leaders of the earlier walkout, were bystanders in 1920. In fact union members denounced Soga as a spy for the planters, and practically ignored Makino. Makino reacted by calling strike leaders "crooks, incompetents, and cockroaches." The scholar John E. Reinecke speculated that Makino "was probably piqued because the union officers did not treat him as an elder statesman on the strength of his leadership in the strike of 1909." Soga, on the other hand, supported the strikers. Referring to the Americanization movement that had engulfed Hawaii, Soga argued that the strike was a demand for an American standard of living. He pointed out that preaching high ideals of Americanism to laborers while they lived and worked under "wretched conditions" was like "throwing . . . diamonds to swines [sic]." He questioned the sincerity of planters and English language newspaper editors who called for the Americanization of plantation workers and in the next breath advocated importing laborers from China.[16]

Ironically, by subsidizing the building of Buddhist temples, plantation managers had provided workers with an organizing device. At Young Men's Buddhist Association meetings in the 1910s, Nisei workers discussed their concerns about wages, hours, working conditions, "and, above all, the question of dignity." As a result of these discussions, delegates from YMBAs throughout the territory met on the various islands in 1919, to discuss common grievances. From these meetings came the idea of a labor organization modeled after the American Federation of Labor.[17]

Most of the strike leaders, whose average age was thirty-two, were young men raised in Hawaii. One of them, Takashi Tsutsumi, declared, "The Americanization movement swamped the Japanese, hitherto saturated with Oriental thoughts and philosophy of meek obedience, with democratic ideas."[18]

Recognition that the process of acculturation had worked its way into the plantation labor force appeared in an advertisement in the *Pacific Commercial Advertiser*, in which HSPA Secretary Royal D. Mead accused strikers of intimidating other workers. "The older married men of the Japanese strikers," Mead said, "have told the Managers that it is the younger element of the Japanese, those born here into American citizenship, who are the most radical among the agitators and the most active in taking measures to prevent the men from seeking their former employment." Tsutsumi agreed. In his account of the strike he wrote that leaders split into two factions as the strike dragged on. Older Japanese advised caution and younger Japanese urged a more aggressive stance.[19]

Five long and difficult months after walking out, strike leaders conceded defeat. As in 1909, plantation managers made some improvements once they had broken the strike. Wages went up, the bonus system improved, and plantations offered improved medical services, better housing and sanitation, and more recreational facilities. A majority of the Japanese laborers returned to the plantations after the strike, but as many as 2,100 found other jobs.[20]

Within ten years after the strike most Japanese had left plantation work for other occupations such as coffee farming, fishing, retailing, and sales, and had made inroads in the professions. By 1940, when many Nisei had reached adulthood, Japanese males were proportionately or overrepresented in most areas of employment outside the plantations. In this way they were like the Chinese who came before them and who preceded them in attaining remarkable advancements in professional and other preferred occupations.[21]

The achievements of Nisei men in Hawaii in 1940 stood in contrast to Nisei men in Los Angeles. In the mainland city they remained underrepresented as professionals and semiprofessionals, proprietors and managers, and craftsmen and foremen. They were slightly overrepresented as clerks and salesmen, considerably so as nonfarm laborers and domestic servants, and enormously overrepresented as unpaid family farm laborers. Nisei men in Hawaii, too, were overrepresented as domestic servants and unpaid family farmers, but much less so. While Nisei men in Hawaii were almost ten times the normal proportion as unpaid family farm laborers, in Los Angeles they were seventy-eight times, and

Table 1

Ratio of Ethnic Occupancy for Employed Males
in Occupational Categories, by Ethnic Group, for 1940.

	Hawaiian	Part-Hawaiian	Caucasian	Chinese	Japanese	Filipino	All Others
Professional	0.66	1.11	2.17	1.44	0.97	0.08	0.72
Semiprofessional	0.55	2.08	1.07	2.35	1.30	0.18	0.63
Farm Mgr.	1.08	0.55	0.21	0.77	6.34	0.24	0.91
Prop. Mgr.	0.28	0.80	1.57	2.41	1.26	0.10	0.78
Sales Clerks	0.34	1.27	0.84	3.91	1.57	0.16	0.51
Craft Workers	1.12	1.64	0.67	0.96	2.55	0.18	0.92
Operatives	1.72	2.29	0.58	1.23	1.25	0.77	1.41
Domestic Service Workers	0.30	0.32	0.05	0.79	6.27	0.62	1.57
Other Service Workers	0.38	0.36	9.31	0.49	0.17	0.18	0.33
Farm Wage Earnmers	0.63	0.38	0.11	0.20	0.77	6.14	1.29
Unpaid Family Farmers	0.78	0.78	0.12	0.46	9.87	0.16	0.53
Other Laborers	4.02	2.26	0.31	0.94	1.19	1.04	2.14
Not Reported	1.33	1.86	0.44	0.44	1.92	0.46	4.59

Key: Caucasian = includes Portuguese and Spanish; Farm Mgr. = farmers and farm managers; Prop. Mgr. = other proprietors, managers, and officials; Sales Clerks = salesmen, clerks, and kindred workers; Craft Workers = craftsmen, foremen, and kindred workers; Farm Wage Earners = farm wage laborers and farm foremen; All Others = excludes farm and mine laborers.
Note: A ratio of more than 1 indicates overrepresentation; a ratio of less than 1 indicates underrepresentation.
Source: Tamura, "Americanization Campaign," 469, 476.

in the rest of Los Angeles County almost one hundred times the normal proportion in that category. More than in Hawaii, racial discrimination in Los Angeles and the rest of California prevented the Nisei there from acquiring professional and other white collar jobs. School boards in Los Angeles county, for example, refused to hire Nisei who had been trained as teachers. Additionally, with a larger concentration of Japanese in Hawaii compared to California, Japanese small businessmen and professionals could count on having clients from among their own ethnic group (see table 1).[22]

In contrast to Nisei men in Hawaii, Nisei women in the territory were like their counterparts in Los Angeles. In both locations Nisei women were underrepresented in many areas of employment, especially in jobs requiring a high school and post-high school education, and overrepresented as unskilled laborers (see table 2).[23]

Table 2
Ratio of Ethnic Occupancy for Employed Females
in Occupational Categories, by Ethnic Group, for 1940

	Hawaiian	Part-Hawaiian	Caucasian	Chinese	Japanese	Filipino	All Others
Professional	0.55	1.60	3.27	1.60	0.25	0.27	0.62
Semiprofessional	0.69	1.60	3.11	0.69	0.27	2.41	1.64
Farm Mgr.	2.81	0.92	0.14	0.28	2.94	0.10	0.21
Prop. Mgr.	1.40	0.64	1.30	1.25	0.81	0.73	1.45
Sales Clerks	0.41	1.16	1.85	1.74	0.55	0.56	0.50
Craft Workers	1.77	1.45	0.78	1.25	0.69	1.74	2.80
Operatives	2.84	1.38	0.48	1.25	0.93	1.05	1.88
Domestic Service Workers	0.57	0.60	0.38	0.28	2.60	1.45	1.13
Other Service Workers	1.06	1.33	0.80	1.03	1.01	1.01	1.09
Farm Wage Earnmers	0.70	0.20	0.13	0.00	5.14	2.45	0.86
Unpaid Family Farmers	0.24	0.17	0.05	0.14	10.14	0.99	0.39
Other Laborers	1.44	0.60	0.70	1.32	1.25	1.25	0.82
Not Reported	2.23	1.50	1.66	0.00	0.56	2.98	1.84

Key: Caucasian = includes Portuguese and Spanish; Farm Mgr. = farmers and farm managers; Prop. Mgr. = other proprietors, managers, and officials; Sales Clerks = salesmen, clerks, and kindred workers; Craft Workers = craftsmen, foremen, and kindred workers; Farm Wage Earners = farm wage laborers and farm foremen; All Others = excludes farm and mine laborers.

Note: A ratio of more than 1 indicates overrepresentation; a ratio of less than 1 indicates underrepresentation.

Source: Tamura, "Americanization Campaign," 471, 477.

Progress in the professions is a prime indicator of the extent of Japanese occupational advancement and acculturation into the American middle class. The following story describes the experiences of one of Hawaii's Nisei.

Masaji Marumoto, son of a plantation laborer turned storeowner, grew up in the rural immigrant community of Kona on the island of Hawaii, where practically everyone spoke Japanese. There Marumoto attended a one-room school serving grades one through eight. At the end of his sixth grade year, he asked his father to send him to Honolulu, where he felt he could learn more. His father agreed and found him a place to live, at the home of a family friend in Kalihi Valley. Once in Honolulu, Marumoto attended both Japanese and English schools, as he had in Kona.

His attempt to enroll at Central Grammar, a select public school for

Standard English speaking students, proved futile. "The principal's name was Miss Overend," Marumoto recalled. "She asked me, 'What grade are you applying for?' And country kid that I was, not speaking good English, I hesitated. I suppose I didn't answer her intelligibly because she said, 'Well, my fourth graders speak better English than you.' She chased me out." So Marumoto attended the Normal School, where he was "a guinea pig" for aspiring teachers.[24]

After the eighth grade Marumoto entered McKinley High, the only public high school on Oahu, but his "English was so bad . . . the first semester" that he "almost flunked out" because of a C minus in English. "I pulled up my English grade to a B plus by the end of the year," he recalled, "and then I completed McKinley at the top of the class."[25]

At the end of his junior year, his English teacher told him, " 'Masaji, I think you should go to college.' At that time," Marumoto recalled, "I never thought of going to college." He did not pursue the idea because his family could not afford the expense. At graduation in 1924, Marumoto won the gold medal for having earned the highest grades in the class. "I got an A-plus in math," he remembered, "and Clarence [who had come in second] just got an A." The evening after graduation the Buddhist bishop and his wife took Marumoto to dinner at the Seaside Hotel. "That was the best hotel in Honolulu at that time," said Marumoto. "That was the first time in my life I ever ate at a table with a tablecloth on it." The bishop urged him to go on to college. When he replied that he didn't have the money, the bishop said he would talk to a scholarship society made up of prominent Issei. A few weeks later Marumoto received an offer of a scholarship to attend a mainland university.[26]

"My father wanted me to go to a college," Marumoto recalled, "where there would be somebody I knew. It so happened that the son of a plantation laborer who came from the same village as my father was a dentist in Chicago. So I decided to go to Chicago. When I applied to the University of Chicago, very frankly, I did not know its standing, that it was as good as I found it to be."[27]

At the University of Chicago, he majored in philosophy because of "a wonderful professor" he had. When he told his father of his major, his father "raised hell" with him and told him to change it to something more practical. So Marumoto switched to a major in political economy. At graduation, having earned all A's, he was offered a fellowship at the University of Chicago, but he decided that there was no future for him as an Asian political economist. So he decided to become a lawyer. "I had never been in a lawyer's office; I had never been in a courthouse either, in Hawaii or in Chicago," he recalled.[28]

He applied to Harvard Law School, and in 1927, became the first non-

Caucasian, non-black student there. During his first year, the professors never called on him. "By the second year, when 30 percent of the class had washed out," Marumoto said, "they gave me more attention."[29]

After having earned his law degree in 1930, he returned to Hawaii. He made the rounds to five or six law offices in Honolulu, but was rejected each time. Even his Harvard degree did not help. "Haole firms didn't really hire Orientals before the war," he recalled. "I finally got a job with Mr. [Frank E.] Thompson [an attorney]. . . . Thompson had a Japanese office manager who had no formal education. He was a son of a sugar plantation worker. . . . He was self-educated but he had lots of common sense, was a good bookkeeper and Mr. Thompson trusted him. So because my family knew him, being neighbors in Kona, I went to see this fellow . . . and he introduced me to Mr. Thompson and Mr. Thompson said, 'Come over, we can take care of you.' " Marumoto stayed with Thompson for a year and a half before he opened his own office. Remembering his rough start, Marumoto later made a point of hiring young Nisei lawyers as assistants to help them start out in the profession. One assistant was Spark Matsunaga, later to become U.S. senator from Hawaii.[30]

After twenty-five years of practice Marumoto was tapped for the judiciary. At that time, because Hawaii was a territory, circuit court judges and Supreme Court justices were nominated by the president of the United States and confirmed by the U.S. Senate. William P. Rogers, then deputy attorney general of the United States, first asked Marumoto to accept the nomination as circuit court judge, but Marumoto refused because it would mean a major reduction in his income. Two years later Rogers asked Marumoto to accept the nomination as associate justice of the Territorial Supreme Court. Marumoto replied, "I will accept if my nomination should be confirmed by the Senate, but I will not accept an interim appointment." Mississippi Senator James O. Eastland, known for his racist views, was chairman of the Senate Judiciary Committee. "I didn't want to take a chance on closing my office up and taking an interim appointment," Marumoto explained, only to be later rejected by Eastland's committee. But his confirmation went without a hitch, and on 1 August 1956, Marumoto became Hawaii's first non-Caucasian supreme court justice in ninety-four years and the first in the United States.[31]

Half a century after he had graduated from McKinley High School, he recalled his English teacher, Esther Thomas, who had interested him in Shelley, Keats, Byron, and Pope. " 'A little learning is a dangerous thing; Drink deep, or taste not the Pierian spring: There shallow draughts intoxicate the brain. And drinking largely sobers us again.' That's Pope," said Marumoto, "and it was pretty heady stuff for a seventeen-year-old Kona boy."[32]

Marumoto's story is unique. His achievements attest not only to his hard work and perseverance, but also to his fine intellect. But Marumoto's story is also common in that it illustrates the barriers facing children of immigrants. And while perhaps not as spectacularly, other ambitious and persistent Nisei, like Marumoto, made gains against great odds.

The proportion of professionals in an ethnic group is a good indicator of where the group ranks in the larger community. Professionals are the best educated occupational group. Their jobs generally carry as much, if not more, status than other occupations, and their income places them among the middle or upper-middle class.[33]

Japanese men in the territory reached a normal proportion in the professions by 1930 and generally remained at that level for the next thirty years. In comparison Chinese men were somewhat overrepresented as professionals from 1940 to 1960; and between 1910 and 1960 Caucasian men were considerably overrepresented, Part-Hawaiian men descended from over- to proportional representation, and Hawaiian men went from over- to underrepresentation (see figure 8).[34]

Unlike Japanese men, Japanese women in Hawaii, while steadily increasing their standing between 1910 and 1960, continued to be considerably underrepresented in the professions when compared to women of all other ethnic groups. Caucasian women, like Caucasian men, were considerably overrepresented, Chinese women were somewhat overrepresented, Part-Hawaiian women, like Part-Hawaiian men, went from over- to proportional representation, and Hawaiian women, like Hawaiian men, descended from over- to underrepresentation. Note that women professionals during this time were mainly teachers and nurses (see figure 9).

The progress of Nisei occupational advancement in Hawaii differed markedly between males and females, reflecting the status of Japanese males within families. Japanese men moved up the occupational ladder quickly, but Japanese women advanced slowly. As was the practice in Japan, Nisei men took precedence over Nisei women. If families could not afford sending all children for further schooling, choices had to be made. In such cases Issei parents sacrificed much for their sons and Nisei sisters worked to support the schooling and occupational advancement of their Nisei brothers. Old-world practices thus played an important role in determining how the Nisei acculturated into American society.[35]

Yet, while Nisei men rose rapidly in the professions, they were not overrepresented from 1910 to 1960. This was in contrast to Caucasian

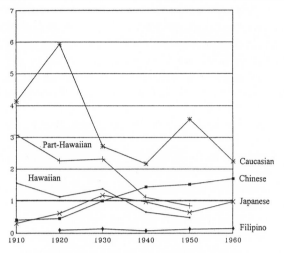

ratio

Figure 8. Ratio of Ethnic Occupancy of Male
Professionals by Ethnic Group, 1910–60.

Source: Tamura, "Americanization Campaign," 475.
Note: Caucasian includes Portuguese. A ratio of
more than 1 indicates overrepresentation; a ratio
of less than 1 indicates underrepresentation.

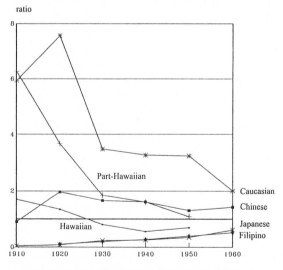

ratio

Figure 9. Ratio of Ethnic Occupancy of Female
Professionals by Ethnic Group, 1910–60.

Source: Tamura, "Americanization Campaign," 475.
Note: Caucasian includes Portuguese. A ratio of
more than 1 indicates overrepresentation; a ratio
of less than 1 indicates underrepresentation.

men, who were disproportionately overrepresented, and Chinese men, who became overrepresented after 1930 and remained so for the next three decades. Because Japanese were a large numerical group in Hawaii, they were more conspicuous than smaller groups and may have seemed to some to be overrepresented in jobs when they actually were not.[36]

Marumoto broke through the barriers excluding Nisei from one of the professions most difficult to enter before World War II. In addition to law, faculty positions at the University of Hawaii during this time were also generally closed to Nisei and other non-Caucasians. Young, bright, ambitious Nisei men therefore entered other professions, gravitating to dentistry, followed by medicine, then engineering, and finally law.

For a Nisei who was upwardly mobile, dentistry offered certain advantages. Unlike law, oral fluency in Standard English was not a prerequisite. Then too, a dentist was not at the mercy of employers who might not hire him, since he functioned as an independent practitioner. And with so many Japanese in the community, a dentist would not be short of patients. Kazuo Hosaka recalled that he had first considered pharmacy, but "it was hard to get a job," so he switched to dentistry. By 1930, Japanese were overrepresented in this profession. Chinese and Caucasians were even more highly overrepresented, Part-Hawaiians went from proportional to underrepresentation, and Hawaiians remained underrepresented. (See figures 10–13; note that the figures include both Issei and Nisei in the professions of dentistry, medicine, engineering, and law.)[37]

Medicine offered another attractive avenue of upward mobility. As with dentistry a doctor could set up his own practice. He was probably helped in starting out by Issei doctors, who originally worked for the plantations and then later moved to the towns. During the late nineteenth century, Queen's Hospital, the only major hospital in Hawaii, refused to allow Japanese doctors to practice there, even those trained in the United States. To overcome this barrier a group of Japanese doctors in 1900 established the Japanese Hospital in Honolulu, providing a place where both Issei and Nisei doctors could send their patients. Although remaining underrepresented in medicine, the Japanese gradually improved their standing in the field from 1910 to 1930, but dropped somewhat in 1950. In comparison the Chinese moved dramatically from under to overrepresentation, Caucasians were substantially overrepresented, and Part-Hawaiians and Hawaiians remained underrepresented.[38]

In 1928 Toshiyuki Kuninobu became the first Nisei in Hawaii to pass the National Medical Board Examination, entitling him to practice medicine anywhere in the United States. Originally from Kauai, young Kuninobu had moved with his parents to Honolulu, where his father became a building contractor. Kuninobu graduated from McKinley High

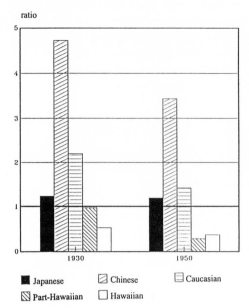

ratio

Figure 10. Ratio of Ethnic Occupancy
of Male Dentists by Ethnic Group,
1930 and 1950.

Source: Tamura, "Americanization Campaign,"
Note: Caucasian includes Portuguese. A ratio
more than 1 indicates overrepresentation; a rat
of less than 1 indicates underrepresentation.

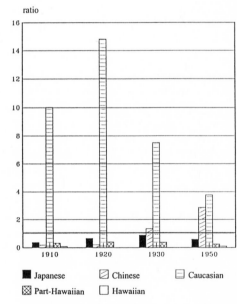

Figure 11. Ratio of Ethnic Occupancy of M
Physicians and Surgeons by Ethnic Group,
1910–50.

Source: Tamura, "Americanization Campaign," 482
Note: Caucasian includes Portuguese. A ratio of
more than 1 indicates overrepresentation; a ratio
of less than 1 indicates underrepresentation.

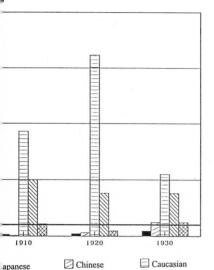

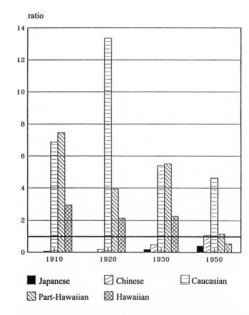

Figure 12. Ratio of Ethnic Occupancy
of Male Engineers by Ethnic Group,
1910–30.

Source: Tamura, "Americanization Campaign," 482.
Note: Caucasian includes Portuguese. A ratio of
more than 1 indicates overrepresentation; a ratio
of less than 1 indicates underrepresentation.

Figure 13. Ratio of Ethnic Occupancy of Male
Lawyers and Judges by Ethnic Group,
1910–50.

Source: Tamura, "Americanization Campaign," 482.
Note: Caucasian includes Portuguese. A ratio of
more than 1 indicates overrepresentation; a ratio
of less than 1 indicates underrepresentation.

in 1921, enrolled at the University of Hawaii for two years of pre-med courses, and then attended the College of Medical Evangelists in Loma Linda, California.[39]

Japanese men did not flock to engineering as they did to the more independent professions of dentistry and medicine. It was difficult for them to find jobs in large companies, which were controlled by the haole elite. Mitsuo Kuramoto, for example, had graduated from college as an electrical engineer. He could not find a job in Hawaii during the late 1920s, so he decided to return to school to become a doctor. He took pre-med courses at the University of Hawaii and then attended Northwestern University Medical School. He eventually became the house physician at the Japanese Hospital. Japanese men made modest gains and remained considerably underrepresented in engineering from 1910 to 1950, during which time Caucasians dominated the profession, Part-Hawaiians remained considerably overrepresented until 1930, and Chinese achieved remarkable gains.[40]

Of the four professions, law remained the least accessible to the Japanese. As with public school teaching, it was closed to the Issei, who lacked American citizenship. Not until 1930 did the Nisei begin making a dent in the profession, although they remained considerably underrepresented even in 1950. In comparison Hawaiians and even more so Part-Hawaiians were considerably overrepresented until 1930, and as in engineering, Chinese made remarkable gains and Caucasians dominated the field.

After World War II more Nisei entered the legal profession. The career decisions of former Hawaii State Supreme Court Associate Justice Edward Nakamura illustrate that opportunities for Nisei lawyers had widened after the war, but they also illustrate the effects of perceived barriers on the choices he made at critical junctures of his life. After graduating from McKinley High School in 1940, he enrolled at the University of Hawaii. He had decided to become a secondary school teacher because, he later explained, "that was one of the things you could aspire to if you were Japanese American. You couldn't aspire to managerial positions in the public or private sector," because "Haoles were the managerial class." But the war interrupted his college career. He enlisted with the Territorial Guard, then the Varsity Victory Volunteers, and finally joined the 442nd Regimental Combat Team. After returning to Hawaii in 1946, he enrolled once again at the University of Hawaii. This time, however, he majored in government instead of education. The war had changed his view of the world, exposing him "to something more than the island culture." As graduation approached, Nakamura considered a career as a professor of government. But after discussing this with his academic advisor, he realized that the chances of returning to Hawaii and being appointed professor at the University of Hawaii were slim, so he decided to enter law school.[41]

Japanese began making inroads in Hawaii's government from about 1930, as an increasing number of Nisei came of age. The percentage of adult citizens of Japanese ancestry grew steadily from 5.5 percent in 1920, to 15.3 percent in 1930, and 26.6 percent in 1940, increasing the chances that Nisei would be elected and appointed to government posts. In 1934 Nisei made up 21.5 percent of all registered voters. Although the Chinese had arrived a generation earlier than the Japanese, it was not until 1920 that a Chinese was elected to office (the first Asian American to do so). This was probably because the Chinese population was not large enough to make a difference at the polls.[42]

Although the percentage of Nisei registered voters and Nisei citizen adults grew impressively from 1930 on, the percentage of elected officials lagged behind, and that of appointed officials fell even further behind. In 1940, for example, Japanese made up 26.6 percent of all adult citizens but only 14.3 percent of all elected officials and 2.9 percent of all appointed officials. While citizens could elect their representatives, government leaders controlled government appointments. In 1950 Nisei were still underrepresented as elected officials and even more so as appointed officials.[43]

A number of Nisei candidates ran for public office in 1926 and 1928. Racism entered the political arena during the 1928 campaign, when Democratic stump speaker E. R. J. "Sonny" Gay attacked James C. Moriyama, deputy city and county auditor, who was running as a Republican for the House of Representatives. At a rally in Honolulu Gay railed, "Why elect this Jap Moriyama to the House? It is bad enough to have a Jap as deputy city and county auditor. He ought to be deported to Japan where the rest of the Japs belong." That year all Nisei candidates ran as Republicans and none were elected.[44]

But the likes of Gay could not stop eventual Nisei success at the polls. In 1930 Noboru Miyake, a Republican, became the first Japanese American elected to office in Hawaii. A veteran of World War I, a member of the American Legion, and a businessman, Miyake was elected outright to the Kauai County Board of Supervisors in the primary election. In the 1930 general election two Japanese Americans, Tasaku Oka, a Republican from the island of Hawaii, and Andy Yamashiro, a Democrat from Honolulu, won seats to the Territorial House of Representatives.[45]

The first Nisei to be appointed to a relatively high government position was also the second Nisei to pass the Hawaii Bar, Wilfred C. Tsukiyama, a 1924 graduate of the University of Chicago Law School. In 1929 he became deputy attorney for the City and County of Honolulu and in 1933 was promoted to city and county attorney.[46]

The first Japanese American appointed to a judicial position was Tomekichi Okino. In 1934 he became district magistrate for the island of Hawaii. Twenty years later another Nisei was appointed to a more coveted position; in 1953 Robert K. Murakami began serving as circuit court judge, four years before Masaji Marumoto became associate justice of the Territorial Supreme Court.[47]

As with high government positions, employment and promotion opportunities in large businesses remained limited for Japanese. While the two English language dailies preached racial harmony, they refused to hire Asians as reporters. The *Honolulu Advertiser* said in 1926 that it was against its policy to hire Asians. Fluency in Standard English was not an issue. Similarly the manager of a large firm in Honolulu told a group of college YMCA boys in 1927 that he could not hire Asians "to wait on the public in his office because that would result in a loss of business."[48]

When Asians were hired, promotions rarely came. On the plantations Caucasians were favored over non-Caucasians for promotion. This held true in pineapple canneries. "Many of these Haoles working in this cannery [as foremen] are nothing but the figure heads," complained a young Nisei man in the late 1920s. "Whenever any difficult problems come up, they come and consult us." So it went with other businesses. Another Nisei in the late 1920s said, "You know that Mr. E. T. has been working for one of the local firms for nearly fifteen years. He knows everything from A to Z about the organization and the business dealings of the firm. . . . Some few months ago there came a Haole man, who knew nothing of the business, but how much do you think he gets? He receives $200.00, while Mr. T, who has been working for nearly fifteen years gets only $150.00. Surely we Japanese have no chance just as long as we work for the Haoles," concluded the Nisei. "That's why we have today so many of the second generation Japanese [who] are eager to enter into independent business and professional activities."[49]

One profession that welcomed the Nisei was teaching. Unlike Caucasian businesses, public schools opened their doors to aspiring Nisei teachers and thereby provided the Japanese with an avenue for upward mobility. Ironically the institution that was supposed to mold young minds and Americanize Japanese and other Asian children accepted Nisei, the very targets of suspicion, as teachers. Although Americanizers proclaimed the importance of schools in Americanizing children of immigrants, teaching the masses of working-class children in Hawaii as elsewhere in America held less prestige and paid less than many other professions. Nisei youths understood this. "In the Hawaiian Islands," wrote an eighth grade Nisei boy in 1927, "most good jobs are done by the white people, so I am deciding to be a teacher."[50]

Nevertheless Nisei recognized the benefits and opportunities teaching provided. Compared to other occupations, there was little race discrimination in the public school system. Teaching was open to all citizens, regardless of ancestry, who met professional requirements. And with a standard salary schedule, teaching provided Asians with the same pay as Caucasians. At the same time teaching fit in well with traditional Japanese values, in which the *sensei*, or teacher, was a respected member of the community. As a Honokaa High School boy said in 1927, "It is a government position, a benefit to humanity and to myself, [and] a secure, steady profession with a fair wage."[51]

Young Nisei men often turned to grammar school teaching when other professions seemed beyond their financial reach. Katsumi Onishi, who found little discrimination in his career as an educator during the 1920s and 1930s, chose teaching partly because it meant two years of Normal School; he could not afford four years of college. He taught for a number of years and then became a principal. Clarence Kobayashi decided to attend Normal School because it took two years and "a job was almost guaranteed after you finished your schooling." His father gave him about $30 in 1925 so that he could travel from the island of Hawaii to Honolulu, settle down, get a job, and go to Normal School.[52]

"[At] McKinley [High School] . . . my ambition was to become an electrical engineer," wrote a Normal School student. "I took four years of science and I am proud of the fact that I received an average of 'A' for the four years. During my senior year, I was made assistant to the physics instructor and . . . enjoyed the privilege of [using] the . . . laboratory after school hours." With no one to advise him at McKinley, however, the student learned upon graduation in 1925 that his "cherished ambition" to study electrical engineering was "shattered." He explained, "During my four years in high school, I had spent so much of my time on science that I neglected my English and language studies. Consequently, graduation time found me minus the necessary two credits of foreign language (Latin in my case) to enable me to enter the 'U.'" At about the same time, his parents returned to Japan, and the student realized that his brother could not afford to send him to the university. "Some of my close friends suggested my going to the Normal School," he recalled. "At first I laughed over the thought of my becoming a 'school ma'am,' but upon second consideration, I began to feel that I had to do something." His brother agreed to loan him the money for Normal School. "Today," concluded the Nisei, "I have completely changed my purpose. I realize the great possibilities of the teaching profession as an aid to the people of Hawaii."[53]

Sometimes Nisei youths who had political ambitions turned to teaching instead. "I used to identify . . . [with] Cicero, Webster, Clay, Calhoun or Douglas," wrote a nineteen-year old Normal School student in 1927. "I used to imagine myself in Congress," he said, demonstrating the influence of his American education. "On Saturdays I used to help father at his work. During the lunch hour I . . . read famous speeches. . . . Sometimes father used to command me to stop reading aloud like an insane person," the student recalled. "Gradually, as months went by, I began to realize that it was useless for anyone of my station in life to try to become a politician because . . . money was needed and money was what I lacked." Another Normal School student in 1927 saw teaching as a stepping-stone to a different career. He planned to teach for about four years and then use the money he saved to attend a mainland university.[54]

Similarly, Japanese women decided teaching "was the only thing to do if you wanted to earn money." "There were so many kids at home I had to go out and support them," recalled Aiko Tokimasa Reinecke. "When I went out to teach I sent my checks home, because I lived in the teacher's cottage, which was free of rent, and all I needed to do was pay for my food."[55]

Teaching attracted young Nisei women who wanted to escape poverty and the plantation, and enjoy the benefits of American middle-class life. A high school girl who aspired to become a teacher wrote in 1927, "My neighbors influenced me in this more than anything else. At first they were very poor but since these girls became teachers, they became happy and wealthy. At present they have a large tract of land, a beautiful and comfortable home located on an upland where one can get a beautiful view. They also have an automobile and a telephone."[56]

Sometimes death in the family was the catalyst. "Before father died," recalled one young woman in the 1920s, "he called me to his bedside and said that he would be watching over me even though he is not with me. He wanted me to be somebody and not an ordinary person working in the cane fields. Right there and then I made up my mind to become a school teacher."[57]

The first Nisei teacher at any level in the public school system was a woman. In 1909 Masa Nakamura received her Normal School certificate and began teaching at Koloa Grammar School on Kauai. The next year two more Nisei women joined her at the grammar school level. By 1914 there were ten Nisei grammar school teachers, all women.[58]

From the mid-1920s until 1931, when the Normal School merged with the University of Hawaii to form a Teacher's College for all teachers, aspiring senior high school teachers attended the university instead of the Normal School. Senior high school teachers received a higher salary than other teachers. In 1928, the average salary for senior high school teachers was $2,098, compared with $1,737 and $1,657 for junior high and elementary school teachers. Only a small percentage of all teachers taught at the senior high level, 9 percent, for example, during the 1929–30 school year. The vast majority were Caucasian women: 97 percent were Caucasians and 72 percent were women. Japanese Americans made up 1 percent of all senior high school teachers that year.[59]

The situation changed as more children of immigrants could afford a university education. Of the 174 aspiring secondary teachers enrolled at the University of Hawaii during the 1927–28 school year, 33 percent were Nisei. The same year 27 percent of the 336 students enrolled at the Normal School were Nisei. (Note that the Nisei were still underrepresented in terms of their proportion—54 percent—as public school students in 1930.) Nisei men who chose a career in teaching tended to choose the senior high school level. Of the 59 Nisei males in 1927–28 who were studying to become teachers, 63 percent planned to teach at the senior high level.[60]

Among public senior high schools McKinley held the greatest prestige during the first thirty years of the twentieth century. Not only was it the oldest public high school in the territory, its standards were considered higher than most public and private high schools. Bert Itoga became the first Japanese American teacher there in 1935, and one of the two first Asian American teachers at the school.[61]

In comparison, it was some time before Japanese Americans entered the teaching staffs of the select public English Standard schools and the private Punahou senior high school. Millicent Arimizu began teaching at Hilo Standard School in 1942, seventeen years after the first Standard school opened, while Hazel Inouye began teaching General Business, Shorthand, and Bookkeeping at Punahou in 1958.[62]

Another way in which teachers could rise in their profession was by becoming principals. Hatsu E. Miyake became the first principal-teacher, a grammar school principal who also taught. Graduating from the Territorial Normal School in 1916, she began her principalship that year, at Ainakea School in Kohala, on the island of Hawaii. She and another teacher taught the sixty-two students there. Eight years later she was still the only Nisei out of 167 elementary and junior high school principals. The following year there were four Nisei principals, and from that point on the numbers grew steadily. By 1930, 5 percent of all principals were Nisei, increasing to 10 and 19 percent in 1940 and 1950. Since the Nisei constituted 42 percent of all those employed in 1950, however, they were still considerably underrepresented as principals.[63]

Nisei principals were even more underrepresented at the senior high level. It was not until 1939 that a Japanese American, Stanley M. Miya-moto, became principal of a senior high school, Kahuku High and Gram-mar. That year, of the twenty senior high school principals in the terri-tory, only three were non-haole, and all were principals of rural schools. One was Japanese, one Portuguese, and one Hawaiian or Part-Hawaiian.[64]

Nearly a quarter of a century would pass before a Nisei became prin-cipal of a Honolulu high school. The first non-Caucasian principals of Farrington and Kalani High Schools, in 1962, were Japanese Ameri-cans Stephen S. Kanda and Thomas Takamune. McKinley's first non-Caucasian principal the following year was also a Japanese American, Timmy T. Hirata.[65]

During the early 1920s, when relatively few Nisei had reached adult-hood, few Japanese Americans were employed as public school teachers. While Nisei made up 9 percent of all public school teachers, they con-stituted 53 percent of all public school students. In contrast Caucasians made up 45 percent of the teaching staff and only 4 percent of the student body. But this changed as increasing numbers of Nisei became adults. As reflected by the numbers and percentages of Normal School graduates in 1929, Japanese joined Chinese and Part-Hawaiians in being among the larger groups of new teachers.[66]

Teaching became, then, an important avenue of upward mobility for the Nisei. In 1930, Japanese men were overrepresented as teachers, but by 1950, other professions had opened up, and teaching no longer played such a crucial role for younger Nisei men. Although Japanese women continued to be considerably underrepresented as teachers in 1930 and 1950, they gradually improved their standing in the profession. In com-parison Caucasian men and women and Chinese women were highly overrepresented as teachers from 1910 to 1950 and Part-Hawaiian men and women decreased from substantial overrepresentation to underrep-resentation for men and slight overrepresentation for women (see figure 14).[67]

Besides teaching most Nisei women seeking a profession during the first half of the twentieth century turned to nursing, a field dominated by Caucasian women. As in teaching, Nisei women were considerably underrepresented in nursing between 1910 and 1950, but their propor-tion increased steadily. Chinese and Korean women progressed more dramatically than Nisei women, and Part-Hawaiian women went from over- to underrepresentation (see figure 15).[68]

Although not given the same status as teaching in Japanese culture, nursing was an attractive profession for young Nisei women who had higher aspirations but could not afford the expense of school. The Japa-nese Hospital, which trained nurses, charged no tuition and furnished

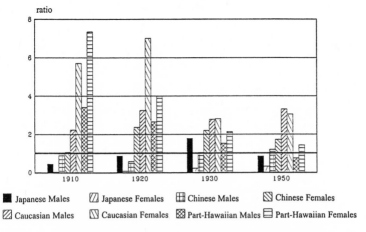

Figure 14. Ratio of Ethnic Occupancy of Teachers,
by Sex and Ethnic Group, 1910–50.

Source: Tamura, "Americanization Campaign," 486.
Note: Caucasian includes Portuguese. A ratio of
more than 1 indicates overrepresentation; a ratio
of less than 1 indicates underrepresentation.

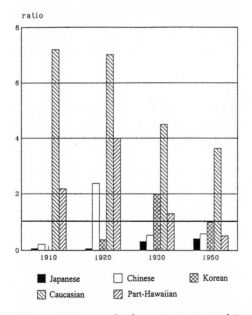

Figure 15. Ratio of Ethnic Occupancy of Female
Nurses by Ethnic Group, 1910–50.

Source: Tamura, "Americanization Campaign," 488.
Note: Caucasian includes Portuguese. A ratio of
more than 1 indicates overrepresentation; a ratio
of less than 1 indicates underrepresentation.

a dormitory for its student nurses. In addition "in those days they paid us . . . about ten dollars a month," recalled Marie, who was a nursing student from 1937 to 1940 with ten other young Nisei women. "Because we were working there, you know. . . . Those days [the hospital] didn't have anybody to clean, so we used to do it all. And bathe the patients. We used to do that." Marie had quit public school at the end of the eighth grade at her father's insistence, and worked as a housekeeper for a number of years before deciding on her own to take the entrance test at the Japanese Hospital. "Some of [the other students] didn't go to high school, but most of them did," she said. "For three years we did lots of studying."[69]

Nursing and teaching, then, served an increasing number of Nisei women, and dentistry, teaching, and medicine, and to a lesser extent engineering and law, served an increasing number of Nisei men as avenues to American middle-class life. Blocked in particular occupations by the haole elite, the Nisei turned to other jobs open to them. In dentistry and medicine Nisei men could establish their own businesses and serve Japanese patients. Other Nisei men turned to teaching, one of the few professions with little race discrimination. Although Nisei women remained underrepresented in the professions in the decades before World War II, they turned to teaching and nursing in increasing numbers.

While Nisei activity in the occupations indicated increased acculturation, it also showed signs of cultural persistence, reflected by the dominant roles assumed by Japanese men. Thus Nisei advancement in professional, skilled, and semiskilled occupations by 1940 was substantial for men but not for women. As they did in their pursuit of schooling and in their social and cultural acculturation, the Nisei, in their occupational advancement, incorporated Japanese values into the American setting as they sought to enter American middle-class society. And, in fact, even those Nisei who remained in the working class and on the plantations demonstrated progressively greater acculturation. They increasingly took on leadership roles among the rank and file and infused the work force with American ideas of union organization.

Epilogue

The acculturation of the Japanese community began slowly during the
sojourner period of 1890 to 1907, picked up some momentum during
the settlement period of 1907 to 1924, and became progressively more
substantial during the 1920s and 1930s as the Nisei grew up, attended
school, and reached adulthood. Japanese American men responded over-
whelmingly to the call for volunteers to join the U.S. Army during World
War II. Forty percent of all male Japanese Americans of military age in
Hawaii enlisted, constituting 60 percent of Hawaii's fighting forces. This
demonstrated not only the Nisei's desire to prove their loyalty, but also
the extent of their acculturation.[1]

By 1940 the Issei, too, had acculturated into American life, although
to a lesser extent than the Nisei. To be sure, the Issei continued to feel
nostalgia for their homeland. A survey taken in 1942 showed that they
had grown attached to America as a result of having lived in the country
for many years, having maintained a higher standard of living than they
could have in Japan, and having seen their children grow up as American citizens. At the same time they carried a sense of kinship with the
Japanese in Japan.[2]

Americanizers interpreted Issei ties to Japan simplistically as evidence of anti-Americanism, but the situation was far more complex than
that. Immigrants naturally held a warm spot for their motherland, the
land of their birth and childhood. Yet they also felt growing attachment
to their adopted country. In times of peace this ambivalence remained
in the background, but in times of war national anxieties pushed the
question of loyalty onto center stage.

Lingering Issei attachment to their homeland became apparent immediately after World War II ended, when rumors spread among the Issei
in Hawaii that Japan had won the war. A Japanese fleet was said to be
in Pearl Harbor to take over Hawaii, the American fleet was said to be
flying the Japanese flag, Japanese officers were said to be stationed at the
military bases of Schofield and Pearl Harbor, and President Truman was
said to be on his way to Japan to officially apologize to the emperor. The

Nisei rejected these rumors with annoyance and impatience. Veterans, especially, were dismayed at what seemed like the undoing of all their efforts during the war to win respect for the Japanese as loyal to America. The contrasting reactions of Issei and Nisei to these rumors point to their different degrees of acculturation.[3]

The rumors that spread among the Issei also reflected their increasing tension, disorientation, and frustration during the course of the war, as they witnessed the destruction of Japanese artifacts, the rejection of long-held practices, and the collapse of familiar cultural institutions. It was not that the Issei wanted the United States to lose the war; it was more that they believed that Japan was invincible.[4]

The end of the war brought jubilation and relief to most Nisei, but humiliation and depression to many of their parents and many Kibei. "I am happy about the surrender," said a Nisei, "but the old folks—they are the ones I feel sorry for. . . . Deep down inside they feel bad." The Nisei explained, "You can't blame them though because this is the first time Japan was ever defeated and now they are no longer that powerful nation they used to be." A Nisei college student, a decorated veteran of the 442nd, offered further insights. "The history of Japan has been one of continuous conquests and of victories up to V-J Day," he said. "The idea that she was a divine nation which cannot lose any war was deeply inculcated into the minds of the Japanese from time immemorial." The veteran continued, "Even the official announcements of surrender through the radio and newspapers for a while couldn't make them see the truth. They simply didn't want to." The veteran then pointed to the mixture of loyalties felt by the immigrants. "The behavior of these Issei seems to indicate their complete disloyalty to the United States," he said. "But I think this is not so. These are the same parents who willingly gave their sons to Uncle Sam for combat duty."[5]

While rumors of Japan's victory reflected Issei attachment to their motherland, the war actually hastened their acculturation by forcing Issei to discard Japanese customs. Because imported Japanese food was no longer available, Issei ate more American-style food. Many burned shrines, paintings, photographs of relatives in Japanese uniforms, portraits of the imperial family, and Japanese books, magazines, and personal letters. They stopped speaking Japanese in public. Women stopped wearing *kimono* and had their hair cut and curled.[6]

The war also changed family life in Hawaii. Nisei called old-world practices contrary to the American way, telling their parents "Don't talk in Japanese," "Don't wear a kimono," "Don't bow like a Japanese." Parent-child roles reversed overnight. Issei had to depend on their children to interpret "regulations governing the conduct of enemy aliens." Some Issei tried to learn English, and many transferred their properties and businesses to their citizen children.[7]

The war further accelerated Issei acculturation by bringing them in contact with Caucasian servicemen. A Nisei, whose family lived next to a reservoir that was taken over by the army, told of soldiers camping in the family's yard. "My alien parents of course felt very uncomfortable in this situation," said the Nisei. At first his parents barely communicated with the soldiers, but as time passed the couple became friendlier until one day the Nisei's father invited the soldiers into the house. This contact helped him better understand American ways. "Father was very narrow-minded about social dancing," explained the Nisei. "To these boys, dancing was a natural pastime and they talked about the good time they had at the U.S.O. dances. They told him how well these dances were conducted and mentioned some of the people who took charge of the dances. Before long, Father stopped condemning dancing and soon accepted it as just another social activity." Another Nisei said, "Until a year ago, I know Father never even thought of inviting service men from the mainland to the house. Today, however, he has a number of very good friends in the service who come regularly to our home. The boys, who have found something of a home at our house, refer to father as 'Pop' and he seems to be rather fond of this affectionate name."[8]

The war also accelerated Nisei acculturation. Those who joined the military came in contact with mainland Caucasians, mainland life, and the world outside Hawaii. Some gained greater self-confidence through their military jobs. "In the war," explained a veteran, "we were given responsibility and were rated accordingly. That was the beginning of a confidence in myself and my ability." Nisei veterans returned to Hawaii more determined than ever to push through barriers that had kept them back. During the postwar period they attended college on the G.I. Bill, worked, raised families, and entered leadership positions in government, education, and politics.[9]

Some scholars have emphasized the speed at which the Nisei acculturated. It is more accurate to characterize their acculturation as substantial in some ways and moderate in others. In areas in which Japanese and American cultural values were compatible, as in schooling and occupational advancement for men, acculturation was substantial. But in areas in which there was cultural incompatibility and thus resistance to change, as in occupational advancement for women and intermarriage, acculturation was only moderate. It is also important to recognize that while there were some impressive success stories, they were not out of proportion to the size of their group. The sheer number of Japanese in Hawaii made them conspicuous and their progress seem greater than it was.[10]

Further understanding of Nisei acculturation can be seen in the acculturation of their children, the Sansei. Sansei have highly developed middle-class American attitudes, but with their own distinctive variations. In them the forces of acculturation and ethnic identity continue to intersect.

In intermarriage Sansei have shown substantial integration with the larger community. While about 4 percent of Nisei men and 6 percent of Nisei women in Hawaii intermarried in the 1930s, about 25 percent of Sansei men and 42 percent of Sansei women in Hawaii outmarried in 1970, and 42 percent of Sansei and Yonsei (fourth generation Japanese American) men and women intermarried in 1980.[11]

But the Sansei have been able to maintain a degree of subcultural distinctiveness. The sociologist Colleen L. Johnson found that Sansei as well as Nisei in Honolulu during the early 1970s formed a "cohesive subcultural identification." Both Sansei and Nisei maintained "well-marked boundaries between themselves and other groups both in their social relationships and their value systems." Like Nisei, Sansei spent most of their time with other Japanese Americans, and preferred kin to non-kin relationships. Although not as strong as with the first two generations, family solidarity remained high among Sansei. Similarly, the political scientist Yasumasa Kuroda found that Japanese Americans in Honolulu in the 1970s were developing a subculture of their own, different from the American or Japanese cultures and different from the subculture of Japanese Americans on the mainland.[12]

Studies on mainland Sansei in the 1960s and 1970s have produced similar results. Sansei in the greater Seattle area maintained strong kin relationships and a strong sense of ethnic pride. California Sansei were generally indifferent to Japanese culture and maintained more contacts with non-Japanese than California Nisei, yet retained their own subcultural identity. While their occupations, customs, education, language, and style of life were American, they tended to maintain friendships with those of their own ethnic group. Like Sansei in Hawaii, mainland Sansei tended to behave biculturally. Their Japanese sub-identity pertained to certain areas of their lives, and their American sub-identity to other areas.[13]

The Sansei subculture has fostered a distinctive personality structure. In a number of studies, Sansei in Hawaii and on the mainland indicated a greater need for "deference" and "abasement," and a lesser need for "dominance" and "exhibition" than Caucasians. Sansei were also more "apprehensive," "diffident," "reserved," "serious," "conscientious," and "unpretentious" than Caucasians. Johnson found that Sansei in Hawaii grew up in families that encouraged collective over self orientation. Dependency, modesty, consideration for others, and sensitivity to others' feelings were encouraged, while independent, pushy, individualistic, and aggressive behaviors were discouraged. This emphasis on the group explains a concept that continues to influence Sansei behavior, *enryo*, to hold back. It means that one is supposed to refrain from imposing oneself on others.[14]

Using Milton Gordon's terms, the Sansei have manifested greater marital, cultural, structural, and identificational assimilation than the Nisei. At the same time the Sansei have evolved a subculture of their own, demonstrating the validity of the dynamic view of cultural persistence proffered by scholars of ethnicity.

The foregoing description of the Sansei underscores what their Nisei parents had demonstrated before World War II, the failure of Americanizers to direct the process whereby Japanese immigrants and their children adapted to their American environment. For all their prestige and power during this period, industrialists, politicians, and school leaders failed to control educational, social, occupational, and cultural developments. Their failure furnished clear evidence of the triumph of acculturation over Americanization.

Appendix

Firsts among Japanese Americans in Hawaii

1909 *First Public School Teacher*
Masa Nakamura (female) began teaching at Koloa School on Kauai.

1910 *First to Pass the Hawaii Bar*
Arthur K. Ozawa graduated from the University of Michigan Law School and passed the bar in 1910. It would be fourteen years before another Nisei, Wilfred C. Tsukiyama, passed the bar. Robert K. Murakami and then Masaji Marumoto passed the bar soon after Tsukiyama.

1913 *First Graduate of the University of Hawaii*
Seigei Yogi (male), entered the College of Hawaii in 1910, two years after it was founded, and graduated in 1913. Few graduated after that until the 1920s, when more Nisei reached college age.

1916 *First Public School Principal*
Hatsu E. Miyake (female) became principal and teacher at Ainakea School in Kohala, on the island of Hawaii.

1927 *First to Attend Harvard Law School*
Masaji Marumoto (male) was the first Asian American, and first non-Caucasian and non-black at Harvard Law School.

1928 *First Medical Doctor*
Toshiyuki Kuninobu (male) was the first Japanese American from Hawaii to pass the National Medical Board Examination, entitling him to practice medicine anywhere in the United States.

1929 *First Appointed Government Official*
Wilfred C. Tsukiyama became deputy attorney for the city and county of Honolulu. In 1933 he became Honolulu City and County Attorney.

1930 *First Elected Official*
Noboru Miyake (male), a Republican, was elected outright in the primary election, to serve on the Kauai County Board of Supervisors. In the general election, Andy Yamashiro, a Democrat from Honolulu, and

Tasaku Oka (male), a Republican from the island of Hawaii, won seats in the Territorial House of Representatives.

1934 *First Judge*
Tomekichi Okino (male) became district magistrate for the island of Hawaii.

1935 *First Female Medical Doctors*
Shizue Komu and Ethel Omori graduated from Tufts Medical School in 1935.

1935 *First Teacher at McKinley High School*
Bert Itoga and Dai Ho Chun were the first Asian American teachers at McKinley.

1935 *First Principal of a Honolulu school*
Stanley M. Miyamoto became principal of Pauoa Elementary School.

1937 *First Deputy Public Prosecutor*
Ralph T. Yamaguchi was assigned to the Honolulu district court as an assistant public prosecutor.

1939 *First Principal of a High School*
Stanley M. Miyamoto was appointed principal of Kahuku High and Grammar School. Of the twenty high schools in the territory in 1939, there were three non-Caucasian principals: a Japanese, a Portuguese, and a Hawaiian or Part-Hawaiian.

1942 *First Teacher at an English Standard School*
Millicent Arimizu taught third graders at Hilo Standard School.

1953 *First Circuit Court Judge*
Robert K. Murakami became circuit court judge on Oahu.

1957 *First Associate Justice of the Hawaii Supreme Court*
Masaji Marumoto was appointed associate justice.

1958 *First Teacher at the senior high level at Punahou School*
Hazel Inouye taught General Business, Shorthand, and Bookkeeping at Punahou.

1962 *First Principal of a Honolulu high school*
Stephen S. Kanda was the first non-Caucasian as well as the first Japanese American principal of Farrington High School. Thomas Takamune was the first non-Caucasian and first Japanese American principal of Kalani High. (The first non-Caucasian Honolulu high school principal was William T. S. Wong of Roosevelt High, appointed in 1958.)

1963 *First Principal of McKinley High School, the oldest public high school in Hawaii*
Timmy T. Hirata was the first non-Caucasian as well as the first Japanese American principal of McKinley.

1967 *First Superintendent of the Hawaii school system*
Ralph Kiyosaki became superintendent of the Hawaii State Department of Education.

Notes

Abbreviations

DPI	Department of Public Instruction, Territory of Hawaii
HA	*Honolulu Advertiser*
HH	*Hawaii Hochi*
NJ	*Nippu Jiji*
PCA	*Pacific Commercial Advertiser*
RASRL	Romanzo Adams Social Research Laboratory
SB	*Honolulu Star-Bulletin*
WCS	William Carlson Smith Collection

Preface

1. Geertz, *Interpretation of Cultures*, 3–30.

2. Social control historians have argued that the middle and upper classes have used institutions to maintain their favored position and control the rest of the population. See, for example, Platt, *Child Savers;* Rothman, *Discovery of the Asylum;* and Violas, *Training of the Urban Working Class.* Chapter 6 further discusses social control historians.

3. DeVos, "Ethnic Pluralism," 9. For other discussions of ethnicity and ethnic groups, see Appleton, *Cultural Pluralism*, 40–48; and Abramson, "Assimilation and Pluralism," 151.

4. Daniels and Kitano, *American Racism*, 2–5. See also Van den Berghe, *Race and Racism*, 9–18; and Horsman, *Race and Manifest Destiny.* Dower (*War without Mercy*) chronicles blatant American and Japanese racism during World War II.

5. The successive constitutions of the nineteenth-century Hawaiian monarchy do not discuss the citizenship status of those born in Hawaii. When Hawaii became a republic in 1894, Asians born in Hawaii automatically became citizens. Unlike the Nisei, the Issei saw their legal rights constrict progressively during the nineteenth century. Before 1894, Asian immigrants could become naturalized subjects of the Hawaiian kingdom. After 1894, they could become naturalized citizens of the Republic only if they could read, write, and speak English, a provision that effectively disqualified most of them. Before 1887, voting rights were accorded adult Asian males who had been naturalized. Under the 1887 Constitu-

tion, however, Hawaiian citizenship was no longer a basis for voting. Residents, even those who were citizens of another country, could vote, as long as they were of Hawaiian, American, or European descent. Asians born in Hawaii could vote, but those naturalized could not, a situation that continued under the Republic of Hawaii. See *Roster Legislatures of Hawaii, 1841–1918; Constitutions of Monarchy and Republic; Speeches of Sovereigns and President;* Jones, "Naturalization in Hawaii," 31–33, 50; and Jones, "Naturalization of Orientals in Hawaii," 66–69.

6. The school initials are H for University of Hawaii, N for Territorial Normal and Training School, SL for St. Louis College (a private high school), HH for Hilo High School, HA for Honokaa High School, HJ for Honokaa Junior High School, J for Japanese High School (a private Japanese language school), L for Lahainaluna High School, LJ for Laupahoehoe Junior High School, M for Maui High School, MK for McKinley High School, and MP for Mid-Pacific Institute (a private school). See William C. Smith, "Second Generation Oriental," 32–36, for the list of questions Smith used.

Prologue

1. Goldman, *Ancient Polynesian Society,* 210; Emory, "Origins of the Hawaiians."

2. Kuykendall, *Hawaiian Kingdom,* 1:28, 82–95, 307.

3. Daws, *Shoal of Time,* 57–65.

4. Goldman, *Ancient Polynesian Society,* 202–3; Kuykendall, *Hawaiian Kingdom,* 1:22–51, 153–69; Daws, *Shoal of Time,* 32–47, 106–11.

5. Kelly, "Land Tenure in Hawaii," 57, 67.

6. Kuykendall, *Hawaiian Kingdom,* 1:330; Stannard, *Before the Horror,* pass.; Schmitt, *Demographic Statistics of Hawaii,* 43; Beechert, *Working in Hawaii,* 37–38, 183; Blaisdell, "Health and Social Services," 102–3; Liu, "Race, Ethnicity," 189.

7. Lind, "Immigration to Hawaii," 12.

8. Kuykendall, *Hawaiian Kingdom,* 3:24–29, 47, 385–97.

9. Ibid., 57–59, 466, 488, 508–12.

10. Daws, *Shoal of Time,* 240–92.

11. Roger Bell, *Last among Equals,* 41–43.

12. Ibid., 14–15, 44–45.

13. Fuchs, *Hawaii Pono,* 21–24, 43–46.

14. Glick, *Sojourners and Settlers,* 67; Fuchs, *Hawaii Pono,* 37.

15. Glick, *Sojourners and Settlers,* x–xi, 12, 18, 23.

16. Lind, *Hawaii's People,* 27–29.

17. Ibid., 28, 31; Carr, "Puerto Ricans in Hawaii," 1–2, 224, 449; Pomerantz, "Background of Korean Emigration," 277, 300; Hernanz, "Life and Misadventures," 61. The first attempt by sugar planters to import Japanese laborers in 1868 had been largely unsuccessful.

18. Daniels and Kitano, *American Racism,* 66; Dorita, "Filipino Immigration," 17–18, 100–107, 124–29.

19. See Chan, *Asian Americans,* for comparisons of the experiences among different Asian American groups in Hawaii and on the mainland.

Chapter 1: Sojourners

1. For accounts of Perry's voyage to Japan, see Walworth, *Black Ships off Japan,* 3–80; and Barr, *Coming of the Barbarians,* 19–27.

2. Clyde and Beers, *Far East,* 112–25.

3. Moriyama, "Causes of Emigration," 248–61; see Moriyama, *Imingaisha,* 2–6.

4. Irwin and Conroy, "Robert Walker Irwin," 46–47. An earlier group had arrived in 1868, but this attempt to use Japanese laborers for Hawaii's plantations was unsuccessful, and most of the immigrants returned to Japan; 1885 began the steady flow of Japanese laborers.

5. Adams, *Japanese in Hawaii,* 11.

6. Yamamoto, "Evolution of an Ethnic Hospital," 34–44, 47–48; Yukiko Kimura, *Issei: Japanese Immigrants,* 123–24.

7. Conroy, *Japanese Frontier in Hawaii,* 106–18; Wakukawa, *History of the Japanese People,* 89–95.

8. Conroy, *Japanese Frontier in Hawaii,* 81–85; Glick, *Sojourners and Settlers,* 102–3; Sharma, "Pinoy in Paradise," 112. The Europeans, like the Japanese, had been dislocated by the forces of industrialization. They, too, were marginal landowners who hoped to return with enough money to increase their holdings, or owning no land at all, to buy the land they desired. They, too, came to America to seek their fortune. See Bodnar, *The Transplanted,* 56.

9. Masuoka, "Westernization of the Japanese Family," 161–62; Usaku Morihara interview, 857.

10. Takaki, *Pau Hana,* 57–126.

11. Ibid., 92–93, 99–101; Beechert, *Working in Hawaii,* 104.

12. "Toden Higa," 513; Masuoka, "Westernization of the Japanese Family," 205; Takaki, *Pau Hana,* 94, 105; Beechert, *Working in Hawii,* 102–4.

13. Beekman and Beekman, "Hawaii's Great Japanese Strike," B1; Takaki, *Pau Hana,* 120.

14. Masuoka, "Westernization of the Japanese Family," 162; Usaku Morihara interview, 855–56.

15. Minoru Inaba interview, 330; WCS R5 N269; Liu, "Race, Ethnicity," 202.

16. Glick, *Sojourners and Settlers,* 38–39.

17. Pimps and gamblers, organized into gangs, operated from Honolulu's Chinatown. After the Chinatown fire in 1900, government officials arrested many gang members, and the groups never reorganized. See Joan Hori, "Japanese Prostitution in Hawaii," 117–20. In a heartbreaking account, Akemi Kikumura described the misery her mother suffered as her father gambled away whatever money both of them earned as migrant farm laborers in California. Theirs was a story of poverty, disillusionment, and degradation. See Kikumura, *Through Harsh Winters,* 39–49.

18. Hori, "Japanese Prostitution in Hawaii," 115–16; Hane, *Peasants, Rebels, and Outcasts,* 207–25; Ichioka, *"Ameyuki-san,"* 1–22; Sissons, *"Karayuki-san,"* 323–41.

19. Lind, "Assimilation in Rural Hawaii," 203; William C. Smith, "Changing Personality Traits," 925.

20. Okahata, *History of Japanese in Hawaii,* 155–56; Uyehara, "Horehore-Bushi," 111–17. "Horehore" is also spelled "holehole" because the Japanese pronunciation falls somewhere between an "r" and an "l." Day-to-day living conditions among the Japanese on the plantations during the fifteen years before Hawaii was annexed to the United States are sparsely documented. Oral histories began in the 1970s, after many Issei had died or returned to Japan.

21. Hunter, *Buddhism in Hawaii,* 70–72; Okahata, *History of Japanese in Hawaii,* 229.

22. Okahata, *History of Japanese in Hawaii,* 48.

23. Ibid., 56–58; Ramsour, "Study of the Entrance and Activity," 236. The Hawaiian Board, an offshoot of the Congregational mission that had begun in Hawaii in 1820, created departments to proselytize the Hawaiians and the growing numbers of Chinese, Portuguese, Japanese, and Filipinos in Hawaii. Heading the Japanese Department in succession were Orramel Gulick, Frank Scudder, and John Erdman. See Erdman, "Hawaiian Board of Missions," 65–66; and Hunter, *Buddhism in Hawaii,* 78.

24. Hunter, *Buddhism in Hawaii,* 136, 149–50.

25. Okumura, *Seventy Years of Divine Blessings,* 17; Tajima, "Japanese Buddhism in Hawaii," 16; Conroy, *Japanese Frontier in Hawaii,* 101.

26. Hunter, *Buddhism in Hawaii,* 42–45; Conroy, *Japanese Frontier in Hawaii,* 101–2; Okahata, *History of Japanese in Hawaii,* 229.

27. Hunter, *Buddhism in Hawaii,* 83.

28. U.S. Commissioner of Labor, *Report of the Commissioner of Labor on Hawaii, 1902,* 37; Hunter, *Buddhism in Hawaii,* 71–73.

29. Hunter, *Buddhism in Hawaii,* 77–78, 80–81; Okahata, *History of Japanese in Hawaii,* 230.

30. Hunter, *Buddhism in Hawaii,* 103. After Japan's defeat in World War II, Emperor Hirohito disavowed his divinity.

31. Conroy, *Japanese Frontier in Hawaii,* 102; Hunter, *Buddhism in Hawaii,* 77; Tajima, "Japanese Buddhism in Hawaii," 11; Yukiko Kimura, "Psychological Aspects," 18.

32. Harrington, "Loyalties: Dual and Divided," 677; Glick, *Sojourners and Settlers,* 273–92; Lyu, "Korean Nationalist Activities," part 1: 23–90; part 2: 53–100.

33. Wakukawa, *History of the Japanese People,* 84; Conroy, *Japanese Frontier in Hawaii,* 94.

34. *PCA,* 3 January 1905, quoted in Wakukawa, *History of the Japanese People,* 164–65.

35. Conroy, *Japanese Frontier in Hawaii,* 94; Stephan, *Hawaii under the Rising Sun,* 30–31; Farrington Papers, Miscellaneous, "Japanese Training Squadron."

36. The Gentlemen's Agreement comprised a series of six notes exchanged by

the United States and Japan. See U.S. Department of State, *Foreign Relations of the United States, 1924*, 339–69.

37. Later chapters discuss other actions against the Japanese, nationally, on the West Coast, and in Hawaii, including alien land laws, foreign press laws, foreign language school laws, the U.S. Supreme Court decision confirming the denial of citizenship to Issei, and the 1924 Immigration Act.

38. Conroy, *Japanese Frontier in Hawaii*, 131–32; Reinecke, *Feigned Necessity*, 10–11.

39. Beechert, *Working in Hawaii*, 122, 146; Adams, *Japanese in Hawaii*, 12; Yukiko Kimura, "Comparative Study of Collective Adjustment," 129.

40. Beechert, *Working in Hawaii*, 132–33.

41. Adams, *Japanese in Hawaii*, 12; Anonymous A interview.

42. U.S. Department of Commerce and Labor, *Bulletin 1906*, 397–99, 485; Aller, "Evolution of Hawaiian Labor Relations," 171–72; Ichihashi, *Japanese in the United States*, 244–45.

43. Ichihashi, *Japanese in the United States*, 283; Strong, *Second Generation Japanese Problem*, 38.

44. Levering, *Public and American Foreign Policy*, 58–61; Ichihashi, *Japanese in the United States*, 284–85.

45. For details of the San Francisco Board incident and its relationship to the Gentlemen's Agreement, see Roger Daniels, *Politics of Prejudice*, 31–44. West Coast agitation against Japanese immigration was enormously out of proportion to the numbers entering the continent. In 1907, the year of heaviest Japanese immigration to the West Coast, about 30,000 arrived. That same year some 1.25 million immigrants entered the United States. In California, the proportion of Japanese in the population peaked at 2 percent. See Daniels, "Japanese Immigrants," 78.

Chapter 2: Settlers

1. Richard Inouye interview. Chinese, Filipino, German, Greek, Irish, and Mexican immigrants, among others, regularly sent millions of dollars to their families in their home countries. See Glick, *Sojourners and Settlers*, 102–3; Cariaga, "Filipinos in Hawaii," 86; and Dinnerstein, Nichols, and Reimers, *Natives and Strangers*, 171.

2. Ichioka, *The Issei*, 246; U.S. Department of Commerce and Labor, *Bulletin 1911*, 715; Masuoka, "Westernization of the Japanese Family," 148; U.S. Department of Commerce and Labor, *Bulletin 1911*, 715; Conroy, *Japanese Frontier in Hawaii*, 91; S. Frank Miyamoto, "Social Solidarity," 87–88.

3. Ichioka, *The Issei*, 164–65; Okahata, *History of Japanese in Hawaii*, 164; Adams, *Japanese in Hawaii*, 16.

4. According to Houchins and Houchins ("Korean Experience in America," 140), about a thousand Korean men in Hawaii also sent for picture brides. Patriarchal Chinese cultural values and American governmental actions combined to limit the number of Chinese women entering the United States after 1882.

United States Chinese exclusion laws did not mention women, but federal courts often ruled against their entry. Some unmarried men returned to China to find wives and then left them behind when re-entering the United States. Until the end of World War II, an excessively large number of married Chinese men living on the mainland and in Hawaii had wives in China. See Chan, "Exclusion of Chinese Women," 94–146. Many Portuguese, Spanish, and Puerto Ricans came as families, so their male marital rates were relatively high. See Adams, *Peoples of Hawaii*, 28; and Adams, Livesay, and VanWinkle, "Statistical Study of the Races," 16.

5. Okahata, *History of Japanese in Hawaii*, 194; *NJ*, 15 September 1922; *NJ*, 22 September 1922.

6. "Tsuru Yamauchi," 488–90.

7. Masuoka, "Westernization of the Japanese Family," 192–94.

8. Osame Manago interview, 1365–74.

9. Raku Morimoto interview, 192–94. Few records remain of the early years of the Susannah Wesley Home. United Methodist missionaries established the home in Waipahu on Oahu in 1899, then moved it to Kalihi in Honolulu in 1901. Besides providing shelter for Japanese and Korean orphan girls and troubled women, the home offered classes in sewing and English. This information is from Ron Higashi, executive director of the Susannah Wesley Community Center, 20 March 1991. Many picture brides arriving on the West Coast also experienced shock and disappointment. See Ichioka, *"Amerika Nadeshiko,"* 345–47.

10. Kame Okano interview, 599; Misae Yano interview.

11. Of the nineteen temples and shrines existing in Kona in 1939, sixteen had been built between 1908 and 1925. See Lind, "Assimilation in Rural Hawaii," 207–8.

12. U.S. Department of Commerce and Labor, *Bulletin 1911*, 730; Okahata, *History of Japanese in Hawaii*, 173; Beekman and Beekman, "Hawaii's Great Japanese Strike," B2.

13. Scudder, "Hawaii's Experience with the Japanese," 111–12; Gulick, *Hawaii's American-Japanese Problem*, 5–6, 11–12; Taylor, *Advocate of Understanding*, 76–77, 87–89, 111–19. A 1924 Japanese consulate survey discussed in Okumura and Okumura, *Hawaii's American-Japanese Problem* (21), found that 80 to 90 percent of the Issei had decided to make Hawaii their permanent homes.

14. Beechert, *Working in Hawaii*, 174; Takaki, *Pau Hana*, 96–97, 104, 112–16.

15. For accounts of group solidarity among mainland Japanese, see Miyamoto, "Immigrant Community in America," 128; and Modell, *Economics and Politics*, 86–93. For discussions of rotating credit associations among Asian immigrants, see Light, *Ethnic Enterprise in America*, 19–36; Glick, *Sojourners and Settlers*, 104–5; and Cariaga, "Filipinos in Hawaii," 93.

16. Ruth N. Masuda, "Japanese Tanomoshi," 16–19.

17. Adams, *Japanese in Hawaii*, 10–12; *NJ*, 2 March 1928; Yukiko Kimura, "Comparative Study of Collective Adjustment," 129; Ichihashi, *Japanese in the United States*, 65–66.

18. Lind, *Hawaii's People*, 27; Dorita, "Filipino Immigration to Hawaii," 130–31; Cariaga, "Filipinos in Hawaii," 2; Houchins and Houchins, "Korean Experience in America," 135; Beechert, *Working in Hawaii*, 146; Archdeacon, *Becoming*

American, 115–19. These percentages are rough estimates because the U.S. government did not keep complete records of alien emigration. Archdeacon's figures on the Turks, Rumanians, Greeks, and Poles are conservative because they do not include those who returned to their homelands after 1924.

19. Adams, *Japanese in Hawaii*, 11. More specific figures for 1907 are as follows: 11,940 men, 1,877 women, and 158 children arrived; 1,810 men, 692 women, and 986 children departed. For 1912: 1,270 men, 2,019 women, and 176 children arrived; 1,787 men, 742 women, and 911 children departed.

20. Adams, *Japanese in Hawaii*, 10; Masuoka, "Westernization of the Japanese Family," 246.

21. Sueno Matsushita interview.

22. Edward Fukunaga interview.

23. Tom Ige, *Boy from Kahaluu*, 11–13.

24. Misako Yamamoto, "Cultural Conflicts and Accommodations," 41–42.

25. Osame Manago interview, 1381–84.

26. Adams, "The Japanese," n.p.

27. Masuoka, "Westernization of the Japanese Family," 144, 146. Hane describes the devastating impact of modernization on the masses of poverty-stricken farmers in Japan during the late nineteenth and early twentieth centuries (*Peasants, Rebels, and Outcasts*).

28. Lind, *Hawaii's Japanese*, 14; U.S. Department of Commerce, Bureau of Census, *Fourteenth Census, 1920: Population*, 1174, 1177.

29. Hawaii Territory, Department of Public Instruction, *Biennial Report*, 1928, 161; hereafter cited as *Biennial Report*. Most Nisei were born between 1905 to 1920. Thus few Nisei reached college-age before 1925. See Japanese Students' Association of Hawaii, *Students' Annual, 1927*, 76. It should be noted that there were some Nisei-Sansei (those having one Issei parent and one Nisei parent) born during the second and third decades of the century. For example, state School Superintendent Timmy Hirata, born in 1915, and U.S. Senator Daniel Inouye, born in 1924, had Nisei mothers. Shichiro Miyamoto's "Study of the Japanese Language Ability of the Second and Third Generation Japanese Children in a Honolulu Language School" reported that 23 percent of the Japanese language school students he surveyed in 1937 were Nisei-Sansei, and 13 percent were Sansei. With few exceptions, the Japanese Americans in my study were Nisei.

30. Richard Inouye interview; Ethel Kina interview.

31. WCS R8 N61.

32. Ibid.

33. WCS R3 HH125; Sueno Matsushita interview.

34. Edythe Yamamoto interview; Charles Sakai interview, 457.

35. I include a discussion of the Issei worldview with the understanding that cultures constantly undergo change. The values expressed by the Issei, in their words and actions, were diverse and continually in the process of change. Nevertheless, some generalizations can be made. See Yanagisako, *Transforming the Past*, 17–20, for a discussion of culture and tradition.

36. Kikumura and Kitano, "Japanese-American Family," 46; Hayashida, "Japanese Moral Instruction," 12.

37. Maykovich, *Japanese American Identity Dilemma*, 27–33; Kikumura and

Kitano, "Japanese-American Family," 46; DeVos, *Socialization for Achievement,* 3; Rogers and Izutsu, "The Japanese," 84.

38. Iwado, " 'Hagakure Bushido,' " 44–45; Maykovich, *Japanese American Identity Dilemma,* 30–33.

39. Maykovich, *Japanese American Identity Dilemma,* 28, 33; DeVos, *Socialization for Achievement,* 12; Lebra, *Japanese Patterns of Behavior,* 22–37; Caudill and Weinstein, "Maternal Care and Infant Behavior," 225–76; Doi, "Amae," 121, 125; Yamamoto and Iga, "Emotional Growth of Japanese-American Children," 170.

40. Kikumura, *Through Harsh Winters,* 10; Masuoka, "Westernization of the Japanese Family," 34.

41. Masuoka, "Westernization of the Japanese Family," 18–19, 31–32, 38–39; Kikumura, *Through Harsh Winters,* 158.

42. Hayashida, "Japanese Moral Instruction," 12.

43. DeVos, *Socialization for Achievement,* 3, 13, 143; Maykovich, *Japanese American Identity Dilemma,* 2, 35–36.

44. Kikumura, *Through Harsh Winters,* 148–49.

45. Maykovich, *Japanese American Identity Dilemma,* 34–35; Passin, *Society and Education in Japan,* 57; Dore, *Education in Tokugawa Japan,* 291.

46. Dore, *Education in Tokugawa Japan,* 1–3, 292–93.

47. The figures on years of schooling are based on table 23 in Strong, *Second Generation Japanese Problem,* 186. According to Strong, U.S. government reports on Issei schooling are inaccurate. See also Petersen, *Japanese Americans,* 123. The data on school attendance and completion in Japan during the nineteenth century, in Passin, *Society and Education in Japan* (6–7), are consistent with these figures. The WCS student essays support these statistics: most of the Nisei said that their parents had from three to six years of education. According to Strong (*Second Generation Japanese Problem,* 160) and Petersen (*Japanese Americans,* 122–23), the Issei who migrated to Hawaii had about one to three fewer years of schooling than those who went directly to the West Coast of the United States. According to Passin (*Society and Education in Japan,* 56–77), by the end of the Tokugawa era (1868) about 50 percent of the men and women farmers were literate. Since the Issei arrived twenty to fifty years later, during the Meiji era, a time of increased intellectual and social stimulation, probably about 70 percent of the immigrants to Hawaii were literate.

48. U.S. Department of Commerce and Labor, *Bulletin 1911,* 691; Adams, *Japanese in Hawaii,* 14–15; Wakukawa, *History of the Japanese People,* 188, 411; Beechert, *Working in Hawaii,* 123, 145; Lind, *Island Community,* 255. Note that Japanese percentages among both skilled and unskilled workers were high because during most of the period between 1890 and 1920, they made up the bulk of all plantation workers. See Lind, *Island Community,* 204, for an excellent stack graph showing the various ethnic groups employed on sugar plantations from 1882 to 1934.

49. Beechert, *Working in Hawaii,* 125; Takaki, *Pau Hana,* 23; Adams, *Peoples of Hawaii,* 35; Adams, *Japanese in Hawaii,* 14–15; Reinecke, *Feigned Necessity,* 138–39; Okahata, *History of Japanese in Hawaii,* 185. The ratio of ethnic occu-

pancy of Japanese plantation laborers in 1920 was 1.0, indicating proportional representation. A ratio above 1.0 indicates overrepresentation, while a ratio below 1.0 indicates underrepresentation. See Tamura, "Americanization Campaign" (426–29), for an explanation of the ratio of ethnic occupancy.

50. Richard Inouye interview.

51. Shoicki Kurahashi interview; Misae Yano interview.

52. Yoshiko Oda interview; Kazuo Hosaka interview; Lowell Takahashi interview, 508–61; Tetsuko Tamura interview.

53. Adams and Kai, "Education of the Boys of Hawaii," 52; WCS R6 N137.

54. Adams and Kai, "Education of the Boys of Hawaii," 50; Charles Sakai interview, 479.

55. U.S. Department of Commerce and Labor, *Bulletin 1906*, 388.

56. Beechert, *Working in Hawaii*, 145; U.S. Department of Commerce and Labor, *Bulletin 1906*, 388–96; Choy, "Moiliili: A Historical Analysis," 70–79; Sueno Matsushita interview.

57. *Planters Monthly*, 187; Aller, "Evolution of Hawaiian Labor Relations," 139–42.

58. Lind, *Island Community*, 269–70; Griffiths, "More Race Questions," 4; U.S. Department of Commerce and Labor, *Bulletin 1906*, 392.

59. Glick, *Sojourners and Settlers*, 217; U.S. Department of Commerce and Labor, *Bulletin 1906*, 402–3.

60. U.S. Department of Commerce, Bureau of the Census, *Fourteenth Census, 1920: Population*, 1277–78.

61. Tamura, "Americanization Campaign," 465–66. Caucasians included Portuguese and Puerto Ricans in 1910 and Portuguese in 1950.

62. Richard Inouye interview; Miyo Asuka interview, 897, 903. Similar comments are found in Fumiko Nunotani interview, 258–59.

63. Lind, "Occupational Trends," 296–97; Lind, *Island Community*, 327; Adams and Kai, "Education of the Boys of Hawaii," 50–52; Goto, "Ethnic Groups and the Coffee Industry," 121.

64. Lind, "Occupational Trends," 297–98.

65. Harold Aoki interview, 725–31; Lind, *Island Community*, 327; Lind, "Occupational Trends," 294–95. Note that Japanese shopkeepers depended on Caucasian wholesalers for the bulk of their supplies; they received some goods from Japan through Japanese wholesalers in Honolulu. For a discussion of the Chinese leaving the plantations for other occupations, see Glick, *Sojourners and Settlers*, 45–84.

66. Misae Yano interview.

Chapter 3: Americanization Fever

1. Interviews with family members and friends. Fujita died in 1976, when she was fifty-nine years old.

2. Wist Papers, "Fujita, Tatsue," *NJ*, 24 June 1939, translated.

3. Wist Papers, "Fujita, Tatsue," Fujita to Wist, 21 June 1939.

4. Fujita to Wist, 21 June 1939.

5. Wist Papers, "Fujita, Tatsue," Wist to Fujita, 23 June 1939.

6. Wist Papers, "Fujita, Tatsue," *NJ*, 3 July 1939, translated.

7. *HH*, 11 July 1939; *NJ*, 11 July 1939.

8. Wist Papers, "Fujita, Tatsue," Makino to Crawford, 27 July 1939; Wist Papers, "Fujita, Tatsue," Crawford to Makino, 28 July 1939; Wist Papers, "Fujita, Tatsue," Wist to Crawford, 1 August 1939.

9. *HH*, 6 July 1939.

10. Abramson, "Assimilation and Pluralism," 151–53.

11. Gordon, *Assimilation in American Life*, 120–21, 128; Greenbaum, "America in Search of a New Ideal," 419–20; Gleason, "American Identity and Americanization," 38–39.

12. A collection of Park's essays on race relations are in Park, *Race and Culture*, published posthumously. For an excellent analysis of Park's work and the studies it generated, see Lyman, "Race Relations Cycle of Robert E. Park," 16–22. Park discussed his views on assimilation in Park and Burgess, *Introduction to the Science of Sociology* (756–62). This book was for some time a standard text in university classes in sociology.

13. Hansen, "Third Generation in America," 492–500; Herberg, *Protestant, Catholic, Jew*, 201. Hansen's 1937 address attracted little notice until it was reprinted in *Commentary* fifteen years later. Fifty years after Hansen enunciated his thesis at Augustana College, a group of historians and social scientists assembled at Augustana to discuss Hansen's contributions to the study of immigrants and their descendants. Results of the discussions were published in Kivisto and Blanck, *American Immigrants and Their Generations*.

14. Gordon, *Assimilation in American Life*, 68–71.

15. Ibid., 80–81; Metzger, "American Sociology and Black Assimilation," 627–47; Paul Takagi, "Myth of 'Assimilation in American Life,'" 149–58; Kagiwada, "Confessions of a Misguided Sociologist," 159–64; Endo, "Social Science and Historical Materials," 307–8.

16. Bodnar, *The Transplanted*, 118. Some studies have questioned specific parts of Gordon's analysis. Wang, "Korean Assimilation," found no evidence supporting the pivotal role Gordon gave to structural assimilation. Wang found no consistent relationship among cultural assimilation, structural assimilation, and identificational assimilation, and concluded that immigrants adjust to a host country in a variety of ways (iv, 114, 120). Gordon's "ethclass" hypothesis, stating that people tend to socialize with members of the same ethnic group and social class, was not borne out by Leon's "Test of the Milton M. Gordon Ethclass Hypothesis," a study of public high school students in Hawaii.

17. Lebra, "Acculturation Dilemma," 6. Lebra does not deny a degree of validity to the linear model, saying that some cultural replacement and cultural conflict do occur. She used linear and nonlinear models in her analysis of Japanese language schools.

18. Abramson, "Assimilation and Pluralism," 154; Gleason, "American Identity and Americanization," 43–45. For critiques of Kallen's views, see Gordon,

Assimilation in American Life, 141–54; and Sollors, "Critique of Pure Pluralism," 250–79.

19. Glazer and Moynihan, *Beyond the Melting Pot,* pass.; Novak, *Rise of the Unmeltable Ethnics,* pass.; Greeley, *Ethnicity in the United States,* 308–10; Gleason, "American Identity and Americanization," 54; Abramson, "Assimilation and Pluralism," 150; Appleton, *Cultural Pluralism,* 34–37; Conzen, Gerber, Morawska, Pozzetta, and Vecoli, "Invention of Ethnicity." Fujita and O'Brien (*Japanese American Ethnicity,* 20) similarly discuss the idea of an emergent ethnicity. The concepts of ethnogenesis, the invention of ethnicity, and an emergent ethnicity seem to capture the experiences of the Sansei, or third generation, whom I discuss briefly in the epilogue.

20. Hartmann, *Movement to Americanize,* 7–8; Solomon, *Ancestors and Immigrants,* 59–61. This Anglo-Saxon complex was criticized during the heyday of the Americanization movement by some contemporaries. See, for example, Berkson, *Theories of Americanization,* 55–67.

21. Daniels, *Coming to America,* 104–9.

22. Ibid., 117.

23. Higham, *Strangers in the Land,* ii, 3–4.

24. Hartmann, *Movement to Americanize,* 64, 105, 267; Higham, *Strangers in the Land,* 236–37; Gordon, *Assimilation in American Life,* 99.

25. Gordon, *Assimilation in American Life,* 98; Hartmann, *Movement to Americanize,* 105–7.

26. Hartmann, *Movement to Americanize,* 216–17; Higham, *Strangers in the Land,* 251, 255; Murray, *Red Scare,* 196–97, 212–17, 264–66.

27. Hartmann, *Movement to Americanize,* 269. Americanization continued to draw interest well into the 1920s. Esther A. Smith, *International Index to Periodicals,* lists a sizable number of articles on the subject from 1920 to 1927, after which articles are few and far between.

28. *Webster's New International Dictionary of the English Language,* 1948 edition, gave the same definition as its 1935 edition.

29. Bierstadt, *Aspects of Americanization,* 114–15; Hartmann, *Movement to Americanize,* 269.

30. Cremin, *Transformation of the School,* 71; Olneck and Lazerson, "Education," 306; Violas, *Training of the Urban Working Class,* 59.

31. Ettinger, "Americanization," 129–33; Krug, *Shaping of the American High School,* 9.

32. Gleason, "American Identity and Americanization," 40; Lazerson, *Origins of the Urban School,* 233; Cremin, *Transformation of the School,* 66; Krug, *Shaping of the American High School,* 9.

33. Flanders, *Legislative Control,* 7–63.

34. Edward P. Irwin, "Ed Irwin More Than Suggests," 55; Steiner, "Some Factors," 116–19.

35. *SB,* 7 January 1919; *PCA,* 11 March 1919; *SB,* 8 January 1919; cited in Weinberg, "Movement to Americanize," 24–25. In March 1921 the *Pacific Commercial Advertiser* was renamed the *Honolulu Advertiser.*

36. Weinberg, "Movement to Americanize," 29, 32–35.

37. Murray, *Red Scare*, 267–69; Beechert, *Working in Hawaii*, 214–15.

38. Olneck, "Americanization and the Education of Immigrants," 398–401.

39. In 1920 the Japanese totaled 109,274 and were proportionately at their peak.

40. Weinberg, "Movement to Americanize," 10–12.

41. Lind, *Hawaii's People*, 30; Lind, *Hawaii's Japanese*, 11–12; Reinecke, *Feigned Necessity*, 6–10, 161–435; Okihiro, *Cane Fires*, 82–123.

42. Weinberg, "Movement to Americanize," 12–16, 30–32; Okumura and Okumura, *Hawaii's American-Japanese Problem*, 25. Like the Japanese, the Germans, once admired for their impressive rise out of the working class, became objects of distrust during and after World War I. German Americans were accused of conspiring with Germany and of being disloyal to the United States. See Higham, *Strangers in the Land*, 196–97.

43. Weinberg, "Movement to Americanize," x, 49–53. In his research on the Americanization campaign as expressed in Hawaii's Caucasian press, Weinberg found a strikingly dramatic increase from 1919 in the amount of newspaper space devoted to issues of Americanization. Coverage began subsiding in 1923.

44. *NJ*, 1 January 1920; *NJ*, 1 January 1922.

45. Weinberg perused locally written articles, editorials, and letters to the editor in the two English language dailies, the *Advertiser* and *Star-Bulletin*, and the English language monthly, *Paradise of the Pacific*, to find out how Caucasians in Hawaii between 1919 and 1923 defined Americanization. He came up with this list: getting an American education; ability to read, write, and speak English; being a Christian; loyalty to the United States only; obeying the law; participating actively in American community life; establishing an American home; using American business methods; being a good sport; rejecting class and race divisions; venerating democracy; having good moral character; continuing American traditions; and being a good American citizen (see Weinberg, "Movement to Americanize," viii, 54–56). Americanizers failed to live up to key elements of their definition as given by Weinberg, that of rejecting class and race divisions and of venerating democracy, insofar as these elements meant equal opportunity for all.

46. Citizenship Education Committee of the Territorial YMCA, *American Institute Papers*, 22; Allen, "Education and Race Problems," 620. In 1923 the territorial legislature passed a law stipulating that only U.S. citizens could be employed as public school teachers. See Robert E. Potter, "Public School Teachers," 29.

47. *Biennial Report*, 1920, 71–72; Clarence Kobayashi interview.

48. *SB*, 11 April 1932; *SB*, 17 June 1941.

49. Stephan, *Hawaii under the Rising Sun*, 35–37, 41–43.

50. Ibid., 42.

51. Takagi, "Moral Education," 23–24.

52. See Higham, *Ethnic Leadership in America*, for essays on the conflict between views of accommodation and protest among different ethnic groups. In

the same book, Roger Daniels's "The Japanese" (36–63) discusses the victory of the accommodationist view among Japanese Americans on the mainland during World War II.

53. Okumura and Okumura, *Hawaii's American-Japanese Problem*, 2; Hunter, *Buddhism in Hawaii*, 136, 149.

54. New Americans Conference, *Proceedings of Annual Conference*, 1939, 6–7; Okumura, "Test of Japanese Assimilation," 45; Okumura, *Seventy Years of Divine Blessings*, 11. Phrases like "blood that flows in their veins" and *"bushido, the way of the samurai"* were often used by Issei and Nisei who wrote about Americanization.

55. Okumura, "Test of Japanese Assimilation," 46.

56. Hawaii Hochi, *Fred Kinzaburo Makino*, n.p.

57. Ibid.

58. Shunzo Sakamaki, "History of the Japanese Press," 98–101. These words, which reflected Makino's views, came from the pen of the *Hochi* editor George W. Wright.

59. New Americans Conference, 1934, 47–48.

60. *HH*, 24 July 1926.

61. *NJ*, 9 December 1919.

62. *NJ*, 12 August 1922; *NJ*, 29 April 1921.

63. *NJ*, 16 November 1925; *NJ*, 3 October 1925; *NJ*, 23 July 1924; *NJ*, 23 July 1924; *NJ*, 27 October 1920. Although Makino and Soga used the term *Americanization* in their advice to Nisei, their definition of the word differed from that of Americanizers. Therefore I avoid using the term when explaining their views. Most Japanese believed that the Nisei should fuse the best of both cultures. Tasuku Harada, professor of Japanese language and culture at the University of Hawaii, told the Nisei in 1924, "Your Americanization does not require the wholesale abandonment of all things Japanese. . . . East and West meet in you." See Japanese Students' Association of Hawaii, *Students' Annual*, 1924, 14–15.

64. *NJ*, 17 April 1920; *NJ*, 25 March 1923; *NJ*, 29 March 1921; *NJ*, 9 December 1919; *NJ*, 10 April 1920.

65. WCS R5 N263; WCS R5 N256; Japanese Students' Association of Hawaii, *Students' Annual*, 1924, 9, 24. Patriotic statements were also given in WCS R8 L8; WCS R3 HH204; WCS R3 HH99; WCS R14 MK110; WCS R14 MK111; WCS R14 MK130; WCS R9 HJ6; and WCS R16 MP261.

66. Poindexter Papers, Miscellaneous, "Japanese Newspapers."

67. *SB*, 11 December 1941; *SB*, 5 January 1942.

68. WCS R3 HH204; WCS R5 N261. Similar views were expressed in WCS R2 N9 and WCS R8 N65.

69. Japanese Students' Association of Hawaii, *Students' Annual*, 1924, 31.

70. WCS R3 N21. Ralph Honda recalled a similar reaction to discrimination. "From 1940 on," he said, "sometimes I [wondered] . . . why didn't the Constitution say that United States citizenship shall be only for the white, then I'd be Japanese and [wouldn't] have to worry. But to be told you are American and not be treated as American, this hurt very much."

258 Notes to Pages 68–73

71. Japanese Students' Association of Hawaii, *Students' Annual*, 1928, 26; WCS R3 HH166. Similar sentiments were expressed in WCS R4 HH6; WCS R7 N164; and Shoichi Kurahashi interview.

72. "What Can American Citizens of Japanese Descent Do to Serve Hawaii and Contribute to Her Progress?" *NJ*, 1928, 5–7.

73. Kobayashi, "Don't Give Me That Rubbish!" 3; Lyman, "Generation and Character," 285; Glenn, *Issei, Nisei, War Bride*, 52; Connor, "Acculturation and Family Continuities," 163; Makabe, "Ethnic Identity and Social Mobility," 112. Other immigrant groups, too, "never construed ethnic preservation as inimical to American citizenship and loyalty." See Olneck and Lazerson, "Education," 308.

74. Shoichi Kurahashi interview; Edythe Yamamoto interview; Yoshiko Oda interview; Tetsuko Tamura interview; Marie interview.

Chapter 4: Discrimination and Americanization

1. Park, *Immigrant Press*, 12–13, 253–54.

2. Ayer and Son, *N. W. Ayer & Son's Directory*, 1900, 1920, pass. "Publications" refers to newspapers, magazines, and periodicals issued daily, three times a week, semiweekly, weekly, semimonthly and monthly, including religious as well as nonreligious publications.

3. Ibid., 1900, 1920, pass. According to Kloss, the number of German speakers in the United States reached a peak of nine million in 1910, the largest proportion of all non-English speaking groups in the history of the United States before World War II ("German-American Language," 211–52).

4. Park, *Immigrant Press*, 359.

5. Wakukawa, *History of the Japanese People*, 331; Hawaii Hochi, *Fred Kinzaburo Makino*, n.p.; Glick, *Sojourners and Settlers*, 299–304; Ma, *Revolutionaries, Monarchists, and Chinatowns*, 41–44, 132–41; Lyu, "Korean Nationalist Activities," part 2, 59–60, 73, 80.

6. Wakukawa, *History of the Japanese People*, 330; Park, *Immigrant Press and Its Control*, 359; Dinnerstein, Nichols, and Reimers, *Natives and Strangers*, 172; Soltes, *Yiddish Press*, 176–77; *NJ*, 17 August 1920; *NJ*, 30 January 1927; *NJ*, 1 December 1927.

7. Wakukawa, *History of the Japanese People*, 331.

8. Ibid., 326; Odo and Sinoto, *Pictorial History of the Japanese*, 148; Morris and Marumoto, "Inventory of Newspapers," pass.

9. Morris and Marumoto, "Inventory of Newspapers," pass.; Tamura, "Americanization Campaign," 432–33.

10. *Hawaii Times 60th Anniversary*, 1; Shunzo Sakamaki, "History of the Japanese Press," 76.

11. *NJ*, 15 November 1920; Shunzo Sakamaki, "History of the Japanese Press," 60.

12. Hawaii Hochi, *Fred Kinzaburo Makino*, n.p.

13. *PCA*, 20 February 1920, cited in Weinberg, "Movement to American-

ize," 58; Reinecke, *Feigned Necessity*, 45; Memo dated 3 May 1921, quoted in Reinecke, *Feigned Necessity*, 153.

14. *HA*, 5 April 1921; Reinecke, *Feigned Necessity*, 157–58.

15. *SB*, 2 April 1921; *HA*, 2 April 1921; *NJ*, 16 March 1921; *NJ*, 3 March 1921; *NJ*, 6 April 1921; *NJ*, 11 April 1921.

16. Wakukawa, *History of the Japanese People*, 332–34; Reinecke, *Feigned Necessity*, 158–60; *NJ*, 29 April 1921.

17. Stephan, *Hawaii under the Rising Sun*, 6, 27. See Shunzo Sakamaki, "History of the Japanese Press" for a discussion of the radio news services used by Japanese language newspapers in Hawaii (15–16).

18. Sakamaki, "History of the Japanese Press," 87; *Hawaii Herald*, 18 September 1987, B1; Hawaiian Sugar Planters' Association, pass. I worked with a translator in comparing the English and Japanese language editorials of *Nippu Jiji*. The HSPA had translations made of a number of Japanese language papers. I have not used the HSPA translations because of their questionable nature. Ralph Honda recalled that when he was working in the public relations office of Castle and Cooke in 1936–37, his supervisor asked him to translate an article from a Japanese language paper. At the same time the HSPA asked its employee, Umetaro Okumura, son of Takie Okumura, to translate the same article. Okumura's translation turned out to be harsher than Honda's. So Honda's supervisor asked another person for a translation; the result was very close to Honda's. When questioned, Okumura said he wanted to give the feeling of the writer, not just a literal translation. This caused Honda to believe that Okumura intended to arouse antagonism against that Japanese language newspaper.

19. Ueda, "Naturalization and Citizenship," 737–40; Daniels, *Asian America*, 43.

20. Ueda, "Naturalization and Citizenship," 741; Hunter, *Buddhism in Hawaii*, 110–11.

21. Scudder, "What is White?" 3–4; *NJ*, 5 October 1922; Ueda, "Naturalization and Citizenship," 741; Bradford Smith, *Americans from Japan*, 148; Petersen, *Japanese Americans*, 47–48. For a full discussion of the naturalization issue and Ozawa's case, see Ichioka, *The Issei*, 210–26.

22. *NJ*, 23 June 1924; WCS R2, Life history of S_____. Until 1931, when a provision of the Cable Act of 1922 was repealed, a woman who married an alien ineligible to citizenship lost her U.S. citizenship. This affected Nisei women who married Issei men. The McCarran-Walter Act of 1952 ended discrimination in naturalization by making it "color blind." See Daniels, *Coming to America*, 281, 329.

23. Hunter, *Buddhism in Hawaii*, 178–79; Stephan, *Hawaii under the Rising Sun*, 33. According to Burrows, both the Chinese and Japanese in Hawaii contributed to their respective countries, but the bulk of the money sent was for "relief" rather than military hardware (*Chinese and Japanese*, 32).

24. Burrows, *Chinese and Japanese*, 33.

25. Embree, *Acculturation among the Japanese*, 137–42.

26. Ichihashi, *Japanese in the United States*, 250–51, 271–72, 287–89. Japan

presented the twenty-one demands on China in five groups. The first would pre-
vent Germany's return to Shantung; the second would have China recognize
Japan's interests in South Manchuria and Inner Mongolia; the third would give
Japan a monopoly in mining in designated parts of China; the fourth would have
China declare her coastal territory inalienable; and the fifth would, among other
things, provide for Japanese advisors in the Chinese government, establish joint
Sino-Japanese police forces, and grant Japan railway construction rights in South
China. These sweeping demands caused governments in the rest of the world to
view Japan suspiciously. For a detailed account of the alien land law, see Daniels,
Politics of Prejudice, 46–64.

27. Ichihashi, *Japanese in the United States,* 261–67, 278–80; *Annals of the
American Academy of Political and Social Science,* 13–16; Daniels, *Politics of
Prejudice,* 63, 88.

28. *SB,* 31 August 1921; *SB,* 2 September 1921; *NJ,* 2 September 1921.

29. Ichihashi, *Japanese in the United States,* 279; Modell, *Economics and
Politics,* 102–4; Daniels, *Asian America,* 146–47. For an account of the alien
land laws and their test cases, see Ichioka, *The Issei,* 153–56, 226–43. That these
anti-Japanese actions carried serious foreign relations implications could be seen
in the decision of the editors of *Annals of the American Academy of Political
and Social Science* to devote their 1921 issue to the question of Japanese immigration. In their foreword they stated that the 1920 California alien land law
might have "international complications," and called the "Japanese question . . .
in many ways the most important of the immigration topics."

30. Daniels, "Japanese Immigrants," 84; Daniels, *Coming to America,* 278–79.

31. Levering, *The Public and American Foreign Policy,* 48–49; Ichihashi,
Japanese in the United States, 310; *United States Statutes at Large, 1923–25:
1924 Immigration Law,* 153–69.

32. Ichioka, *The Issei,* 247; *NJ,* 9 February 1923; *NJ,* 28 May 1924; *New
Americans,* 5 (Apr. 1924): 4; *NJ,* 11 April 1924.

33. Ichihashi, *Japanese in the United States,* 311, 314–15; Ichioka, *The Issei,*
247, 250; *NJ,* 24 June 1924; *NJ,* 25 June 1924; *NJ,* 31 May 1924; *NJ,* 4 June 1924.
An immigration law passed in 1965 put Asian immigration on the same footing
as other immigration.

34. Ichioka, *The Issei,* 245–46.

35. *NJ,* 1 November 1924.

36. Ogawa, *Jan Ken Po,* 140.

37. Ibid., 140.

38. Hawaii Hochi, *Fred Kinzaburo Makino,* 72–73; Raku Morimoto interview;
Ralph Honda interview.

39. Myrick, "Open Letter to Governor Wallace R. Farrington," 13, 15, 17–18,
24. Myrick gives more details of the Fukunaga case. See also Ogawa, *Jan Ken Po,*
116–46; and Kotani, *Japanese in Hawaii,* 59–65.

40. *NJ,* 7 January 1929; *NJ,* 5 February 1929; *NJ,* 19 June 1929; *NJ,* 23 October 1929.

41. Sueno Matsushita interview; Miya Soga interview; Tetsuko Tamura interview; Shizue Kuramoto interview.

42. Marie interview; Raku Morimoto interview.

43. Ogawa, *Jan Ken Po*, 141–42; *HA*, 20 October 1930.

44. Daws, *Shoal of Time*, 319–31.

45. New Americans Conference, *Proceedings of Annual Conference*, 1933, 44.

46. Daws, *Shoal of Time*, 336–37; Marumoto, "Personal History," part 2, 17.

47. Weinberg, "Movement to Americanize," 60; Matsubayashi, "Japanese Language Schools," 73–77; Huber, "Dual Citizenship," 23; Burrows, *Chinese and Japanese*, 5; Bradford Smith, *Americans from Japan*, 149–50.

48. *NJ*, 16 October 1925; *NJ*, 19 October 1925; Aiko Tokimasa Reinecke interview; *HA*, 29 June 1932.

49. *NJ*, 22 October 1924; *NJ*, 3 January 1925; *NJ*, 29 October 1926; Okumura, "Problem of Expatriation," 1; Shunzo Sakamaki, "History of the Japanese Press," 99; *HH*, 23 August 1939; *HH*, 14 October 1941.

50. New Americans Conference, *Proceedings of Annual Conference*, 1928, 21; Ibid., 1938, 31–32, 62; Ibid., 1940, 76.

51. Ichihashi, *Japanese in the United States*, 323; Huber, "Dual Citizenship," 23; Jones, "Naturalization in Hawaii," 51–52.

52. Petersen, *Japanese Americans*, 50; Huber, "Dual Citizenship," 24; Ichihashi, *Japanese in the United States*, 323–24. Nisei dual citizenship was also controversial on the mainland. See Toyotomi Morimoto, "Language and Heritage Maintenance," 84–85.

53. "Statement of approval, whenever required" was not explained in the information packet given by the Japanese consulate. See New Americans Conference, *Proceedings of Annual Conference*, 1940, 82–85; and George Sakamaki, "Dual Citizenship and Expatriation," 35.

54. Wray, "Menace of Dual-Citizenship," 9. According to Hawaii Territory, Board of Health, Bureau of Vital Statistics ("Annual Report for Fiscal Year Ended June 30, 1939," 78; and "Board of Health Report for Fiscal Year 1940," 12), there were 3,130 Japanese American births in the fiscal year ending June 1939 and 3,337 in the fiscal year ending June 1940. The average of 3,234 births means that 799 corresponds to 25 percent of the births in 1939.

55. Adams, "Why Japanese Parents Register Their Children," n.p.

56. New Americans Conference, *Proceedings of Annual Conference*, 1928, 21; Ibid., 1930, 19. By the end of 1933, only 4,353 males and 1,097 females had voluntarily expatriated since passage of the new law in 1924, and among those born after 1924, 13,923 males and 13,038 females were not registered at the Japanese consulate. See Okahata, *History of Japanese in Hawaii*, 246.

57. *SB*, 1 January 1941; New Americans Conference, *Proceedings of Annual Conference*, 1940, 86.

58. Petersen, *Japanese Americans*, 150; George Sakamaki, "Dual Citizenship and Expatriation," 35.

59. New Americans Conference, *Proceedings of Annual Conference*, 1930, 19; Marumoto, "Personal History," part 2, 25.

60. George Sakamaki, "Dual Citizenship and Expatriation," 8; *HA*, 26 June 1932.

Chapter 5: Schools as Avenues to Middle-Class Life

1. For discussions on the importance of schooling among mainland Japanese, see S. Frank Miyamoto, "Social Solidarity," 104–10; Modell, *Economics and Politics,* 156–58; and Shimada, "Education, Assimilation, and Acculturation," 68–92.

2. WCS R1 H37. All students quoted in this chapter and in the entire study are of Japanese descent unless otherwise specified.

3. Ibid.

4. Ibid., emphasis in original.

5. Perlmann ("Who Stayed in School") reported a strong relationship between high school grades—reflecting intelligence, work habits, interest in school and other individual characteristics—and graduation from high school. Social background factors, however, made a difference in determining whether or not a student dropped out of school before reaching high school.

6. Hawaii Territory, Department of Public Instruction, *Biennial Report,* 1920, 4–7 (hereafter cited as *Biennial Report,* by year); McCarthy Papers, Territorial Departments, Public Instruction, "Schedule, Teachers' Salaries."

7. Wist, *Century of Public Education,* 141–43; U.S. Department of the Interior, Bureau of Education, *Survey of Education in Hawaii,* 54–55.

8. Wist, *Century of Public Education,* 143–44; *Biennial Report,* 1910, 77; *Biennial Report,* 1920, 205; Hawaii Territory, Department of Public Instruction, "Term Reports, 1940"; hereafter cited as "Term Reports" by year.

9. U.S. Department of the Interior, Bureau of Education, *Survey of Education in Hawaii,* 212; Hawaii Territory, Department of Public Instruction, *School Directory,* 1925–41; Wist, *Century of Public Education,* 177.

10. Tyack, "Pilgrim's Progress," 263–65; Hawaii Territory, Department of Public Instruction, *School Directory,* 1924–40, pass., 1967–68, 6. Hawaii became a state in 1959.

11. U.S. Department of the Interior, Bureau of Education, *Survey of Education in Hawaii,* 146; Shaw, "Output of the Territorial Normal and Training School," 25a.

12. WCS R4 HH8; WCS R6 N145.

13. WCS R6 N175; WCS R16 MP27; WCS R5 N270.

14. WCS R2 N9.

15. Masuoka, "Sociological Study," 263.

16. *Biennial Report,* 1920, 205; *Biennial Report,* 1930, 51; "Term Reports, 1940, 1947."

17. Tyack, *One Best System,* 230.

18. Adams, *Peoples of Hawaii,* 46; Raku Morimoto interview, 172, 181; WCS R1 H19; Sueno Matsushita interview.

19. WCS R6 N173; see also Richard Funai interview, 22–51.

20. *Biennial Report,* 1926, 30–31; *Biennial Report,* 1932, 65, 68; "Term Reports, 1936." See Adams, *Peoples of Hawaii,* 45–47, for comparable data. According to *Biennial Report* (1926, 30–31), six-and-a-half years old was considered the normal age of children entering first grade. For purposes of tabulation the DPI

considered children to be at the normal age if they were younger than eight years old when completing grade one in June (see "Term Reports"). Some students in each grade were younger than the normal ages, but the numbers were minimal.

21. Rose Falconer interview, 166; U.S. Department of the Interior, Bureau of Education, *Survey of Education in Hawaii*, 37; Tsuzaki, "Hawaiian-English," 25–28; Simson, "Use of Hawaiian-Creole," 3. See Sato, "Nonstandard Approach to Standard English" (262–63) Lourie and Conklin, *Pluralistic Nation* (10–13), and Milroy and Milroy, *Authority in Language* (22–23) for discussions of Standard English.

22. Wist, *Century of Public Education*, 181; *Biennial Report*, 1916, 10; *Biennial Report*, 1934, 16; Timmy Hirata interview; Akira Sakima interview; Francis Miyake interview; Richard Funai interview; Tokio Okudara interview. Until 1922, the Territorial Normal and Training School, which was a division of the DPI until 1931, and which prepared prospective grammar school teachers, accepted eighth grade graduates, who attended the Normal School for four years. A Normal School degree was then about equivalent to a high school diploma. From 1922, the Normal School began accepting only high school graduates into a two-year program to prepare grammar school teachers. In the 1920s the University of Hawaii established a department of education that began preparing prospective high school teachers. In 1931, the Normal School merged with the University of Hawaii and was renamed Teachers College, at which time prospective elementary and secondary teachers both matriculated for four years. Teachers College also offered a fifth year to those interested in continuing their training. See *Biennial Report*, 1924, 61; *Biennial Report*, 1928, 110; and Potter, "Public School Teachers," 28–29.

23. Hawaiian-Caucasian female retired teacher interview; Mark and Zelie Sutherland interview; Eileen Tam interview. Modell discusses similar assessments of Nisei students by Los Angeles teachers (*Economics and Politics*, 160).

24. WCS R4 HH19; Masuoka, "Westernization of the Japanese Family," 272. Similar comments are found in WCS R3 HH126; WCS R6 N196; WCS R3 HH99; and WCS R3 HH213.

25. WCS R1 H39.

26. WCS R1 H18; WCS R1 H19; WCS R11 L15; WCS R4 HH34.

27. William C. Smith, *Americans in Process*, 52.

28. Mitamura, "Life on a Hawaiian Plantation," 53; William C. Smith, *Americans in Process*, 163–64.

29. William C. Smith, *Americans in Process*, 164–65.

30. WCS R6 N145. This is the same Takie Okumura who organized the New Americans Conferences, to be discussed more fully in chapter 6. While Okumura held to the idea that the vast majority of Nisei should work on the plantation, he also believed that a select few should pursue higher education. To that end he established two low-cost dormitories, one for boys and another for girls, where he attempted to Christianize his charges by requiring their attendance at religious services.

31. Yoshiko Oda interview; Tetsuko Tamura interview.

32. Kazuo Hosaka interview.

33. WCS R8 N61.

34. WCS R12 M20.

35. The 1929 figure is from Livesay, *Study of Public Education,* 105. The 1935 percentage is from table 5 in Tamura, "Americanization Campaign," 440. Three percent is a rough estimate based on an extrapolation of available data. Livesay (110) reported that forty-one Nisei graduated from the University of Hawaii in 1930. If we say that about twenty more graduated from mainland colleges, we have sixty college graduates. These students would have been in the second grade in 1915–16. Livesay (105) estimated 2,839 Japanese students in second grade in 1919–20. If we say that roughly 2,000 Nisei were in the second grade in 1915–16, we have 3 percent of them graduating from college fourteen years later. Nisei school attendance in Hawaii was similar to that of American-born children of white immigrants on the mainland. In 1920, for example, 35.1 percent of Nisei in Hawaii who were sixteen or seventeen years old attended school, compared to 34.5 percent of American-born children of white immigrants. Note that the age of a student did not necessarily indicate grade level, since a number of sixteen and seventeen-year-olds were still in grammar school. See Adams, *Japanese in Hawaii,* 24.

36. Livesay, *Study of Public Education,* 75–76.

37. Ibid., 105; Tamura, "Americanization Campaign," 440. No figures are available for continuance to college.

38. Kim, "Koreans in Hawaii," 79–80, 136–37; Pomerantz, "Background of Korean Emigration," 277–315; Patterson, "Upward Social Mobility," 8–11; Patterson, *Korean Frontier in America,* 21–22, 103–5; Cariaga, "Filipinos in Hawaii," 109–10. In 1930 only 12 percent of Filipino men aged twenty to twenty-four, and only 35 percent aged fifteen and older, were married. To explain differences among minority groups in school achievement, John U. Ogbu has posited an incentive thesis, which is compatible with my research findings on the Japanese in Hawaii. Research is needed to see how well his thesis explains the experiences of Portuguese, Hawaiians, Filipinos, Samoans, and other ethnic groups in Hawaii. According to Ogbu, volunatary minorities like the Issei came to the United States in search of better opportunities, and this was reflected in their drive to succeed. Involuntary minorities like African Americans and native Americans, on the other hand, became part of American society against their will, and as a result, formed a set of secondary cultural characteristics that worked against school achievement. See, for example, Ogbu, "Class Stratification," 163–82; Ogbu, "Minority Status and Literacy," 141–68; Ogbu, "Minority Coping Responses," 433–56; and Gibson and Ogbu, *Minority Status and Schooling.*

39. Sueno Matsushita interview.

40. Clarence Kobayashi interview; WCS student essays.

41. Richard Inouye interview; Teiki Yoshimoto interview, 308–9; Masayuki Yoshimura, 1475–79.

42. Shoichi Kurahashi interview.

43. William Ishida interview, 431–38; Minoru Kimura interview, 271; WCS R4 HH46. Similar comments are found in WCS R2 H49, and WCS R2 H49. Paula Fass's *Outside In* (64–65) discusses similar educational choices made by Euro-

pean immigrant families in New York City during the first three decades of the twentieth century; when families could afford to send only one child to high school, that child was likely to be the youngest in the family. Moreover, in New York City as in Hawaii, second generation Americans went to high school with the intention of improving their lives.

44. Shoichi Kurahashi interview; Ethel Kina interview; Mitamura, "Life on a Hawaiian Plantation," 54. Similar accounts of elder siblings having to quit school to help support the family are given in WCS R5 HH43; Choy, "Moiliili: A Historical Analysis," 70–79; *HA*, 11 October, C1, C4; Yoshitaka Takashiba interview, 15; Yosoto Egami interview, 261; Charles Sakai interview, 457; and Edith Yonenaka interview, 100.

45. WCS R12 M19.

46. WCS R3 HH80. A similar story is found in WCS R7 N128.

47. Stratford, "Cross-Section of a High School Student's Life," 85–86, 89; WCS R1 H39; WCS R4 HH8; WCS R4 HH33; WCS R14 MK123; WCS R4 HH20; WCS R8 N56; Shoichi Kurahashi interview; Misao Kawakami interview.

48. Richard Inouye interview; Lowell Takahashi interview. Similar accounts are found in WCS R6 N134; WCS R7 N156; and WCS R8 N61.

49. Minoru Inaba interview.

50. WCS R6 N173.

51. WCS R4 HH19.

52. WCS R4 HH23; WCS R3 HH125; WCS R6 N180; WCS R6 N225.

53. "Joseph Y. Kurihara, Autobiography," 10. Similar accounts are found in WCS R1 H30, and Adams and Kai, "Education of the Boys of Hawaii," 35.

54. WCS R1, H-BSK; WCS R5 N263.

55. WCS R7 N166. A similar account is found in WCS R4 HH10.

56. Yuzuru Morita interview, 143.

57. WCS R2 N7.

58. WCS R1 H19.

59. In regard to figures 2 through 4: In calculating school persistence, I combined private and public school students. Private school enrollment in the lower grades during this interwar period ranged from 6 to 11 percent of all students attending school. In high school, private school enrollment ranged from 13 to 19 percent of all students. Additionally, I chose grade, not age, in charting school persistence, because students' ages did not indicate what grades they were in. Moreover, because first grade enrollment was disproportionately large, I began with grade two. The University of Hawaii sociologist Thayne Livesay wrote in 1932: "First grade figures would not give a true picture of conditions. Quite a large proportion of children entering the public schools in the Territory come from homes where no English is spoken and this means that they are apt to remain in the first grade for more than one year" (*Study of Public Education*, 98).

It should be kept in mind that ethnic designations were probably not uniform from school to school and year to year. Japanese students were generally easy to identify because their parents had rarely intermarried and their family names were easily recognizable. On the other hand, because of intermarriage, other students might have been mis-classified because of their last names and/or their physiognomy. Part-Chinese, Part-Hawaiians, and Caucasians were especially susceptible to mis-identification. In addition, about half of all students attending public schools were Japanese, and for this reason the mis-designation of individual non-Japanese students had a much more exaggerated effect on statistics than did the miscounting of the Japanese. Finally, students moving from grade to grade from year to year, when known only by their ethnicity, were not necessarily the same individuals. There was certainly some inflow of new students in each grade in rates that varied from group to group. For example, among 600 sixth graders and 550 eighth graders two years later, 70 may have dropped out and 20 others may have newly enrolled. The effects of such changes cannot be measured and are not reflected in the graphs. Yet, except for Other Caucasians—that is, Caucasians other than Portuguese, Spanish, and Puerto Ricans—enrollment by ethnic groups in Hawaii's public schools was relatively stable. Immigration to Hawaii largely ended by 1924, except for adult male Filipinos, who continued to arrive during the next eight years.

The greatest fluctuations in school enrollment, shown in figure 4, occurred among Other Caucasians in the years during and surrounding World War II. In the 1930s, thousands of defense construction workers and their families arrived from the mainland. Thus there was a sharp increase among Other Caucasian students, shown in figure 4 between 1939 and 1941. Their dramatic drop between 1941 and 1943 reflects departures from Hawaii to the mainland after the attack on Pearl Harbor, and their increase from 1945 to 1947 reflects their return to Hawaii after the war (*SB*, 31 March 1941, 20).

It should also be noted that a small percentage of seniors did not graduate from high school. See Hawaii Territory, Governor's Advisory Committee on Education, "University of Hawaii," 11. A survey found that 33 percent of the Nisei living in Honolulu in 1971 had gone beyond high school, to college or to technical or business schools; 23 percent had received college degrees; and 5 percent, graduate degrees. See Research Committee on the Study of Japanese Americans in Honolulu, Hawaii, *Honolulu's Japanese Americans in Comparative Perspective*, 80–81. Chinese and Filipino students showed a similar pattern of staying in school progressively longer during the interwar period. The different rates of school persistence of the Chinese, followed by the Japanese and then the Filipinos, reflect the different times of each group's initial arrival to Hawaii. The Part-Hawaiians and Portuguese made more modest percentage gains.

60. For persistence rates of twelfth graders in 1943, see Tamura, "Americanization Campaign," 443–44. The Koreans outperformed the Japanese until 1943, but their numbers were so small that I do not include them in figures 3 and 4. For numbers and percentages for Korean students, see Ibid., 440–64. My findings agree with the 1950 census report, which indicated that the median number of school years completed by Japanese Americans born between 1926 and 1930 was 12.36, exceeding the overall median of 11.93 years and second to the median of 12.47 for Chinese Americans. See U.S. Department of Commerce, Bureau of the Census, *Seventeenth Census, 1950*, 52–71.

61. Wist, *Century of Public Education*, 161; Allen, "Education and Race Problems," 616.

62. Allen, "Education and Race Problems," 617; Wist, *Century of Public Education*, 161; Masuoka, "Race Attitudes of the Japanese People," 114. Masaji Marumoto, who had come to Honolulu from rural Kona, a bright young man who would become the first associate justice of the Territorial Supreme Court in 1957, was rejected at Central Grammar because of his spoken English. Chapter 10 discusses his experiences.

63. U.S. Department of the Interior, Bureau of Education, *Survey of Education in Hawaii*, 246–47; McCarthy Papers, Territorial Departments, Public Instruction, "Superintendent, September 1920," MacCaughey to Farrington 1 July 1920; Allen, "Education and Race Problems," 617; Towse, "Proposed School," 75. Frank E. Bunker, director of the survey, had recommended segregating students in separate schools based on their proficiency in English, but Washington officials had omitted the recommendation from the final report because doing so would have been "embarrassing to the Bureau in regions of the United States where conditions were different from those of Hawaii." See Bunker, "Education of the Children," 1.

64. Allen, "Education and Race Problems," 617.

65. At least there were no more complaints about it, and the English Standard schools that developed after 1924 did not segregate the students they admitted. Farrington Papers, Territorial Departments, Public Instruction, "January–December, 1922," MacCaughey to Farrington, 25 October 1922 (emphasis in original).

66. For a listing of all English Standard schools and the years they were established, see Tamura, "Americanization Campaign," 447. Most of the Standard schools were grammar schools that included grades one to eight and elementary schools that included grades one to six. There was one Standard junior high school, Stevenson Intermediate School in Honolulu, and one standard high school, Roosevelt High School in Honolulu. In 1927 and 1931 the territorial legislature expressly provided for English Standard schools. Particularly during the 1940s, the DPI established English Standard "sections—a sort of school within a school"—in other elementary schools. See Meller, "Hawaii's English Standard Schools," 4–10. The *Hawaii Educational Review* (23 [May 1935]: 267) mentions the Annex at Lihue School. For data on population by ethnic group in cities and islands of Hawaii in 1930, see Hawaii Territory, Board of Health, Bureau of Vital Statistics, "Report of the Registrar General . . . 30 June 1930," 85.

67. *NJ*, 19 June 1920; and *SB*, 19 April 1925, cited in Stueber, "Hawaii: A Case Study," 249–50.

68. Hawaii Territory, Department of Public Instruction, "Miscellaneous Reports," 9; *NJ*, 31 March 1925; *Friend* 95 (Apr. 1925): 75.

69. *NJ*, 31 March 1925; *NJ*, 19 June 1920; *NJ*, 23 February 1925; *HH*, 22 July 1926; *HH*, 20 February 1931; *SB*, 19 April 1925.

70. Stueber, "Hawaii: A Case Study," 247.

71. Ibid., 253.

72. Hormann, "English Standard School."

73. Tamura, "Americanization Campaign," 449–50.

74. Enrollment figures do not include students in the English Standard divi-

sion at Lihue School, nor those in English Standard sections of other public schools, which were prevalent in the 1940s. Complete data for these sections are unavailable. Additionally, enrollment in English Standard sections was often based on general ability rather than solely on oral English. See Meller, "Hawaii's English Standard Schools," 10.

75. Stueber, "Hawaii: A Case Study," 254.

76. *HA*, 3 June 1948; Westminster School District of Orange County et al. v. Mendez et al., No. 11310 (9th Cir. 1947). The teachers B. K. Hyams interviewed seemed to accept the English Standard schools as a fact of life. The papers of Governors McCarthy, Farrington, and Judd (who served successively from 1918 to 1934) contained few references to the English Standard schools, and did not include files of petitions, correspondence, and news articles on Standard schools as they did on language schools.

77. In contrast, in the foreign language school issue, the Issei, being noncitizens, had no political influence, so they used the courts to protect their rights. In the same way citizens whose views are in the minority often use the courts when they are blocked by the legislature.

78. Allen, "Education and Race Problems," 616; Tamura, "Americanization Campaign," 454. About 11 percent of all second through twelfth graders in Hawaii attended private school in 1925 and 1937, a figure that increased to almost 18 percent in 1947.

79. The ratios of ethnic occupancy in figure 6 exclude first graders because data for 1925 combine first graders with kindergartners. I deliberately exclude kindergartners from my data on private school enrollment because their numbers distort the overall private school enrollment figures. Often, parents who worked had no choice but to send their children to private kindergartens, since there were no public school kindergartens available until 1943. When separate figures are available for kindergartners, their huge enrollment becomes evident. In 1937, for example, 4,133 students attended private kindergartens. One year later, fewer than one-third of them attended private schools as first graders. The difference was even greater for Japanese. In 1937, 1,855 Japanese students attended private kindergartens. A year later, only 8 percent of them continued in private school as first graders. Once public school was available, most parents sent their children there. A few "free kindergartens," subsidized by private organizations, operated in the 1920s and 1930s ("Term Reports, 1937, 1938," n.p.; *Biennial Report, 1920*, 156; *Biennial Report, 1944*, 21. In compliance with Act 220, passed by the territorial legislature, the DPI opened its first kindergartens that fall).

Because of the substantial enrollment in private kindergartens, figures in the Department of Public Instruction's *Biennial Reports* can be misleading. According to the 1928 report, for example, 2,395 Japanese students were attending private schools. The report failed to point out, however, that only 21 percent of these students were in regular private schools. The rest were in kindergarten (63 percent) or special schools and classes, including post-secondary commercial schools (16 percent) (*Biennial Report, 1928*, 161).

80. Stroupe, "Significant Factors"; Hormann, "Integration in Hawaii's

Schools," 8; Harold Aoki interview, 768–69; Mia Soga interview. Punahou was established in 1841 to educate the children of missionaries.

81. WCS R6 N180.

82. Lowell Takahashi interview, 508–61; WCS R16 MP29. For private school enrollment figures, see Tamura, "Americanization Campaign," 455–57. Mid-Pacific was established in 1905 from a merger of two Congregational mission schools, Kawaiahao Seminary for Hawaiian girls and Mills School for Chinese boys, and developed as a Christian, nonsectarian coeducational boarding high school. See Wist, *Century of Public Education,* 121–22; "Mid-Pacific Institute," 264; and Gulick, *Mixing the Races,* 70. Iolani School for boys and St. Andrew's Priory for girls were Episcopal schools that accepted nonchurch members as students. Iolani also offered boarding facilities. See Gulick, *Mixing the Races,* 156; and Wist, *Century of Public Education,* 17–19. Hawaiian Mission Academy, a Seventh-day Adventist school in Honolulu, also accepted nonchurch members.

83. Aiko Tokimasa Reinecke interview; Hajime Warashima interview, 563–622.

84. Kazuo Hosaka interview; Simonson, "Brief History," 62–63, 70–73.

85. Hormann, "Integration in Hawaii's Schools," 10.

86. Masakazu Shimoda interview, 145–214; Ralph Honda interview.

87. Shoho arrived at conclusions broadly similar to mine: that girls took second place to boys in educational priority, that parents emphasized schooling, and that public schools were agents of acculturation ("Americanization through Public Education," 228–44, 352–55).

88. Shizue Komu Kuramoto interview.

89. Tamura, "Americanization Campaign," 460; Misae Yano interview; Anonymous A interview; Marie interview.

90. WCS R3 HH184; WCS R16 MP27.

91. Tetsuko Tamura interview.

92. WCS R7 N80.

93. WCS R7 N164.

94. WCS R6 N185.

95. WCS R2 N10; Misao Kawakami interview.

96. WCS R11 L4.

97. Brown, "Fear of Feminization," 496, 504; Krug, *Shaping of the American High School,* 11–12, 171–73; Rury, *Education and Women's Work,* 4; Seller, *History of Women's Education,* 97.

98. Figure 7 compares girl-boy ratios of Japanese and Other Caucasian students. A ratio of less than one means that fewer girls than boys attended high school. A ratio of more than one reflected the American norm. The 1945 ratios reflect wartime influences. As figure 7 shows, Japanese girls increasingly went on to high school. Whereas in 1918 the girl-boy ratio was only 0.15, it had advanced to 0.61 by 1933. By the eve of Pearl Harbor, the ratio had reached 1.0, indicating that just as many Japanese girls as Japanese boys were attending high school.

99. For girl-boy ratios of different ethnic groups from 1918 to 1947, see Tamura, "Americanization Campaign," 460–64.

Chapter 6: Schools as Channels for Plantation Work

1. Michael Katz originated the revisionist thesis in his seminal study, *The Irony of Early School Reform.* See also Katz, *Class, Bureaucracy, and Schools,* 175; and Katz, "Apology for American Educational History," 75–76. Other revisionist works include Violas, *Training of the Urban Working Class;* Nasaw, *Schooled to Order;* Feinberg and Rosemont, *Work, Technology, and Education;* Spring, *Sorting Machine;* and Bowles and Gintis, *Schooling in Capitalist America.* Gail Miyasaki's "Schooling of the Nisei" applied the revisionist thesis to Hawaii. Among those not considered revisionists but who have argued the social control thesis are Wiebe, *Search for Order;* and Buenker, "The Progressive Era: A Search for a Synthesis." Historians have both applauded and criticized the revisionist thesis. See, for example, Greene, "Identities and Contours: An Approach to Educational History"; Lazerson, "Revisionism and American Educational History"; Muraskin, "Social-Control Theory in American History: A Critique"; Cohen, "History of the History of American Education"; Ravitch, *Revisionists Revised;* Kantor, "Great School Warriors"; and Altenbaugh, "'Our children are being trained like dogs and ponies.'"

2. See Weiss, *American Education and the European Immigrant* (xi–xxviii), for a similar discussion of the interaction between immigrants and their host culture.

3. Beechert, *Working in Hawaii,* 240–41; Adams and Kai, "Education of the Boys of Hawaii," 23.

4. *SB,* 2 January 1920, cited in Stueber; U.S. Department of the Interior, Bureau of Education, *Survey of Education in Hawaii,* 205–6, 224–28; Farrington Papers, Territorial Departments, Public Instruction, January–June 1922; Farrington, "Hawaii's Opportunities," n.p.; Farrington, "Opportunities in Hawaii," 1–2.

5. Adams and Kai, "Education of the Boys of Hawaii," 42–43.

6. McCarthy Papers, Territorial Departments, Public Instruction, "Superintendent, June 1918 to June 1919."

7. Ibid.; and *Christian Science Monitor,* n.d., in McCarthy Papers, Territorial Departments, Public Instruction, "Superintendent, July to December 1920."

8. *Paradise of the Pacific* 34 (Dec. 1921): 75; Beechert, *Working in Hawaii,* 243.

9. *HA,* 16 June 1931.

10. Lind, *Island Community,* 325.

11. Lazerson and Grubb, *American Education and Vocationalism,* 48–49; Cohen and Lazerson, "Education and the Corporate Order," 318–23; Hogan, *Class and Reform,* 152–54.

12. Sol Cohen, "Urban School Reform," 300; Lazerson and Grubb, *American Education and Vocationalism,* 17–18; Hogan, *Class and Reform,* 174.

13. Okumura and Okumura, *Hawaii's American-Japanese Problem,* 2; Sanjume, "Analysis of the New Americans Conference," 13–14.

14. Sanjume, "Analysis of the New Americans Conference," 18–29.

15. Ibid., 2, 41–58, 61; New Americans Conference, *Proceedings of the Annual Conference,* 1930, 5, 20.

16. *HH,* 4 August 1928; *HA,* 8 August 1928; New Americans Conference,

1940, *Proceedings of the Annual Conference*, 98. Acting Consul-General Takeuchi, like other representatives of the Japanese government in Hawaii and on the mainland, encouraged acculturation. For the mainland experience, see Daniels, *Asian America*, 173.

17. Sanjume, "Analysis of the New Americans Conference," 31–39; New Americans Conference, *Proceedings of the Annual Conference*, 1927–41. See also Nomura, "Debate over the Role of Nisei," pass.; and *HH*, 9 August 1928.

18. New Americans Conference, *Proceedings of the Annual Conference*, 1927, 6–7; Ibid., 1930, 30; Ibid., 1931, 7.

19. *New Americans* 14 (May 1929): 2.

20. New Americans Conference, *Proceedings of the Annual Conference*, 1927, 8, 11; Ibid., 1929, 7; Ibid., 1931, 17, 27; Ibid., 1935, 17–18; Ibid., 1937, 19–23.

21. Ibid., 1936, 27–28.

22. Ibid., 1934, 25; Ibid., 1937, 6.

23. Governor's Coordinating Committee, *Kansha: In Appreciation*, n.p.; New Americans Conference, 1928, 6. Others who had urged the Nisei to work on the plantation were invited back to speak time and again. According to Keiko Yamamoto ("Oral History of Miles Cary," 23–24), Cary had wanted to be on the faculty at the University of Hawaii, but was rejected by the Board of Regents. When he announced his decision to accept a position at the University of Minnesota in his letter of resignation as McKinley High School principal, he mentioned "certain feelings that should remain unexpressed," as well as his desire to teach at the college level. See *HA*, 4 February 1948. See also Williams, "Educational Theory and Philosophy" (46–90), for a discussion of Cary's educational philosophy.

24. New Americans Conference, *Proceedings of the Annual Conference*, 1937, 6.

25. Judd Papers, Territorial Departments, Public Instruction, "Educational Survey," November–December 1929.

26. Hawaii Territory, Governor's Advisory Committee on Education, *Survey of Schools and Industry*, Appendix, 8–10.

27. Hawaii Territory, Governor's Advisory Committee on Education, *Survey of Schools and Industry*, v, Section 2, 8–9; Stueber, "Hawaii: A Case Study," 299.

28. Hawaii Territory, Governor's Advisory Committee on Education, "Report on the Sugar Cane Industry," 2; Hawaii Territory, Governor's Advisory Committee on Education, *Survey of Schools and Industry*, Section 1, 14–17, Section 2, 72.

29. *NJ*, 23 April 1920.

30. *NJ*, 19 November 1925; *NJ*, 16 November 1925.

31. Stueber, "Hawaii: A Case Study," 297.

32. *SB*, 1931, from RASRL, Cabinet 2, File 37.

33. *New Freedom*, 26 December 1931.

34. *SB*, January 1932, from RASRL, Cabinet 2, File 37.

35. *SB*, 1 January 1929; *SB*, 6 September 1933; *SB*, 11 May 1937; *SB*, 29 May 1937; *Biennial Report*, 1934, 41.

36. *Biennial Report*, 1924, 73; *Biennial Report*, 1926, 105–6. In September 1925, Hawaii began using federal money for vocational education, but because

the territorial legislature had failed to appropriate sufficient matching funds, the DPI was unable to use all available federal money that year.

37. *Biennial Report, 1926*, 105, 110; Lazerson, *Origins of the Urban School,* 97–154.

38. *Biennial Report, 1928*, 116; *Biennial Report, 1926*, 106.

39. *Biennial Report, 1928*, 119–20; *Biennial Report, 1930*, 111.

40. *SB*, 16 April 1931.

41. *Biennial Report, 1928*, 117–18; *Biennial Report, 1930*, 106.

42. *Biennial Report, 1930*, 19, 107; *Biennial Report, 1928*, 111; *Biennial Report, 1936*, 25.

43. Sanjume, "Analysis of the New Americans Conference," 16–17; New Americans Conference," *Proceedings of the Annual Conference, 1930*, 20; *NJ,* 6 August 1927.

44. New Americans Conference, *Proceedings of the Annual Conference, 1928*, 22.

45. Ibid., 1929, p. 6; Ibid., 1931, 9; Ibid., 1932, 21; Ibid., 1941, 28, 58.

46. *HH*, 13 August 1928.

47. Ibid.

48. *HH*, 30 April 1926.

49. Adams and Kai, "Education of the Boys of Hawaii," 40–42, 46.

50. Hawaii Territory, Governor's Advisory Committee on Education, "Report on the Sugar Cane Industry," 49–53; Symes, "Other Side of Paradise," 41.

51. *HH*, 29 August 1927.

52. Richard Inouye interview; WCS R4 HH10; WCS R8 N97. A similar account is found in WCS R3 HH133.

53. Hawaii Territory, DPI, "Annual Descriptive Report," 1; William C. Smith, "Second Generation Oriental," 10; WCS R1 N10; Mitamura, "Life on a Hawaiian Plantation," 51. Similar statements are found in WCS R7 N79; WCS R3 HH207; and WCS R1 H35. See also Takaki, *Pau Hana,* 138.

54. William C. Smith, *Americans in Process,* 87; WCS R3 HH166; WCS R7 N156.

55. WCS R7 N79; WCS R1 N10. A similar view is found in WCS R3 HH204. See also Takaki, *Pau Hana,* 80–81.

56. Adams and Kai, "Education of the Boys of Hawaii," 47.

57. WCS R1 N10; WCS R17 MP38; Adams and Kai, "Education of the Boys of Hawaii," 47; WCS R12 M22; WCS R11 L2; WCS R11 L1; WCS R11 L10.

58. Farrington Papers, Territorial Departments, Public Instruction, July–Sept. 1922. According to Adams and Kai, four years later the attitudes of Hawaii's youth were similar ("Education of the Boys of Hawaii," 26–28). Lind found that, except for the smaller proportion actually entering the skilled trades, the grammar school graduates of 1927 entered jobs in roughly the same proportions as Adams and Kai's survey indicated they would ("Occupational Attitudes," 252). In 1925, Eddy reported on the life vocations public and private high school seniors in the territory expected to have. Teaching, medicine and dentistry, and office work ranked at the top of the list for all seniors. Plantation work, agriculture, and skilled trades ranked at the bottom. Like the Chinese, a larger proportion of

Japanese boys chose office work over the skilled trades. And when compared with other groups, the proportion of Japanese boys who chose teaching was relatively modest. Since 41 percent (twenty-four out of fifty-nine) of the Japanese students who chose teaching were boys, compared to 17 percent of the other groups, Eddy concluded that Japanese boys, more than other groups, tended to choose teaching. What he failed to take into account was that Japanese boys made up a large proportion (77 percent) of Japanese seniors. When choices made by boys in each group are seen in relative proportion to one another, teaching no longer stood out as a primary choice for Japanese boys. Teaching was the most popular choice among girls of all ethnic groups. More than other groups, however, Caucasian girls saw more options for themselves; a smaller proportion of them chose teaching and a larger proportion looked to professions such as medicine and dentistry ("Study of the Vocational Opportunities").

59. *SB*, 4 June 1929; *HH*, 6 June 1929; Hawaii Territory, Governor's Advisory Committee on Education, "Report on the Sugar Cane Industry," 49–53.

60. *HH*, 29 August 1927; *HH*, 11 December 1931; emphasis in original.

61. *NJ*, 28 August 1926; *NJ*, 16 April 1927; Eddy, "Study of the Vocational Opportunities," 66; Gay, "Study of the Development of the Senior High Schools," 46.

62. *NJ*, 15 April 1926; *NJ*, 18 April 1928; *NJ*, 28 January 1925; *NJ*, 16 February 1928; Adams and Kai, "Education of the Boys of Hawaii," 41.

63. *NJ*, 6 September 1931; *NJ*, 9 December 1932.

64. Hawaii Territory, Governor's Advisory Committee on Education, "Report on the Sugar Cane Industry," 51; Hyams, "School Teachers as Agents," 213.

65. Eddy, "Study of the Vocational Opportunities," 70, 75; Hyams, "School Teachers as Agents," 213–14.

66. Hyams, "School Teachers as Agents," 214; Gladys Feirer interview.

67. Hyams, "School Teachers as Agents," 214–15.

68. Adams and Kai, "Education of the Boys of Hawaii," 47.

69. *Biennial Report*, 1928, 120; Judd Papers, Territorial Departments, Public Instruction, "Educational Survey," November–December 1929; *SB*, 15 July 1931. Probably due to fewer available jobs during the depression, the 1930s witnessed an increase in enrollment in vocational agriculture. In 1930, 476 boys over 14 years and older enrolled in vocational agriculture, increasing to 1,031 in 1933 and 1,272 in 1936. See *Biennial Report*, 1936, 26.

70. *HA*, 16 February 1931; Uyeunten, "Struggle and Survival," 185–89. Hawaii Nisei were 48 to 53 percent of all seniors from 1925 to 1930. No such figures are available for the years 1918 to 1924, but about 44 to 51 percent of all students in public school at that time were Nisei. See "Term Reports, 1925–30"; *Biennial Report*, 1918, 50; *Biennial Report*, 1920, 205; *Biennial Report*, 1922, 4; and *Biennial Report*, 1924, 113. With the exception of McKinley and Hilo High Schools, for which alumni names and addresses were available beginning with the classes of 1920 and 1922, all other high schools began with their original graduating class. Only Maui High and Grammar School and Kauai High and Grammar School, established in 1913 and 1914, included graduates from as early as 1918. All other high schools, excluding McKinley and Hilo, opened after 1922, and their first graduation would occur four years later.

71. *HH,* 12 February 1931; Japanese Students' Association, *Students' Annual,* 1924, 41.

72. Hawaii Territory, DPI, School Directory, 1931–41; *Biennial Report,* 1934, 41; Wist, *Century of Public Education,* 174, 182–83.

Chapter 7: Japanese Language Schools

1. Onishi, "Study of the Attitudes," 7–9; Okahata, *History of Japanese in Hawaii,* 216; Lind, *Hawaii's Japanese,* 23. Christian ministers opened the second and third schools: Takie Okumura in Honolulu, in 1896, and Shiro Sokabe in Honomu, near Hilo on the island of Hawaii in 1897. The first Buddhist-sponsored language school opened in 1902.

2. Onishi, "Study of the Attitudes," 11. Like Onishi, Shichiro Miyamoto ("Study of the Japanese Language Ability," 11) found that most Japanese children attended language school: out of the 12,517 children attending public schools in Honolulu in 1930, 12,060 also attended Japanese language schools.

3. Takagi, "Moral Education," 112; Okahata, *History of Japanese in Hawaii,* 217.

4. Okahata, *History of Japanese in Hawaii,* 217, 219; *PCA,* 14 February 1919, cited in Weinberg, "Movement to Americanize," 112. For discussions on the Japanese language school issue in California, see Matsubayashi, "Japanese Language Schools," 148–51; and Toyotomi Morimoto, "Language and Heritage Maintenance," 72–104.

5. Matsubayashi, "Japanese Language Schools," 83–86, 108, 140; Halsted, "Sharpened Tongues," 9–8, 144–45; Hunter, *Buddhism in Hawaii,* 109–10; Okahata, *History of Japanese in Hawaii,* 218–20. See also Hawkins, "Politics, Education, and Language Policy" (39–56), for a discussion of the language school case.

6. That territorial officials hoped to abolish Japanese language schools can be seen, for example, in private correspondence between Superintendent MacCaughey and Governor Farrington in 1922, which referred to "a policy looking forward to the elimination of foreign language schools in the territory." See Halsted, "Sharpened Tongues," 114–15. In addition, Caucasian members (including K. C. Leebrick, a political science professor at the University of Hawaii, Henry Butler Schwartz, who later became the DPI's Supervisor of Foreign Language Schools, and Arthur L. Dean, president of the University of Hawaii) of a Joint Committee on foreign language schools suggested, as had the 1920 federal survey of education in Hawaii, that public schools offer Asian language courses to end the need for private language schools, "charging tuition if necessary" to finance them. See Japanese Educational Association of Hawaii, *Brief Survey of the Foreign Language School Question,* 8–10. For a discussion of the Joint Committee, see Halsted, "Sharpened Tongues," 104–7, 112.

7. Hawaii Territory, *Laws of the Territory of Hawaii,* 1920, 30–33, 36–37. California legislators enacted a similar foreign language school law in August 1921. See Matsubayashi, "Japanese Language Schools," 148–58, 262; and Toyotomi Morimoto, "Language and Heritage Maintenance," 80.

8. Halsted, "Sharpened Tongues," 107, 112–14.

9. Aiko Tokimasa Reinecke interview.

10. Japanese Educational Association of Hawaii, *Brief Survey,* 14–15; Halsted, "Sharpened Tongues," 182–83; *Biennial Report,* 1922, 102–3.

11. *Hawaii Herald,* 18 September 1987, 13; Wakukawa, *History of the Japanese People,* 184.

12. *SB,* 3 February 1923; Matsubayashi, "Japanese Language Schools," 159. Note: *NJ,* 6 February 1923, and *NJ,* 2 May 1925, said that both parties appealed.

13. Halsted, "Sharpened Tongues," 118, 190–91; Onishi, "Study of the Attitudes," 11. Act 171 also created the position of supervisor of foreign language schools, a position filled by Henry Butler Schwartz on 4 May 1923, and required that pupils complete the first grade before being allowed to attend a foreign language school. See Matsubayashi, "Japanese Language Schools," 164; Hawaii Territory, *Laws of the Territory of Hawaii,* 1923, 204–7; and Hawaii Territory, *Laws of the Territory of Hawaii,* 1925, 178–80.

14. *NJ,* 23 April 1923; Matsubayashi, "Japanese Language Schools," 164; Onishi, "Study of the Attitudes," 11.

15. *HH,* 7 July 1925; *SB,* 8 July 1925.

16. Farrington v. Tokushige 11 Fed. (2d) 710 (9th Cir. 1926); Meyer v. Nebraska 262 U.S. 390 (1923); Bartels v. Iowa 262 U.S. 404 (1923); Pierce v. Society of Sisters 268 U.S. 510 (1925).

17. Tyack, "Perils of Pluralism," 74–98.

18. Farrington v. Tokushige 273 U.S. 284 (1927). Meyer v. Nebraska, 395, notes that in 1923, twenty-one states and Nebraska had anti-foreign language school laws. For a discussion of these court cases, see O'Brien, "Education, Americanization, and the Supreme Court."

19. *HA,* 12 May 1923; *NJ,* 17 August 1923; Embree, *Acculturation among the Japanese,* 136.

20. *NJ,* 10 August 1922; *NJ,* 11 August 1922; Okihiro, *Cane Fires,* 211–24. Soga wrote that the American members of the joint committee had intimated that if the Japanese members did not agree to the recommendations, the legislature would abolish all Japanese language schools.

21. *HH,* 14 June 1926, emphasis in original; Compilation Committee for the Publication of Kinzaburo Makino's Biography, *Life of Kinzaburo Makino,* 65–66.

22. Hawaii Hochi, *Fred Kinzaburo Makino,* n.p.

23. Scudder, "Language Schools," 13–16; U.S. Department of the Interior, Bureau of Education, *Survey of Education in Hawaii,* 134–40; Talbott, "Making Americans in Hawaii," 284.

24. *HA,* 1 December 1922; Farrington Papers, Miscellaneous, "Language Schools, 1922."

25. McCarthy Papers, Miscellaneous, "Japanese Language Schools, Petitions"; WCS R3 HH80; WCS R4 HH32; WCS R2 N7. Like the Japanese, other ethnic groups believed that maintaining the mother language and culture was compatible with being good Americans. Kloss noted that "at German American festivals, it became customary to exclaim that in order to be loyal to his bride, a man did not have to forsake his mother" ("German-American Language," 229).

26. Takagi, "Moral Education," 112; Okahata, *History of Japanese in Hawaii*, 217; Hawaii Territory, *Laws of the Territory of Hawaii*, 1920, 30–33, 36–37; Halsted, "Sharpened Tongues," 107.

27. Hunter, *Buddhism in Hawaii*, 173–74, 179; *NJ*, 10 October 1935; *HH*, 22 July 1938; *HA*, 25 September 1940; *SB*, 9 July 1940; *SB*, 23 October 1940; *HA*, 10 October 1940; *HH*, 21 October 1940.

28. Okahata, *History of Japanese in Hawaii*, 216–17; Matsubayashi, "Japanese Language Schools," 257; Hunter, *Buddhism in Hawaii*, 88; Takagi, "Moral Education," 23–24.

29. Okahata, *History of Japanese in Hawaii*, 217; Takagi, "Moral Education," 24, 28–30. According to Halsted ("Sharpened Tongues," 125, 169–71), a territorial textbook revision project in 1924, directed by Henry Butler Schwartz, supervisor of foreign language schools, proved to be a fiasco. Schwartz himself knew little Japanese, and those he hired to translate the English stories to Japanese filled the books with vocabulary errors that were offensive to Japanese teachers. Moreover, the books, printed by *Star-Bulletin*, cost the schools more than ones that had been printed in Japan. Ultimately, because of their numerous errors, the books were unusable.

30. Takagi, "Moral Education," 111–16; Onishi, "Study of the Attitudes," 24–25. Bradford Smith included some pro-Japanese compositions written by Hawaii Nisei students in 1940 that probably reflected sentiments of teachers more than those of students. The Nisei who sent Smith the compositions explained that students who wrote the essays were writing for a good grade, and they wrote what they thought would please the teacher (*Americans from Japan*, 113). U.S. Senator Daniel Inouye, in his autobiograpy, *Journey to Washington* (35–38), recalled a teacher in 1939 who was strongly pro-Japan.

31. WCS R8 N39; Ige, *Boy from Kahaluu*, 5; Edith Yonenaka interview, 79; Timmy Hirata interview.

32. U.S. Department of the Interior, Bureau of Education, *Survey of Education in Hawaii*, 134–40; Takagi, "Moral Education," 17, 117–18; Kaigo, *Japanese Education*, 53–55; Hayashida, "Japanese Moral Instruction," 15; Lebra, "Acculturation Dilemma," 8–9. Classes focused on three main areas: moral education; penmanship; and reading, writing, and speaking.

33. WCS R8 N61; WCS R6 N181; Shoichi Kurahashi interview. Hayashida found a high correlation in values between Japanese students and students of all other ethnic groups in 1933, when Japanese schools were at their prime ("Japanese Moral Instruction," 38).

34. Hunter, *Buddhism in Hawaii*, 99, 172; *NJ*, 22 November 1919; *NJ*, 6 August 1920; Onishi, "Study of the Attitudes," 16.

35. Matsubayashi, "Japanese Language Schools," 233; Harada, "Survey of the Japanese Language Schools," 50–53.

36. Among those who concluded that language schools hampered students in acquiring the English language were Bachman, "Reading Program," 203; Barrett, "Mathematical Achievement," 73; Harris, "Reading Ability of Maui High School Students," 61; and Madorah E. Smith, "Direction of Reading," 422–51. Among those who found that language schools had no measurable effects on chil-

dren's mastery of English were Symonds, "Effect of Attendance," 411–23; Lewis, "Study of the Speech Attitudes," 8–9, 34–35, 49; and Reginald Bell, *Public School Education*, 98–103.

37. Kono, "Language as a Factor," 92–94; Strong, *Second Generation Japanese Problem*, 167–68; Hawaii Territory, DPI, "Reports of the Supervisor of Foreign Language Schools," emphasis in original.

38. Kosaki, "Culture Conflicts and Guidance Needs," 49. Modell discusses the Issei's desire to improve communication with their children as an important reason for sending them to Japanese language schools (*Economics and Politics*, 159–60).

39. Misako Yamamoto, "Cultural Conflicts and Accommodations," 47.

40. Ichihashi, *Japanese in the United States*, 331–32; Interviews with Nisei; Kosaki, "Culture Conflicts and Guidance Needs," 51; Farrington Papers, Miscellaneous, "Language Schools, 1922," M.E.; WCS R8 N56; WCS R8 N55.

41. Paulston, "Bilingualism and Education," 470, 474.

42. For similar Chinese views of their language schools, see Lai, "Natural History of the Chinese Language School," 93–94.

43. *NJ*, 21 November 1919; Farrington Papers, Territorial Departments, Public Instruction, "Foreign Language Schools."

44. WCS R1 H29.

45. WCS R8 N97; Shoichi Kurahashi interview. WCS R12 M24, WCS R1 H30, and WCS R2 H49 also did well and enjoyed Japanese school. Most Japanese High School students who wrote essays found in the WCS collection saw value in attending Japanese school. They said that knowledge of Japanese helped them better communicate with their parents; they also expected it to help them in their future career.

46. WCS R7 N177; WCS R8 N39.

47. WCS R5 N256; WCS R3 HH176; WCS R5 HH45; Ethel Kina interview; WCS R3 HH133. Similar views were expressed in Vivian Nakamura interview; WCS R2 N11; and WCS R9 HJ6.

48. Tetsuko Tamura interview; Aiko Tokimasa Reinecke interview; WCS R9 HJ3; Kazuo Hosaka interview. Similar comments are found in WCS R6 N185; WCS R8 N69; WCS R5 N269; and WCS R3 HH180.

49. WCS R6 N173; Minoru Inaba interview; 341; Tetsuko Tamura interview; Tokio Okudara interview, 421–22.

50. WCS R9 N70. Similar comments are found in Kosaki, "Culture Conflicts and Guidance Needs," 52; and WCS R6 N225. For a discussion of the mainland Nisei's lack of interest in Japanese language school, see Svensrud, "Attitudes of the Japanese," 259–64. For discussions of mainland and Hawaii Nisei's lack of fluency in Japanese, see Ano, "Loyal Linguists," 274–76; and Shibutani, *Derelicts of Company K*, 196. Although 45 percent of some Los Angeles Nisei who were surveyed in the late 1930s said that they attended language school willingly, that willingness did not translate into diligence in studying the language, nor did it result in fluency in the language. See Toyotomi Morimoto, "Language and Heritage Maintenance," 140–42. Many Nisei who were not interested in attending Japanese school when they were young later regretted that they had not been

more serious about learning Japanese. This regret was common among those I interviewed, and in WCS R7 N98; WCS R4 HH29; WCS R4 HH27; WCS R5 N261; WCS R5 HH43; and Onishi, "Study of the Attitudes," 52–137, 147.

51. Lind, "Japanese Language Schools," 1–15.

52. Shoichi Kurahashi interview.

Chapter 8: Social Changes

1. *HA*, 20 July 1930; Lind, *Island Community*, 266–67. The Chinese and Portuguese, who had immigrated earlier, showed higher amounts of savings. The Chinese had a per capita savings of $13.35 in 1910, $59.32 in 1920, and $150.76 in 1930; for the Portuguese, the amounts were $40.85 in 1910, $95.37 in 1920, and $116.11 in 1930. In real estate the Portuguese per capita investment was $105.80 in 1911, $236.35 in 1920, and $522.62 in 1930; for the Chinese the amounts were $40.79 in 1911, $176.24 in 1920, and $570.26 in 1930.

2. Beechert, *Working in Hawaii*, 123–24; Yoshiko Oda interview; Okada, *No-No Boy*, 120.

3. Lind, "The Camps," 2–6.

4. Choy, "Moiliili: A Historical Analysis," 19.

5. Coulter and Serrao, "Manoa Valley, Honolulu," 109–30.

6. S. Frank Miyamoto, "Immigrant Community in America," 221–22; Modell, *Economics and Politics*, 66, 75; Lind, "The Camps," 2–6.

7. Hartmann, *Movement to Americanize*, 16; Balch, *Our Slavic Fellow Citizens*, 410.

8. Kikumura, *Through Harsh Winters*, 11–12; Modell, *Economics and Politics*, 66, 85.

9. Connor, "Acculturation and Family Continuities," 162–63; Kitano, "Japanese-American Crime and Delinquency," 169.

10. Strong and Bell, *Vocational Aptitudes*, 165–68; Hayner, "Delinquency Areas in the Puget Sound Region," 314–28. Lind (*Island Community*, 292), Adams (*Peoples of Hawaii*, 49–57), and *Glimpses of Japanese in Hawaii* (27) have similarly shown low figures for the Japanese when compared with other groups.

11. Lind, "The Camps," 2–6.

12. Ibid.

13. Ogawa, *Jan Ken Po*, 142–43. Chapter 4 discusses the Fukunaga case in greater detail.

14. On the mainland, European immigrants sometimes Anglicized their family names in their eagerness to become "more American." Adamic's *What's Your Name?* provides touching case studies of identity issues involved in name-changing.

15. Hawaii Territory, DPI, "Years Average Mark, 1921–35." There were 301 Honolulu and 684 rural eighth graders in 1924. The few Nisei who were given English first names by their parents were probably born after 1920. In my own interviews and in reading interviews done by others, I did not come across Nisei who said their parents gave them English first names.

16. Hawaii Territory, DPI, "Years Average Mark, 1921–35"; Reinecke, "Personal Names in Hawaii," 351. There were 1,620 rural eighth graders in 1934. Reinecke also found that only 5.5 percent of the 180 Japanese students in a rural intermediate school in 1934 wrote English names on their registration forms ("Personal Names in Hawaii," 351). Records for Honolulu eighth graders in 1934 are missing.

17. Hawaii Territory, DPI, *School Directory*, 1926–44.

18. Hawaii Territory, University, "Catalogue and Announcement of Courses, 1927–28," 122–23; Hawaii Territory, University, *University of Hawaii Bulletin* 16:6: 155–57; Hawaii Territory, University, "Report of the President for 1945–46," 33. The numbers of Japanese students graduating from the university were sixteen in 1926, ninety-four in 1936, and one hundred in 1946.

19. Kuroda, "Study of Japanese-Americans," 25. The eighth graders of 1924 would have been in their sixties in 1971.

20. Timmy Hirata interview; Richard Inouye interview; Ige, *Boy from Kahaluu*, 8.

21. Edythe Yamamoto interview; WCS R9 HJ3; Anonymous B interview. Ralph Honda, whose given name was Chikato, also chose his American name himself in 1925, when he was eighteen. He later legalized it.

22. Marie interview; Vivian Nakamura interview; Ethel Kina interview.

23. Thelma Izumi interview, 47; and Tokio Okudara interview.

24. WCS R7 N164; WCS R1 H39.

25. WCS R7 N80; WCS R1 H17; Aiko Tokimasa Reinecke interview.

26. WCS R3 HH203; WCS R7 N164.

27. WCS R7 N80; WCS R1 M.M.

28. Akira Sakima interview, 370; Keiko Yamamoto, "Oral History of Miles Cary," 46; Timmy Hirata interview. See also Williams, "Educational Theory and Philosophy," 66–82, 95–97, 106–7.

29. WCS R2 N11; Misako Yamamoto, "Cultural Conflicts and Accommodations," 46.

30. WCS R12 M22; WCS R2 H49; WCS R3 N20; Bernard K. Yamamoto, "Assimilation of the Japanese," 53–54. Modell discusses mainland Issei's objections to the "evils" of social dancing (*Economics and Politics*, 159).

31. WCS R1 H39; WCS R11 L4.

32. WCS R3 HH201; Japanese Students' Association of Hawaii, *Students' Annual*, 1924, 3; Ibid., 1929, 24.

33. Chinese Students' Alliance of Hawaii, *Students' Annual*, pass.; Korean Students' Alliance of Hawaii, *Students' Annual*, pass.

34. Richard Inouye interview.

35. WCS R1 H27; WCS R14 MK120.

36. Ethel Kina interview. In their interviews, Vivian Nakamura and Marie also spoke of learning American ways while working as maids. Census reports give the following figures for Japanese male and female servants ten years of age and older: 1,982 females in 1910; 1,559 males and 1,728 females in 1920; and 923 males and 2,589 females in 1930. See U.S. Department of Commerce, Bureau of the Census, *Thirteenth Census, 1910: Population*, 609–10; U.S. Department of

Commerce, Bureau of the Census, *Fourteenth Census, 1920: Population*, 1278; and U.S. Department of Commerce, Bureau of the Census, *Fifteenth Census, 1930: Outlying Territories*, 89–90.

37. Masuoka, "Westernization of the Japanese Family," 278. Although the woman was Issei, the fact that she was unmarried meant that she had probably come to Hawaii as a young child and therefore had experiences like many Nisei.

38. William C. Smith, "Born American, But ——," 15; WCS R8 N56. According to Glenn, Nisei domestic servants in the San Francisco Bay area also used their jobs to learn about American ways (*Issei, Nisei, War Bride*, 124–27).

39. WCS R6 N134; Yukiko Kimura, "Psychological Aspects," 16; Opler, "Cultural Dilemma of a Kibei Youth," 305.

40. Caudill, "Japanese-American Personality," 9–10.

41. Stonequist, *Marginal Man*, vii; Gordon, *Assimilation in American Life*, 56–58; Maykovich, *Japanese American Identity Dilemma*, 12–13. A *Hochi* editorial on 3 November 1941 called the Nisei the "lost generation."

42. Miya Soga interview.

43. WCS R1 H39; Misako Yamamoto, "Cultural Conflicts and Accommodations," 40; Mihata, "Americans of Japanese Ancestry," 16; Stonequist, "Marginal Man in Hawaii," 19.

44. Maykovich, *Japanese American Identity Dilemma*, 30; Kikumura, *Through Harsh Winters*, 14.

45. Doi, "Omote and Ura," 258–61.

46. Rogers and Izutsu, "The Japanese," 96–97.

47. Kikumura, *Through Harsh Winters*, 209–10.

48. Kimura and Freeman, "Problem of Assimilation," 61.

49. WCS R3 HH123; WCS R3 HH156; WCS R6 N180. Similar comments are found in WCS R2 N10 and WCS R6 N173.

50. Masuoka, "Westernization of the Japanese Family," 241.

51. Misako Yamamoto, "Cultural Conflicts and Accommodations," 42–43.

52. Masuoka, "Westernization of the Japanese Family," 241.

53. Misako Yamamoto, "Cultural Conflicts and Accommodations," 42, 46.

54. Yoshiko Oda interview; Tetsuko Tamura interview; Ethel Kina interview; Choy, "Moiliili, A Historical Analysis," 70–79, 87–97; Marie interview; Richard Inouye interview.

55. For discussions of conflict between Issei and Nisei on the mainland, see S. Frank Miyamoto, "Immigrant Community in America," 230; Modell, *Economics and Politics*, 154–56; Shimada, "Education, Assimilation, and Acculturation," 149–55; and Uyeunten, "Struggle and Survival," 190–93.

56. *NJ*, 21 February 1921; *NJ*, 22 February 1921; *NJ* 4 January 1924.

57. WCS R3 N19; WCS R1 H39. Similar comments are found in WCS R3 HH180 and WCS R14 MK110.

58. Misako Yamamoto, "Cultural Conflicts and Accommodations," 43; Masuoka, "Westernization of the Japanese Family," 280, 285–86.

59. Masuoka, "Westernization of the Japanese Family," 257.

60. Hayashida, "Japanese Moral Instruction," 12; Kosaki, "Culture Conflicts and Guidance Needs," 23, 41.

61. *NJ*, 27 April 1928; Masuoka, "Westernization of the Japanese Family," 209–10.

62. Masuoka, "Westernization of the Japanese Family," 270–72.

63. Ibid., 273; Embree, *Acculturation among the Japanese*, 145.

64. Misako Yamamoto, "Cultural Conflicts and Accommodations," 45. According to Tsurumi, this Issei view of marriage was the result of the spread of samurai practices to the Japanese peasantry in Japan during the late nineteenth century (*Women in Japan*, 2–3).

65. Tsuruyo Kimura interview; Yosoto Egami interview; Choy, "Moiliili, A Historical Analysis," 87–97. Mrs. C is the only identification given in Choy's study. Yanagisako found that among Seattle Nisei, earlier pre–World War II marriages tended to be arranged by Issei parents, while later pre-war marriages were the result of Nisei initiatives (*Transforming the Past*, 68–69).

66. WCS R4 HH10; WCS R2 J49; WCS R14 MK137; William C. Smith, "Second Generation Oriental," 21.

67. Spickard, *Mixed Blood*, 97, 103.

68. Lind, *Hawaii's People*, 108.

69. Ibid. With the influx of Caucasian men to Hawaii during World War II, the outmarriage rate for Nisei women jumped 10 percent while remaining the same for Nisei men.

70. Kikumura and Kitano, "Interracial Marriage," 26–35; Tinker, "Intermarriage and Ethnic Boundaries," 50–60, 63; Spickard, *Mixed Blood*, 75, 80–81.

71. Kikumura and Kitano, "Interracial Marriage," 29–33. Spickard discusses various theories on intermarriage (*Mixed Blood*, 6–9, 14). Others have argued that Japanese females acculturated more quickly than Japanese males and have used the higher intermarriage rates among Japanese women as evidence. See Arkoff, Meredith, and Iwahara, "Dominance-Deference Patterning," 61–66; Caudill, "Japanese-American Personality," 3–102; and DeVos, "Quantitative Rorschach Assessment," 50–87.

72. Bernard K. Yamamoto, "Assimilation of the Japanese," 54.

73. *NJ*, 2 March 1926; *NJ*, 16 June 1928.

74. Masuoka, "Race Attitudes," 178.

75. Ibid.

76. Nagoshi and Nishimura, "Some Observations Concerning Haole-Japanese Marriages," 57; Kosaki, "Culture Conflicts and Guidance Needs," 65.

77. George Yamamoto, "Social Adjustment," 49.

78. WCS R4 HH10; Ozaki, "Student Attitudes on Interracial Marriage," 24. This was a common theme among the essays in the WCS collection.

79. Yoshizawa, "Japanese Family in Rural Hawaii," 56–63; George Yamamoto, "Social Adjustment," 33.

80. Spickard, *Mixed Blood*, 87; Aiko Tokimasa Reinecke interview; George Yamamoto, "Social Adjustment," 40–41. This does not mean that in the 1920s and 1930s Caucasians favored intermarriage with all ethnic groups. There was a tension in America between ideas of independence, individuality, and tolerance on the one hand, and racism on the other.

Even before American independence, anti-miscegenation statutes sought to prevent intermarriage between blacks and whites in colonies such as Maryland, North Carolina, Massachusetts, and Pennsylvania. Such statutes continued to be enacted after independence. At one time or another as many as thirty-eight states prohibited some form of intermarriage. By the end of the 1940s all southern and some western states prohibited marriage between blacks and whites; western states forbade marriage between Asians and Caucasians; and some states prohibited American Indian and white, or American Indian and black, marriages. Hawaii's tolerance of intermarriage stood in sharp contrast to the rest of the country. In 1948 the California Supreme Court declared California's anti-miscegenation law unconstitutional, and in 1967, when sixteen states still carried anti-miscegenation laws on their books, the U.S. Supreme Court ruled that states could not prohibit intermarriage. See Barron, "The Church, the State, and Intermarriage," 77–84. See also Cretser and Leon, *Intermarriage in the United States*, 3, 35–48, 61–74, and 75–90 for essays on intermarriage among Chinese, Japanese, and Koreans in the United States.

Chapter 9: Cultural Changes

1. Spickard, *Mixed Blood*, 42; Maykovich, *Japanese American Identity Dilemma*, 36; *NJ*, 25 April 1927.

2. Wagatsuma, "Social Perceptions of Skin Color," 407, 412. See also Wagatsuma, "Some Problems of Interracial Marriage," 247–64.

3. Masuoka, "Race Attitudes," 61, 94; Ozaki, "Student Attitudes on Interracial Marriage," 23–26. African Americans were not included in the list because so few lived in Hawaii before World War II that most Japanese had no contact with them.

4. WCS R11 L1; WCS R14 MK123; Samuels, *The Japanese and the Haoles of Honolulu*, 70–72. See also WCS R3 HH201; WCS R7 N73.

5. WCS R14 MK130; WCS R5 N270.

6. WCS R12 M23.

7. WCS R5 SL185; WCS R14 MK129; WCS R3 HH217; "Term Reports, 1927."

8. "Joseph Y. Kurihara, Autobiography," 2–3; William C. Smith, *Americans in Process*, 16–17, 24. Nisei I interviewed who lived both in Hawaii and on the mainland said they generally did not experience as much race prejudice in Hawaii as they did on the mainland.

9. William C. Smith, *Americans in Process*, 32, 39; Reinecke, *Feigned Necessity*, 25–33.

10. *PCA*, 4 January 1911.

11. WCS R6 MP1; WCS R6 N227.

12. Burrows, *Chinese and Japanese*, 90–92. According to Spickard, there was less discrimination on the mainland than in Hawaii because of the looser community structure there (*Mixed Blood*, 94). The pejorative term *eta*—often translated as "much filth"—has been replaced in Japan by the more neutral term *burakumin*—citizens (*min*) of special communities. In Hawaii, *eta* and *chorinbo* were the more common terms used. Japan's treatment of minorities like the *burakumin*, Koreans, and Ainu, is discussed in DeVos and Wetherall, *Japan's*

Minorities. See also DeVos, "Minority Status and Delinquency in Japan," in his *Socialization for Achievement,* and Hane, *Peasants, Rebels, and Outcasts,* 139–71.

13. *NJ,* 20 July 1930; *SB,* 2 December 1930; *NJ,* 20 July 1930. Spickard listed the marriage preferences for mainland Issei in this order: Japanese from their home village or prefecture, *Naichi* or Japanese from Japan proper, Caucasians, Chinese, Koreans, Okinawans, *eta,* Filipinos, Mexicans, Puerto Ricans, and blacks (*Mixed Blood,* 103–4).

14. Ethnic Studies Oral History Project, *Uchinanchu,* includes a variety of essays on the Okinawan experience in Hawaii.

15. Sakihara, "History and Okinawans," xxi–xxiv; Yukiko Kimura, "Social-Historical Background," 51–71; Sueno and Yoshino, "Minorities," 195; Sakai and Sakihara, "Okinawa," 87; Stires, "The Ryukyus," 17–21.

16. Percentage from Matsumoto, "Okinawa Migrants to Hawaii," 128.

17. Toyama and Ikeda, "Okinawan-Naichi Relationship," 59–60.

18. Higa, "Okinawa in Hawaii," 41; Philip K. Ige, "Okinawan Nisei," 157.

19. Toyama and Ikeda, "Okinawan-Naichi Relationship," 51–65; Samuels, *The Japanese and the Haoles of Honolulu,* 70.

20. WCS R3 HH166; WCS R8 N22.

21. WCS R7 N79; WCS R3 HH118. Nisei continued to express this view even into the 1960s. One Nisei in the 1960s said, "Haoles see themselves as being superior to the other races, because they have the blond hair and the blue eyes and speak better English than anyone else." Another said, "They have a tendency to look down on people, laborers, peons." See Samuels, *The Japanese and the Haoles of Honolulu,* 61.

22. WCS R7 N104.

23. Samuels, *The Japanese and the Haoles of Honolulu,* 61; Masuoka, "Race Attitudes," 83.

24. WCS R9 HJ3; Masuoka, "Race Attitudes," 113; WCS R14 MK123.

25. WCS R6 N177.

26. WCS R12 M24; WCS R14 MK120; WCS R6 N199; WCS R6 N173.

27. WCS R4 HH73.

28. WCS R5 N270; WCS R6 N134; WCS R2 N9. Similar comments were made in WCS R3 HH200; WCS R3 HH207; WCS R3 HH210.

29. Marie interview; WCS R1 H29.

30. WCS R14 MK110. Similar comments were made by Nisei in other essays in the WCS collection.

31. *Biennial Report,* 1924, 30; Hawaii Territory, DPI, "Miscellaneous Reports and Statistical Tables," 21 January 1927.

32. *Biennial Report,* 1926, 91–92. I define my use of the term Standard English in my discussion of English Standard Schools in chapter 5.

33. Stueber, "Hawaii: A Case Study," 305; *Biennial Report,* 1926, 91–92.

34. *Biennial Report,* 1928, 108–9; WCS R2 H49.

35. Reinecke and Tsuzaki, *Language and Dialect in Hawaii,* 160; Sato, "Linguistic Inequality in Hawaii," 256. Sato notes that the line between dialects and creoles is unclear ("Nonstandard Approach," 262). Reinecke used the terms "cre-

ole dialect" to refer to Pidgin English and "colonial dialect" to refer to Hawaii Creole English. See Nichols, "Creoles of the USA," 70, for a clear explanation of pidgins and creoles.

36. Derek Bickerton and William Wilson, "Pidgin Hawaiian," 61–76; Reinecke, "Pidgin English in Hawaii," 780–81; Reinecke and Tsuzaki, *Language and Dialect in Hawaii*, 193–94. According to Reinecke and Tsuzaki (148–52), although a number of non-haole public school teachers in the earlier days of the territory spoke non-Standard English, their language was closer to Standard English than Pidgin English. Sato ("Linguistic Inequality in Hawaii," 256) states, "[A] creole's basic vocabulary is usually taken from the standard or colonial language of the community, while its grammatical structure derives from its antecedent pidgin, the donor languages to the pidgin, and from innovations by creole speakers." Sato ("Sociolinguistic Variation," 648–49) discusses linguistic differences between Hawaii Pidgin English and Hawaii Creole English.

37. Reinecke, "Pidgin English in Hawaii," 780–81. According to U.S. Department of the Interior, Bureau of Education (*Survey of Education in Hawaii*, 22, 37), about 38 percent of public school students in 1919 were of Japanese descent. According to *Biennial Report*, 1920 (205), 47 percent of all public school students were Japanese in 1920. According to Reinecke, the 1930 census report, claiming that 301,514 spoke English and 66,824 spoke no English, ignored the widespread use of non-Standard English. Milroy and Milroy explain why absolute standardization of a spoken language never occurs (*Authority in Language*, 22–23).

38. WCS R3 N21. Similar comments were made in WCS R14 MK130; WCS R6 N177; and WCS R16 MP29.

39. Reinecke and Tsuzaki, *Language and Dialect in Hawaii*, 107; Stratford, "Cross-Section of a High School Student's Life," 57; Shichiro Miyamoto, "Study of the Japanese Language Ability," 27. Thirteen percent of the Japanese students at the Honolulu language school Miyamoto studied in 1937 were Sansei or third generation Japanese Americans, and 23 percent were Nisei-Sansei, Japanese Americans having one Nisei parent.

40. Reinecke and Tsuzaki, *Language and Dialect in Hawaii*, 179–80, 190. Reinecke speculated that Hawaiian Creole English was probably spoken by 1900 and well established by 1920.

41. WCS R8 N63; Yoshitake Takashiba interview; Misako Yamamoto, "Cultural Conflicts and Accommodations," 47. The Nisei whose essays are in the WCS collection, who were born between 1900 and 1912, said that they spoke Japanese at home with their parents and English to siblings and friends. A few said they spoke Japanese with their siblings and friends. Although they used the words "Japanese" and "English," to describe their languages, more than likely they spoke non-Standard versions of each.

42. Kono, "Language as a Factor," 92–94; Brigance, "How Good is the English?" 133–34; Reinecke and Tsuzaki, *Language and Dialect in Hawaii*, 183. See also Breed, "Study of the English Vocabulary," 1–44. According to the "Term Reports, 1936," 55 percent of the public high school seniors in December 1936 were of Japanese descent.

43. Shizuko Morimoto, "Study of Oral English Usage," 46; Richard Inouye interview; Yoshitaka Takashiba interview, 13–14; WCS R14 MK110.

44. Misaki, "Effect of Language Handicap," 102.

45. WCS R5 N270; Timmy Hirata interview; Yoshitaka Takashiba interview, 13–14; Ralph Honda interview.

46. WCS R3 HH99; WCS R2 N7; WCS R17 R.M.; WCS R7 N166; WCS R16 MP29.

47. Reinecke, "Pidgin English in Hawaii," 783, 787–88; Reinecke and Tsuzaki, *Language and Dialect in Hawaii*, 156–57, 178. Similarly, in an analysis of local culture in Hawaii, Okamura, in "Aloha Kanaka Me Ke Aloha 'Aina" (126, 135) has pointed to Hawaii's economic and social context during the early decades of the twentieth century, "the collective historical subordination of Hawaiians and the immigrant plantation groups to the Haole planter and merchant oligarchy." A ramification of this ethclass structure, according to Okamura, appears in the present use of the term "local." The common understanding defines a "local" as one born and raised in Hawaii. Often included is the notion of a casual, easygoing, friendly, family-oriented lifestyle. Caucasians born and raised in Hawaii are usually (but not always) excluded from this definition, in spite of their long historical presence in Hawaii and their considerable historical influence in the government, economy, education, language, and society of Hawaii. Portuguese, because they came as plantation workers, are considered "local." The term is often used as a way to exclude others, and there is an element of prejudice and racism in its use. "Indeed," wrote Okamura, "it would be somewhat remarkable if the local concept did not include some prejudicial views and understandings given the fact that the concept itself is a product of a historical period of blatant racism." It is in fact the "common subordinate status of [the non-white] to the dominant Haole group" during plantation days that is the basis of the former's present common local identity.

48. *Friend*, July 1917, cited in Reinecke, *Feigned Necessity*, 42; *PCA*, 17 March 1919; Judd, "Repaganization of Hawaii," 188.

49. *SB*, 24 January 1920; Hunter, *Buddhism in Hawaii*, 129, 140.

50. Murphy, "Japanese Problem in Hawaii," 130–31; Hunter, *Buddhism in Hawaii*, 75.

51. MacCaughey, "Some Outstanding Educational Problems," 29. Similar thoughts were expressed in articles cited in Weinberg, "Movement to Americanize," 73: *SB*, 24 May 1920; *PCA*, 18 May 1920; *SB*, 12 May 1920; *SB*, 24 January 1920; *SB*, 28 July 1919. Matsubayashi, "Japanese Language Schools," 235; Imamura, *History of the Hongwanji Mission*, 1–11; Hunter, *Buddhism in Hawaii*, 105.

52. Imamura, *Democracy According to the Buddhist Viewpoint*, 21–22, 26–27; *SB*, n.d., cited in Matsubayashi, "Japanese Language Schools," 235.

53. Gulick, *Mixing the Races*, 184; Hunter, *Buddhism in Hawaii*, 131; Tajima, "Japanese Buddhism in Hawaii," 10.

54. Horinouchi, "Americanized Buddhism," iii; Embree, *Acculturation among the Japanese*, 107.

55. Onishi, "Second Generation Japanese," 46; Hunter, *Buddhism in Hawaii*,

131–32; Tajima, "Japanese Buddhism in Hawaii," 29, 47–49, 55; Embree, *Acculturation among the Japanese*, 107–10. In his study of the Sacramento Buddhist church in California, Horinouchi, in "Americanized Buddhism," found that compared to Hawaii, Buddhism on the mainland was slow to adapt to the American environment. Greater changes came after World War II. Modell discussed the relatively slow response of Buddhist leaders, in contrast to their Christian counterparts, to the needs of the Japanese in Los Angeles (*Economics and Politics*, 75–79). S. Frank Miyamoto, in "Social Solidarity among the Japanese in Seattle" (99–102), similarly concluded that Buddhism did not actively "Americanize" to meet the needs of the Issei as they settled in the Seattle area.

56. WCS R2 H49; William C. Smith, *Americans in Process*, 143.

57. Hunter, *Buddhism in Hawaii*, 132–34, 151–54; Gulick, *Mixing the Races*, 181; WCS R5 N260; WCS R8 N63.

58. Hunter, *Buddhism in Hawaii*, 159.

59. Ibid., 157.

60. Ibid., 161; WCS R4 HH32; WCS R2 N10; WCS R2 N7; WCS R5 HH45; WCS R15 MK145.

61. WCS R13 MK54; WCS R7 N104.

62. WCS R3 HH200; WCS R6 N133; WCS R3 HH156.

63. Sueno Matsushita interview; WCS R3 HH80; WCS R7 N163; WCS R7 N156; WCS R5 N261; WCS R6 N196; WCS R3 HH88; WCS R6 N199; WCS R6 N145; Misao Kawakami interview.

64. WCS R6 N180.

65. WCS R7 N165; WCS R4 HH33.

66. WCS R8 N69; WCS R5 N263; WCS R8 N70.

67. The 1917 figure is from Hunter, *Buddhism in Hawaii*, 95. According to the 1920 census, 76,961 Japanese were ten years of age or older; according to the 1910 census, 62,950 Japanese were ten years and older. If we say that, very roughly, 73,000 were ten years and older in 1917, then 1,714 divided by 73,000 gives 2.3 percent Christian Japanese. The 1927 estimate is from *HA*, 15 August 1927. Of the 131,971 Japanese in Hawaii, 127,000 were Buddhists, 2,464 Protestants, and 500 Mormons. No figures were given for Japanese Catholics. The article did not give its source, and the number of Buddhists seems inflated. The 1937 information is from Gulick, *Mixing the Races*, 181. Onishi says that the Honpa Hongwanji had 18,500 members and 10,000 Sunday School children in 1937 ("Second Generation Japanese," 43). The 1941 figure is from *SB*, 8 May 1941. During World War II, all Buddhist temples were closed, and Buddhist priests were interned, but Buddhism successfully revived after the war, during the 1950s and 1960s (see Hunter, 186, 189). The 1971 figures are from Research Committee on the Study of Japanese Americans in Honolulu, Hawaii, *Honolulu's Japanese Americans in Comparative Perspective*, 32, 95, 107–8. The percentage of Christians increased with Honolulu Sansei, third generation Japanese Americans. Of the 57 percent of the Sansei in 1971 who professed having a religion, 36 percent said they were Buddhists, while 53 percent said they were Christians (47 percent Protestants; 6 percent Catholics). In contrast, in Japan only 30 percent said they had a religion. Of these, 75 percent said they were Buddhists and 3 percent Christians.

68. According to Miyamoto, there were somewhat more Japanese Christians than Buddhists in Seattle in 1936 ("Social Solidarity," 99–102). A survey of religious preferences among Japanese in three internment camps shows from 19 to 57 percent of the Nisei, and from 3 to 38 percent of the Kibei and Issei, identifying themselves as Christians (see Thomas, *The Salvage*, 607–8). According to the War Relocation Authority, 35 percent of the Nisei and 23 percent of the Issei in internment camps identified themselves as Christians, while 49 percent of the Nisei and 69 percent of the Issei identified themselves as Buddhists. The percentage of Nisei and Issei Buddhists was probably higher than these figures indicate, since many of those interned were probably afraid to declare themselves Buddhists (see Kashima, *Buddhism in America*, 53–54).

According to Loftin ("Japanese in Brazil," 167), about 70 percent of all Issei and Nisei in Brazil were Buddhists or Shintoists in 1940; according to Fujii ("Acculturation of the Japanese Immigrants," 21), about 46 percent were Buddhists in 1950; and according to Suzuki ("Japanese Immigrant in Brazil," 295–97), about 28 percent of all Nisei were Buddhists and 62 percent were Catholics in 1958. In comparing these percentages with those for Hawaii, it should be kept in mind that immigration to Brazil was later than to Hawaii and the mainland; many Japanese immigrated to Brazil in the 1920s and 1930s, after the United States had closed its doors to them.

69. Hilo and Himeno, "Some Characteristics," 41.

70. Tao, "Fifty Years of Constant Struggle," 3–4; Watanabe, "Japanese Christian Church Situation," 148–50.

71. Petersen, *Japanese Americans*, 178–80. Onishi argued that the Honpa Hongwanji mission spread successfully in Hawaii because it provided a tie with Japanese culture while adapting itself to its American environment ("Second Generation Japanese," 43). Bodnar noted that churches served to extend tradition, Americanize their followers, and foster communal solidarity and ethnic consciousness (*The Transplanted*, 167).

Chapter 10: Occupational Changes

1. Lind, *Island Community*, 325; Sam Uyehara interview, 1519–22.

2. Richard Inouye interview.

3. Lind, *Island Community*, 240–41.

4. Adams, *Japanese in Hawaii*, 14–15; Wakukawa, *History of the Japanese People*, 188.

5. Reinecke, "Labor disturbances in Hawaii," n.p.; Takaki, *Pau Hana*, 127–28; Wakukawa, *History of the Japanese People*, 169.

6. Wakukawa, *History of the Japanese People*, 169; Okahata, *History of Japanese in Hawaii*, 173–74, 180; Beechert, *Working in Hawaii*, 171–74. Details of the 1909 strike are discussed in Beechert, *Working in Hawaii*, 169–76; Takaki, *Pau Hana*, 153–64; Wakukawa, *History of the Japanese People*, 169–92; Okahata, *History of the Japanese in Hawaii*, 170–81; and U.S. Department of Commerce and Labor, *Bulletin of the Bureau of Labor*, No. 94, 726–62.

7. Hane, *Peasants, Rebels, and Outcasts*, 7, 21–27, 193–204.

8. Reinecke, *Feigned Necessity*, 41, 87.

9. Ibid., 90; Beechert, *Working in Hawaii*, 197.

10. Reinecke, *Feigned Necessity*, 93, 95–96.

11. Ibid., 93.

12. Ibid., 101, 104; Lind, *Hawaii's Japanese*, 21; Probasco, "Japanese Filipino Labor Unions," 40; Beechert, *Working in Hawaii*, 204.

13. Reinecke, *Feigned Necessity*, 108–9; Okahata, *History of Japanese in Hawaii*, 190; Beechert, *Working in Hawaii*, 204.

14. Okumura, *Seventy Years of Divine Blessings*, 57–60.

15. Weinberg, "Movement to Americanize," 69–71, quoting *PCA*, 27 January 1920; *PCA*, 2 February 1920; *PCA*, 8 February 1920; *SB*, 30 January 1920; *SB*, 30 November 1920. Hunter, *Buddhism in Hawaii*, 121–22; *SB*, 13 February 1920; Reinecke, *Feigned Necessity*, 93, 124–27.

16. Beechert, *Working in Hawaii*, 212; Reinecke, *Feigned Necessity*, 123; *NJ*, 9 December 1919; *NJ*, 10 April 1920. Numerous editorials in *Nippu Jiji* from December 1919 through 1920 supported laborers in their efforts to gain higher wages. Reinecke's *Feigned Necessity* (123) said that Soga was more conciliatory in his English section, but working with a translator, I found that editorials in the English section were direct translations of editorials in the Japanese section.

17. Beechert, *Working in Hawaii*, 197–99.

18. Tsutsumi, "History of Hawaii's Labor Movement," 9.

19. *PCA*, 3 April 1920; Probasco, "Japanese Filipino Labor Unions," 15.

20. Reinecke, *Feigned Necessity*, 116. The 1920 strike is discussed in Ibid., 87–160; Beechert, *Working in Hawaii*, 196–215; Takaki, *Pau Hana*, 164–76.

21. Lind, *Island Community*, 325; Glick, *Sojourners and Settlers*, 110–18.

22. Modell, *Economics and Politics*, 129–37; Uyeunten, "Struggle and Survival," 186–89.

23. Modell, *Economics and Politics*, 129–37; Uyuenten, "Struggle and Survival," 189.

24. Masaji Marumoto interview, 10–11.

25. Ibid.

26. Ibid., 12–14; *SB*, 7 May 1979.

27. Masaji Marumoto interview, 15.

28. Ibid., 15, 25; Masaji Marumoto, "Personal History," Winter 1980, 27.

29. *SB*, 7 May 1979, B1.

30. Marumoto, "Personal History," Winter 1980, 27; Masaji Marumoto interview, 32, 63.

31. Marumoto, "Personal History," Fall 1981, 19; Masaji Marumoto interview, 18–20, 67. The first non-white justice, serving from 1846 to 1862, was Hawaiian.

32. *SB*, 7 May 1979, B1.

33. A similar argument is made by Samuels, *The Japanese and the Haoles of Honolulu*, 25.

34. The military buildup in Hawaii during the 1920s and 1930s affected the ratios for figure 8. The large influx of Caucasians from the mainland dramatically increased the 1930 and 1940 population totals. Employed Caucasians increased by 14,783 in the 1920s and 23,512 in the 1930s. The partial military withdrawal

after the war caused a dramatic drop in the number of employed Caucasians, from 48,772 in 1940 to 24,811 in 1950. Census reports for 1930 and 1940 do not separate out armed forces personnel from among total employed persons.

If military-related employees were deleted, Japanese ratios would drop to about 1.08 for 1930 and .87 for 1940. Thus the 1930 increase in the ratio for Japanese male professionals was actually more modest than figure 8 indicates. (Subtracting 10,000 from each of the totals of employed males for 1930 and 1940 results in a decrease of about .10 in the Japanese ratios for those years.) The relatively low Japanese ratio of .65 in 1950 might be partly explained by the effects of the war. Those Japanese men who might have been professionals by 1950 postponed their college education by enlisting in the military. After the war, many of them went on to college. The results of their college education would not be seen until after 1950. (In July 1945, Japanese men constituted 60 to 65 percent of all men from Hawaii in the armed forces, while Japanese citizens and noncitizens made up only 33 percent of the population of the territory. See Hawaii Territory, Office of the Military Governor, Morale Section, *The AJA—Their Present and Future,* n.p.)

Although the ratio for Japanese male professionals dropped from 1940 to 1950, the number of Japanese male professionals actually increased during this ten-year period, from 1,198 in 1940 to 2,504 in 1950. However, the increase was not substantial enough to offset the decrease in total number of employed males, from 145,659 in 1940 to 119,860 in 1950, which affected the Japanese ratio. Similarly, although the proportion of Part-Hawaiian professional men decreased between 1910 and 1950, their raw numbers in the professions actually increased. This increase was insufficient, however, because there was a larger increase of professionals among the rest of the population. For the numbers of male professionals and total employed males by ethnic group, see Tamura, "Americanization Campaign," 476.

35. Despite the almost equal number of Japanese female professionals (1,197) to Japanese male professionals (1,198) in 1940, female Nisei did not pursue schooling in the same way male Nisei did. The professions women chose, teaching and nursing, required less schooling and less financing than the professions men chose. Overall a larger proportion of women of all ethnic groups entered the professions, mainly teaching and nursing (5,264 out of 35,137), when compared with men (4,228 out of 145,659), resulting in a smaller ratio for Japanese professional women (0.25 as compared to 0.97 for Japanese male professionals).

36. The ratio for Japanese male professionals in 1970 was 0.89, and that for Japanese female professionals was 0.88, indicating slight underrepresentation. Because of the different ways ethnic categories were recorded in different census years, these ratios are only general indicators. But in 1970 most Japanese adults were still ethnically pure, since few Nisei had intermarried. Japanese professionals in 1970 mainly included the second and third generations.

37. Kazuo Hosaka interview.

38. Eriko Yamamoto, "Evolution of an Ethnic Hospital," 78–84, 141, 330–31. During World War II the Japanese Hospital was renamed Kuakini Hospital after the street it was on.

39. *NJ,* 5 October 1928.

40. Shizue Komu Kuramoto interview; Tamura, "Americanization Campaign," 482–83. Although Japanese were underrepresented in engineering, there were numerically more Japanese than Chinese or Part-Hawaiian engineers in 1920 and 1930. In proportion to the numbers of employed males in each group, however, the Japanese were underrepresented. In 1930 there were 35,496 employed Japanese males, compared to 8,571 Chinese and 4,368 Part-Hawaiian employed males.

41. *HH*, 17 November 1989.

42. *NJ*, 4 February 1935; George K. Yamamoto, "Political Participation," 360. In 1920, citizens of Chinese ancestry constituted about 7 percent of the adult population.

43. Ibid.

44. *NJ*, 6 September 1928; *NJ*, 21 October 1928.

45. *Garden Isle*, 30 September 1930; *NJ*, 7 October 1930; *NJ*, 6 November 1930.

46. *Who's Who: Americans of Japanese Ancestry*, 157. The first Nisei passed the Hawaii bar in 1910, a time when few Nisei had reached adulthood. See the appendix, "Firsts among Japanese Americans in Hawaii."

47. *All about Hawaii*, 1920–53.

48. *HH*, 17 July 1926; William C. Smith, *Americans in Process*, 86.

49. Masuoka, "Race Attitudes," 120.

50. WCS R9 HJ28.

51. WCS R4 HH8.

52. Tom Kaser, "Japanese Americans," C-2; Clarence Kobayashi interview.

53. WCS R8 N55. A similar story of wanting to become an engineer but being unable to afford four years of college is found in WCS R6 N223.

54. WCS R5 N270; WCS R7 N156.

55. Aiko Tokimasa Reinecke interview.

56. WCS R4 HH48.

57. William C. Smith, "Changing Personality Traits," 926. A similar account is found in WCS R8 N39.

58. *Biennial Report*, 1910, 105–21; *Biennial Report*, 1914, 101–32.

59. *Biennial Report*, 1927–28, 165; Hawaii Territory, Governor's Advisory Committee on Education, *Survey of Schools and Industry in Hawaii*, Appendix, 102. Before the 1920s senior high school teachers came from the mainland.

60. William C. Smith, *Americans in Process*, 79–80.

61. *NJ*, 31 May 1935. The other teacher was a Chinese American.

62. "Term Report, 1925–42," pass.; *The Oahuan*, 1927–58, pass.

63. *Biennial Report*, 1916, 74, 115; Hawaii Territory, DPI, *School Directory*, 1924–25, 1925–26, 1930–31, 1940–41, 1950–51; Tamura, "Americanization Campaign," 476–77. In 1924 the smallest rural school retained one teacher for eleven students, while the largest school in Honolulu employed forty-nine teachers for about 1,679 students. The Nisei ratio of ethnic occupancy for school principals in 1950 was 0.18.

64. Hawaii Territory, DPI, *School Directory*, 1939–40, 16–22.

65. Hawaii Territory, DPI, *School Directory*, 1925–63.

66. Shaw, "Output of the Territorial Normal and Training School," 25a.

67. Figure 14, based on census data, includes both public and private (includ-

ing language) school teachers. Because of this, the 1930 ratio for Japanese men (1.79) is much higher than it would be if it included only public school teachers. Only American citizens could become public school teachers. Figure 14, like figures 8 through 13, includes Issei as well as Nisei, and thus reflects the progression of the entire Japanese community instead of only that of the second generation. The DPI did not regularly keep data on public school teachers by ethnic group.

68. There was a sharp numerical increase from 140 nurses in 1910 to 1,447 in 1920, reflecting the aftermath of World War I. Census reports for 1910 to 1930 list only teaching and nursing under female professionals. The small size of the Korean population meant that an increase of just thirteen nurses in 1930 resulted in a dramatic increase in their 1930 ratio (1.99).

69. Marie interview. Nisei girls talk about parents objecting to their becoming nurses in WCS R11 L1 and WCS R6 N177. According to Carlson, the Japanese Hospital's nursing school opened in 1931 ("Will Hawaii's Nurses Win Clio?" 8).

Epilogue

1. The Nisei paid a high price to demonstrate their loyalty. They suffered a casualty rate more than three times the average in the U.S. Army, and contributed to 80 percent of Hawaii's casualties. See Daws, *Shoal of Time*, 351; Fuchs, *Hawaii Pono*, 306. In contrast to the Japanese on the West Coast, less than 1 percent of the 160,000 Japanese in Hawaii were interned. Not only were ships unavailable to transport them to mainland internment camps, but interning one-third of Hawaii's population presented a logistical nightmare and would have brought the territory's economy to a standstill. There were simply too many Japanese working in too many of the territory's essential services. Fortunately, haole leaders in the Islands understood this. See Daws, *Shoal of Time*, 347–48.

2. Lind, *Hawaii's Japanese*, 118.

3. Yukiko Kimura, "Rumor among the Japanese," 84–85, 87–88; War Research Laboratory, What People Are Saying, Report No. 8, 2–3, 6. Right after World War II ended, rumors of Japan's victory also spread among the Issei in the Immigration and Naturalization Service (INS) internment camps at Santa Fe, New Mexico and Crystal City, Texas, and among some of the Japan-bound Issei in the partially segregated relocation center at Tule Lake, California. Those returning to Hawaii were told that a Japanese fleet would meet them at Seattle and escort them home. In one INS camp, only about a hundred out of two thousand internees accepted Japan's defeat. Others became angry and violent when told that Japan had lost the war.

4. Yukiko Kimura, "Rumor among the Japanese," 84–93; War Research Laboratory, What People Are Saying, Report No. 8, 1–6.

5. Lind, *Hawaii's Japanese*, 222–24.

6. Kawahara and Hatanaka, "Impact of War," 36–40.

7. Yukiko Kimura, "Some Effects of the War," 23. The acculturation of mainland Japanese also accelerated during the war. According to Kitano, the evacuation of the Japanese from the West Coast broke up Japanese ghettoes, diminished the

power of the Issei, and made many renounce things Japanese (*Japanese Americans*, 111).

8. Kawahara and Hatanaka, "Impact of War on an Immigrant Culture," 41–42.

9. Kimura and Freeman, "Problem of Assimilation," 57.

10. For studies that have emphasized the speed of Nisei acculturation, see, for example, Caudill, *Japanese American Personality*; Petersen, *Japanese Americans*,

11. Spickard, *Mixed Blood*, 80. By 1960 most Nisei were already married, so 1970 figures represent Sansei marriages. Kikumura and Kitano ("Interracial Marriage," 30) show a higher rate of intermarriage (47 percent) in 1970 among male and female Japanese because they use married couples as their base unit. I prefer Spickard's figures because his calculations are based on individuals instead of pairs. See Spickard, *Mixed Blood* (396), for the reasoning behind his method of calculating intermarriage percentages.

12. Johnson, "Alternatives to Alienation," 370; Johnson, "Japanese-American Family," 1–3; Johnson, "Interdependence, Reciprocity, Indebtedness," 351–63; Kuroda, "Uniqueness of the Japanese Americans," 9–10.

13. Masuda, Matsumoto, and Meredith, "Ethnic Identity in Three Generations," 199; Connor, "Acculturation and Family Continuities," 159–65; Yanagita, "Familial, Occupational, and Social Characteristics," 100–101; Levine and Montero, "Socioeconomic Mobility," 33–48; Montero, *Japanese Americans*, 61; Woodrum, "Japanese American Social Adaptation"; Israely, "Exploration into Ethnic Identity," 368–70. See also Fujita and O'Brien, *Japanese American Ethnicity*, 61–62, 116–17.

14. Arkoff, "Need Patterns in Two Generations," 75–79; Arkoff, Meredith, and Iwahara, "Dominance-Deference Patterning," 65; Meredith, "Amae and Acculturation," 171–80; Meredith, "Acculturation and Personality," 175–82; Connor, "Acculturation and Family Continuities," 164; Johnson, "Alternatives to Alienation," 347, 355, 366–67. In Japan, *enryo* originally referred to the deferential way people behaved toward superiors. In America the concept was generalized to other situations and included such behaviors as hesitancy to speak out at meetings, refusal of a second helping, and acceptance of the lesser of two objects when given a choice. See Kitano, *Japanese Americans*, 124–25.

Works Cited

Archival Documents

Farrington, Wallace R. Papers, 1921 to 1929. Miscellaneous. "Japanese Training Squadron." Hawaii State Archives. Honolulu.

———. Miscellaneous. "Language Schools, Foreign, Petitions, Correspondence, 1922." Hawaii State Archives. Honolulu.

———. Territorial Departments. Public Instruction. "Foreign Language Schools." Hawaii State Archives. Honolulu.

———. Territorial Departments. Public Instruction. "January–December, 1922." Hawaii State Archives. Honolulu.

Hawaii Territory. Department of Public Instruction. "Miscellaneous Reports and Statistical Tables, 1921–30." Hawaii State Archives. Honolulu.

———. "Reports of the Supervisor of Foreign Language Schools, 15 April–December 1925." Hawaii State Archives. Honolulu.

———. "Term Reports, December 1925–47." Hawaii State Archives. Honolulu. (From 1925 to 1947 the Territorial Department of Public Instruction collected enrollment data of public and private school students, separated by grade and ethnic group, and compiled them in bound volumes called Term Reports. These reports provided the data for many of the graphs in this study.)

———. "Years Average Mark, 1921–35," 4 vols. Hawaii State Archives. Honolulu.

Judd, Lawrence M. Papers, 1929 to 1934. Territorial Departments. Public Instruction. "Education, Teacher Training." Hawaii State Archives. Honolulu.

———. Territorial Departments. Public Instruction. "Educational Survey." Hawaii State Archives. Honolulu.

McCarthy, Charles J. Papers, 1918 to 1921. Miscellaneous. "Japanese Language Schools, Petitions." Hawaii State Archives. Honolulu.

———. Territorial Departments. Public Instruction. "Schedule, Teachers' Salaries." Hawaii State Archives. Honolulu.

———. Territorial Departments. Public Instruction. "Superintendent, June 1918 to June 1919." Hawaii State Archives. Honolulu.

———. Territorial Departments. Public Instruction. "Superintendent, July to December 1920." Hawaii State Archives. Honolulu.

Poindexter, Joseph B. Papers, 1934 to 1942. Miscellaneous. "Japanese Newspapers, Articles, etc." Hawaii State Archives. Honolulu.

Romanzo Adams Social Research Laboratory (RASRL). Hawaiian Collection.

Hamilton Library. University of Hawaii, Honolulu. (The RASRL collection includes working papers of the University of Hawaii sociology professor Romanzo Adams and newspaper clippings on a variety of topics from 1927 to the 1960s.)

Wist, Benjamin O. Papers. Teachers College, 1938–39. "Fujita, Tatsue." Hawaiian Collection. Hamilton Library. University of Hawaii, Honolulu.

Newspapers and Periodicals Covering Hawaii

Friend. 1917 to 1925
Garden Isle. 1930
Hawaii Educational Review. 1931 to 1935
Hawaii Herald. 1987, 1989
Hawaii Hochi. 1925 to 1939
Hawaii Mainichi. 1931
Honolulu Advertiser. 1921 to 1938
Honolulu Star-Bulletin. 1919 to 1941, 1979
New Freedom. 1931
New Americans. 1924 to 1929
Nippu Jiji. 1919 to 1939
Pacific Commercial Advertiser. 1919 to 1921
Paradise of the Pacific. 1919 to 1938

Personal Accounts

Ethnic Studies Oral History Project, University of Hawaii at Manoa. *Five Life Histories.* Honolulu: Ethnic Studies Oral History Project, 1983.
———. *Kalihi: Place of Transition,* 3 vols. Honolulu: Ethnic Studies Oral History Project, 1984.
———. *Social History of Kona,* 2 vols. Honolulu: Ethnic Studies Oral History Project, 1981.
———. *Stores and Storekeepers of Paia and Puunene, Maui,* 2 vols. Honolulu: Ethnic Studies Oral History Project, 1981.
———. *Waialua and Haleiwa: The People Tell Their Story,* 9 vols. Honolulu: Ethnic Studies Oral History Project, 1981.
Hyams, B. K. Interviews done in 1983 in Hawaii with fifteen retired teachers who taught in Hawaii in the 1920s and 1930s, on seven cassette tapes. Hawaiian Collection. Hamilton Library. University of Hawaii, Honolulu.
Oral History Project, Social Science Research Institute, University of Hawaii at Manoa. *Waikiki, 1900–1985,* 4 vols. Honolulu: Oral History Project, 1985.
Watumull Foundation Oral History Project. *Watamull Foundation Oral History Project.* Honolulu, 1987.
William Carlson Smith Papers. "Life Histories of Students, Selected Series from

the William Carlson Smith Papers," 1926–27. Nineteen microfilm reels. Hamilton Library. University of Hawaii, Honolulu.

Interviews Cited

Anonymous A. Female Nisei. Interview by author, 30 April 1988, Honolulu.

Anonymous B. Male Nisei. Interview by author, 10 April 1989, Honolulu.

Aoki, Harold. Interview by Michiko Kodama-Nishimoto, 19 March 1985, transcript. *Waikiki, 1900–1985*, 2:723–74.

Asuka, Miyo. Interview by Michiko Kodama-Nishimoto, 20 February 1985, transcript. *Waikiki, 1900–1985*, 2:885–915.

Egami, Yosoto. Interview by Faye Komagata, 18 November 1980, transcript. *Social History of Kona*, 1:261–326.

Falconer, Rose. Interview by Faye Komagata, 9 December 1980, transcript. *Social History of Kona*, 1:155–82.

Feirer, Gladys. Interview by B. K. Hyams, 1983, untranscribed, tape 7.

Fukunaga, Edward. Interview by Michiko Kodama, 23 January 1981, transcript. *Social History of Kona*, 2:963–1016.

Funai, Richard. Interview by Dale Hayashi, 31 July 1976, transcript. *Waialua and Haleiwa: The People Tell Their Story*, 5:22–51.

Hawaiian-Caucasian female retired teacher. Interview by B. K. Hyams, 1983, untranscribed, tape 3.

Hirata, Timmy T. Interview by author, 30 June 1988, Honolulu.

Honda, Ralph. Interview by author, 29 June 1988, Honolulu.

Hosaka, Kazuo. Interview by author, 28 June 1989, Honolulu.

Inaba, Minoru. Interview by Faye Komagata, 24 November 1980, transcript. *Social History of Kona*, 1:329–408.

Inouye, Richard. Interview by author, 10 July 1989, Honolulu.

Ishida, William. Interview by Faye Komagata, 11 February 1981, transcript. *Social History of Kona*, 1:411–63.

Izumi, Thelma Y. Interview by Michiko Kodama, 11 January 1984, transcript. *Kalihi: Place of Transition*, 1:42–69.

Kawakami, Misao. Interview by B. K. Hyams, 1983, untranscribed, tape 4.

Kimura, Minoru. Interview by Michiko Kodama, 20 December 1983, transcript. *Kalihi: Place of Transition*, 1:255–98.

Kimura, Tsuruyo. Interview by Faye Komagata, 20 December 1980, transcript. *Social History of Kona*, 2:1073–1128.

Kina, Ethel. Interview by author, 26 June 1989, Honolulu.

Kobayashi, Clarence. Interview by B. K. Hyams, 1983, untranscribed, tape 5.

Kurahashi, Shoichi. Interview by author, 29 June 1989, Honolulu.

Kuramoto, Shizue Komu. Interview by author, 19 August 1989, Honolulu.

Manago, Osame. Interview by Michiko Kodama, 24 November 1980, transcript. *Social History of Kona*, 2:1357–94.

Marie. Female Nisei born in 1916 who preferred to be otherwise anonymous. Interview by author, 23 June 1989, Honolulu.

Marumoto, Masaji. Interview by Lila Sahney, 1985 and 1986, transcript. *Watumull Foundation Oral History Project.*

Matsushita, Sueno. Interview by author, 27 June 1989, Honolulu.

Miyake, Francis. Interview by Howard Nonaka, 8 July 1976, transcript. *Waialua and Haleiwa: The People Tell Their Story,* 5:126–69.

Morihara, Usaku. Interview by Michiko Kodama, 6 November 1980, transcript. *Social History of Kona,* 2:841–84.

Morimoto, Raku. Interview by Michiko Kodama, 9 June 1983, transcript. *Five Life Histories,* 165–236.

Morita, Yuzuru. Interview by Warren Nishimoto, 2 June 1983, transcript. *Five Life Histories,* 131–63.

Nakamura, Vivian. Interview by author, 3 July 1989, Honolulu.

Nunotani, Fumiko. Interview by Michael Mauricio, 25 March 1985, transcript. *Waikiki, 1900–1985,* 1:243–77.

Oda, Yoshiko. Interview by author, 24 June 1988, Honolulu.

Okano, Kame. Interview by Faye Komagata, 1 November 1980, transcript. *Social History of Kona,* 1:591–626.

Okudara, Tokio. Interview by Michiko Kodama, 22 December 1983, transcript. *Kalihi: Place of Transition,* 2:407–43.

Reinecke, Aiko Tokimasa. Interview by author, 23 June 1988, Honolulu.

Sakai, Charles. Interview by Dale Hayashi, 10 July 1976, transcript. *Waialua and Haleiwa: The People Tell Their Story,* 7:454–96.

Sakima, Akira. Interview by Michiko Kodama, 26 January 1984, transcript. *Kalihi: Place of Transition,* 2:349–404.

Shimoda, Masakazu. Interview by Warren Nishimoto, 7 November 1979, transcript. *Storekeepers of Paia and Puunene, Maui,* 1:145–214.

Soga, Miya. Interview by author, 16 March 1988, Honolulu.

Sutherland, Mark and Zelie. Interview by B. K. Hyams, 1983, untranscribed, tape 4.

Takahashi, Lowell G. Interview by Norma Carr, 22 July 1976, transcript. *Waialua and Haleiwa: The People Tell Their Story,* 7:508–61.

Takashiba, Yoshitaka. Interview by Michiko Kodama, 23 January 1981, transcript. *Social History of Kona,* 1:2–47.

Tam, Eileen. Interview by B. K. Hyams, 1983, untranscribed, tape 4.

Tamura, Tetsuko. Interview by author, 26 March 1988, Honolulu.

Uyehara, Sam. Interview by Warren Nishimoto, 3 March 1986, transcript. *Waikiki, 1900–1985,* 4:1519–22.

Warashima, Hajime. Interview by Dale Hayashi, 9 August 1976, transcript. *Waialua and Haleiwa: The People Tell Their Story,* 7:563–622.

Yamamoto, Edythe. Interview by author, 28 June 1989, Honolulu.

Yano, Misae. Interview by author, 12 June 1989, Honolulu.

Yonenaka, Edith. Interview by Michiko Kodama, 2 June 1983, transcript. *Five Life Histories,* 71–129.

Yoshimoto, Teiki. Interview by Michael Mauricio, 27 March 1985, transcript. *Waikiki, 1900–1985,* 1:281–323.

Yoshimura, Masayuki. Interview by Michiko Kodama-Nishimoto, 23 April 1986, transcript. *Waikiki, 1900–1985,* 3:1451–84.

Other Sources

Abramson, Harold J. "Assimilation and Pluralism." In *Harvard Encyclopedia of American Ethnic Groups,* ed. Stephan Thernstrom, 150–60. Cambridge, Mass.: Belknap Press, 1980.

Adamic, Louis. *What's Your Name?* New York: Harper and Brothers, 1942.

Adams, Romanzo. *Japanese in Hawaii.* New York: National Committee on American Japanese Relations, 1924.

——. "Why Japanese Parents in Hawaii Register Their Children as Citizens of Japan." *Universal Review* 2 (Aug. 1928). Box 1, file 3. Romanzo Adams Social Research Laboratory (RASRL), Hawaiian Collection. Hamilton Library. University of Hawaii. Honolulu.

——. "The Japanese, [1929]" 10 page typescript, box 6, file 57. Romanzo Adams Social Research Laboratory, Hawaiian/Pacific Collections. Hamilton Library. University of Hawaii. Honolulu.

——. *The Peoples of Hawaii.* Honolulu: Institute of Pacific Relations, 1933.

——, and Dan Kane-zo Kai. "The Education of the Boys of Hawaii and Their Economic Outlook." *University of Hawaii Research Publications* 4 (Jan. 1928): 1–59.

——, T. M. Livesay, and E. H. VanWinkle. "A Statistical Study of the Races in Hawaii, 1925." Hawaiian/Pacific Collections, Hamilton Library, University of Hawaii, Honolulu.

All about Hawaii: Thrum's Hawaiian Almanac, 1920–53, Honolulu.

Allen, Riley. "Education and Race Problems in Hawaii." *American Review of Reviews* (Dec. 1921): 613–24.

Aller, Curtis C. "The Evolution of Hawaiian Labor Relations: From Benevolent Paternalism to Mature Collective Bargaining." Ph.D. diss., Harvard University, 1958.

Altenbaugh, Richard J. "'Our children are being trained like dogs and ponies': Schooling, Social Control, and the Working Class." *History of Education Quarterly* 21 (Summer 1981): 213–22.

Ano, Masaharu. "Loyal Linguists: Nisei of World War II Learned Japanese in Minnesota." *Minnesota History* 45 (1977): 273–87.

Annals of the American Academy of Political and Social Science 93 (1921).

Appleton, Nicholas. *Cultural Pluralism in Education.* New York: Longman, 1983.

Archdeacon, Thomas J. *Becoming American: An Ethnic History.* New York: Free Press, 1983.

Arkoff, Abe. "Need Patterns in Two Generations of Japanese-Americans in Hawaii." *Journal of Social Psychology* 50 (1959): 75–79.

——, Gerald Meredith, and Shinkuro Iwahara. "Dominance-Deference Patterning in Motherland-Japanese, Japanese-American and Caucasian-American Students." *Journal of Social Psychology* 58 (1962): 61–66.

Ayer, N. W., and Son. *N. W. Ayer & Son's Directory of Newspapers and Periodicals.* Philadelphia: N. W. Ayer & Son, 1900–1940.

Bachman, Ross W. "The Reading Program of a Small, Rural, Elementary School." M.A. thesis, University of Hawaii, 1938.

Balch, Emily G. *Our Slavic Fellow Citizens*. New York: Charities Publications Committee, 1910.

Barr, Pat. *The Coming of the Barbarians: A Story of Western Settlement in Japan, 1853–1870*. London: Macmillan, 1967.

Barron, Milton L. "The Church, the State, and Intermarriage." In *The Blending American: Patterns of Intermarriage*, ed. Milton L. Barron, 52–86. Chicago: Quadrangle Books, 1972.

Barrett, Charles B. "The Mathematical Achievement of Eighth Grade Pupils from the Standpoint of Racial Ancestry." M.A. thesis, University of Hawaii, 1939.

Beechert, Edward D. *Working in Hawaii: A Labor History*. Honolulu: University of Hawaii Press, 1985.

Beekman, Take and Allan Beekman. "Hawaii's Great Japanese Strike." *Pacific Citizen*, 23 Dec. 1960, 14(A) and 1–8, 23–24(B).

Bell, Reginald. *Public School Education of Second-Generation Japanese in California*. Palo Alto: Stanford University Press, 1935.

Bell, Roger. *Last among Equals: Hawaiian Statehood and American Politics*. Honolulu: University of Hawaii Press, 1984.

Berkson, Isacc B. *Theories of Americanization: A Critical Study, with Special Reference to the Jewish Group*. New York: Teachers College, Columbia University, 1920.

Bickerton, Derek and William Wilson. "Pidgin Hawaiian." In *Pidgin and Creole Languages: Essays in Memory of John H. Reinecke*, ed. Glen Gilbert, 61–76. Honolulu: University of Hawaii Press, 1987.

Bierstadt, Edward Hale. *Aspects of Americanization*. Cincinnati: Stewart Kidd, 1922.

Blaisdell, Richard Kekuni. "Health and Social Services." In *Report on the Culture, Needs, and Concerns of Native Hawaiians Pursuant to Public Law 96–565, Title III. Vol. I*, ed. Native Hawaiians Study Commission, 99–122. Honolulu: Native Hawaiians Study Commission, 1983.

Bodnar, John. *The Transplanted: A History of Immigrants in Urban America*. Bloomington: Indiana University Press, 1985.

Bowles, Samuel and Herbert Gintis. *Schooling in Capitalist America: Eduational Reform and the Contradictions of Economic Life*. New York: Basic Books, 1976.

Breed, Eleanor D. "A Study of the English Vocabulary of Junior High School Pupils." M.A. thesis, University of Hawaii, 1928.

Brigance, William N. "How Good is the English of High School Graduates in Hawaii?" *Hawaii Educational Review* 26 (Jan. 1938): 133–34.

Brown, Victoria Bissell. "The Fear of Feminization: Los Angeles High Schools in the Progressive Era." *Feminist Studies* 16 (Fall 1990): 493–518.

Buenker, John D. "The Progressive Era: A Search for a Synthesis." *Mid-America* 51 (1969): 175–93.

Bunker, Frank E. "The Education of the Children of the American-born Parents in Hawaii." *Hawaii Educational Review* 11 (Sept. 1922): 1–3.

Burrows, Edwin G. *Chinese and Japanese in Hawaii during the Sino-Japanese Conflict*. Honolulu: Institute of Pacific Relations, 1939.

Cariaga, Roman R. "The Filipinos in Hawaii: A Survey of Their Economic and Social Conditions." M.A. thesis, Univeristy of Hawaii, 1936.

Carlson, LoRaine. "Will Hawaii's Nurses Win Clio? A Historical Perspective on the Pursuit to Professionalism." A methodological paper presented to the Department of Educational Foundations, 29 June 1987. Hawaiian/Pacific Collections, Hamilton Library, University of Hawaii, Honolulu.

Carr, Norma. "The Puerto Ricans in Hawaii, 1900–1958." Ph.D. diss., University of Hawaii, 1989.

Caudill, William. *Japanese-American Personality and Acculturation*. Provincetown, Maine: Journal Press, 1952.

———. "Japanese-American Personality and Acculturation." *Genetic-Psychology Monographs* 45 (1952): 3–102.

———, and H. Weinstein. "Maternal Care and Infant Behavior in Japan and America." In *Japanese Culture and Behavior*, ed. Takie Sugiyama Lebra and William P. Lebra, 225–76. Honolulu: University of Hawaii Press, 1974.

Chan, Sucheng. *Asian Americans: An Interpretive History*. Boston: Twayne Publishers, 1991.

———. "The Exclusion of Chinese Women, 1870–1943." In *Entry Denied: Exclusion and the Chinese Community in America, 1882–1943*, ed. Sucheng Chan, 94–146. Philadelphia: Temple University Press, 1991.

Chinese Students' Alliance of Hawaii. *Students' Annual*. Honolulu: Chinese Students' Alliance of Hawaii, 1920–31.

Choy, Ellen, et al. "Moiliili: A Historical Analysis, 1900–1945." Honolulu, 1977. Hawaiian Collection. Hamilton Library. University of Hawaii, Honolulu.

Citizenship Education Committee of the Territorial YMCA. *American Institute Papers*. Honolulu: Citizenship Education Committee, 1919.

Clyde, Paul H. and Burton F. Beers. *The Far East: A History of the Western Impact and the Response, 1830–1970*. 5th ed. Englewood Cliffs, N.J.: Prentice-Hall, 1971.

Cohen, David K. and Marvin Lazerson. "Education and the Corporate Order." In *Education in American History: Readings on the Social Issues*, ed. Michael B. Katz, 318–33. New York: Praeger, 1973.

Cohen, Sol. "Urban School Reform." *History of Education Quarterly* 9 (Fall 1969): 298–304.

———. "The History of the History of American Education, 1900–1976: The Uses of the Past." *Harvard Educational Review* 46 (Aug. 1976): 298–330.

Compilation Committee for the Publication of Kinzaburo Makino's Biography. *Life of Kinzaburo Makino*. Honolulu: n.p., [1965].

Connor, John W. "Acculturation and Family Continuities in Three Generations of Japanese Americans." *Journal of Marriage and the Family* 36 (Feb. 1974): 159–65.

Conroy, Hilary. *The Japanese Frontier in Hawaii, 1868–1898*. Berkeley: University of California Press, 1953.

Conzen, Kathleen Neils, David A. Gerber, Ewa Morawska, George E. Pozzetta, and Rudolph J. Vecoli. "The Invention of Ethnicity: A Perspective from the U.S.A." *Journal of American Ethnic History* 12 (Fall 1992): 3–63.

Coulter, John W. and Alfred G. Serrao. "Manoa Valley, Honolulu: A Study in Economic and Social Geography." *Bulletin of the Geographical Society of Philadelphia*, 30 April 1932, 109–30.

Cremin, Lawrence A. *The Transformation of the School: Progressivism in American Education, 1876–1957.* New York: Alfred A. Knopf, 1961.

Cretser, Gary A. and Joseph J. Leon, ed. *Intermarriage in the United States.* New York: Haworth Press, 1982.

Daniels, Roger. *The Politics of Prejudice: The Anti-Japanese Movement in California and the Struggle for Japanese Exclusion.* Berkeley: University of California Press, 1962.

———. "Japanese Immigrants on a Western Frontier: The Issei in California, 1890–1940." In *East across the Pacific: Historical and Sociological Studies of Japanese Immigration and Assimilation*, ed. Hilary Conroy and T. Scott Miyakawa, 76–91. Santa Barbara: ABC-Clio Press, 1972.

———. "The Japanese." In *Ethnic Leadership in America*, ed. John Higham, 36–63. Baltimore: Johns Hopkins University Press, 1978.

———. *Asian America: Chinese and Japanese in the United States since 1850.* Seattle: University of Washington Press, 1988.

———. *Coming to America: A History of Immigration and Ethnicity in American Life.* New York: HarperCollins Publishers, 1990.

———, and Harry H. L. Kitano. *American Racism: Exploration of the Nature of Prejudice.* Englewood Cliffs, N.J.: Prentice-Hall, 1970.

Daws, Gavan. *Shoal of Time: A History of the Hawaiian Islands.* Honolulu: University Press of Hawaii, 1968.

DeVos, George A. "Quantitative Rorschach Assessment of Maladjustment and Rigidity in Acculturating Japanese-Americans." *Genetic Psychology Monographs* 52 (1955): 50–87.

———. *Socialization for Achievement: Essays on the Cultural Psychology of the Japanese.* Berkeley: University of California Press, 1973.

———. "Ethnic Pluralism: Conflict and Accomodation." In *Ethnic Identity, Cultural Continuities and Change*, ed. George A. DeVos and Lola Romanucci-Ross, 5–41. Palo Alto: Mayfield Publishing Co., 1975.

———, and William O. Wetherall. *Japan's Minorities: Burakumin, Koreans, Ainu and Okinawans.* London: Minority Rights Group, 1974.

Dinnerstein, Leonard, Roger L. Nichols, and David M. Reimers. *Natives and Strangers: Ethnic Groups and the Building of America.* New York: Oxford University Press, 1979.

Doi, L. Takeo. "Omote and Ura: Concepts Derived from the Japanese Two-Fold Structure of Consciousness." *Journal of Nervous and Mental Disease* 4 (1973): 258–61.

———. "Amae: A Key Concept for Understanding Japanese Personality Structure." In *Japanese Culture and Behavior: Selected Readings*, ed. William P. Lebra, 121–29. Honolulu: University of Hawaii Press, 1986.

Dore, Ronald P. *Education in Tokugawa, Japan.* Berkeley: University of California Press, 1965.

Dorita, Sister Mary. "Filipino Immigration to Hawaii." M.A. thesis, University of Hawaii, 1954.

Dower, John W. *War without Mercy*. New York: Pantheon Books, 1986.

Eddy, John M. "A Study of the Vocational Opportunities for High School Graduates in the Territory of Hawaii." M.A. thesis, University of Chicago, 1926.

Embree, John F. *Acculturation among the Japanese of Kona, Hawaii*. Menasha, Wis.: American Anthropological Association, 1941.

Emory, Kenneth. "Origin of the Hawaiians." *Journal of the Polynesian Society* 68 (1959): 29–35.

Endo, Russell. "Social Science and Historical Materials on the Asian American Experience." In *Asian-Americans: Social and Psychological Perspectives*, vol. 2, ed. Russell Endo, Stanley Sue, and Nathaniel N. Wagner, 304–31. Ben Lomond: Science & Behavior Books, Inc., 1980.

Erdman, John P. "The Hawaiian Board of Missions." *Friend* 107 (Apr. 1937): 65–66.

Ethnic Studies Oral History Project, ed. *Uchinanchu*. Honolulu: Ethnic Studies Oral History Project, 1981.

Ettinger, William, L. "Americanization." *School and Society* 9 (Feb. 1919): 129–33.

Farrington, Wallace R. "Hawaii's Opportunities for Its Boys Who Know Agriculture." Address before the Committee on Trade, Commerce, and Industrial Development, Chamber of Commerce of Honolulu, 2 July 1928. Hawaiian/Pacific Collections, Hamilton Library, University of Hawaii, Honolulu.

———. "Opportunities in Hawaii." *New Americans* 10 (May 1929): 1–2.

Fass, Paula S. *Outside In: Minorities and the Transformation of American Education*. New York: Oxford University Press, 1989.

Feinberg, Walter and Henry Rosemont, Jr. *Work, Technology, and Education: Dissenting Essays in the Intellectual Foundations of American Education*. Urbana: University of Illinois Press, 1975.

Flanders, Jesse K. *Legislative Control of the Elementary Curriculum*. New York: Teachers College, Columbia University, 1925.

Fuchs, Lawrence H. *Hawaii Pono: A Social History*. New York: Harcourt, Brace, and World, 1961.

Fujii, Yukio. *The Acculturation of the Japanese Immigrants in Brazil*. Gainesville: University of Florida Press, 1959.

Fujita, Stephen S. and David O'Brien. *Japanese American Ethnicity: The Persistence of Community*. Seattle: University of Washington Press, 1991.

Gay, Floy T. "A Study of the Development of the Senior High Schools." M.A. thesis, University of Hawaii, 1945.

Geertz, Clifford. *The Interpretation of Cultures: Selected Essays*. New York: Basic Books, 1973.

Gibson, Margaret A. and John U. Ogbu. *Minority Status and Schooling: A Comparative Study of Immigrant and Involuntary Minorities*. New York: Garland, 1991.

Glazer, Nathan and Daniel Patrick Moynihan. *Beyond the Melting Pot: The*

Negroes, Puerto Ricans, Jews, Italians, and Irish of New York City, 2d ed. Cambridge: MIT Press, 1963.

Gleason, Philip. "American Identity and Americanization." In *Harvard Encyclopedia of American Ethnic Groups,* ed. Stephan Thernstrom, 36–58. Cambridge, Mass.: Belknap Press, 1980.

Glenn, Evelyn Nakano. *Issei, Nisei, War Bride: Three Generations of Japanese American Women in Domestic Service.* Philadelphia: Temple University Press, 1986.

Glick, Clarence E. *Sojourners and Settlers: Chinese Migrants in Hawaii.* Honolulu: University of Hawaii Press, 1980.

Glimpses of Japanese in Hawaii. Honolulu: Nippu Jiji, 1925.

Goldman, Irving. *Ancient Polynesian Society.* Chicago: University of Chicago Press, 1970.

Gordon, Milton M. *Assimilation in American Life: The Role of Race, Religion, and National Origins.* New York: Oxford University Press, 1964.

Goto, Baron. "Ethnic Groups and the Coffee Industry in Hawaii." *Hawaiian Journal of History* 16 (1982): 118–23.

Governor's Coordinating Committee. *Kansha: In Appreciation, the 100th Anniversary of Japanese in Hawaii.* Honolulu: Japanese Junior Chamber of Commerce, 1985.

Greeley, Andrew M. *Ethnicity in the United States.* New York: Wiley, 1974.

Greenbaum, William. "America in Search of a New Ideal: An Essay on the Rise of Pluralism." *Harvard Educational Review* 44 (1974): 411–40.

Greene, Maxine. "Identities and Contours: An Approach to Educational History." *Educational Researcher* 2 (Apr. 1973): 5–10.

Griffiths, Arthur F. "More Race Questions." Paper read at a meeting of the Social Science Association, 1 March 1915. Hawaiian/Pacific Collections, Hamilton Library, University of Hawaii, Honolulu.

Gulick, Sidney L. *Hawaii's American-Japanese Problem.* Honolulu: Star-Bulletin, 1915.

———. *Mixing the Races in Hawaii.* Honolulu: The Hawaiian Board Book Rooms, 1937.

Halsted, Ann L. "Sharpened Tongues: The Controversy over the 'Americanization' of Japanese Language Schools in Hawaii, 1919–1927." Ph.D. diss., Stanford University, 1988.

Hane, Mikiso. *Peasants, Rebels, and Outcasts: The Underside of Modern Japan.* New York: Pantheon, 1982.

Hansen, M. L. "The Third Generation in America: A Classic Essay in Immigrant History." *Commentary* 14 (Nov. 1952): 492–500.

Harada, Koichi G. "A Survey of the Japanese Language Schools in Hawaii." M.A. thesis, University of Hawaii, 1934.

Harrington, Mona. "Loyalties: Dual and Divided." In *Harvard Encyclopedia of American Ethnic Groups,* ed. Stephan Thernstrom, 676–86. Cambridge, Mass.: Belknap Press, 1980.

Harris, Arthur L. "Reading Ability of Maui High School Students." M.A. thesis, University of Hawaii, 1935.

Hartmann, Edward. G. *The Movement to Americanize the Immigrant*. New York: Columbia University Press, 1948.

Hawaii Hochi. *Fred Kinzaburo Makino*. Honolulu: Hawaii Hochi, 1986.

Hawaii Territory. Board of Health. Bureau of Vital Statistics. "Report of the Registrar General for the Fiscal Year Ended 30 June 1930."

————. Board of Health. Bureau of Vital Statistics. "Annual Report of the Board of Health, Territory of Hawaii for Fiscal Year Ended June 30, 1939." State of Hawaii Office of Health Status Monitoring, Honolulu.

————. "Board of Health, Territory of Hawaii Bureau of Vital Statistics Report for Fiscal Year 1940." State of Hawaii Office of Health Status Monitoring, Honolulu.

————. Department of Public Instruction. *Biennial Report to the Governor and Legislature*. Honolulu: Department of Public Instruction, 1914–42.

————. Department of Public Instruction. *School Directory*. Honolulu: Department of Public Instruction, 1924–46.

————. Department of Public Instruction. "Annual Descriptive Report of the Territorial Board for Vocational Education to the Federal Board for Vocational Education," 1928. Cited in Floy Gay, "A Study of the Development of the Senior High Schools," 45. M.A. thesis, University of Hawaii, 1945.

————. Governor's Advisory Committee on Education. "Report on the Sugar Cane Industry." Mimeographed. Hawaiian/Pacific Collections, Hamilton Library, University of Hawaii, Honolulu, 1931.

————. Governor's Advisory Committee on Education. *Survey of Schools and Industry in Hawaii*. Honolulu: The Printshop Co., 1931.

————. Governor's Advisory Committee on Education. "University of Hawaii." Mimeographed. Hawaiian/Pacific Collections, Hamilton Library, University of Hawaii, Honolulu, 1931.

————. *Laws of the Territory of Hawaii, Passed by the Eleventh Legislature, Special Session*. 1920.

————. *Laws of the Territory of Hawaii, Passed by the Twelfth Legislature, Regular Session*. 1923.

————. *Laws of the Territory of Hawaii, Passed by the Thirteenth Legislature, Regular Session*. 1925.

————. Office of the Military Governor. Morale Section. *The AJA—Their Present and Future*. Honolulu: Office of the Military Governor, 1945.

————. University. "Catalogue and Announcement of Courses, 1927–28." *Quarterly Bulletin*, vol. 6, no. 2. Honolulu: University of Hawaii, 1927.

————. University. *The University of Hawaii Bulletin*, vol. 16, no. 6. Honolulu: University of Hawaii, 1938.

————. University. "Report of the President for 1945–46." *University of Hawaii Bulletin*, vol. 26, no. 1. Honolulu: University of Hawaii, 1946.

Hawaii Times 60th Anniversary, 1895–1955. Special Edition, 1 October 1955.

Hawaiian Sugar Planters Association. "Translations from the Japanese Press, 1923." Hawaiian/Pacific Collections, Hamilton Library, University of Hawaii, Honolulu.

Hawkins, John N. "Politics, Education, and Language Policy: The Case of Japanese Language Schools in Hawaii." *Amerasia* 5:1 (1978): 39–56.

Hayashida, Akiyoshi. "Japanese Moral Instruction as a Factor in the Americanization of Citizens of Japanese Ancestry." M.A. thesis, University of Hawaii, 1933.

Hayner, Norman S. "Delinquency Areas in the Puget Sound Region." *American Journal of Sociology* 39 (Nov. 1933): 314–28.

Herberg, Will. *Protestant, Catholic, Jew: An Essay in American Religious Sociology.* Garden City, N.Y.: Doubleday, 1956 [1955].

Hernanz, German Rueda. "The Life and Misadventures of Eight Thousand Spaniards in Hawaii during the First Decades of the Twentieth Century." *Anglo-American Studies* 1 (Apr. 1985): 55–70.

Higa, Masanori. "Okinawa in Hawaii." In *Uchinanchu*, ed. Ethnic Studies Oral History Project, 37–47. Honolulu: Ethnic Studies Oral History Project, 1981.

Hilo, M. and Emma K. Himeno. "Some Characteristics of American and Japanese Culture." *Social Process in Hawaii* 21 (1957): 34–41.

Higham, John. *Strangers in the Land: Patterns of American Nativism.* New Brunswick, N.J.: Rutgers University Press, 1955.

———, ed. *Ethnic Leadership in America.* Baltimore: Johns Hopkins University Press, 1978.

Hogan, David. *Class and Reform: School and Society in Chicago, 1880–1930.* Philadelphia: University of Pennsylvania Press, 1985.

Hori, Joan. "Japanese Prostitution in Hawaii during the Immigration Period." *Hawaiian Journal of History* 15 (1981): 113–24.

Horinouchi, Isao. "Americanized Buddhism: A Sociological Analysis of Protestantized Japanese Religion." Ph.D. diss., University of California at Davis, 1973.

Hormann, Bernard L. "The English Standard School." What People Are Saying and Doing, Report No. 9. War Research Laboratory, University of Hawaii, 8 May 1946.

———. "Integration in Hawaii's Schools." *Social Process in Hawaii* 21 (1957): 5–15.

Horsman, Reginald. *Race and Manifest Destiny: The Origins of American Racial Anglo-Saxonism.* Cambridge: Harvard University Press, 1981.

Houchins, Lee and Chang-su Houchins. "The Korean Experience in America, 1903–24." In *The Asian American: The Historical Experience*, ed. Norris Hundley, Jr., 129–56. Santa Barbara: Clio Books, 1976.

Huber, S. C. "Dual Citizenship." *Paradise of the Pacific* 50 (Jan. 1938): 24.

Hunter, Louise H. *Buddhism in Hawaii: Its Impact on a Yankee Community.* Honolulu: University of Hawaii Press, 1971.

Hyams, B. K. "School Teachers as Agents of Cultural Imperialism in Territorial Hawaii." *Journal of Pacific History* 20 (Oct. 1985): 202–19.

Ichihashi, Yamato. *Japanese in the United States.* New York: Arno Press, 1969 [1932].

Ichioka, Yuji. "*Ameyuki-san:* Japanese Prostitutes in Nineteenth-Century America." *Amerasia Journal* 4: 1 (1977): 1–22.

———. "*Amerika Nadeshiko:* Japanese Immigrant Women in the United States, 1900–1924." *Pacific Historical Review* 49 (1980): 339–57.

———. *The Issei: The World of the First Generation Japanese Immigrants, 1885–1924.* New York: Free Press, 1988.

Ige, Philip K. "An Okinawan Nisei." In *Uchinanchu,* ed. Ethnic Studies Oral History Project, 149–60. Honolulu: Ethnic Studies Oral History Project, 1981.

Ige, Tom. *Boy from Kahaluu: An Autobiography.* Honolulu: Kin Cho Jin Kai, 1989.

Imamura, Yemyo. *Democracy According to the Buddhist Viewpoint.* Honolulu: Honpa Hongwanji Mission, 1918.

———. *A History of the Hongwanji Mission in Hawaii.* Honolulu: Hongwanji Mission, 1918.

Inouye, Daniel K. and Lawrence Elliott. *Journey to Washington.* Englewood Cliffs, N.J.: Prentice-Hall, 1967.

Irwin, Edward P. "Ed Irwin More Than Suggests That We Should Not Try to 'Americanize' Orientals in Hawaii, Even if We Can." *Paradise of the Pacific* 37 (Dec. 1924): 54–56.

Irwin, Yukiko and Hilary Conroy. "Robert Walker Irwin and Systematic Immigration to Hawaii." In *East across the Pacific: Historical and Sociological Studies of Japanese Immigration and Assimilation,* ed. Hilary Conroy and T. Scott Miyakawa, 40–55. Santa Barbara: ABC Clio Press, 1972.

Israely, Hilla K. "An Exploration into Ethnic Identity: The Case of Third-Generation Japanese Americans." Ph.D. diss., University of California, Los Angeles, 1975.

Iwado, Z. Tamotsu. " 'Hagakure Bushido' or the Book of the Warrior." *Cultural Nippon* 7 (Nov. 1939): 33–55.

Japanese Educational Association of Hawaii. *A Brief Survey of the Foreign Language School Question.* Honolulu: Japanese Educational Association of Hawaii, 1923.

Japanese Students' Association of Hawaii. *Students' Annual.* Honolulu: Japanese Students' Association of Hawaii, 1924–35.

Johnson, Colleen L. "The Japanese-American Family and Community in Honolulu: Generational Continuities in Ethnic Affiliation." Ph.D. diss., Syracuse University, 1972.

———. "Alternatives to Alienation: A Japanese-American Example." In *Education and Community: A Radical Critique of Innovative Schooling,* ed. Donald. W. Oliver, 348–74. Berkeley: McCutchan Publishing Corp., 1976.

———. "Interdependence, Reciprocity, Indebtedness: An Analysis of Japanese American Kinship Relations." *Journal of Marriage and the Family* 39 (May 1977): 351–63.

Jones, Maude. "Naturalization in Hawaii, 1795–1900," [unpublished manuscript, 1930s]. Hawaiian Collection. Hamilton Library. University of Hawaii, Honolulu.

———. "Naturalization of Orientals in Hawaii Prior to 1900." In *Forty-First Annual Report of the Hawaiian Historical Society for the Year 1932,* 66–69. Honolulu: Hawaiian Historical Society, 1933.

"Joseph Y. Kurihara, Autobiography." Japanese American Evacuation and Resettlement Collection. Bancroft Library, University of California, Berkeley.

Judd, Henry P. "The Repaganization of Hawaii." *Friend* 89 (July 1920): 188.

Kagiwada, George. "Confessions of a Misguided Sociologist." *Amerasia Journal* 2 (Fall 1973): 159–64.

Kaigo, Tokiomi. *Japanese Education: Its Past and Present*. Tokyo: Kokusai Bunka, 1968.

Kantor, Harvey. "The Great School Warriors: A Review of Diane Ravitch's *The Revisionists Revised*." In *Revisionists Respond to Ravitch*, Walter Feinberg, Harvey Kantor, Michael Katz, and Paul Violas, 43–59. Washington, D.C.: National Academy of Education, 1980.

Kaser, Tom. "Japanese Americans Largest Group in the DOE." *Honolulu Advertiser* (19 July 1974): C-2.

Kashima, Tetsudan. *Buddhism in America: The Social Organization of an Ethnic Religious Institution*. Westport, Conn.: Greenwood Press, 1977.

Katz, Michael B. *The Irony of Early School Reform*. Cambridge: Harvard University Press, 1968.

———. *Class, Bureaucracy, and Schools: The Illusion of Educational Change in America*. Expanded edition. New York: Praeger, 1975.

———. "An Apology for American Educational History." In *Revisionists Respond to Ravitch*, Walter Feinberg, Harvey Kantor, Michael Katz, and Paul Violas, 60–87. Washington, D.C.: National Academy of Education, 1980.

Kawahara, Kimie and Yuriko Hatanaka. "The Impact of War on an Immigrant Culture." *Social Process in Hawaii* 8 (1943): 36–45.

Kelly, Marion. "Land Tenure in Hawaii." *Amerasia Journal* 7 (Fall 1980): 57–74.

Kikumura, Akemi. *Through Harsh Winters: The Life of a Japanese Immigrant Woman*. Novato, Calif.: Chandler & Sharp, 1981.

———, and Harry H. L. Kitano. "Interracial Marriage: A Picture of the Japanese Americans." In *Asian-Americans: Social and Psychological Perspectives*, vol. 2, ed. Russell Endo, Stanley Sue, and Nathaniel N. Wagner, 26–35. Ben Lomond: Science and Behavior Books, 1980.

———. "The Japanese American Family." In *Ethnic Families in America*, ed. Charles H. Mindel and Robert W. Habenstein, 43–60. New York: Elsevier, 1981.

Kim, Bernice B. H. "The Koreans in Hawaii." M.A. thesis, University of Hawaii, 1937.

Kimura, Evelyn Yama and Margaret Zimmerman Freeman. "The Problem of Assimilation." *Social Process in Hawaii* 19 (1955): 55–64.

Kimura, Yukiko. "Psychological Aspects of Japanese Immigration." *Social Process in Hawaii* 6 (1940): 10–22.

———. "Some Effects of the War Situation upon the Alien Japanese in Hawaii." *Social Process in Hawaii* 8 (1943): 18–28.

———. "Rumor among the Japanese." *Social Process in Hawaii* 11 (1947): 84–92.

———. "A Comparative Study of Collective Adjustment of the Issei, the First Generation Japanese, in Hawaii and in the Mainland United States since Pearl Harbor." Ph.D. diss., University of Chicago, 1952.

———. "Social-Historical Background of the Okinawans in Hawaii." In *Uchinanchu*, ed. Ethnic Studies Oral History Project, 51–71. Honolulu: Ethnic Studies Oral History Project, 1981.

———. *Issei: Japanese Immigrants in Hawaii.* Honolulu: University of Hawaii Press, 1988.

Kitano, Harry H. L. "Japanese-American Crime and Delinquency." In *Asian-Americans: Psychological Perspectives,* ed. Stanley Sue, Nathaniel N. Wagner, and Russell Endo, 161–70. Ben Lomond: Science and Behavior Books, 1973.

———. *Japanese Americans: The Evolution of a Subculture.* Englewood Cliffs, N.J.: Prentice-Hall, 1976.

Kivisto, Peter and Dag Blanck, eds. *American Immigrants and Their Generations: Studies and Commentaries on the Hansen Thesis after Fifty Years.* Chicago: University of Illinois Press, 1990.

Kloss, Heinz. "German-American Language Maintenance Efforts." In *Language Loyalty in the United States: The Maintenance and Perpetuation of Non-English Mother Tongues by American Ethnic and Religious Groups,* ed. Joshua A. Fishman, 211–52. London: Mouton and Co., 1966.

Kobayashi, Hisashi J. "Don't Give Me That Rubbish!" *Hokubei Mainichi,* 26 March 1970. Cited in Minako K. Maykovich, *Japanese American Identity Dilemma,* 3. Tokyo: Waseda University Press, 1972.

Kono, Ayako. "Language as a Factor in the Achievement of American-born Students of Japanese Ancestry." M.A. thesis, University of Hawaii, 1934.

Korean Students Alliance of Hawaii. *Students' Annual.* Honolulu: Korean Students Alliance of Hawaii, 1932.

Kosaki, Mildred. "The Culture Conflicts and Guidance Needs of Nisei Adolescents." M.Ed. thesis, University of Hawaii, 1949.

Kotani, Roland. *The Japanese in Hawaii: A Century of Struggle.* Honolulu: Hawaii Hochi, 1985.

Krug, Edward A. *The Shaping of the American High School, 1920–1941,* vol. 2. Madison: University of Wisconsin Press, 1972.

Kuroda, Yasumasa. "A Study of Japanese-Americans in Honolulu: Subculture and Subsociety." Prepared for delivery at the annual meeting of the Association for Asian Studies, New York, 27–29 March 1972.

———. "The Uniqueness of the Japanese-Americans: A Comparative Analysis of Japanese-Americans, Mainlanders, and Other Islanders in Hawaii and Japanese in Japan." Paper delivered before the Hawaii Chapter of the American Studies Association, April 1980.

Kuykendall, Ralph S. *The Hawaiian Kingdom, Vol. 1, 1778–1854.* Honolulu: University of Hawaii Press, 1968 (1938).

———. *The Hawaiian Kingdom, Vol. 3, 1874–1893.* Honolulu: University of Hawaii Press, 1967.

Lai, Kum Pui. "The Natural History of the Chinese Language School in Hawaii." M.A. thesis, University of Hawaii, 1935.

Lazerson, Marvin. *Origins of the Urban School: Public Education in Massachusetts, 1870–1915.* Cambridge: Harvard University Press, 1971.

———. "Revisionism and American Educational History." *Harvard Educational Review* 43 (May 1973): 270–83.

———, and W. Norton Grubb. *American Education and Vocationalism.* New York: Teachers College Press, 1974.

Lebra, Takie Sugiyama. "Acculturation Dilemma: The Function of Japanese Moral

Values for Americanization." *Council on Anthropology and Education Newsletter* 3 (1972): 6–13.

——. *Japanese Patterns of Behavior*. Honolulu: University of Hawaii Press, 1976.

Leon, Joseph J. "A Test of the Milton M. Gordon Ethclass Hypothesis on Samples of Public High School Youth in Hawaii." Ph.D. diss., University of Hawaii, 1975.

Levering, Ralph B. *The Public and American Foreign Policy, 1918–1978*. New York: William Morrow, 1978.

Levine, G. N. and D. M. Montero. "Socioeconomic Mobility among Three Generations of Japanese Americans." *Journal of Social Issues* 29 (1973): 33–48.

Lewis, Helen Marion. "A Study of the Speech Attitudes of the University of Hawaii Freshmen." M.A. thesis, University of Hawaii, 1949.

Light, Ivan H. *Ethnic Enterprise in America: Business and Welfare among Chinese, Japanese, and Blacks*. Berkeley: University of California Press, 1972.

Lind, Andrew W. "Occupational Trends among Immigrant Groups in Hawaii." *Social Forces* 7 (Dec. 1928): 290–99.

——. "Occupational Attitudes of Orientals in Hawaii." *Sociology and Social Research* 12 (Jan.–Feb. 1929): 245–55.

——. "The Camps." *New Americans* 14 (June 1933): 2–6.

——. *An Island Community*. Chicago: University of Chicago Press, 1938.

——. "Assimilation in Rural Hawaii." *American Journal of Sociology* 45 (Sept. 1939): 200–214.

——. *Hawaii's Japanese: An Experiment in Democracy*. Princeton: Princeton University Press, 1946.

——. "Japanese Language Schools, 1948." Hawaii Social Research Laboratory, University of Hawaii, 7 December 1948.

——. *Hawaii's People*. 3d ed. Honolulu: University of Hawaii Press, 1967.

——. "Immigration to Hawaii." *Social Process in Hawaii* 29 (1982): 1–14.

Liu, John M. "Race, Ethnicity, and the Sugar Plantation System: Asian Labor in Hawaii, 1850 to 1900." In *Labor Immigration under Capitalism: Asian Workers in the United States before World War II*, ed. Lucie Cheng and Edna Bonacich, 186–210. Berkeley: University of California Press, 1984.

Livesay, Thayne M. *A Study of Public Education in Hawaii*. No. 7. Honolulu: University of Hawaii Research Publications, 1937.

Loftin, Marion T. "The Japanese in Brazil: A Study in Immigration and Acculturation." Ph.D. diss., Vanderbilt University, 1951.

Lourie, Margaret A. and Nancy Faires Conklin, eds. *A Pluralistic Nation*. Rowley, Mass.: Newbury House Publishers, 1978.

Lyman, Stanford. "The Race Relations Cycle of Robert E. Park." *Pacific Sociological Review* 11 (Spring 1968): 16–22.

——. "Generation and Character: The Case of the Japanese-Americans." In *East across the Pacific*, ed. Hilary Conroy and T. Scott Miyakawa, 279–314. Santa Barbara: ABC-Clio Press, 1972.

Lyu, Kingsley. "Korean Nationalist Activities in Hawaii and the Continental United States, 1900–1945." Part 1: 1900–1919. Part 2: 1919–45. *Amerasia Journal* 4:1 (1977): 23–90; 4:2 (1977): 53–100.

Ma, L. Eve Armentrout. *Revolutionaries, Monarchists, and Chinatowns: Chinese Politics in the Americas and the 1911 Revolution.* Honolulu: University of Hawaii Press, 1990.

MacCaughey, Vaughan. "Some Outstanding Educational Problems." *Paradise of the Pacific* 32 (July 1919): 29.

Makabe, Tomoko. "Ethnic Identity and Social Mobility: The Case of the Second Generation Japanese in Metropolitan Toronto." *Canadian Ethnic Studies* 10:1 (1978): 106–23.

Marumoto, Masaji, "A Personal History," 3 parts. *East-West Journal* 1 (Winter 1980): 22–27; 2 (Spring 1981): 16–26; 3 (Fall 1981): 20–27.

Masuda, Minoru, Gary H. Matsumoto, and Gerald M. Meredith. "Ethnic Identity in Three Generations of Japanese Americans." *Journal of Social Psychology* 81 (1970): 199–207.

Masuda, Ruth N. "The Japanese Tanomoshi." *Social Process in Hawaii* 3 (1937): 16–19.

Masuoka, Jitsuichi. "Race Attitudes of the Japanese People in Hawaii." M.A. thesis, University of Hawaii, 1931.

———. "A Sociological Study of the Standard of Living." *Social Forces* 15 (1936): 262–67.

———. "The Westernization of the Japanese Family in Hawaii." Ph.D. thesis, State University of Iowa, 1940.

Matsubayashi, Yoshihide. "The Japanese Language Schools in Hawaii and California, from 1892–1941." Ph.D. diss., University of San Francisco, 1984.

Matsumoto, Y. Scott. "Okinawa Migrants to Hawaii." *Hawaii Journal of History* 16 (1982): 125–33.

Maykovich, Minako K. *Japanese American Identity Dilemma.* Tokyo: Waseda University Press, 1972.

Meller, Norman. "Hawaii's English Standard Schools." Legislative Reference Bureau, Report No. 3, 1948.

Meredith, Gerald M. "Acculturation and Personality among Japanese-American College Students in Hawaii." *Journal of Social Psychology* 68 (1966): 175–82.

———. "Amae and Acculturation among Japanese-American College Students in Hawaii." *Journal of Social Psychology* 70 (1968): 171–80.

Metzger, L. Paul. "American Sociology and Black Assimilation: Conflicting Perspectives." *American Journal of Sociology* 76 (Jan. 1971): 627–47.

"Mid-Pacific Institute." *Hawaii Educational Review* 23 (May 1935): 264.

Mihata, Walter Y. "Americans of Japanese Ancestry." *Universal Review* 2 (Aug. 1928): 16. Romanzo Adams Social Research Library, Box 1, File 3.

Milroy, James and Lesley Milroy. *Authority in Language: Investigating Language Prescription and Standardisation,* 2d ed. London: Routledge, 1991.

Misaki, Hisakichi. "The Effect of Language Handicap on Intelligence Tests of Japanese Children." M.A. thesis, Stanford University, 1927. Cited in Shizuko Morimoto, "A Study of Oral English Usage among Pupils of Japanese Ancestry Attending Public Schools in Hawaii," 6. M.A. thesis, University of Hawaii, 1938.

Mitamura, Machiyo. "Life on a Hawaiian Plantation." *Social Process in Hawaii* 6 (1940): 50–58.

Miyamoto, S. Frank. *Social Solidarity among the Japanese in Seattle*. Seattle: University of Washington Press, 1939.

———. "An Immigrant Community in America." In *East across the Pacific: Historical and Sociological Studies of Japanese Immigration and Assimilation*, ed. Hilary Conroy and T. Scott Miyakawa, 217–43. Santa Barbara: ABC-Clio Press, 1972.

Miyamoto, Shichiro. "A Study of the Japanese Language Ability of the Second and Third Generation Japanese Children in a Honolulu Language School." M.A. thesis, University of Hawaii, 1937.

Miyasaki, Gail. "The Schooling of the Nisei." M.A. thesis, University of Hawaii, 1977.

Modell, John. *The Economics and Politics of Racial Accommodation: The Japanese of Los Angeles, 1900–1942*. Urbana: University of Illinois Press, 1977.

Montero, Darrel. *Japanese Americans: Changing Patterns of Ethnic Affiliation over Three Generations*. Boulder, Colo.: Westview Press, 1980.

Morimoto, Shizuko. "A Study of Oral English Usage among Pupils of Japanese Ancestry Attending Public Schools in Hawaii." M.A. thesis, University of Hawaii, 1938.

Morimoto, Toyotomi. "Language and Heritage Maintenance of Immigrants: Japanese Language Schools in California, 1903–1941." Ph.D. diss., University of California, Los Angeles, 1989.

Moriyama, Alan T. "The Causes of Emigration: The Background of Japanese Emigration to Hawaii, 1885 to 1894." In *Labor Immigration under Capitalism: Asian Workers in the United States before World War II*, ed. Lucie Cheng and Edna Bonacich, 248–76. Berkeley: University of California Press, 1984.

———. *Imingaisha: Japanese Emigration Companies and Hawaii, 1894–1908*. Honolulu: University of Hawaii Press, 1985.

Morris, Nancy and Claire Marumoto. "Inventory of Newspapers Published in Hawaii, Preliminary List, 1984." Hawaiian Collection. Hamilton Library. University of Hawaii, Honolulu.

Muraskin, William A. "The Social Control Theory in American History: A Critique." *Journal of Social History* 9 (Fall-Summer 1975–76): 559–69.

Murphy, U. G. "The Japanese Problem in Hawaii." *Friend* 91 (June 1922): 130–31.

Murray, Robert K. *Red Scare: A Study in National Hysteria, 1919–1920*. New York: McGraw-Hill, 1955.

Myrick, Lockwood. "An Open Letter to Governor Wallace R. Farrington on Fukunaga's Insanity." 5 November 1928. Hawaiian Collection. Hamilton Library. University of Hawaii, Honolulu.

Nagoshi, Kunio and Charles Nishimura. "Some Observations Regarding Haole-Japanese Marriages in Hawaii." *Social Process in Hawaii* 18 (1954): 57–65.

Nasaw, David. *Schooled to Order: A Social History of Public Schooling in the United States*. New York: Oxford University Press, 1979.

New Americans Conference. *Proceedings of Annual Conference*. First to Fifteenth Conferences. Honolulu: n.p., 1927–42.

Nicholas, Patricia C. "Creoles of the USA." In *Language in the USA*, ed. Charles A Ferguson and Shirley B. Heath, 69–91. Cambridge: Cambridge University Press, 1981.

Nomura, Gail M. "The Debate over the Role of Nisei in Prewar Hawaii: The New Americans Conference, 1927–1941." *Journal of Ethnic Studies* 15 (Spring 1987): 95–115.

Novak, Michael. *The Rise of the Unmeltable Ethnics: Politics and Culture in the Seventies.* New York: Macmillan, 1972.

The Oahuan. Honolulu: Punahou School, 1927–58.

O'Brien, Kenneth B., Jr. "Education, Americanization, and the Supreme Court: The 1920s." *American Quarterly* 13 (1961): 161–71.

Odo, Franklin and Kazuko Sinoto. *A Pictorial History of the Japanese in Hawaii, 1885–1924.* Honolulu: Bishop Museum Press, 1985.

Ogawa, Dennis M. *Jan Ken Po: The World of Hawaii's Japanese Americans.* Honolulu: University Press of Hawaii, 1973.

Ogbu, John U. "Class Stratification, Racial Stratification, and Schooling." In *Class, Race, and Gender in American Education,* ed. Lois Weiss, 163–82. Albany: SUNY Press, 1988.

———. "Minority Status and Literacy in Comparative Perspective." *Daedalus: Proceedings of the American Academy* 119 (Spring 1990): 141–68.

———. "Minority Coping Responses and School Experiences." *Journal of Psychohistory* 18 (Spring 1991): 433–56.

Okada, John. *No-No Boy.* San Francisco: Combined Asian-American Research Project, [1957] 1976.

Okahata, James H., ed. *A History of Japanese in Hawaii.* Honolulu: United Japanese Society of Hawaii, 1971.

Okamura, Jonathan Y. "Aloha Kanaka Me Ke Aloha 'Aina: Local Culture and Society in Hawaii." *Amerasia Journal* 7 (1980), 119–37.

Okihiro, Gary Y. *Cane Fires: The Anti-Japanese Movement in Hawaii, 1865–1945.* Philadelphia: Temple University Press, 1991.

Okumura, Takie. "The Problem of Expatriation." *New Americans* 13 (Mar. 1933): 1.

———. "Expatriation—Back to the Soil." *Mid-Pacific Magazine* 48 (Jan.–Mar. 1935): 81–86.

———. "Test of Japanese Assimilation." *Friend* 110 (Mar. 1940): 45.

———. *Seventy Years of Divine Blessings.* Honolulu: Okumura, 1940.

———, and Umetaro Okumura. *Hawaii's American-Japanese Problem: A Campaign to Remove Causes of Friction between the American People and Japanese.* Honolulu: n.p., 1927.

Olneck, Michael R. "Americanization and the Education of Immigrants, 1900–1925: An Analysis of Symbolic Action." *American Journal of Education* 97 (Aug. 1989): 399–423.

———, and Marvin Lazerson. "Education." In *Harvard Encyclopedia of American Ethnic Groups,* ed. Stephan Thernstrom, 303–19. Cambridge, Mass.: Belknap Press, 1980.

Onishi, Katsumi. "The Second Generation Japanese and the Hongwanji." *Social Process in Hawaii* 3 (1937): 43–48.

———. "A Study of the Attitudes of the Japanese in Hawaii toward the Japanese Language Schools." M.A. thesis, University of Hawaii, 1943.

Opler, Marvin K. "Cultural Dilemma of a Kibei Youth." In *Clinical Studies in*

Culture Conflict, ed. Georgene H. Seward, 297–316. New York: Ronald Press Co., 1958.

Ozaki, Shigeo. "Student Attitudes on Interracial Marriage." *Social Process in Hawaii* 6 (1940): 23–28.

Park, Robert E. *Immigrant Press and Its Control.* New York: Harper and Bros., 1922.

——. *Race and Culture.* Glencoe: The Free Press, 1950.

——, and Ernest W. Burgess. *Introduction to the Science of Sociology.* 2d ed. Chicago: University of Chicago Press, 1924.

Passin, Herbert. *Society and Education in Japan.* New York: Teachers College Press, [1965].

Patterson, Wayne. "Upward Social Mobility of the Koreans in Hawaii." Paper presented at the Center for Korean Studies Conference on Korean Migrants Abroad, University of Hawaii at Manoa, Honolulu, 8–11 January 1979.

——. *The Korean Frontier in America: Immigration to Hawaii, 1896–1910.* Honolulu: University of Hawaii Press, 1988.

Paulston, Christina Bratt. "Bilingualism and Education." In *Language in the USA,* ed. Charles A. Ferguson and Shirley B. Heath, 469–85. Cambridge: Cambridge University Press, 1981.

Perlmann, Joel. "Who Stayed in School? Social Structure and Academic Achievement in the Determination of Enrollment Patterns, Providence, R.I., 1880–1925." *Journal of American History* 72 (Dec. 1985): 588–614.

Petersen, William. *Japanese Americans: Oppression and Success.* New York: Random House, 1971.

Planters' Monthly 1 (1882): 187. Cited in Edward D. Beechert. *Working in Hawaii: A Labor History.* Honolulu: University of Hawaii Press, 1985.

Platt, Anthony. *The Child Savers: The Invention of Delinquency.* 2d ed. Chicago: University of Chicago Press, 1977.

Pomerantz, Linda. "The Background of Korean Emigration." In *Labor Immigration under Capitalism: Asian Workers in the United States before World War II,* ed. Lucie Cheng and Edna Bonacich, 277–315. Berkeley: University of California Press, 1984.

Potter, Robert E. "Public School Teachers and Teacher Education in Territorial Hawaii." *Educational Perspectives* 20 (Fall 1981): 22–32.

Probasco, Herbert. "Japanese Filipino Labor Unions and the 1920 Plantation Strike in Hawaii." Paper prepared for History 665, University of Hawaii, Honolulu, 1966.

Ramsour, H. B. "A Study of the Entrance and Activity of Evangelical Christianity in Hawaii." M.A. thesis, Southwestern Baptist Theological Seminary, 1952.

Ravitch, Diane. *The Revisionists Revised.* New York: Basic Books, 1977.

Reinecke, John E. "Pidgin English in Hawaii." *American Journal of Sociology* 43 (Mar. 1938): 778–89.

——. "Personal Names in Hawaii." *American Speech* 15 (Dec. 1940): 345–52.

——. "Labor Disturbances in Hawaii, 1890–1925: A Summary." Unpublished draft, 1966.

——. *Feigned Necessity: Hawaii's Attempt to Obtain Chinese Contract Labor,*

1921–1923. San Francisco: Chinese Materials Center, 1979.

————, and Stanley M. Tsuzaki. *Language and Dialect in Hawaii: A Sociological History to 1933.* Honolulu: University of Hawaii Press, 1969.

Research Committee on the Study of Japanese Americans in Honolulu, Hawaii. *Honolulu's Japanese Americans in Comparative Perspective.* Tokyo: Institute of Statistical Mathematics, 1984.

Rogers, Terence and Satoru Izutsu. "The Japanese." In *People and Cultures of Hawaii: A Psychocultural Profile,* ed. John F. McDermott et al., 73–99. Honolulu: University of Hawaii Press, 1980.

Roster Legislatures of Hawaii, 1841–1918; Constitutions of Monarchy and Republic; Speeches of Sovereigns and President. Honolulu: Archives of Hawaii, 1918.

Rothman, David. *Discovery of the Asylum.* Boston: Little, Brown, 1971.

Rury, John L. *Education and Women's Work: Female Schooling and the Division of Labor in Urban America, 1870–1930.* Albany: State University of New York Press, 1991.

Sakai, Robert K. and Mitsugu Sakihara. "Okinawa." In *Kodansha Encyclopedia of Japan,* 6:86–88. Tokyo: Kodansha, 1983.

Sakamaki, George. "Dual Citizenship and Expatriation." *Paradise of the Pacific* 50 (Apr. 1938): 35.

Sakamaki, Shunzo. "A History of the Japanese Press in Hawaii." M.A. thesis, University of Hawaii, 1928.

Sakihara, Mitsugu. "History and Okinawans." In *Uchinanchu,* ed. Ethnic Studies Oral History Project, xxi–xxiv. Honolulu: Ethnic Studies Oral History Project, 1981.

Samuels, Frederick. *The Japanese and the Haoles of Honolulu.* New Haven, Conn.: College and University Press, 1970.

Sanjume, Jisoo. "An Analysis of the New Americans Conference from 1927 to 1938." M.A. thesis, University of Hawaii, 1939.

Sato, Charlene J. "Linguistic Inequality in Hawaii: The Post-Creole Dilemma," in *Language of Inequality,* ed. Nessa Wolfson and Joan Manes, 255–72. Berlin: Mouton, 1985.

————. "A Nonstandard Approach to Standard English." *TESOL Quarterly* 23 (June 1989): 259–82.

————. "Sociolinguistic Variation and Language Attitudes in Hawaii." In *English around the World: Sociolinguistic Perspectives,* ed. Jenny Cheshire, 647–63. Cambridge: Cambridge University Press, 1991.

Schmitt, Robert. *Demographic Statistics of Hawaii 1778–1965.* Honolulu: University of Hawaii Press, 1968.

Scudder, Doremus. "What is White?" *New American* 2 (June 1917): 3–4.

————. "The Language Schools." *The Friend* 89 (Jan. 1920): 13–16.

————. "Hawaii's Experience with the Japanese." *Annals of the American Academy of Political and Social Science* 93 (1921): 111–12.

Seller, Maxine Schwartz. "*A History of Women's Education in the United States:* Thomas Woody's Classic—Sixty Years Later." *History of Education Quarterly* 29 (Spring 1989): 95–107.

Sharma, Miriam. "Pinoy in Paradise: Environment and Adaptation of Filipinos in Hawaii, 1906–1946." *Amerasia Journal* 7:2 (1980): 91–118.

Shaw, Ruth C. "The Output of the Territorial Normal and Training School." M.A. thesis, University of Hawaii, 1929.

Shibutani, Tamotsu. *The Derelicts of Company K.* Berkeley: University of California Press, 1978.

Shimada, Koji. "Education, Assimilation, and Acculturation: A Case Study of a Japanese-American Community in New Jersey." Ed.D. diss., Temple University, 1974.

Shoho, Alan R. "Americanization through Public Education of Japanese-Americans in Hawaii, 1930–1941." Ph.D. diss., Arizona State University, 1990.

Simonson, Jacob A. "A Brief History of the Origin, Growth, and Organization of Seventh-Day Adventist Schools in Hawaii." M.A. thesis, University of Hawaii, 1940.

Simson, Rebecca L. "The Use of Hawaiian-Creole (HCE) and Standard English (SE) by Two Hawaiian-American Elementary School Students." M.A. thesis, University of Hawaii, 1984.

Sissons, D. C. S. "*Karayuki-san:* Japanese Prostitutes in Australia, 1887–1916." *Historical Studies* 17 (1977): 323–41.

Smith, Bradford. *Americans from Japan.* Philadelphia: Lippincott, 1948.

Smith, Esther A., ed. *International Index to Periodicals.* New York: H. W. Wilson, 1924–41.

Smith, Madorah E. "The Direction of Reading and the Effect of Foreign Language School Attendance on Learning to Read." *Journal of Genetic Psychology* 40 (June 1932): 422–51.

Smith, William C. "Born American, But——," in *Survey Graphic,* May 1926. Quoted in Yamato Ichihashi, *Japanese in the United States,* 345. New York: Arno Press, 1969 [1932].

———. "The Second Generation Oriental in America." Preliminary Paper Prepared for the Second General Session of the Institute of Pacific Relations, 15–27 July 1927. Hawaiian/Pacific Collections, Hamilton Library, University of Hawaii, Honolulu.

———. "Changing Personality Traits of Second Generation Orientals in America." *American Journal of Sociology* 33 (1928): 922–29.

———. *Americans in Process.* Ann Arbor: Edwards Brothers, 1937.

Sollors, Werner. "A Critique of Pure Pluralism." In *Reconstructing American Literary History,* ed. Sacvan Bercovitch, 250–79. Cambridge: Harvard University Press, 1986.

Solomon, Barbara Miller. *Ancestors and Immigrants.* Cambridge: Harvard University Press, 1956.

Soltes, Mordecai. *The Yiddish Press: An Americanizing Agency.* New York: Arno Press, 1969.

Spickard, Paul R. *Mixed Blood: Intermarriage and Ethnic Identity in Twentieth-Century America.* Madison: University of Wisconsin Press, 1989.

Spring, Joel. *The Sorting Machine.* New York: McKay, 1976.

Stannard, David. *Before the Horror: The Population of Hawaii on the Eve of*

Western Contact. Honolulu: University of Hawaii Social Science Research Institute, 1989.

Steiner, Jesse F. "Some Factors Involved in Minimizing Race Friction on the Pacific Coast." *Annals of the American Academy of Political and Social Science* 93 (1921): 116–19.

Stephan, John J. *Hawaii under the Rising Sun: Japan's Plans for Conquest after Pearl Harbor.* Honolulu: University of Hawaii Press, 1984.

Stires, Frederick H. "The Ryukyus: An American Dependency—An Analysis of the Military and Civil Administrations of the Ryukyu Islands, 1945–1958." Ph.D. diss., Georgetown University, 1960.

Stonequist, Everett V. "The Marginal Man in Hawaii." *Social Process in Hawaii* 1 (1935): 18–20.

———. *The Marginal Man: A Study in Personality and Culture Conflict.* New York: C. Scribner's Sons, 1937.

Stratford, Jane. "Cross-Section of a High School Student's Life." M.A. thesis, University of Hawaii, 1930.

Strong, Edward K. *The Second Generation Japanese Problem.* [Palo Alto]: Stanford University Press, [1934] 1970.

———, and Reginald Bell. *Vocational Aptitudes of Second-Generation Japanese in the United States.* [Palo Alto]: Stanford University Press, 1933.

Stroupe, Connor B. "Significant Factors in the Influx to Private Schools on Oahu Since 1900." M.A. thesis, University of Hawaii, 1955.

Stueber, Ralph. "Hawaii: A Case Study in Development Education, 1778–1960." Ph.D. diss., University of Wisconsin, 1964.

Sueno, Murakoshi and I. Roger Yoshino. "Minorities." In *Kodansha Encyclopedia of Japan,* 5:195. Tokyo: Kodansha, 1983.

Suzuki, Teiiti. *The Japanese Immigrant in Brazil.* Tokyo: University of Tokyo Press, 1969.

Svensrud, Marian. "Attitudes of the Japanese toward Their Language Schools." *Sociology and Social Research* 17 (1933): 259–64.

Symes, Lillian. "The Other Side of Paradise: Americanization versus Sugar in Hawaii." *Harper's Monthly Magazine* 166 (Dec. 1932): 38–47.

Symonds, Percival M. "The Effect of Attendance at Chinese Language Schools on Ability with the English Language." *Journal of Applied Psychology* 8 (Dec. 1924): 411–23.

Tajima, Paul. "Japanese Buddhism in Hawaii." M.A. thesis, University of Hawaii, 1935.

Takagi, Mariko. "Moral Education in Pre-War Japanese Language Schools in Hawaii." M.A. thesis, University of Hawaii, 1987.

Takagi, Paul. "The Myth of 'Assimilation in American Life.'" *Amerasia Journal* 2 (Fall 1973): 149–58.

Takaki, Ronald. *Pau Hana: Plantation Life and Labor in Hawaii, 1835–1920.* Honolulu: University of Hawaii Press, 1983.

Talbott, E. Guy. "Making Americans in Hawaii." *American Review of Reviews* 73 (Mar. 1926): 280–85.

Tamura, Eileen H. "The Americanization Campaign and the Assimilation of the

Nisei in Hawaii, 1920 to 1940." Ph.D. diss., University of Hawaii, 1990.

Tao, Ichizo. "Fifty Years of Constant Struggle for God." *Friend* 110 (Jan. 1940): 3–4.

Taylor, Sandra C. *Advocate of Understanding: Sidney Gulick and the Search for Peace with Japan.* Kent State: Kent State University Press, 1984.

Thomas, Dorothy S., with the assistance of Charles Kikuchi and James Sakoda. *The Salvage: Japanese American Evacuation and Resettlement.* Berkeley: University of California Press, 1952.

Tinker, John N. "Intermarriage and Ethnic Boundaries: The Japanese American Case." *Journal of Social Issues* 29 (1973): 49–66.

"Toden Higa." In *Uchinanchu*, ed. Ethnic Studies Oral History Project, 510–20. Honolulu: Ethnic Studies Oral History Project, 1981.

Towse, Ed. "Proposed School for English Speaking Students." *Friend* 91 (Apr. 1922): 75.

Toyama, Henry and Kiyoshi Ikeda. "The Okinawan-Naichi Relationship." *Social Process in Hawaii* 14 (1950): 51–65.

"Tsuru Yamauchi." In *Uchinanchu*, ed. Ethnic Studies Oral History Project, 488–509. Honolulu: Ethnic Studies Oral History Project, 1981.

Tsurumi, Kazuko. *Women in Japan: A Paradox of Modernization.* Tokyo: Sophia University, 1977.

Tsutsumi, Takashi. "History of Hawaii's Labor Movement." Translated by Umetaro Okumura. Honolulu: n.p., 1921. Quoted in John E. Reinecke. *Feigned Necessity: Hawaii's Attempt to Obtain Chinese Contract Labor, 1921–1923*, 121. San Francisco: Chinese Materials Center, 1979.

Tsuzaki, Stanley M. "Hawaiian-English: Pidgin, Creole, or Dialect?" *Pacific Speech* 1 (Dec. 1966): 25–28.

Tyack, David B. "The Perils of Pluralism: The Background of the Pierce Case." *American Historical Review* 74 (Oct. 1968): 74–98.

———. *The One Best System: A History of American Urban Education.* Cambridge: Harvard University Press, 1974.

———. "Pilgrim's Progress: Toward a Social History of the School Superintendency, 1860–1960." *History of Education Quarterly* 16 (Fall 1976): 257–95.

Ueda, Reed. "Naturalization and Citizenship." In *Harvard Encyclopedia of American Ethnic Groups*, ed. Stephan Thernstrom, 734–48. Cambridge, Mass.: Belknap Press, 1980.

U.S. Commissioner of Labor. *Report of the Commissioner of Labor on Hawaii, 1902.* Senate Documents, No. 181, 57th Congress, 2d Session, 1903.

U.S. Department of Commerce. Bureau of the Census. *Thirteenth Census, 1910: Population.* Vol. 4. Washington, D.C.: Government Printing Office, 1911.

———. *Fourteenth Census, 1920: Population.* Vol. 4. Washington, D.C.: Government Printing Office, 1921.

———. *Fifteenth Census, 1930: Outlying Territories.* Washington, D.C.: Government Printing Office, 1931.

———. *Sixteenth Census, 1940: Population, Hawaii.* Washington, D.C.: Government Printing Office, 1941.

———. *Seventeenth Census, 1950: Population.* Washington, D.C.: Government Printing Office, 1951.

———. *Eighteenth Census, 1960: Population.* Vol. 1, pt. 13. Vol. 2, pt. 1c. Washington, D.C.: Government Printing Office, 1961.

U.S. Department of Commerce and Labor. *Bulletin of the Bureau of Labor, No. 66—September 1906, Third Report of the Commissioner of Labor on Hawaii.* Washington, D.C.: Government Printing Office, 1906.

———. *Bulletin of the Bureau of Labor, No. 94—May 1911, Fourth Report of the Commissioner of Labor on Hawaii.* Washington, D.C.: Government Printing Office, 1911.

U.S. Department of the Interior. Bureau of Education. *A Survey of Education in Hawaii.* Bulletin 1920, No. 16. Washington, D.C.: Government Printing Office, 1920.

U.S. Department of State. *Foreign Relations of the United States, 1924.* Washington, D.C.: Government Printing Office, 1939.

Uyehara, Yukuo. "The Horehore-Bushi." *Social Process in Hawaii* 28 (1980–81): 110–20.

Uyeunten, Sandra O. "Struggle and Survival: The History of Japanese Immigrant Families in California, 1907–1945." Ph.D. diss., University of California at San Diego, 1988.

Van den Berghe, Pierre L. *Race and Racism: A Comparative Perspective.* New York: Wiley, 1978.

Violas, Paul C. *The Training of the Urban Working Class: A History of Twentieth Century American Education.* Chicago: Rand McNally, 1978.

Wagatsuma, Hiroshi. "The Social Perceptions of Skin Color in Japan." *Daedalus* 96 (Spring 1967): 407–43.

———. "Some Problems of Interracial Marriage for the Japanese." In *Interracial Marriage: Expectations and Realities,* ed. Irving R. Stuart and Lawrence E. Abt, 247–64. New York: Grossman Publishers, 1973.

Wakukawa, Ernest K. *A History of the Japanese People in Hawaii.* Honolulu: Toyo Shoin, 1938.

Walworth, Arthur. *Black Ships off Japan: The Story of Commodore Perry's Expedition.* New York: Alfred A. Knopf, 1946.

Wang, Jerry H. "Korean Assimilation in the Multi-Ethnic Setting of Hawaii: An Examination of Milton Gordon's Theory of Assimilation." Ph.D. diss., University of Hawaii, 1981.

War Research Laboratory. What People Are Saying and Doing, Report No. 8. War Research Laboratory, University of Hawaii, 1 March 1946.

Watanabe, T. "The Japanese Christian Church Situation on the Island of Hawaii." *Friend* 110 (Aug. 1940): 148–50.

Weinberg, Daniel E. "The Movement to Americanize the Japanese Community in Hawaii: An Analysis of One Hundred Percent Americanization Activity in the Territory of Hawaii as Expressed in the Caucasian Press, 1919–1923." M.A. thesis, University of Hawaii, 1967.

Weiss, Bernard J., ed. *American Education and the European Immigrant: 1840–1940.* Urbana: University of Illinois Press, 1982.

Who's Who: Americans of Japanese Ancestry. Wailuku, Hawaii: Maui Publishing Co., 1941.

Wiebe, Robert H. *The Search for Order, 1877–1920.* New York: Hill and Wang, 1967.

Williams, Shirley Joann. "The Educational Theory and Philosophy of Education of Miles Elwood Cary: Implications for Democracy in a Global Civic Culture." Ph.D. diss., Northern Illinois University, 1991.

Wist, Benjamin O. *A Century of Public Education in Hawaii.* Honolulu: Hawaii Educational Review, 1940.

Woodrum, Eric M. "Japanese American Social Adaptation over Three Generations." Ph.D. diss., University of Texas at Austin, 1978.

Wray, Albert. "The Menace of Dual-Citizenship." *Paradise of the Pacific* 52 (May 1940): 9.

Yamamoto, Bernard K. "The Assimilation of the Japanese and Juvenile Delinquency." *Social Process in Hawaii* 5 (1939): 51–54.

Yamamoto, Eriko. "The Evolution of an Ethnic Hospital in Hawaii: An Analysis of Ethnic Processes of Japanese Americans through the Development of the Kuakini Medical Center." Ph.D. diss., University of Hawaii, 1988.

Yamamoto, George K. "Social Adjustment of Caucasian-Japanese Marriages in Honolulu." M.A. thesis, University of Hawaii, 1949.

———. "Political Participation among Orientals in Hawaii." *Sociology and Social Research* 43 (May–June 1959): 359–64.

Yamamoto, Joe and Mamoru Iga. "Emotional Growth of Japanese-American Children." In *The Psychosocial Development of Minority Group Children,* ed. Gloria J. Powell, 167–78. New York: Brunner Mazel, 1983.

Yamamoto, Keiko. "An Oral History of Miles Cary at McKinley High School." Unpublished manuscript prepared for Educational Foundations 699, 1979.

Yamamoto, Misako. "Cultural Conflicts and Accommodations of the First and Second Generation Japanese." *Social Process in Hawaii* 4 (1938): 40–48.

Yamamura, Douglas Y. and Raymond Sakumoto. "Residential Segregation in Honolulu." *Social Process in Hawaii* 18 (1954): 35–46.

Yanagisako, Sylvia Junko. *Transforming the Past: Tradition and Kinship among Japanese Americans.* Stanford: Stanford University Press, 1985.

Yanagita, Yuki. "Familial, Occupational, and Social Characteristics of Three Generations of Japanese Americans." M.A. thesis, University of Southern California, 1968.

Yoshizawa, Emi. "A Japanese Family in Rural Hawaii." *Social Process in Hawaii* 3 (1937): 56–63.

Index

Accommodation: as reaction to discrimination, 150

Acculturation, 49–51; agents of, 171–75; and Buddhism, 209–10; compared with Americanization, 52; and Issei-Nisei conflicts, 172–73; and cultural persistence, 210; and cultural values, 40–41; and first names, 169–71; of Issei, 29, 40–41, 151, 165, 178–80, 235–37; and Japanese language schools, 154–55, 158–60; of Nisei, 187, 235, 237–38; of Sansei, 238–39; and strike of 1920, 215–16; and Tatsue Fujita, 48–49; use of term, 52; and World War II, 236–37. *See also* Assimilation

Act 30, 147; provisions of, 147

Act 152: provisions of, 148–49

Act 171: provisions of, 148

Adams, Romanzo, 125–26, 139

Ad Club: and Japanese language schools, 157

Agriculture: employment in, during 1920s, 137

Akina, Ernest A., 135

Americanization: and Anglo-conformity, 52–53; and anti-Japanese sentiment, 57–61; compared with acculturation, 52; crusade in Hawaii, 56–61; crusade on mainland, 52–56; defined, 59, 129; and discrimination, 70–88; foreshadowed, 20–21; Issei attitude toward, 61; Nisei attitude toward, 48–49; primary impetus of, 53–54; and Red Scare, 54; schools' role in, 60; and Tatsue Fujita, 48–49; and World War I, 54. *See also* Americanizers

Americanizers, 48–49; and definition of good citizenship, 151–52; and earlier American attitudes, 53; failure of, 124, 145, 239; and Hawaii Creole English, 198–99; and Japanese language schools, 147, 151–55, 158; and labor agitation, 203; and Buddhism, 203–4, 206–7; and schools as key to Americanization, 124–25. *See also* Americanization

Anglo-conformity: and Americanization, 52–53; and assimilation, 49

Assimilation, 49–51; and Anglo-conformity, 49. *See also* Acculturation

Atherton, Frank C., 131

Banks, Judge James J., 148

Bartels v. Iowa, 149–50

Board of Commissioners. *See* Territorial Board of Education

Buddhism, 203–10; and acculturation, 17, 209–10; accusations against, 17; adapts to America, 204–6; and control of laborers, 16; efforts to spread, 15–17; followers of, 208–9; and Gakuo Okabe, 16; and Japanese language schools, 152, 155; plantation managers' encouragement of, 15–16; and Soryu Kagahi, 15–16; and Yemyo Imamura, 16. *See also* Imamura, Yemyo

Burakumin, 192–93, 282n.12

Butler, John K., 73

California: discriminates against Japanese, 19–20

Cary, Miles E.: on Americanizers' views, 132, 144; on dual citizenship of Nisei,

Cary, Miles E. (*continued*)
84; and Hawaii, 132; and New Americans Conference, 132; on students thinking for themselves, 144, 172
Caucasians: and control of Hawaii, 3–4
Caudill, William, 175–76
Central Grammar School, 218–19; as prototype of English Standard schools, 108–10
Chamber of Commerce (Hawaii): and Charles A. Prosser, 133; on high school tuition, 133–34
Christianity: followers of, 208–9; among Japanese, 15, 207–9; and Kanichi Miyama, 15; plantation managers' encouragement of, 15; and Takie Okumura, 15
Citizenship: of Asians, 245–46n.5; of Issei, 245–46n.5
Coffee farming: among Japanese, 38–39
Collins, George M., 127–28, 131–33
Community cohesion: and first names, 169; and juvenile delinquency, 167–68
Conflicts: and democratic vs. aristocratic tendencies, 145
—between Issei and Nisei, 179–80; on choosing marriage partners, 182–83; on filial piety, 181–82; on roles of husbands and wives, 180; on social functions, 172–73
Confrontation: as reaction to discrimination, 150
Crawford, David L., 130, 143
Crawford, Will C.: and English Standard schools, 111; on Hawaii Creole English, 198; and high school tuition, 135; and New Americans Conferences, 137; on Nisei ambitions, 131; and school expenditures, 135; and training in agriculture, 127, 143
Crime. *See* Juvenile delinquency; Fukunaga, Myles Yutaka
Cultural misunderstanding: and language school controversy, 151–52; and picture bride marriages, 23
Cultural persistence: and acculturation, 210, 238–39; and occupational advancement, 234; and schooling of females, 119–24. *See also* Ethnic identity

Cultural values: and acculturation, 40–41

Dean, Arthur L.: on discrepancy between expectations and employment, 141–42; on educational costs, 134; and English Standard schools, 112
Debolt, Judge John T., 149
Department of Public Instruction (DPI): and Act 30, 147. *See also* Schools, public
Discrimination: and Americanization, 79–88; and Fukunaga case, 81–83; and immigration law of 1924, 78–81; inhibits acculturation, 61; and Issei, 150; and Japanese language press, 70–75; and naturalization, 76–77; and Nisei, 48–49, 195. *See also* Prejudice; Racism
Dual citizenship: Americanizers' on, 84; among Americans, 84; and conflicting nationality laws, 85; discussed at New Americans Conferences, 85, 130; and expatriation difficulties, 86–88; Issei on, 84–85; and Japan's revision of nationality laws, 86; and Nisei, 84–88; and Nisei public school teachers, 84
Dual identities, 67–68

Employment: and acculturation, 174–75; agricultural, in 1920s, 137, 142; Caucasian-run businesses, 228; coffee farming, 38–39; dentistry, 223–24; domestic service, 174–75; engineering, 225–26; ethnic group representation, 217–18, 222; fishing, 38–40; gender differences among Japanese professionals, 221, 234; government, 227–28; among Japanese, 217–18, 221–22; law, 225–27; medicine, 223–24; non-agricultural, 144–45; nursing, 232–34; plantations, 211; small businesses, 38–40; teaching, 228–33; among Territorial youths, 142
Erdman, John P., 129
Eta. *See* Burakumin
Ethnic communities, 166–67
Ethnic identity: and acculturation, 238; and cultural pluralism, 51–52. *See also* Cultural persistence

Picture bride marriages, 23–25
Pidgin English. *See* Hawaii Creole English
Pierce v. Society of Sisters, 149–50
Plantations: discrimination on, 137–41; and *holehole bushi*, 14; Japanese move off, 35–37, 211–14, 216; living/working conditions on, 11, 14, 212; rejecting work on, 137–41; and runaways, 12–13; social segregation on, 140; and Wallace R. Farrington, 126; workers move off, 128
Poindexter, Joseph P., 148
Population: by ethnic group, 58
Portuguese: vs. haole, 5
Prejudice: decreases, 191–92; in Hawaii, 190–91; of Japanese toward others, 188–89; among Japanese, 189–90, 192–95. *See also* Discrimination; Racism
Press
—foreign language: and acculturation, 71; discrimination against, 70–75, 140–44; on mainland, 70
—Japanese language: vs. English language sections, 75; value of, to Issei, 71–72. *See also Hawaii Hochi; Nippu Jiji*
Professionals, by ethnic group: female, 222; male, 222
Prosser, Charles A., 133, 135
Punahou School, 116–17, 176; Japanese American teachers at, 231

Racism: among Japanese, 184, 192; and English Standard schools, 112. *See also* Discrimination; Prejudice
Reinecke, John E., 199, 215
Rice, Charles A., 135
Rice farming: among Japanese, 38–40
Rudkin, Judge Frank H., 149
Russo-Japanese war: Americans on, 20; Issei on, 18

St. Andrews Priory, 269n.82
Sakamaki, George, 87–88
Sakamaki, Shunzo, 66–67
Sansei: acculturation of, 238–39, 255n.19; on mainland, 238; and subcultural identity, 238–39, 255n.19

Schooling: costs of, 101; among Japanese females, 119–24; Japanese on, 91; among non-Japanese and mainland females, 122–24; and patriarchal authority, 120–21; and plantation work, 137–41
School principals: Nisei, 231–32
Schools: and acculturation, 124, 171; and Americanization, 60; and Americanizers' goals, 124
—Catholic, 118
—English Standard, 107–15, 267n.66; absent in DPI documents, 114–15; arguments for and against, 111–12; and elitism, 112–13; ethnic groups in, 113–14; Japanese American teachers at, 231; legacy of, 115; public school students in, 113; and racism, 112
—Japanese language, 9; and Americanizers, 147, 151–55, 158; attendance at, 146; beginnings of, 146; challenge Territorial laws, 148–50; as cultural centers, 146; and cultural transmission, 158; and good citizenship, 151–54; and Japanese, 151–55, 158–60; laws against, 147; and learning English, 155–56; and learning Japanese, 156–57; and moral education, 154–55; Ninth Circuit Court decision on, 14; and Nisei, 153–55, 158–60; and plantation managers, 146; Supreme Court decision on, 150; textbooks used in, 61, 153; and WWII, 160–61. *See also* Act 30; Act 152; Act 171; Banks, Judge James J.; *Bartels v. Iowa*; Debolt, Judge John T.; Farrington, Wallace R.; Lightfoot, Joseph; *Meyer v. Nebraska*; Palama Japanese Language School; *Pierce v. Society of Sisters*; Poindexter, Joseph P.; Rudkin, Judge Frank H.
—private, 115–19; enrollment in, 93; ethnic group representation in, 115–16; and Nisei continuing education, 118–19. *See also* Hawaiian Mission Academy; Iolani School; Mid-Pacific Institute; Punahou School; St. Andrews Priory; Students, private school
—public: administration of, 93; and

Uchinanchu, 193–95
University of Hawaii, 223–31; aspiring
    teachers at, 231; ethnic groups at, 100;
    and Governor's Advisory Committee
    on Education, 133. *See also* Crawford,
    David L.; Dean, Arthur L.

Vocational education: in agriculture,
    136–37, 142–44; beginnings in
    Hawaii, 135; definition of, 135–36;
    failure of, 144–45; and Honolulu Voca-
    tional School, 136; and ties among
    industry/government/schools, 128;
    and Washington School, 136. *See also*
    Smith-Hughes Act

"Weep into silence," 150
Wilcox, Elsie, 135
Wist, Benjamin O.: on Hawaii Creole
    English, 198; on training in agricul-
    ture, 127; and Tatsue Fujita, 45–47
World War I, 147
World War II, 234–37; and acculturation,
    236–37; rumor of Japanese victory,
    235–36
Wright, George W.: as *Hawaii Hochi*
    editorial writer, 75; on Japanese em-
    phasis on education, 138–39; on Nisei
    plantation work, 138–39; and Tatsue
    Fujita, 48. *See also Hawaii Hochi*;
    Makino, Fred Kinzaburo

Eileen H. Tamura, Ph.D., is an educational historian and director of social studies projects at the Curriculum Research & Development Group, College of Education, University of Hawaii. She has authored articles on the Nisei in Hawaii, education in Hawaii, and social studies education. A book she co-authored, *A History of Hawaii*, received an excellence award from the American Association for State and Local History.